# WOMEN AND CRIME IN AMERICA

Edited by

**LEE H. BOWKER**

University of Wisconsin, Milwaukee

**A GLENCOE Book**

**Macmillan Publishing Co., Inc.**
**NEW YORK**

**Collier Macmillan Publishers**
**LONDON**

**Macmillan Publishing Co., Inc.**
866 Third Avenue, New York, New York 10022

Collier Macmillan Canada, Ltd.

Library of Congress Catalog Card Number: 80-81794


Printing    2 3 4 5 6 7 8        Year:    2 3 4 5 6 7 8

ISBN    0-02-476830-8

# CONTENTS

# Preface

When I created a new course on females and the criminal justice system at the University of Wisconsin, Milwaukee, in 1977, I found that there were no texts on the subject on the commercial market. *Women and Crime in America* is my response to that problem.

This book of readings is designed to be used in three ways. The first is as a basic text in courses on female crime, female victimization, and the criminal justice system. The second is as a supplementary reader in courses that focus on criminology, the law, the criminal justice system, or victimology in general but that include a unit on one or more of the subjects covered in the reader. It is expected that the availability of *Women and Crime in America* will encourage more instructors to include units on women in their courses. The third is as a resource for individuals interested in research in this important area. A major accomplishment of *Women and Crime in America* is that it brings to light important unpublished work by Pagelow, Adler, Steffensmeier, Giordano, Kerbel, Dudley, Feyerherm, Randall, Rose, Moyer, and White. For this reason, scholars interested in female criminals, the victimization of women, and the response of the criminal justice system to women will want to have *Women and Crime in America* in their libraries.

The book is divided into three parts, with seven to nine articles in each part. Part I, "Statistics and Theory on Female Crime," includes articles on historical and contemporary theory and a number of recent empirical studies of female crime and delinquency. Articles on female participation in organized crime, a race riot, and legalized prostitution round out this section. Part II, "Women as Victims of Crime," includes a general presentation of statistics on the victimization of women, three articles on rape, and four articles on wife-beating. Part III, "The Processing of Female Offenders in the Criminal Justice System," includes three articles on the police and the courts and four articles on women in the correctional system.

In a field that is permeated with ideological considerations, it is important constantly to strive for clarity of logic and for a tight fit between theory and empirical reality. For this reason, I have tried to balance theoretical articles with reports of experiments, data summaries, and accounts of naturalistic field investigations. Taken together, these articles provide the student with both an accurate view of the relationship between women and the criminal justice system and a number of stimulating theoretical notions about this relationship.

Ideologically (and no text is ever ideologically neutral), this text leans more toward feminist perspectives than toward the more reactionary positions in gender politics. A few of the articles set the subject matter in historical perspective, but the emphasis is on contemporary issues. In keeping with the title, the geographical focus of the book is the United States, and crosscultural perspectives have been largely reserved for a later effort. The essays that introduce each topic reflect my belief that, following van den Berghe's position on race relations in South Africa, it is impossible honestly to take a value-neutral stance when discussing the victimization of the innocent and the (relatively) powerless. Therefore, I have only partially muted my personal feelings about criminal victimization and the sometime mistreatment of victims and offenders by criminal justice system personnel in my own comments and in the selection of articles for inclusion in the text.

I would like to express my appreciation to Susan Hunter, Michigan State University; Imogene Moyer, Old Dominion University; and Rita Warren, State University of New York at Albany, for their thoughtful comments. Ann Schlesinger and Penny Thornton, who typed and retyped this manuscript, deserve my special thanks for their hard and diligent work. Judy Ziajka and Robin Seaman at Glencoe were most helpful in the development of this reader.

Putting together a reader provides an excuse to get to know colleagues who are doing exciting things in the field. The many authors who revised papers or wrote original articles for the book were a delight to work with, and I thank them for the use of their materials.

Thanks and apologies are also due to Dee Thomas-Bowker and our daugher Jessica, who put up with endless inconveniences while I was working on this project.

Lee  H.  Bowker

# WOMEN AS CRIMINALS

---

# PART ONE

# STATISTICS AND THEORY
# ON FEMALE CRIME

## 1. EARLY THEORY OF FEMALE CRIME

Cesare Lombroso published the first edition of *The Female Offender* in 1895, the first time in Western history that a work of serious scholarship had been entirely devoted to the examination of crimes committed by women. Lombroso's efforts represented a substantial advance over those of earlier criminologists in that they directed attention to the empirical reality of the existence of criminals rather than dabbling in theoretical and ethical analyses that were unconnected to the actual state of the human condition. Unfortunately, his field studies utilized unrepresentative samples of incarcerated offenders who had often suffered long periods of confinement under terrible conditions and who therefore showed signs of physical deterioration that were partially the result of criminal justice system "treatment" rather than the cause of the criminality. Lombroso also focused too much on exceptionally severe cases, again generalizing inappropriately to criminals as a whole. These errors were compounded when he applied the techniques that had made his studies of male criminals world famous to his subsequent analysis of female criminals, for he also accepted the current sexist stereotypes of womanhood as true and interpreted female criminality in that light.

For Lombroso, serious criminals were atavists, biological throwbacks to an earlier state of human development. This emphasis on the importance of biology in criminality continued for women long after it had been largely abandoned in explanation of male crime, as Pollak's (1950) analysis of the literature on female crime demonstrated. He applied a Freudian interpretation to female behavior, suggesting that women instigate male crimes and mask their own criminality because they learn to conceal their feelings in sexual intercourse. These and other misleading beliefs about female crime have been convincingly rejected by feminist theorists, of which the article on criminological theory by Smart (1977), reprinted in this section, is an excellent example.

## 2. THE "NEW FEMALE CRIMINAL"

In the early 1970s the popular and applied literature began to include articles about a new kind of female criminal who was more violent and "masculine" than any who had existed in the past. The FBI agreed with this redefinition of female crime despite the fact that its own Uniform Crime Reports showed violent crime by women to be rising only just enough to keep up with male violent crime. The "Director's Message" to the readers of the FBI Law Enforcement Bulletin in May 1977 was that female crime had gotten out of hand. Murder, assault, bank robbery, and terrorism were discussed as if there were a major movement of females into these crimes (Kelley, 1977). Since the absolute number of these female criminals was quite modest, perhaps the director's concern was generated more by the unfeminine nature of these crimes than by the nonexistent amazon crime wave.

This argument found its first academic expression in Freda Adler's book, *Sisters in Crime* (1975). She holds that female criminal behavior has become more masculine in recent years, with the women's movement playing an important role in this change. She says that along with the masculinization of female crime, there has been an increase in the frequency and variety of female crime. And, most importantly, these changes have been accompanied by an increase in female violence. Adler believes that the more women become like men (unisex), the greater the similarity there will be between male and female criminal patterns. Adler's evidence for her theory is largely anecdotal rather than a careful study of statistics and field observations of female criminal behavior. Since 1975, other researchers have tried to find out whether her assumptions and conclusions were true. Has female crime become more violent? If so, has the women's movement played a major role in this change? Does the merging of sex roles in general mean that women will shortly be committing as many crimes as men?

Three answers to questions stimulated by Adler's assertions are reprinted in this section in the form of articles by Simon (1976), Steffensmeier (1978), and Giordano, Kerbel, and Dudley (1978). Simon presents official data on female crime from 1932 through 1972 based on the FBI's Uniform Crime Reports. These data show that the major rise in female crime since the beginning of the women's movement has been in property crimes such as larceny/theft, embezzlement, fraud, forgery, and counterfeiting rather than in violent crimes such as homicide, robbery, and aggravated assault. In fact, female arrests for homicide, robbery, and aggravated assault have been remarkably stable since the 1950s. Simon explains the rise in female property crime as being due to the increase in labor force participation, which gives women increased opportunities for committing many types of property crimes. In her opinion, women do not commit fewer crimes than men because of any inherent factors—it is just that they have less opportunity to commit crimes than men. Therefore, the increase in female crime has not been due to the women's movement per se, but rather to broad societal changes that have increased female labor force participation.

3

If the main increase in female crime is in property offenses rather than in violent offenses, then we would examine female property crime in greater detail. This is what Steffensmeier (1978) does in his article on changes in female property crime between 1960 and 1975. Steffensmeier's analysis represents an advance over earlier articles in that he adjusts female crime rates for both the simultaneous rise in male crime and the increase in the female population of the United States. He shows that there has indeed been a significant rise in female property crime, but that this could not possibly be due to the effects of the women's movement because it began before the women's movement came to light. Based on his examination of criminal statistics, Steffensmeier concludes that the progressive equalization of the sexes may result in the eventual equalization of arrest rates for certain property crimes, but it will never have that effect on violent crimes. In his words, "Our analysis of UCR arrest statistics suggests that the new female criminal is more a social invention than an empirical reality . . ." (1978:580). This analysis is further extended in the postscript that Steffensmeier has prepared especially for this text (1979).

Giordano, Kerbel, and Dudley (1978) refined the argument about female criminality by examining police blotters in Toledo, Ohio for selected years between 1890 and 1976. These blotters provide much more accurate and detailed information on female crime than the Uniform Crime Reports. Recorded female crime in 1890 was heavily related to prostitution and did not contain any examples of many of the more serious crime categories. By 1930 this had greatly changed, and although the fequency of female crime was still much lower than male crime, the patterns were as similar as they were in 1976. We again see in these data that fundamental alterations were occurring in the fabric of female crime before the women's movement became a force in American society.

The Toledo study points out the importance of economic conditions in understanding female crime. A high proportion of the female criminals were unemployed or, if working, held only the most menial jobs. The increase in female crime in 1930 as compared with 1890 and 1909 is related to the economic stress created by the depression years. Then, as now, there was an influx of married women into the labor market, which made the economic situation of single women increasingly precarious as they competed with a rising number of older, more experienced women workers. In the depression years, the job pool actually shrank, while the 1970s have seen an only slightly different situation in which jobs have been increasing, but not as fast as the number of women seeking work. Could it be that the increase in female property crime is not due to the employment of more women, but rather to the desperation of young, single, and minority women who find it impossible to obtain the jobs they are qualified to perform?

## 3. FURTHER UNDERSTANDINGS OF FEMALE CRIME

There are two other reasons why we should be suspicious of any direct link between the women's movement and recent developments in female crime rates.

4

The first is that the women's movement has not yet penetrated into the lower classes from which the arrested females counted in official crime statistics are largely drawn. This should come as no surprise to anyone, for an informal content analysis of issues attended to by movement spokeswomen indicates that the movement has retained its focus on middle-class issues with only minimal attention to the needs of women in poverty. The second point is that even among middle-class young women in high school, there is almost no relationship between liberated attitudes and participation in juvenile delinquency (Giordano and Cernkovich, 1979). So we see that regardless of whether the analysis is statistical, historical, structural, or social-psychological, it is impossible to find much support for the idea that the women's movement has had a significant effect on female crime.

The fact that liberated attitudes have been shown to have essentially no relationship to female juvenile delinquency does not mean that psychological factors are unimportant in the decision to commit delinquent acts. Research conducted by Weis (1976) suggests that female juvenile delinquents tend to use their delinquency to reinforce traditional feminine self-images rather than to validate self-images that are more traditionally masculine or new role-convergent self-images. A recent analysis of the psychological approach and other theories about female criminality by Widom (1978) reveals that, although there is much evidence of familial psychopathology, there is no conclusive evidence of an unusually high level of individual psychopathology among female offenders. Widom believes that subcultural theories of crime and delinquency, which have not been appropriate for the explanation of female crime and delinquency in the past, may become more applicable in the future as a subculture of female criminals and delinquents develops.

The final article in this section is an original analysis of self-reported female juvenile delinquency prepared for this text by Feyerherm. All of the studies discussed thus far have used official statistics, which leaves us with the question of to what extent these statistics are representative of the true level, distribution, and character of female crime in America. No data exist that could adequately answer this question for adult crime, but there are a number of studies of unreported female juvenile delinquency of which Feyerherm's article is an outstanding example. In general, these studies suggest that the true gender differences in crime are not as great as they appear in official statistics. It appears that criminal justice system personnel tend to underreport female economic crime more than violent crimes against persons, and that they sometimes inappropriately sexualize the offenses of female defendants. However, the fundamental patterns in self-reported female-crime studies are exactly the same as the patterns displayed in official crime statistics. The differences are in the frequencies, not in the nature or patterns, of the crimes committed.

## REFERENCES

Adler, Freda. *Sisters in Crime.* New York: McGraw-Hill Book Company, 1975.
Bowker, Lee. H. *Women, crime, and the criminal justice system.* Lexington, MA: D.C. Heath, 1978.

Giordano, Peggy C., Kerbel, Sandra, and Dudley, Sandra. *The economics of female criminality: An analysis of police blotters, 1890–1976.* Paper presented at the annual meeting of the Society for the Study of Social Problems, San Francisco, 1978.

————, and Cernkovich, Stephen A. On complicating the relationship between liberation and delinquency. *Social Problems,* April 1979, 26, 467–481.

Kelley, C.M. Message from the director. *FBI Law Enforcement Bulletin,* May 1977, *46,* 1,2.

Lombroso, Cesare. *The female offender.* London: Fisher Unwin, 1895.

Pollak, Otto. *The criminality of women.* Philadelphia: University of Pennsylvania Press, 1950.

Simon, Rita. American women and crime. *The Annals of the American Academy of Political and Social Science,* January 1976, *423,* 31–46.

Smart, Carol. Criminological theory: Its ideology and implications concerning women. *British Journal of Sociology,* March 1977, *28,* 89–100.

Steffensmeier, Darrell J. Crime and the contemporary woman: An analysis of changing levels of female property crime, 1960–75. *Social Forces,* 1978 *57,* 566–584.

————. *Patterns of female property crime, 1960–78: A postscript.* Original paper prepared specially for this volume, 1979.

Weis, Joseph G. Liberation and crime: The invention of the new female criminal. *Crime and Social Justice,* Fall–Winter 1976, *6,* 17–27.

Widom, Cathy S. Toward an understanding of female criminality. *Progress in Experimental Personality Research,* 1978, *8,* 245–308.

ONE

# Criminological Theory: Its Ideology and Implications Concerning Women*

CAROL SMART

Criminological theories have rarely been concerned with the analysis of female criminality. Typically criminologists have either been content to subsume discussion of women offenders under "general" theories, that is to say·they have implicitly assumed the female is dealt with in discussing the male, or they have dealt with them exceptionally briefly in the

*From the *British Journal of Sociology,* Volume 28, Number 1, March 1977. Reprinted by permission of Routledge & Kegan Paul, Ltd, London, 1977.

way that other "marginal or "special" categories are treated. The reason offered for this overwhelming lack of interest is that within the population of known offenders, female offenders constitute a statistically much smaller proportion than male offenders. With the exception of offences like shoplifting and soliciting, the number of female offenders nowhere exceed the numbers of male offenders known to the police. But this statistical "insignificance" alone cannot fully explain why so little work has been attempted in this area. Rather the relative absence of work on crimes by women may be considered as symbolic of the nature of the discipline of criminology. Traditional criminology in both the UK and the USA has always had close links with social and penal policy-making bodies with the result that research has tended to be directed towards areas officially designated as social problems. Female criminality has not generally been treated as a particularly important or pressing social problem, not only because of its comparative rarity, but also because of the nature of the offences committed by women. Official statistics, which are themselves a problematic source of information in criminology,[1] indicate that women engage mostly in petty offences and, with the exception of prostitutes, most appearances by women in court are for first offences. Women do not seem to pose a serious recidivist problem therefore, nor a threat to society, and so fail to constitute a real problem to the agencies of social control. Failing to become a pressing social problem has meant that studies of female criminality have not received much official support or finance with the result that traditional "control oriented" criminology has also shown a lack of interest in this area.

The lack of attention devoted to the question of crimes committed by women and their treatment has given rise to the present unsatisfactory understanding of female offenders and the offences they commit. There has been virtually no development of our knowledge in this area with the result that ostensibly scientific works predicated upon unexplicated ideologies have been allowed to stand uncriticized. Recognition of the under-development of criminology and sociology in this area is explicit in Ward's statement to the U.S. National Commission on Crimes of Violence that:

> Our knowledge of the character and causes of female criminality is at the same stage of development that characterised our knowledge of male criminality some thirty or more years ago.[2]

As a consequence of this lack of development the ideology and methodological limitation inherent in some of the classical works on female criminality still inform contemporary studies and, furthermore, are reflected in the treatment of female offenders.

This paper is therefore concerned to reveal the ideological foundations of the major theories of female criminality, in particular the culturally relative, commonsense conceptions of women on which they are
based. I shall concentrate on the works of Lombroso and Pollak, whose
theories are still influential, as well as the work of Cowie, Cowie and
Slater whose analysis of female delinquents reveals the influence of the
early theorists.[3] The second part of this paper will focus on the possible
implications of the ideologies inherent in these studies of female
criminality.

## THE IDEOLOGY OF THEORIES OF FEMALE CRIMINALITY

The most significant ideology which informs both classical and contemporary accounts of female criminality is a sexist ideology. It is sexist not
because it differentiates between the sexes but because it attributes to
one sex socially undesirable characteristics which are assumed to be
intrinsic or "natural" characteristics of that sex. Such an ideology arises
because the socially structured and culturally given nature of the
assumptions informing these theories are not treated as subjects for
analysis; rather common-sense understandings are taken for granted as a
suitable platform from which to commence theorizing. Working within
the natural attitude, adopting culturally given understandings of the
nature of sexual differences and in particular the characteristics attributed to women, the theorists concerned provide merely a scientific gloss
for common-sense understandings. Myths about the "inherent" evil in
women or their lack of intelligence and ability and their "natural" passivity therefore abound in these studies and they are used uncritically to
supply "evidence" for either the greater or lesser involvement of women
in crime.

An equally persuasive theme implicit in most accounts of female
criminality, which also stems from the uncritical attitudes of the pio-
neers in this field, is that of biological determinism. Biological determi-
nist accounts may take two forms, although they are rarely mutually
exclusive. Firstly women who have committed offences are perceived to
have been motivated by fundamental biological bodily processes. For
example, menstruation or the menopause, by affecting the hormonal
balance in the body, are taken to be precipitating factors leading some
women to commit criminal acts. In such cases action is seen to be
directly related to, or even directly produced by, hormonal or biological
imbalance. Secondly, and more significantly, the female biology is perceived to determine the temperament, intelligence, ability and aggression

of women. In this case it is usually argued that women are "naturally" averse to crime and hence any involvement in criminal activities is treated as symptomatic of a fundamental physical (or more recently mental) pathology. As a consequence of biological factors assuming such a key status in studies of female criminality it has followed that female offenders have been treated as a homogeneous group. Such factors as class, status, power, age, culture and so on are not considered as pertinent to an understanding of female criminality even though these variables are now accepted as relevant to the study of male criminality. As a result, therefore, of both the creation of a narrow stereotypical perception of women which relies upon culturally constituted understandings of the nature of female sexuality and the belief in biological determination, those women who do commit offences are judged to be either criminal by nature[4] or pathological because they deviate from the "true" biologically determined nature of woman which is to be law abiding.[5]The latter perspective which treats female offenders as pathological is prevalent in both classical and contemporary criminological theories, one consequence of this being the continuing implementation of policy decisions predicated upon an understanding that criminal activity by women is a product of pathology located within the individual rather than an exemplification of meaningful action. Indeed it has become a "popular" belief that women who commit criminal offences are "sick" and in need of psychiatric treatment; it is to a much lesser extent that this "sick" analogy has been adopted in the treatment of men as men are generally assumed to be rationally responsible for their actions while women are not.

This theme of the biological basis of female criminality which has become so entrenched in official and academic explanations was first fully formulated by Lombroso in his work entitled *The Female Offender* published in 1895. It is of course true that Lombroso employed biological factors to account for male criminality but with few exceptions this school of thought has been repudiated. As Shoham maintains,

> Today, . . . the Lombrosian myth in criminology, and the few contemporary adherents to the biophysiological approach to the genesis of crime, are considered a sad episode which retarded the development of the field by almost half a century.[6]

This is undoubtedly the case with most of Lombroso's theories and yet the ideological content of his work on female criminality persists in contemporary explanations. In particular his assertion that most women, with the exception of the rare "born" criminal, are "congenitally . . . less inclined to crime" and his belief that women's "natural" passivity and conservatism robs them of the initiative to break the law have become a predominent part of the ideology in contemporary criminological and sociological theories.

The work of Cowie, Cowie and Slater (1968) is perhaps the best exemplar of a modified form of the ideology inherent in Lombroso's work. In analysing the differences between male and female delinquency they state,

> Differences between the sexes in hereditary predisposition (to crime) could be explained by sex-linked genes. Furthermore the female mode of personality, more timid, more lacking in enterprise, may guard her against delinquency.[7]

Clearly, Cowie, Cowie and Slater and other theorists who adopt similar positions, have taken no cognizance of cross-cultural studies nor of historical data which reveal that, rather than there being only one "female mode of personality" there are a multitude of culturally and historically based sets of attitudes and expectations that influence the consciousness or personalities of women, thus producing gender-related behaviour. To suggest, for example, that women are "more lacking in enterprise," or in the case of Lombroso, lead more sedentary lives because of their genetic structure, is to ignore the social situation facing many women which gives no opportunity or outlet for active or creative behaviour.

Interestingly, Lombroso maintains that one sure sign of criminality in women is the lack of a maternal instinct. This deficiency was perceived to mean that "psychologically and anthropologically" the delinquent woman belongs more to the male than the female sex. But this belief, which is echoed in Cowie's work, is based on not only biological determinism but also on a confusion between sex and gender. As Ann Oakley[8] has pointed out sex is a biological term and gender a social, cultural and psychological term such that for a woman to act in a socially defined "masculine" way does not mean that she is sexually or biologically abnormal. However, where gender appropriate behaviour is seen as biologically determined women who adopt "masculine" forms of behaviour become labelled "masculine" themselves and this has connotations of "maleness" which are seen to be linked to hormonal or genetic abnormalities. Cowie et al. in fact failed to distinquish between sex and gender at all, they state,

> Is there any evidence that *masculinity or femininity of bodily constitution* plays any part in predisposing to delinquency and in determining the form it takes? [Emphasis added.]

In response to this question they maintain,

> Delinquents of both sexes tend to be larger than controls, and over-
> grown by population standards. . . . Markedly masculine traits in
> girl delinquents have been commented on by psychoanalytic
> observers. . . . *we can be sure that they have had some physical*
> *basis.* [Emphasis added.][9]

The point is that female delinquents are not perceived to be merely
adopting behaviour more usually associated with males, they are portrayed as being chromosomally or genetically abnormal. This means that
the "treatment" of such offenders becomes justifiable, the aims, inten-
tionality and rationality of the deviant act are overlooked and the social
and cultural conditions under which the act took place can be relegated
to the vague status of "environmental" factors whose only role is to
occasionally "trigger" the inherent pathology of the deviant. Crime and
delinquency can thereby be treated as an individual, not social,
phenomenon.

Inherent in this "individual pathology" model is a control oriented
ideology which serves to locate the causes of "problems" in specific individuals and which supplies the relevant knowledge and understanding to
develop the appropriate technologies and social policies for controlling
deviant members. Criminological theorizing thereby comes a means of
providing new technologies for control or, failing that, a means of legiti-
mating current policies which become justified as forms of treatment
rather than punishment. Moreover, while such theorizing is not concerned to provide the subjects of its study with the means to change their
social situation and status it does provide a damaging anti-intellectual
diet for its consumers which in fact serves to mystify the social phenomenon under research. For example, the way in which Cowie, Cowie
and Slater present their evidence is worth noting for they attempt to
appeal to the reader's "senses" rather than intellect or critical faculties.
They have a tendency to invoke "common-sense" and concepts of the
"natural" to support their claims rather than relying on credible, scientific evidence. Rather than reducing the influence of their work however,
their anti-theoretical and anti-intellectual approach may be conducive to
acceptance by policy-makers who perceive themselves to be concerned
with "practical" issues and not theoretical ones. For example, Cowie et
al. state,

> *Common-sense* suggests that the main factors are somatic ones,
> especially hormonal ones . . . [Emphasis added.]

and again later,

> It is more natural to suppose that the male-female difference, both
> in delinquency rates and in the forms that delinquency takes, would
> be closely connected with the masculine or feminine pattern of
> development of personality. [Emphasis added.][10]

This debunking of a theoretical and intellectual approach to the topic
may be seen as the witting embrace of ideology.[11]

I have implied that the work of Pollak[12] is also of considerable significance to the present state of our knowledge of female criminality. His
work is broadly within the same ideological tradition of Lombroso and
Cowie but the conclusions he draws show some interesting variations.
For example, he does not assume that fewer women than men commit
crimes; in fact, he argues that women are the most able criminals as
biologically and socially they are well equipped for lying, deceiving and
trickery. Consequently, he argues that they commit heinous crimes but
are never apprehended and he thereby gives considerable support to the
theological and common-sensical view that women are inherently more
evil than men. He maintains in fact that women instigate crimes and
manipulate the gullible male sex into enacting them, in other words
women are the cause of the downfall of others.[13] The ability to be manipulative is, according to Pollak, due to the physiologically based fact
that women can conceal their "positive emotion" during sexual intercourse while men cannot as they must achieve an erection. He argues,

> It cannot be denied that this basic physiological difference may well
> have a great influence on the degree of confidence which the two
> sexes have in the possible success of concealment and thus on their
> character pattern in this respect.[14]

Thus, rather than considering the implications of the sexual politics
which produce a situation in which many women face sexual intercourse
when they are neither aroused nor willing, Pollak takes this example as
a basis for further assumptions about women's ambiguous attitude
towards "veracity" and deceit.

There are numerous other examples in Pollak's work where his
uncritical, anti-feminist presuppositions lead him to make authoritative
but unsubstantiated statements about the origins of female criminality.
In this respect his work cannot be differentiated from other ideologically
informed works like Lombroso's and Cowie's. Where he does offer an
important variation however, which is uniquely significant in terms of its
implication, is in relation to the treatment of female offenders by the
Courts and police. He maintains that the chivalrous attitude of men

towards women, which is based on a misconception of women as gentle and passive creatures, leads them to treat female offenders more leniently than their male counterparts. He states

> One of the outstanding concomitants of the existing inequality between the sexes is chivalry and the general protective attitude of man towards woman . . . . Men hate to accuse women and thus indirectly to send them to their punishment, police officers dislike to arrest them, district attorneys to prosecute them, judges and juries to find them guilty and so on.[15]

Such beliefs are extremely prevalent both in common-sense and criminological accounts,[16] in spite of evidence which reveals that in sentencing, magistrates are more likely to be influenced by a previous record or the seriousness of the offence than the sex of offender[17] and that in some cases, particularly in so-called moral offences, female offenders are actually treated more severely[18] than male offenders. The implications of this ideology of chivalry and male benevolence are discussed in the next section.

## THE IMPLICATIONS OF THE IDEOLOGICAL CONTENT OF THEORIES OF FEMALE CRIMINALITY

The implications of theorizing have frequently been overlooked by those sociologists or criminologists who perceive themselves merely to be observers or recorders of everyday life. Yet social theories do have indirect social implications either by confirming common-sense and culturally located beliefs or by altering the consciousness of people in their everyday lives through a criticism and demystification of accepted values and beliefs. Allen recognizes this when he argues that,

> Theories enter into the ideological process and emerge in an abbreviated, often vulgarized, sloganized form embedded in language and thought processes alike. They form the basis of common-sense attitudes. They are transmitted through the family, enter into folklore, get expression through the mass media. In a variety of subtle ways conventional theoretical explanations enter the conscious of individuals and provide them with instant explanations.[19]

Although this process by which theories are translated into common conceptual currency will influence the actors own perception of self, our concern here is more with the way in which particular "scientific" theories of female criminality, operating with conceptions of social science which indicate an interest in technical control rather than emancipation or liberation and emphasizing the biological and pathological nature of criminal offences, may have influenced and/or legitimated the conceptualizations of policy makers such that female criminality is, or continues to be, interpreted as a biologically-rooted sickness.

Indeed there is a clear trend within the English penal system towards adopting a concept of "treatment" for offenders rather than, or in association with, punishment. This development may be simply indicative of an "official" recognition of more "efficient" means of controlling criminals than have been available in the past but it may also indicate a change in the conception of the motivational basis of criminality away from the classical concept of responsibility to a more positivistic orientation which emphasizes individual pathology.

The development is most marked in penal policies relating to female offenders. For example one consequence of the adoption of the "sick" analogy for understanding what is defined as criminal motivation, is the transformation of Holloway from a prison to a secure psychiatric hospital in which women will receive psychiatric treatment related to their perceived individual psychological "needs" rather than to their offence.[20] The assumption underlying this policy is that to deviate in a criminal way is "proof" of some kind of mental imbalance in women. This position is quite consistent with other assumptions about the mental instability of women in general employed to explain or account for the mental health statistics which indicate that women suffer from mental illness more frequently than men.[21] In fact mental illness has been perceived as an alternative to crime for women[22]—both crime and mental illness being treated as phenomena emerging from common "causes" rather than as possible rational and logical action.[23] Nigel Walker lends some credence to this practice when he states that,

> Certainly in practice women offenders have a higher chance of being dealt with as mentally abnormal. . . . We cannot however exclude the possibility that psychiatrists diagnoses . . . are being influenced by the . . . proposition . . . that there is probably something abnormal about a woman delinquent.[24]

The implications of the adoption of the "sick" analogy in the treatment of female offenders does not merely rest with the introduction of therapeutic methods and the removal and denial of responsibility for action. It in fact creates a situation in which realistic and potentially self-determining educational and vocational courses are intentionally excluded or reduced in importance. The women in the new Holloway will not be able to work, except for therapeutic or general domestic work. They will not be given the opportunity to learn skills which will fundamentally improve their life-chances, not only because the average stay in Holloway is so short, but also because it is not the principal aim of penal policy for women. In fact their typically dependent status will be confirmed and their ability to control or possibly change their life styles further damaged. Penal policy for female offenders is geared to preserving the typical female role, its intention is to make women and girls adapt to their pre-given passive social role which by definition is thought to preclude deviant behaviour. The criminological theories discussed in the preceding section (with the exception of Pollak's work) all provide a justification for this policy because they support common-sense understandings of the "natural" role and behaviour of women. Even if it is impossible to show that these theories of female criminality have precipitated some of the changes in the treatment of female criminals it can still be argued that the ideological basis of such works offers a "scientific" legitimation of social policy oriented towards an adoption of the "sick" analogy, the development of more effective techniques of control and the perpetuation of the subordinate position of women.

Lastly, in considering the implication of these ideologically informed theories of female criminality, we must return to the idea of chivalry and male benevolence propounded by Pollak. While it is possible that sexual discrimination plays an important part in differential arrest and sentencing policy, it is misleading to assume that this discrimination is always in favour of the female sex. In fact it is difficult to reconcile the view that the police and legal system are staffed by "chivalrous" men with reports on the treatment of female political prisoners,[25] prostitutes[26] and raped women.[27] It would seem that if sexual discrimination is an influential factor in the treatment of women it is not a simple variable that always leads to greater leniency. However the belief in chivalry and leniency has become a part of our (mis)understanding of the operation of the legal system and it has served to conceal the existence of unfavourable attitudes towards female offenders and the real injustice often meted out in the name of benevolence and paternalism.[28] The very existence of chivalry is synonymous with an inequality of power between the sexes in which a woman must depend on a man for her protection. Women must deserve their protection however, and women and girls of a "bad moral" character who lose their rights in this respect, leave themselves open to the full force of outraged morality. It should also be remembered that the morality co-existent with chivalry imposes double-standards on men and women, frequently condoning the same behaviour in one sex while punishing it in the other. As Chesney-Lind maintains,

> These labels (immoral, incorrigible) allow for the same abuses that
> characterize the labels of "sick" or "insane"—that is, the "savings"

or "helping" of a girl often justifies more radical and severe "treatment" than does the punishment of a male law violator.[29]

The practice of sending adolescent girls to Approved Schools (now community homes) for being found "in need of care and protection" or for being in "moral danger" is an example of the double-edged nature of chivalry and paternalism. The Home Office statistics for 1960 reveal that while 95 per cent of boys are sent to Approved Schools for committing offences, only 36 per cent of girls are similarly committed. Consequently 64 per cent of these girls are committed to penal institutions without having committed any criminal offence.[30] The justification for this discrimination is often couched in humanitarian terms, for example as a form of protection or as an opportunity for moral guidance, but in practice it would seem that juvenile girls are punished severely for behaviour which is usually overlooked in boys. A similar case can be made for prostitutes who are socially stigmatized and punished for their behaviour while their clients remain respected members of society. Such inequitable treatment finds its justification in the ideology which underpins most of the theories of female criminality. Once it is accepted that deviant females are sick individuals or that they are naturally inclined to wrongdoing and this is combined with a belief in the "benefits" of chivalry and paternalism it is not surprising that Cowie can make the statement that,

> These girls had to be removed from society into the security of a residential school much more for their own sakes than to protect society. *And yet, if one looks at their delinquent acts, they are of a very petty and trivial kind.* [Emphasis added.][31]

The frequent injustice and the severity of the "treatment" of female offenders or adolescents involved in so-called sexual or moral deviations is therefore veiled in humanitarianism. Moreover because the courts and other agents of social control reflect the double-standards of morality implicit in our socio-sexual mores and because their attitudes towards women are informed by a common-sense understanding of what a "natural" female should be, negative discrimination towards women in "sexual" offences, including rape cases, is overlooked. Theories of female criminality have tended to preserve this mystification and to justify the differential treatment of male and female offenders in terms of unexplicated assumptions about the "true nature" of men and women. They have in no way served to clarify our understanding of a complex issue. It is to be hoped that new trends in the sociology of deviance and criminology will not merely replicate the major limitations of existing studies of female criminality by treating this phenomenon as marginal to a general understanding of the nature of crime in contemporary society.[32]

# NOTES

1. B. Hindess, *The Use of Official Statistics in Sociology*, Macmillan, 1973; P.N.P. Wiles, "Criminal Statistics and Sociological Explanations of Crime" in P. Wiles and W. G. Carson (eds), *Crime and Delinquency*, Martin Robertson, 1970.

2. D. Ward, "Crimes of Violence by Women," *A report to the National U.S. Commission on Crimes of Violence*, 1968.

3. C. Lombroso, *The Female Offender*, Fisher Unwin, 1895; O. Pollak, *The Criminality of Women*, University of Pennsylvania Press, 1950 (Perpetua Edition, 1961); J. Cowie, V. Cowie and E. Slater, *Delinquency in Girls*, Heinemann, 1968.

4. O. Pollak, op. cit.

5. C. Lombroso, op cit; J. Cowie, op. cit.

6. S. G. Shoham, *Society and the Absurd*, Basil Blackwell, 1974, p. 117.

7. J. Cowie, op. cit., p. 167.

8. A. Oakley, *Sex, Gender and Society*, Temple Smith, 1972.

9. J. Cowie, op. cit., pp. 171-2.

10. J. Cowie, op. cit., pp. 170-71.

11. For a further example of this sort of anti-intellectual approach see G. Konopka, *The Adolescent Girl in Conflict*, Prentice-Hall, 1966.

12. O. Pollak, op. cit.

13. A contemporary version of the belief that women cause the downfall of others, particularly men, is embodied in the "maternal deprivation" debate which argues that unloving or rejecting mothers cause the delinquency and criminality of the next generation. See, for example, T. C. N. Gibbens, "Female Offenders" in *British Journal of Hospital Medicine*, vol. 6, 1971, p. 280.

14. O. Pollak, op. cit., p. 10.

15. O. Pollak, cop. cit., p. 151.

16. See, for example, A. Smith "The Woman Offender" in L. Blom-Cooper, *Progress in Penal Reform*, Clarendon Press, 1974.

17. N. Walker, *Crime and Punishment in Britain*, University of Edinburgh Press, 1973, p. 300.

18. M. Chesney-Lind, "Judicial Enforcement of the Female Sex Role: the Family Court and the Female Delinquent" in *Issues in Criminology*, vol. 8, no. 2 (1973).

19. V.L. Allen, "The Common-Sense Guide to Industrial Relations" in *University of Leeds Review*, vol. 17, no. 1 (1974), p. 10.

20. D.E.R. Faulkner, "The redevelopment of Holloway Prison" in *The Howard Journal of Penalogy and Crime Prevention*, vol. 12, no. 2 (1971).

21. There is a considerable debate about whether women "really" suffer from mental illness more than men or whether a male-oriented health service merely diagnoses women as mentally ill more readily than men. For the part of the debate see P. Chesler, *Women and Madness*, Allen Lane, 1974; D.L. Phillips and B.E. Segal, "Sexual Status and Psychiatric Symptoms," *American Sociological Review*, vol. 34 (1969).

22. M. A. Bertrand, "The Insignificance of Female Criminality," First Conference of the European Group for the Study of Deviance and Social Control, Florence, 1973.

23. R.D. Laing, *The Politics of Experience,* Penguin, 1968.

24. N. Walker, op. cit., p. 302.

25. A. Davis, *If they come in the morning . . .,* Orbach and Chambers, 1971.

26. K. Millet, *The Prostitution Papers,* Paladin, 1975; K. Davis, "Prostitution" in R. K. Merton and R. Nisbet (eds), *Contemporary Social Problems,* Harcourt Brace and World, 1966.

27. S. Griffin, "Rape: The All-American Crime," *Ramparts,* Sept. 1971; K. Weis and S. Borges "Victimology and Rape," *Issues in Criminology,* vol. 8, no. 2 (1973).

28. R. M. Terry, "Discrimination in the Handling of Juvenile Offenders by Social Control Agencies," in P. G. Garabedian (ed.), *Becoming Delinquent,* Adeline Press, 1970; M. Chesney-Lind, op. cit.

29. M. Chesney-Lind, op. cit., pp. 57.

30. H.J. Richardson, *Adolescent Girls in Approved Schools,* Routledge & Kegan Paul, 1969.

31. J. Cowie, op. cit., p. 166.

32. There are some indications that the area of women and crime is being treated more critically now. See, for example, *Issues in Criminology,* vol. 8, no. 2 (1973); K.E. Rosenblum, "Female deviance and the female sex role: a preliminary investigation," *Brit. J. Sociol.,* vol. 26, no. 2 (1975). C. Smart, *Women, Crime and Criminology: A Feminist Critique,* Routledge & Kegan Paul, 1977.

TWO

# American Women and Crime*

RITA J. SIMON

On the occasion of the Hamlyn Lectures at Sheffield University, in 1963, Lady Barbara Wooton observed:

It is perhaps rather curious that no serious attempt has yet been made to explain the remarkable facts of the sex ratio in detected

---

*Reprinted from "American Women and Crime" by Rita J. Simon in Volume no. 423 of the *Annals of the American Academy of Political and Social Science.* © 1976, by the American Academy of Political and Social Science.

criminality; for the scale of the sex differential far outranks all the other tracts (except that of age in the case of indictable offenses) which have been supposed to distinguish the delinquent from the nondelinquent population. It seems to be one of those facts which escape notice by virtue of its very conspicuousness. It is surely, to say the least, very odd that half the population should be apparently immune to the criminogenic factors which lead to the downfall of so significant a proportion of the other half. Equally odd is it, too, that although the criminological experience of different countries varies considerably, nevertheless the sex differential remains.[1]

Much has happened in the dozen or so years since Lady Wooton made these remarks. The main thrust of this article will be to describe those changes, to explain why they have occurred, and to make some prognosis about their implication for the future.

The topic, women and crime, is currently enjoying a wave of interest unknown at any previous time. Interest in the female offender is, I believe, a specific manifestation of the increased general interest and attention that women have been receiving since the latter part of the 1960s. Women themselves have been largely responsible for their increased notoriety. Having organized into a visible and vocal social movement, whose objectives are the attainment of greater freedom and more responsibility, they have also succeeded in drawing attention to themselves. One of the consequences of this attention has been to question and to search many aspects of women's roles that have hitherto been of little interest or concern to social scientists, clinicians, and law enforcement officials.

The movement for women's liberation has changed a lot of things about women's reality; and it has been at least partially responsible for changes in women's behavior vis-à-vis criminal activities, as well as scholars' perceptions of the types of women who are likely to engage in crime. In 1966, Rose Giallombardo characterized the image of the woman offender as follows:

> Women who commit criminal offenses tend to be regarded as erring and misguided creatures who need protection and help rather than as dangerous criminals from whom members of society should be protected.[2]

How similar that sounds to the observations of the Gluecks, who wrote, in 1934:

> The women are themselves on the whole a sorry lot. The major problem involved in the delinquency and criminality of our girls is their lack of control of their sexual impulses.[3]

How strange these observations sound when one notes that, in 1970, four of the FBI's ten most wanted fugitives were women. Daniel Green, writing a few months ago in the *National Observer,* commented:

> Before the advent of militant feminism, female radicals were little more than groupies in the amorphous conglomeration of revolutionary and anti-war groups that came to be known collectively in the '60s as The Movement. Like camp followers of old, they functioned principally as cooks, flunkies, and sex objects.
>
> Sexual equality came to the Movement in the gas-polluted streets of Chicago during the '68 Democratic Convention. Enraged by the tactics of Mayor Daley's police, Middle American daughters raised for gentler things shrieked obscenities and hurled rocks as ferociously as veteran street fighters. From then on, guerrilla women were dominant figures in the splintered Movement, particularly the defiantly militant Weatherman faction, which they purged of *"macho* sexism" and renamed the Weather Underground.[4]

What role has the woman's liberation movement played in changing both the image of the female offender and the types of criminal activities that she is likely to commit? The rhetoric of the woman's movement has emphasized similarity between the sexes. Kate Millet, for example, argues that all of the significant behavioral differences between the sexes are those that have been developed by culture, environment, and sexist training.[5] Others in the movement have emphasized that women are no more moral, conforming, or law-abiding than men. They have urged their sisters to neither bask in feelings of superiority nor entrap themselves into wearing masks of morality and goodness.

In their contact with law enforcement officials, women in the movement are prepared to trade preferential and paternalistic treatment for due process in civil and criminal procedures. Movement lawyers have claimed that women defendants pay for judges' beliefs that it is more in man's nature to commit crimes than it is in woman's. Thus, they argue that when a judge is convinced that the woman before him has committed a crime, he is more likely to overreact and punish her, not only for the specific offense, but also for transgressing against his expectations of womanly behavior.

The existence of such statutes as the "indeterminate sentence" for women, or the sanctioning of a procedure whereby only convicted male defendants have their minimum sentences determined by a judge at an open hearing and in the presence of counsel, while the women's minimum sentence is decided by a parole board in a closed session in which she is not represented by counsel, are cited as evidence of the unfair, punitive treatment that is accorded to women in the court.[6]

The position that some supporters of the Equal Rights Amendment (ERA) have taken vis-à-vis prisons also illustrates the willingness of the woman's movement to accept the responsibilities of equality. The movement recognizes that the stereotypes that are held of women in the larger society provide some advantages to female inmates. For example, physically, penal institutions for women are usually more attractive and more pleasant than the security-oriented institutions for men. The institutions tend to be located in more pastoral settings and they are not as likely to have the gun towers, the concrete walls, and the barbed wire that so often characterize institutions for men. Women inmates usually have more privacy than men. They tend to have single rooms; they may wear street clothes rather than prison uniforms; they may decorate their rooms with such things as bedspreads and curtains, that are provided by the prison. Toilet and shower facilities also reflect a greater concern for women's privacy. Advocates of ERA have written that they would eliminate these differentials by subjecting both men and women to the same physical surroundings in sexually integrated institutions. "Ideally, the equalization would be up to the level presently enjoyed by the women. But, if a State faces an economic roadblock to equalizing up, the ERA would tolerate equalization down to a lower, more economically feasible level."[7]

On the major goals of the contemporary woman's movement is equal opportunities with men for positions and jobs that carry prestige and authority. While the objectives of the woman's movement of the 1920s were to get women out of their homes and into factories and offices, today success is more likely to be measured by the proportion of women in managerial and professional positions, by the proportion of women who have completed college and university, and by the absence of lower salary scales for women who hold the same types of jobs as men.

A review of census data indicates that the gap between men and women who occupy management and professional positions is as great today as it was 25 years ago. In 1948, for example, 29 percent of the women employed in white-collar positions occupied professional and managerial slots; in 1971 the percentage was 33. Among men, in 1948, the proportion of white-collar positions represented in the managerial and professional sub-categories was 61 percent; in 1971 it was 70 percent. Between 1950 and 1970, the proportion of women who graduated from college increased by 70 percent; but as of 1971 there were still almost six men for every four women who completed four years of college. On the matter of income, the annual earnings of women between 1956 and 1970 decreased in comparison to those of men (1956: women—$3,619, men—$5,716; 1970: women—$4,794, men—$8,845).

Notable changes have occurred, however, in the proportion of married women employed on a full-time basis between 1950 and 1970—a shift from 24.8 percent to 41.1 percent—and especially among married women with children of school age (6–17 years), where there has been an increase from 28.3 percent to 49.2 percent.

There is still much to be done before the woman's movement can claim success in achieving equality between men and women in jobs involving occupational prestige and high incomes. But the increase in the proportion of women who hold full-time jobs, the consciousness that the movement's rhetoric has succeeded in raising, along with the changes that have occurred in women's legal rights in such areas as personal property, abortion, and divorce laws, have all contributed to altering women's overall status as well as increasing opportunities and propensities that women have for committing crimes. What changes have already occurred in the area of crime will be described in some detail in the following pages.

## WOMEN AS CRIMINALS

Table 1 describes the proportion of women who have been arrested for all crimes, for all serious crimes, and for serious violent and property crimes from 1932 to 1972.[8] The average rates of change in the proportion of women arrested between 1953 and 1972, between 1958 and 1972, and between 1967 and 1972 are also shown here. The last period is particularly crucial, because we would expect that during this period the rate of change would be marked by the greatest increase.

The average increase in the proportion of women arrested for serious crimes is greater than the average increase in the proportion of women arrested for all crimes. The data also show that the average rate of increase was greatest in the period from 1967 to 1972—.52 for all crimes and .84 for serious offenses. Note also that from 1961 onward the percentage of women arrested for serious crimes was greater than the percentage of women arrested for all offenses.

The popular impression that in recent years women have been committing crimes of violence at a much higher rate than they have in the past is disputed by the statistics in Table 1. In fact, the increase in the proportion of arrests of women for serious crimes is due almost wholly to the increase in property offenses. Indeed, the percentage of women arrested for crimes of violence shows neither an upward nor a downward trend. The news item that, in 1970, four out of the FBI's most wanted fugitives were women must be juxtaposed against those statistics, which tell quite a different story.

**Table 1.** *Percentage of Females Arrested for All Crimes, For All Serious Crimes, and for Serious Violent and Property Crimes: 1932-1972*

| YEAR[a] | ALL CRIMES | SERIOUS CRIMES[b] | VIOLENT CRIMES | PROPERTY CRIMES |
|---|---|---|---|---|
| 1932 | 7.4 | 5.8 | 6.5 | 5.3 |
| 1933 | 7.2 | 5.9 | 7.1 | 5.2 |
| — | — | — | — | — |
| 1935 | 6.9 | 6.0 | 7.3 | 5.3 |
| 1936 | 7.3 | 6.4 | 8.0 | 5.7 |
| — | — | — | — | — |
| 1938 | 6.8 | 5.4 | 7.0 | 4.6 |
| — | — | — | — | — |
| 1942 | 12.0 | 8.9 | 9.8 | 8.3 |
| 1943 | 16.1 | 10.1 | 10.5 | 9.9 |
| — | — | — | — | — |
| 1946 | 10.7 | 7.7 | 7.7 | 7.7 |
| 1947 | 10.3 | 8.0 | 8.3 | 7.8 |
| — | — | — | — | — |
| 1949 | 9.9 | 8.0 | 9.9 | 7.3 |
| 1950 | 9.6 | 8.1 | 9.4 | 7.2 |
| — | — | — | — | — |
| 1953 | 10.8 | 9.4 | 11.9 | 8.5 |
| 1954 | 10.9 | 8.9 | 11.6 | 8.2 |
| 1955 | 11.0 | 9.1 | 12.0 | 8.4 |
| 1956 | 10.9 | 9.0 | 13.5 | 8.0 |
| 1957 | 10.6 | 9.3 | 13.1 | 8.5 |
| 1958 | 10.6 | 9.7 | 11.9 | 9.3 |
| 1959 | 10.7 | 10.5 | 12.7 | 10.0 |
| 1960 | 11.0 | 10.9 | 11.8 | 10.8 |
| 1961 | 11.3 | 11.5 | 11.6 | 11.4 |
| 1962 | 11.5 | 12.4 | 11.5 | 12.6 |
| 1963 | 11.7 | 12.7 | 11.6 | 12.9 |
| 1964 | 11.9 | 13.5 | 11.6 | 13.9 |
| 1965 | 12.1 | 14.4 | 11.4 | 14.9 |
| 1966 | 12.3 | 14.8 | 11.3 | 15.6 |
| 1967 | 12.7 | 15.0 | 10.8 | 16.0 |
| 1968 | 13.1 | 15.0 | 10.3 | 16.1 |
| 1969 | 13.8 | 16.6 | 10.6 | 17.9 |
| 1970 | 14.6 | 18.0 | 10.5 | 19.7 |
| 1971 | 15.0 | 18.3 | 10.9 | 20.1 |
| 1972 | 15.3 | 19.3 | 11.0 | 21.4 |
| Average rate of change (per year) 1953–72 | +0.23 | +0.52 | −0.05 | +0.68 |
| Average rate of change 1958–72 | +0.35 | +0.68 | −0.07 | +0.86 |
| Average rate of change 1967–72 | +0.52 | +0.84 | +0.04 | +1.07 |

**Table 1.** *Percentage of Females Arrested for All Crimes, For All Serious Crimes, and for Serious Violent and Property Crimes: 1932-1972 (continued)*

Source: For the data in tables 1–4, *Uniform Crime Reports* (Washington, D.C.: U.S. Department of Justice, Federal Bureau of Investigation).

[a]Not all of the years between 1933 and 1953 are included; but the periods of the depression, the Second World War, and the immediate postwar years are included in the sample. Between 1933 and 1953, the data reported in tables 1–5 are based on fingerprint records received from local law-enforcement officials throughout the United States. They are limted to arrests for violations of state laws and local ordinances. But not all persons arrested are fingerprinted. Beginning in 1953, the system was changed, and the figures from 1953 through 1972 describe all arrests in cities with a population of more than 2,500. While recognizing that the sources for the pre-1953 data are different than those collected later, I think that for purposes of comparison—for example, male versus female arrests—they are worth presenting.

[b]Serious crimes, according the the *Uniform Crime Reports* published by the FBI, are criminal homicide (murder, nonnegligent manslaughter, and manslaughter by negligence), forcible rape, robbery, aggravated assault, burglary, larceny, and auto theft. We have omitted forcible rape from our calculations because women are never charged with such an offense.

The percentages for property offenses, however, show that big changes have occurred. In 1932, about one in every 19 persons arrested was a woman. In 1972, one in 4.7 persons arrested was a woman. Not only has there been a consistent increase in the percentage of women who have been arrested for property offenses, but also the biggest increases have occurred in the period beginning in 1967. This last finding is most congruent with our major hypothesis—that women's participation in selective crimes will increase as their employment opportunities expand and as their interests, desires, and definitions of self shift from a more traditional to a more liberated view. The crimes that are considered most salient for this hypothesis are various types of property, financial, and white-collar offenses.

Table 2 describes the percentage of female and male arrests, for serious crimes and for serious property and violent offenses within the total male and female arrests for all crimes.

In 1953, one out of 12.8 female arrests was for serious crimes as opposed to one out of slightly less than 10.9 male arrests. But two decades later, more women were arrested for serious offenses (about one out of four) than were males (about one out of five). The average rate of change among the women was greater during each of the three time periods than it was for the men. But the time span from 1967 to 1972 does not show a greater increase when compared with time periods that

**Table 2.** *Females and Males Arrested for Crimes of Violence and Property and for Serious Crimes Combined, as Percentages of All Arrests in their Respective Sex Cohorts: 1953-1972*

| Year | VIOLENT CRIMES | | PROPERTY CRIMES | | SERIOUS CRIMES | |
|---|---|---|---|---|---|---|
| | Females | Males | Females | Males | Females | Males |
| 1953 | 2.2 | 2.0 | 5.6 | 7.2 | 7.8 | 9.2 |
| 1954 | 2.2 | 2.1 | 6.0 | 8.2 | 8.2 | 10.3 |
| 1955 | 2.3 | 2.1 | 6.2 | 8.3 | 8.5 | 10.4 |
| 1956 | 2.3 | 1.9 | 5.9 | 8.4 | 8.2 | 10.3 |
| 1957 | 2.2 | 1.8 | 7.1 | 9.0 | 9.3 | 10.8 |
| 1958 | 2.1 | 1.9 | 7.8 | 9.0 | 9.9 | 10.9 |
| 1959 | 2.3 | 1.9 | 8.3 | 8.9 | 10.6 | 10.8 |
| 1960 | 2.5 | 2.4 | 9.9 | 10.2 | 12.4 | 12.6 |
| 1961 | 2.5 | 2.4 | 10.9 | 10.8 | 13.4 | 13.2 |
| 1962 | 2.4 | 2.4 | 12.2 | 10.9 | 14.6 | 13.3 |
| 1963 | 2.5 | 2.4 | 13.4 | 12.0 | 15.9 | 14.4 |
| 1964 | 2.6 | 2.6 | 15.4 | 13.0 | 18.0 | 15.6 |
| 1965 | 2.6 | 2.7 | 16.3 | 12.8 | 18.9 | 15.5 |
| 1966 | 2.8 | 3.0 | 17.3 | 13.1 | 20.1 | 16.1 |
| 1967 | 2.8 | 3.2 | 18.0 | 13.7 | 20.8 | 16.9 |
| 1968 | 2.5 | 3.5 | 18.2 | 14.3 | 20.7 | 17.8 |
| 1969 | 2.6 | 3.6 | 19.6 | 14.3 | 22.2 | 17.9 |
| 1970 | 2.5 | 3.6 | 21.3 | 14.8 | 23.8 | 18.4 |
| 1971 | 2.7 | 3.2 | 21.5 | 15.3 | 24.2 | 19.2 |
| 1972 | 2.9 | 4.4 | 22.3 | 14.8 | 25.2 | 19.2 |
| Average rate of change, 1953-72 | +0.04 | +0.13 | +0.88 | +0.40 | +0.92 | +0.53 |
| Average rate of change, 1958-72 | +0.06 | +0.18 | +1.04 | +0.41 | +1.11 | +0.59 |
| Average rate of change, 1967-72 | +0.02 | +0.24 | +0.82 | +0.22 | +0.90 | +0.46 |

NOTE: When the data are examined in this way, only the years in which all arrests have been recorded are included.

extend farther back. The percentage increase of men who have been arrested for violent offenses over the two decades is almost four times the percentage increase for women. For property offenses, it is the percentage increase for women who have been arrested that is three times the percentage increase for men.

Table 3 describes women's participation in the specific offense categories that are included in the index of serious offenses from 1932 to 1972 (type I offenses). Note that among all six offenses, only one shows a marked increase over time. After 1960, the proportion of women who have been charged with larceny or theft in any given year is much greater than is the proportion in any of the other offense categories, property as well as violent. It is interesting to note that until about 1960 the proportions of women who were arrested for homicide and aggravated assault were similar to those arrested for larceny, but in 1972 the percentage in the larceny category had almost doubled the 1960 percentage; whereas from 1960 on, the proportions have remained roughly the same for the homicide and aggravated assault offenses.

Table 4 describes trends in the proportion of women arrested for selected offenses in the type II category.[9] The figures show that in 1972 approximately one in four persons arrested for forgery was a woman and one in 3.5 arrests for embezzlement and fraud involved a woman. If present trends in these crimes persist, approximately equal numbers of men and women will be arrested for fraud and embezzlement by the 1990s, and for forgery and counterfeiting the proportions should be equal by the 2010s. The prediction made for embezzlement and fraud can be extended to larceny as well. On the other hand, if trends from 1958 to 1972 continue, fewer women will be arrested for criminal homicide and aggravated assault.

In summary, the data on arrests indicate the following about women's participation in crime: (1) The proportion of women arrested in 1972 was greater than the proportion arrested one, two, or three decades earlier. (2) The increase was greater for serious offenses than it was for all type I and type II offenses combined. (3) The increase in female arrest rates among the serious offenses was caused almost entirely by women's greater participation in property offenses, especially in larceny.

The data show that, contrary to impressions that might have been gleaned from the mass media, the proportion of females arrested for violent crimes has changed hardly at all over the past three decades. Female arrest rates for homicide, for example, have been the most stable of all violent offenses. Further probing of female arrest rates in the type II offenses revealed that the offenses that showed the greatest increases were embezzlement and fraud and forgery and counterfeiting. The increases were especially marked for the period from 1967 to 1972. None of the other offenses included in either type I or type II, save larceny, showed as big a shift as did these two white-collar offenses. Should the average rate of change that occurred between 1967 and 1972 continue, female arrest rates for larceny/theft embezzlement, and fraud will be commensurate to women's representation in the society, or, in other words, roughly equal to male arrest rates. There are no other offenses among those contained in the uniform crime reports, save prostitution, in which females are so highly represented.

**Table 3.** *Females Arrested as Percentage of All Arrests for Type 1 Offenses, 1932–1972*

| YEAR | CRIMINAL HOMICIDE | ROBBERY | AGGRAVATED ASSAULT | BURGLARY | LARCENY/ THEFT | AUTO THEFT |
|------|-------------------|---------|--------------------|----------|----------------|------------|
| 1932 | 8.7 | 3.3 | 8.6 | 1.7 | 9.3 | 1.6 |
| 1933 | 9.7 | 4.4 | 8.3 | 1.9 | 8.4 | 1.4 |
| 1935 | 9.9 | 4.6 | 8.0 | 1.7 | 8.3 | 1.7 |
| 1936 | 10.0 | 4.8 | 8.7 | 1.9 | 8.5 | 1.8 |
| 1938 | 9.6 | 3.9 | 7.9 | 1.5 | 7.1 | 1.5 |
| 1942 | 13.2 | 5.0 | 10.8 | 2.2 | 12.6 | 2.3 |
| 1943 | 13.2 | 5.3 | 11.7 | 3.1 | 15.5 | 2.2 |
| 1946 | 10.8 | 4.6 | 8.5 | 2.5 | 12.9 | 2.1 |
| 1947 | 11.3 | 4.5 | 9.4 | 2.7 | 12.4 | 2.2 |
| 1949 | 12.8 | 4.5 | 10.6 | 2.5 | 11.9 | 2.4 |
| 1950 | 13.5 | 4.3 | 10.6 | 2.5 | 11.5 | 2.7 |
| 1953 | 14.1 | 4.3 | 15.9 | 2.0 | 13.9 | 2.6 |
| 1954 | 14.2 | 4.2 | 15.9 | 2.2 | 13.0 | 2.5 |
| 1955 | 14.2 | 4.2 | 16.0 | 2.3 | 13.3 | 2.6 |
| 1956 | 14.8 | 4.3 | 17.6 | 2.3 | 12.6 | 2.5 |
| 1957 | 14.7 | 3.9 | 17.5 | 2.0 | 13.2 | 2.7 |
| 1958 | 16.4 | 4.5 | 15.7 | 2.4 | 14.3 | 3.2 |
| 1959 | 16.8 | 4.6 | 16.4 | 2.7 | 15.4 | 3.2 |
| 1960 | 16.1 | 4.6 | 15.3 | 2.8 | 16.8 | 3.6 |

Table 3. Females Arrested as Percentage of All Arrests for Type 1 Offenses, 1932–1972 (continued)

| YEAR | CRIMINAL HOMICIDE | ROBBERY | AGGRAVATED ASSAULT | BURGLARY | LARCENY/THEFT | AUTO THEFT |
|---|---|---|---|---|---|---|
| 1961 | 15.9 | 4.9 | 15.2 | 3.2 | 18.0 | 3.7 |
| 1962 | 17.2 | 5.1 | 14.7 | 3.6 | 19.6 | 3.9 |
| 1963 | 15.9 | 4.9 | 14.9 | 3.3 | 20.1 | 3.7 |
| 1964 | 16.6 | 5.3 | 14.4 | 3.7 | 21.4 | 4.3 |
| 1965 | 16.3 | 5.3 | 14.4 | 3.8 | 23.2 | 4.2 |
| 1966 | 15.9 | 5.1 | 14.0 | 3.8 | 24.0 | 4.1 |
| 1967 | 15.4 | 5.2 | 13.6 | 4.1 | 24.8 | 4.3 |
| 1968 | 15.4 | 5.5 | 13.1 | 4.1 | 25.2 | 4.9 |
| 1969 | 14.8 | 6.3 | 13.2 | 4.3 | 27.2 | 5.1 |
| 1970 | 14.8 | 6.2 | 13.3 | 4.6 | 29.0 | 5.0 |
| 1971 | 16.0 | 6.4 | 13.9 | 4.8 | 29.1 | 6.0 |
| 1972 | 15.6 | 6.6 | 13.9 | 5.1 | 30.8 | 5.7 |
| Average rate of change, 1953–72 | +0.08 | +0.12 | −0.10 | +0.16 | +0.89 | +0.16 |
| Average rate of change, 1958–72 | −0.06 | +0.14 | −0.13 | +0.19 | +1.18 | +0.18 |
| Average rate of change, 1967–72 | +0.04 | +0.28 | +0.06 | +0.20 | +1.20 | +0.28 |

**Table 4.** *Other Crimes, Females Arrested as Percentage of All People Arrested for Various Crimes: 1953-1972*

| YEAR | EMBEZZLEMENT AND FRAUD | FORGERY AND COUNTER-FEITING | OFFENSES AGAINST FAMILY AND CHILDREN | NARCOTIC DRUG LAWS | PROSTITUTION AND COMMERCIALIZED VICE |
|---|---|---|---|---|---|
| 1953 | 18.3 | 14.0 | 9.3 | 15.7 | 73.1 |
| 1954 | 14.4 | 13.4 | 9.6 | 17.5 | 70.1 |
| 1955 | 15.6 | 15.2 | 9.8 | 17.1 | 68.8 |
| 1956 | 15.5 | 16.6 | 9.1 | 16.3 | 62.9 |
| 1957 | 14.4 | 14.8 | 9.0 | 15.6 | 69.2 |
| 1958 | 14.3 | 15.1 | 8.6 | 16.4 | 69.0 |
| 1959 | 14.9 | 16.2 | 8.9 | 16.2 | 65.2 |
| 1960 | 15.7 | 16.8 | 9.7 | 14.6 | 73.5 |
| 1961 | 15.7 | 17.5 | 11.2 | 15.4 | 71.8 |
| 1962 | 17.6 | 18.1 | 11.0 | 15.1 | 76.1 |
| 1963 | 18.3 | 18.7 | 11.5 | 14.2 | 77.0 |
| 1964 | 19.5 | 19.3 | 11.3 | 14.1 | 81.2 |
| 1965 | 20.7 | 19.2 | 11.0 | 13.4 | 77.6 |
| 1966 | 21.8 | 20.9 | 12.1 | 13.8 | 79.3 |
| 1967 | 23.4 | 21.4 | 11.4 | 13.7 | 77.2 |
| 1968 | 24.4 | 22.3 | 10.9 | 15.0 | 78.0 |
| 1969 | 26.3 | 23.2 | 11.4 | 15.5 | 79.5 |
| 1970 | 27.8 | 24.4 | 11.3 | 15.7 | 79.1 |
| 1971 | 27.4 | 24.8 | 11.6 | 16.3 | 77.4 |
| 1972 | 29.7 | 25.4 | 12.3 | 15.7 | 73.5 |
| Average rate of change, 1953-72 | +0.60 | +0.60 | +0.16 | 0 | +0.02 |
| Average rate of change, 1958-72 | +1.10 | +0.74 | +0.26 | -0.05 | +0.32 |
| Average rate of change, 1967-72 | +1.26 | +0.80 | +0.18 | +0.40 | -0.74 |

Two final observations: (1) it is plausible to assume that the police are becoming less "chivalrous" to women suspects and that the police are beginning to treat women more like equals; (2) police behavior alone cannot account for both the large increases in larceny, fraud, embezzlement, and forgery arrests over the past six years and for the lack of increase in arrests for homicide, aggravated assault, and other violent crimes.

The more parsimonious explanation is that as women increase their participation in the labor force their opportunity to commit certain types of crime also increases. As women feel more liberated physically, emotionally, and legally, and less subjected to male power, their frustrations and anger decrease. This explanation assumes that women have no greater store of morality or decency than do men. Their propensities to commit crimes do not differ, but, in the past, their opportunities have been much more limited. As women's opportunities increase, so will the likelihood that they will commit crimes. But women will be most likely to commit property, economic, and financial types of offenses. Their greater freedom and independence will result in a decline in their desire to kill the usual objects of their anger or frustration: their husbands, lovers, and other men upon whom they are dependent, but insecure about.

## CROSS-NATIONAL ARREST STATISTICS

A brief comparison of female arrest statistics in the United States with those collected by the International Criminal Police Organization for 25 countries all over the world in 1963, 1968, and 1970 shows that the United States moved from eighth place in 1963 to fourth place in 1968 to third place in 1970.

But the heterogeneity of the countries that rank directly above and directly below the United States makes it difficult to draw any conclusions about the types of societies that are conducive to high female arrest rates. Among those countries closest to the United States, there is, on the one hand, the West Indies, Thailand, and Burma; and, on the other hand, Portugal, West Germany, Luxembourg, France, Austria, and Great Britain.

Perhaps more sense can be made of the rankings when they are broken by types of offenses. The offense categories that are included in the International Criminal Statistics and their definitions are listed in footnote 10. Table 5 compares the United States' female arrest statistics with other countries' for offense categories I, III (A and B), IV, and VI.[10]

**Table 5.** *Ranking of Countries by Percentage of Women Arrested for Various Crimes: 1963, 1968, 1970*

| Country | ALL CRIMES | | MURDER | | MAJOR LARCENY | | MINOR LARCENY | | FRAUD | | DRUGS | |
|---|---|---|---|---|---|---|---|---|---|---|---|---|
| | Rank | Percent | Rank | Percent | Rank | Percent | Rank | Percent | Rank | Percent | Rank | Percent |
| West Indies | 1 | 28.9 | 11. | 13.3 | 13 | 3.4 | 11 | 16.3 | 5.5 | 15.4 | — | — |
| New Zealand | 2 | 25.3 | 4 | 16.9 | 8 | 4.2 | 6 | 19.6 | 5.5 | 15.4 | 5 | 14.2 |
| Thailand | 3 | 17.3 | 19 | 4.2 | 15 | 3.0 | 14 | 14.4 | 13 | 10.1 | 11 | 4.6 |
| West Germany | 4 | 16.4 | 8 | 15.0 | 10 | 3.8 | 1 | 25.5 | 2 | 21.8 | 3 | 14.6 |
| Luxembourg | 5 | 16.2 | — | — | 2.5 | 8.7 | 13 | 15.4 | 14 | 9.5 | — | — |
| United States | 6 | 15.2 | 6.5 | 15.4 | 7 | 5.3 | 2 | 24.8 | 1 | 23.5 | 7 | 11.1 |
| Austria | 7.5 | 13.8 | 3 | 22.0 | 2.5 | 8.7 | 4 | 22.6 | 3 | 20.8 | 4 | 14.3 |
| France | 7.5 | 13.8 | 12 | 12.8 | 1 | 8.8 | 8.5 | 16.6 | 4 | 18.7 | — | — |
| England and Wales | 9 | 13.5 | 6.5 | 15.4 | 16 | 2.6 | 7 | 18.5 | 8 | 14.4 | — | — |
| Tunisia | 10 | 12.8 | 1 | 27.0 | 4 | 8.5 | 18 | 7.3 | 20 | 4.6 | 12 | 3.5 |
| Israel | 11 | 12.1 | 22 | 2.8 | 17 | 2.5 | 19 | 6.8 | 17 | 6.6 | 8 | 7.7 |
| Korea | 12 | 11.5 | 2 | 22.4 | 9 | 4.0 | 16 | 10.0 | 15 | 8.2 | 2 | 23.1 |
| Scotland | 13 | 10.9 | 10 | 13.4 | 11 | 3.7 | 8.5 | 16.6 | 7 | 14.5 | — | — |
| Netherlands | 14 | 10.4 | 15 | 8.1 | 13 | 3.4 | 3 | 23.5 | 9 | 13.1 | — | — |
| Ireland | 15 | 10.1 | 13 | 12.5 | 5 | 6.5 | 10 | 16.5 | 11 | 10.6 | — | — |
| Monaco | 16 | 7.5 | — | — | — | — | — | — | — | — | — | — |
| Tanzania | 17 | 6.9 | 9 | 14.1 | 19 | 2.2 | 21 | 4.2 | 21 | 2.1 | — | — |
| Cyprus | 18 | 6.7 | 17 | 6.5 | 18 | 2.4 | 17 | 7.7 | 19 | 4.7 | 9 | 6.8 |
| Finland | 19 | 6.6 | 16 | 6.9 | 13 | 3.4 | 12 | 15.9 | 12 | 10.3 | — | — |
| Japan | 20 | 4.6 | 5 | 16.5 | 20 | 1.2 | 5 | 20.5 | 16 | 7.0 | 1 | 24.1 |
| Malawi | 21 | 4.2 | 20.5 | 4.0 | 22 | .9 | 23 | 2.6 | 22 | 1.7 | 14 | 1.0 |
| Hong Kong | 22 | 3.0 | 20.5 | 4.0 | 21 | 1.0 | 22 | 4.1 | 18 | 5.5 | 13 | 2.2 |
| Fiji | 23.5 | 1.9 | 18 | 4.5 | 23 | .3 | 20 | 5.1 | 23 | .8 | — | — |
| Brunei | 23.5 | 1.9 | — | — | — | — | — | — | — | — | 10 | 4.8 |
| Canada | — | — | 17 | 10.0 | 6 | 5.5 | 15 | 13.4 | 10 | 11.8 | 6 | 13.9 |

For property and financial crimes—such as larceny, as defined by
the FBI statistics, and fraud—the United States ranks second and first,
respectively. Countries that rank directly above and below are those of
Western Europe such as West Germany, Austria, and the Netherlands.
For crimes of violence and drugs, American women rank sixth and seventh and are surrounded by a heterogeneous collection of countries that
include the West Indies, New Zealand, West Germany, Scotland, and
Canada. The positions of the United States and the countries of Western
Europe in the larceny and fraud rankings are consistent with the
hypothesis that, in those societies in which women are more likely to be
employed in commercial and white-collar positions and to enjoy legal
and social rights, they are also more likely to engage in property and
economic types of crimes.

## CONVICTIONS AND SENTENCES

Examination of convictions and sentencing patterns between men and
women over time is difficult because of the absence of judicial statistics
at the level of state courts. The federal statistics that are available from
1963 to 1972 are consistent with the arrest data in that they show that
over the eight-year time span, the highest proportion of women have
been convicted for fraud, embezzlement, and forgery. These same
offenses also show the greatest increase in the proportion of females who
have been convicted between 1963 and 1971.

California statistics from 1960 through 1972 do not show that the
increase in convictions has followed the increase in arrests for the same
type of offenses.[11] Although there has been an increase of 31 percent in
the proportion of women convicted for all types of crimes from 1962 to
1972, that increase has been due solely to the higher conviction rates for
violent offenses.

New York State statistics on the proportion of female commitments
to correctional institutions by type of offenses from 1963 to 1972 reveal
an overall decline and no significant changes within any of the offense
categories.

The proportion of female commitments to all state penal institutions
declined between 1950 and 1970 from 5.1 percent to 4.7 percent.

On the whole, using the rather meager statistics that are available, it
appears that the courts have not been adapting their behavior to meet
the changing roles that women, and perhaps the police in their interactions with women, are performing. In interviews that were conducted

with about 30 criminal trial court judges in the Midwest in the winter of 1974, we found that most of the judges had not observed, and did not anticipate, any changes either in the numbers or types of women or in the types of offenses that women were likely to be charged with in the immediate future. Most of the respondents said that they expected to continue to be easier on women than on men, when it came to passing sentence.

## WOMEN AS VICTIMS OF CRIMES

This section shifts the focus of this article and turns the issue on its head by examining the role of women as victims of criminal acts. One of the issues to which the woman's movement has directed much of its efforts has been the treatment of women who are victims of rape. The movement has been critical of the legal system and has demanded changes in the standards of proof and identification that are required. It has pointed to the police and demanded that they behave more humanely. It has insisted that medical and psychological facilities be made available and has called for changes in the manner and circumstances under which women who claimed they had been raped are examined. It has also demanded that the services of a therapist be made available to the victim as soon as possible after she has reported the attack. The movement itself has been instrumental in setting up "rape hot lines" in many communities.

For all the attention that has been devoted to the female as "rape victim," it is interesting to note the proportions of men and women who have been victims of all types of criminal acts. For example, Wolfgang reported the characteristics of victims of criminal homicide from 1948 to 1952 and found that 76.4 percent were men and 23.6 percent were women. In 1972, the FBI reported that 22.2 percent of all murder victims were women.

In 1971, under the auspices of the Law Enforcement Assistance Administration, the Bureau of the Census conducted victimization surveys in Montgomery County, Ohio (Dayton), and in Santa Clara County, California (San Jose). In Dayton, 16,000 persons over the age of 16 and in San Jose 28,000 persons over the age of 16 were victims of assault, robbery, or personal larceny at least once during 1970. The proportion of female victims in each city is shown below.

It is obvious that the percentage of women victims is less than their representation in each of the communities. Even when rape victims are

| *Women* as a percent of | Dayton | San Jose |
|---|---|---|
| Assault victims* | 31 | 34 |
| Robbery victims | 36 | 34 |
| Personal larceny victims | 49 | 30 |

*Includes persons who reported they were raped.

included in the assault categories, the proportion of assault victims is less than the 50 percent that one might expect simply on the basis of female representation in the community.

The following statistics allow for comparison between women and other categories in the two communities by showing rates of victimization per 100 population.

| | VICTIMIZATION RATES | |
|---|---|---|
| *Persons* victimized by: | Dayton | San Jose |
| Assault* | 3.2 | 3.3 |
| Robbery | 0.8 | 0.8 |
| Personal larceny | 0.4 | 0.2 |
| *Women* victimized by: | | |
| Assault* | 1.9 | 2.1 |
| Robbery | 0.6 | 0.5 |
| Personal larceny | 0.4 | 0.2 |

*Includes persons who reported they were raped.

These figures, along with the national data on homicide, indicate that women are *less* likely to be victims of crimes than are men, and especially young men. Of course, one might argue that the relevant comparison is not the proportion of female victims by their representation in the society, but the proportion of female victims by the proportion of female offenders. If it is men—and especially men between the ages of 16 and 24—who commit the highest proportion of criminal acts, then perhaps one should expect persons in that category to also account for the highest proportion of victims.

|  | VICTIMIZATION RATES | |
| --- | --- | --- |
| *Young men* between 16 and 24 victimized by: | Dayton | San Jose |
| Assault | 11.7 | 9.2 |
| Robbery | 1.7 | 2.4 |
| Personal larceny | 0.8 | 1.0 |
| *Minority* group members:* | | |
| Assault | 3.1 | 3.9 |
| Robbery | 1.6 | 1.0 |
| Personal larceny | 0.8 | 0.3 |

*Dayton figures are for black persons; San Jose figures are for persons of Spanish origin or descent.

**Table 6.** *Sex of Victim and Offender for Aggravated Assault Arrests, 17 Cities, 1967*

|  | SEX OF VICTIM | | |
| --- | --- | --- | --- |
| Sex of Offender | Male | Female | Total |
| Male | 56.6 | 27.0 | 83.6 (727) |
| Female | 9.3 | 7.1 | 16.4 (142) |
| Total | 65.9 (573) | 34.1 (296) | 100   (869) |

NOTE: The figures represent percentages; those in parentheses are numbers of offenses.

In their report to the *National Commission on the Causes and Prevention of Violence,* Mulvihill and Tumin described the results of a survey of victim and offender patterns for four major violent crimes in 17 large American cities. The crimes were: criminal homicide, aggravated assault, forcible rape, and robbery (armed and unarmed).[12] Table 6 describes the sex of the offender and the sex of victim for one of those types of offenses.

The Mulvihill–Tumin data also show the following characteristics:

1. For all four offense categories, at least two-thirds of both the victims and the offenders are men. Armed robbery is almost exclusively a male situation: 90 percent of the victims and 95 percent of the offenders are men.

2. In the case of criminal homicide, 34 percent of the interactions are intersexual, and the roles performed by the men and women are divided almost equally—16.4 percent female offender/male victim, 17.5 percent male offender/female victim. There is a greater likelihood that the victim of a homicide perpetrated by a woman will be a family member (most likely her spouse) than when the homicide is committed by a man. Women are also more likely to kill members of their family than are men. White and black women share that propensity almost equally.

3. In the other offense categories, when the situation is intersexual, there is a much greater likelihood that the male will be the offender and the female the victim. For aggravated assault cases, the ratio of male-female victims is 3:1, in armed robbery, 2.5:1, and in unarmed robbery, 13:1.

These 1967 data are consistent with those obtained in the 1971 victimization surveys of Dayton and San Jose in that they also portray the male as being the victim much more frequently than the female. These data serve the additional function of dramatizing the extent to which violent crime is still very largely a male enterprise (males are both the perpetrators and the victims). Only 3.8 percent of all the criminal homicides, 7.1 percent of all the aggravated assaults, and .9 and 2.9 percents of all the armed and unarmed robberies were acts perpetrated by females against females. Finally, the 1967 data also show that when violent offenses are intersexual, the woman's role is much more likely to be that of the victim and the male's that of the offender. Homicide is the exception.

## CONCLUDING REMARKS

In the last three or four years, all of the mass media—films, newspapers, television, magazines, and radio—have agreed upon a common theme vis-à-vis women and crime. They have claimed that more women are engaging in more acts of violence than have been engaged in by American women at any time in the past. And they have attributed much of the females' greater propensities for violence to the woman's movement. The fact that, in 1970, four women made the FBI list for the ten most wanted criminals served as prima facie evidence of the accuracy of their perceptions. The Patty Hearst scenario also did much to convince the mass media that the image they were projecting about the increased propensities for violence by American women was indeed an accurate one.

But examination of national statistics over several decades reveals quite a different picture and, admittedly, one that lacks the drama of the media-created image. Women's participation in crime, especially serious crime, has increased. And the increase has been especially marked from 1967 on. But the types of serious crime that women are engaging in, in growing numbers, are crimes of property. They are economic and financial types of offenses. It is larceny, embezzlement, fraud, and forgery that are proving so attractive to women, and not homicide, assault, and armed robbery.

The increase in the first group of offenses and the decline in the second are, I believe, related in the following manner. With the woman's movement, a much greater proportion of women are working outside the home which provides more women with greater opportunities to embezzle, to commit fraud, and to steal than are available to housewives. The fact that these women are working also enhances their feelings of independence. The woman's movement support these feelings by offering women a new image of themselves; and laws have changed so as to provide women with more legal and social independence. All of these factors, I believe, reduce the likelihood that women will attack or kill their most traditional targets: namely, their husbands or their lovers, other women with whom their men have become involved, or their unborn babies.

The factors cited above have provided women with the economic independence to take care of themselves and with a legal and social status that allows them to live without the protection of a man and to determine the fate of their own bodies. At least in the short run, then, I think we will continue to see an increase in women participating in property, fiscal, and economic offenses. Violent offenses will remain relatively stable or decline. The expectation, or the fear, that large numbers of young women will turn to radical politics and become revolutionaries has little evidence to support it. The Patty Hearsts and the Emily Harrises are probably as rare a phenomenon as was Ma Barker.

## NOTES

1. Lady Barbara Wooton, "A Magistrate in Search of the Causes of Crimes," *Crime and the Criminal Law,* 1963, pp. 6–8.

2. Rose Giallombardo, *Society of Women: A Study of a Women's Prison* (New York: John Wiley & Son, Inc., 1966), p. 7.

3. Sheldon Glueck and Eleanor Glueck, *Five Hundred Delinquent Women* (New York: Alfred A. Knopf, Inc., 1934), p. 96.

4. Daniel A. Green, "The Dark Side of Women's Liberation: Crime Takes a Female Turn," *National Observer*, September 1974, p. 2.

5. Ibid., p. 2.

6. For a more detailed discussion of how the indeterminate sentence is applied to women, see: Linda Temen, "Discriminatory Sentencing of Women Offenders," *Criminal Law Review* 11 (winter 1973), p. 355.

7. R.R. Arditi et al., "The Sexual Segregation of American Prisoners," *Yale Law Journal* 82 (November-May 1973), p. 1266.

8. It may appear that this discussion uses arrest statistics as proxies for describing crime tates among men and women without regard for the hazards of doing so. While the hazards are recognized, unfortunately there are no other data prior to these statistics that provide information about the characteristics of the suspect as well as the offense he or she is believed to have committed. Criminologists usually prefer to use statistics for determining crime rates that are computed on the basis of crimes known to the police, but those statistics do not identify the suspect in any way. It is also recognized that the proportions of arrests vary considerably from one type of offense to another. Arrest rates are more accurate proxies for behavior in violent types of crimes than they are for crimes against property.

9. The Type II offenses shown in table 4 have been included because there has been a change in the arrest pattern for women or because they are offenses for which arrest rates for women are consistently high.

10.   I.   Murder: Any act performed, with the purpose of taking human life, no matter under what circumstances. This definition excludes manslaughter and abortion, but not infanticide.

    II.   Sex offenses: Each country uses the definitions of its own laws for determining whether or not an act is a sex crime; rape and trafficking in women are also included.

   III.   Larceny: Any act of intentionally and unlawfully removing property belonging to another person. This category includes such a wide variety of offenses, that it was subdivided into:
   A. major larceny: robbery with dangerous aggravating circumstances (for example, armed robbery, burglary, housebreaking)
   B. minor larceny: all other kinds of larceny (for example, theft, receiving stolen goods)

   IV.   Fraud: Any act of gaining unlawful possession of another person's property other than by larceny. This category includes embezzlement, misappropriation, forgery, false pretenses, trickery, deliberate misrepresentation, swindle in general.

    V.   Counterfeit currency offenses: This includes any violation in connection with manufacture, issuing, altering, smuggling, or traffic in counterfeit currency.

   VI.   Drug offenses: This category covers any violation involving illicit manufacture of, traffic in, transportation of, and use of narcotic drugs.

11. The state of California maintains the most comprehensive crime and judicial statistics in the 50 states.

12. They obtained a 10 percent random sample of 1967 offense and arrest reports from the following cities: Atlanta, Boston, Chicago, Cleveland, Dallas, Denver, Detroit, Los Angeles, Miami, Minneapolis, New Orleans, New York, Philadelphia, St. Louis, San Francisco, Seattle, and Washington.

---

THREE

# Crime and the Contemporary Woman: An Analysis of Changing Levels of Female Property Crime, 1960-1975*†

DARRELL J. STEFFENSMEIER

In recent years there has been a proliferation of popular and scientific writing on the extent to which patterns and levels of female crime have been changing, and the impact of the women's movement and changing sex roles on criminal behavior (Adler; Bruck; Rosenblatt and Greenland; Simon). A common theme of these writings is that the criminal activities of women are coming to resemble those of men in kind and degree as convergence in role expectations and access to illegitimate opportunities increases. Supposedly, women are committing more

---

*Reprinted from *Social Forces* (57, December 1978). "Crime and the Contemporary Woman: An Analysis of Changing Levels of Female Property Crime, 1960-75," by Darrell J. Steffensmeier. Copyright © The University of North Carolina Press.

†I wish to thank several colleagues of the Pennsylvania State University for statistical advice and useful comments on this manuscript. They include Clifford Clogg, Gordon DeJong, Alvin Rosenthal, Renee Hoffman Steffensmeier, Shannon Stokes, and Rex Warland. Thanks are also due to two anonymous referees for helpful suggestions.

crimes, catching up with their male counterparts, and increasingly engaging in traditionally male-dominated crimes. According to Adler, for example, there has been a "skyrocketing increase in the rate at which women steal cars, burglarize stores, forge checks, embezzle funds. . . . While they [women] have demonstrated ability to drive tractor trailers, climb telephone poles, lay bricks, carry mail, perform surgery, defend clients, and judge cases, they have also shown no greater potential than males to remain lawabiding" (250). Similarly, Chief Ed Davis of the Los Angeles Police Department believes that the women's movement has triggered "a crime wave like the world has never seen before."

This intriguing, and to many self-evident, hypothesis has been challenged. In a recent paper on violent crime trends, Steffensmeier et al. outline several shortcomings in current discussions of female crime. Chief among these is the tendency to rely on arrest statistics of the Uniform Crime Reports (UCR) and to use these statistics in an inappropriate and misleading fashion. Most analysts (e.g., Adler; Simon, a) follow the UCR practice of reporting gross arrest figures and percentage changes based on these figures to show that there are more women arrested for criminal offenses today than in the past. Resulting partly from the failure to specify the central questions on female crime trends, this use of UCR arrest statistics overlooks two crucial issues. One is whether the rate of increase in female arrests is greater than increases in the U.S. female population during the same time period. A second issue is whether the rate of increase in female arrests is greater than the increase for males.

In our earlier analysis of female violent crime (Steffensmeier et al.), these issues were dealt with by using U.S. census data in conjunction with UCR arrest data to compute sex-specific arrest rates. Here I apply these same procedures to an analysis of female property crime, procedures which make the UCR arrest figures comparable over time and between the sexes and so permit comparisons of male and female crime levels.

In our analysis of female violent crime, we found substantial increases in rates of violent crime for females since 1960. But this increase is generally matched or exceeded by the increases for males. Most importantly, the relative gap between male and female levels of violence remains about the same as it was sixteen years ago. But one might expect changes in levels of female property crime to be more clear-cut than the changes we found in violent crime. It is anticipated that levels of female property crime (taking into account population changes) have increased since 1960, and that the relative gap between female and male levels has decreased. The rationale for expecting a decrease with respect to property crimes is derived from an argument originally advanced by Clinard and recently supported by Webb and Jacobson that ". . . the influence of functional changes in a society is less in personal crimes than in property offenses which involve the acquisition of things and not necessarily any personal or fortuitous situation" (Clinard, 204). A functional change, as used here, can refer to any structural property change such as in urbanization, industrialization, occupational distributions, educational levels, and so on. We assume that the amelioration of structural inequities between the sexes is a functional change which, while having little impact on person or violent crimes, should lead to a decline over time in differences between the sexes in levels of property crime.

The purpose of this paper, therefore, is to examine trends in female property crime since 1960. As in the previous analysis of female violent crime, we ask whether (1) the rate of increase in female property crime arrests is greater than the increase in the U.S. female population during 1960–75; (2) the rate of increase for females is greater than the increase for males; and (3) whether, within the female arrest population, there has been an increase in the proportion arrested for property crimes. We will also examine the data to assess whether changes in female participation in crime can be attributed to the effects of the women's movement. The approach to this issue is to break the analysis of data into two time periods, 1960–67 and 1968–75, and assess the difference in the rate of change between the two time periods.[1]

In the discussion of our results, we will suggest several factors that may account for the data patterns that were uncovered and assess the extent to which the different factors fit the data.

## METHODS

Data on arrests for the years 1960–75 were obtained from the Uniform Crime Reports in order to assess property crime trends in the United States. Published by the FBI, these statistics are the only nationwide, longitudinal data available which provide the number of arrests in a given year, the offenses for which suspects have been arrested, and the age, sex and race of those arrested. Since 1960 is the comparison year for trend analysis in the UCR, we also used 1960 as our base year. Moreover, sixteen years is enough time to assess crime trends. In the following analysis five indices of property crime were selected: burglary, larceny-theft,[2] auto theft, fraud/embezzlement,[3] and stolen properly.[4] In addition, we used an overall measure of property crime which combined the three index offenses of burglary, larceny, and auto theft.

As noted earlier, previous analysts have generally used UCR gross arrest figures to document their statements about increased levels of female property crime. These figures are computed from the volume or number of persons arrested rather than from rates. The UCR do not provide arrest rates broken down by sex and the use of UCR percentage change figures is hazardous because these tabulations do not adequately take into account changes in population size and composition.[5] "To continue using the traditional UCR expression of percent changes in volume of arrests from one year or decade to another is to perpetuate almost meaningless measures" (Wolfgang, 708). In order to overcome the deficiencies of earlier analyses we will use sex-specific arrest rates as our principal measure of female property crime.

In using arrest rates as our major measure of levels of female property crime, two types of computations were performed on the UCR arrest statistics. First, arrest data from UCR along with data from census reports were combined to compute offense specific arrest rates that have been refined to take into account sex distributions in the population. The standardization procedure (discussed in detail in Rosenthal and Steffensmeier) used to compute these arrest rates makes the UCR arrest figures comparable over time and between the sexes. The formula used to compute the arrest rates is:

$$\text{RATE}/100{,}000 = M/P \times N/T \times 100{,}000$$

where M = the arrest volume figure given in the appropriate UCR table.

P = the population volume figure from the same UCR table.

N = the estimated number of persons who would be in the UCR table if coverage were complete (e.g., total U.S. population, total rural population, etc). This figure is taken from U.S. population estimates.

T = estimated number of persons in the target category for whom the arrest figures are given (e.g., males in rural areas, people under 18 years of age, etc.). This figure is taken from U.S. population estimates.

The figures in the formula are taken from two different sources. M and P come from the applicable table in the UCR. For reasons discussed in detail elsewhere (Rosenthal and Steffensmeier) the figures for specific years are taken from the UCR table with the largest P. N and T are taken from the *Current Population Reports* (U.S. Bureau of the Census, 1974; 1975).

A second type of calculation gave us the percentage that females contribute to the total (male and female) arrest rate for (1) each offense and (2) the combined property crime index. These percentages enable comparison of male and female arrest rates. An illustration will clarify our use of these percentages. If, over sixteen years, we found increases in the arrest rates of females for burglary, but the percentage contribution of females to the total arrest rates for burglary remained fairly stable at say 25 percent, we would conclude that the male arrest rate for burglary was increasing just as fast as the female rate. Conversely, if we found increases over sixteen years in the arrest rates of females for burglary and the percentage contribution of females to the total arrest rate for burglary rose from 25 percent to 45 percent in 1975, we would conclude that the relative gap between the sexes was closing.

This procedure allows us to determine whether the *relative* gap in male and female crime levels has narrowed or widened since 1960. While changes in relative differences are the principal concern of our analysis, changes in absolute differences will also be indicated. Sex differences in absolute gains in crime levels were determined by calculating annual rates of change.

In addition to the calculation of refined arrest rates and percentages based on them, a third set of calculations was performed on the UCR arrest statistics to demonstrate changes in the type of crimes for which persons are likely to be arrested. The arrest volumes of the UCR were used to calculate (1) the percentage of property crime arrests among serious crime arrests, and (2) the percentage of property crime arrests among all arrests. This analysis was performed within each sex cohort using the five individual indices of property crime and the combined property crime index. Comparisons of these percentages shows whether there has been a change in the proportion of females and males arrested for property crimes, so expanding on the type of analysis conducted by Simon, a.[6]

Most students of crime who use the UCR data preface their analysis with a few conventional words of caution about the reliability and validity of these statistics. Although one purpose of this report is to demonstrate how these statistics can be used more appropriately and meaningfully, we too are aware of the vulnerability of UCR arrest datas to measurement errors.[7] If we can assume a random distribution of measurement error between the sexes, then we are reasonably safe in using the UCR arrest data for purposes of examining the relative differences in property crime levels between males and females over a given time period. It is risky, however, to use the UCR arrest data as either an absolute measure of property crime levels for females for a specific year, or to use them to assess relative differences in crime levels for females over time.

## FINDINGS

The findings of this report speak to the following three questions, in each case, for the years 1960–75.

1. Has there been an increase in rates of property crime for females in the United States?
2. Has the gap between males and females in rates of property crime decreased?
3. Within the female arrest population, has there been an increase in the proportion of females arrested for property offenses?

To answer the first question, sex-specific arrest rates were computed for each year 1960 through 1975. Examination of the data for females in Table 1 shows that over the 16-year period the arrest rates per 100,000 increased: (1) from 9.3 to 31.0 for burglary, (2) from 87.3 to 379.6 for larceny, (3) from 5.4 to 10.6 for auto theft, (4) from 14.7 to 67.1 for fraud/embezzlement and (5) from 2.3 to 13.7 for stolen property. For the three combined property index offenses the female arrest rate increased from 101.9 to 421.2. The rates in Table 1 lead to the conclusion that rates of property crime for females in the United States have increased substantially.[8]

The second question, the extent to which rates of female violent crime have changed relative to male rates, involves a comparison of arrest rates for males and females. In any discussion of changing sex roles and its relation to female criminality, the central issue is whether sex differences in levels of crime diminish as men and women move toward greater equality in their rights and privileges. This includes the question whether the women's movement per se has had a unique influence on female criminality.

Examination of the data for males in Table 1 reveals that there have been large increases in arrest rates for each of the property offenses. Comparison of the arrest rates reveals larger relative increases over the years for females than males. We can compare arrest rates for the sexes by calculating the percentage that females contribute to the total arrest rate for each offense. For each property offense (except stolen property) and for the combined property index there has been a gradual upward trend in the percent that females contribute to the total arrest rates. Over the 16-year period, the percent of female contribution increased: (1) from 2.8 to 5.0 for burglary, (2) from 15.2 to 29.3 for larceny-theft, (3) from 3.5 to 6.4 for auto theft, and (4) from 14.4 to 32.1 for fraud/ embezzlement. For the combined property index of burglary, larceny-theft, and auto theft the female contribution increased from 9.6 to 20.3.

**Table 1.** *Property Crime Arrest Rates per 100,000 for Females and Males, and Percent of Female Contribution to Total Arrest Rates*[a]

| Year | 3 PROPERTY-CRIME INDEX | | | BURGLARY | | | LARCENY-THEFT | | | AUTO THEFT | | | FRAUD-EMBEZZLEMENT | | | STOLEN PROPERTY | | |
|---|---|---|---|---|---|---|---|---|---|---|---|---|---|---|---|---|---|---|
| | Female | Male | % Contribution | Female | Male | % Contribution | Female | Male | % Contribution | Female | Male | % Contribution | Female | Male | % Contribution | Female | Male | % Contribution |
| 1975 | 421.2 | 1657.1 | 20.3 | 31.0 | 588.4 | 5.0 | 379.6 | 913.8 | 29.3 | 10.6 | 155.0 | 6.5 | 67.1 | 142.2 | 32.1 | 13.7 | 124.9 | 9.9 |
| 1974 | 428.1 | 1708.0 | 20.0 | 31.7 | 592.9 | 5.1 | 384.5 | 930.5 | 29.2 | 11.9 | 184.5 | 6.1 | 53.7 | 121.0 | 30.7 | 13.4 | 127.3 | 9.5 |
| 1973 | 339.6 | 1364.7 | 19.9 | 25.4 | 479.6 | 5.0 | 303.6 | 706.8 | 30.1 | 10.5 | 178.4 | 5.6 | 41.9 | 101.0 | 29.3 | 10.5 | 101.2 | 9.4 |
| 1972 | 327.0 | 1387.4 | 19.1 | 23.6 | 464.8 | 4.8 | 293.3 | 743.6 | 28.3 | 10.1 | 179.1 | 5.4 | 44.2 | 113.9 | 27.9 | 10.1 | 101.0 | 9.1 |
| 1971 | 321.8 | 1470.1 | 18.0 | 23.4 | 468.1 | 4.6 | 286.7 | 786.3 | 26.7 | 11.8 | 199.6 | 5.6 | 44.0 | 119.3 | 26.9 | 10.6 | 111.0 | 8.7 |
| 1970 | 298.7 | 1400.5 | 17.6 | 20.8 | 455.3 | 4.4 | 267.8 | 742.9 | 26.5 | 10.1 | 202.3 | 4.7 | 35.5 | 104.1 | 25.5 | 8.9 | 93.3 | 8.7 |
| 1969 | 252.1 | 1313.3 | 16.1 | 18.4 | 434.8 | 4.1 | 222.8 | 667.0 | 25.0 | 10.9 | 211.5 | 4.9 | 29.6 | 92.0 | 24.3 | 6.5 | 75.0 | 7.9 |
| 1968 | 213.7 | 1265.0 | 14.5 | 17.6 | 434.1 | 3.9 | 186.0 | 620.3 | 23.1 | 10.2 | 210.6 | 4.6 | 24.3 | 84.6 | 22.3 | 4.8 | 61.6 | 7.2 |
| 1967 | 200.9 | 1210.0 | 14.2 | 16.0 | 406.8 | 3.8 | 176.6 | 602.7 | 22.7 | 8.3 | 200.5 | 4.0 | 24.2 | 87.8 | 21.6 | 3.6 | 46.9 | 7.0 |
| 1966 | 183.2 | 1128.5 | 14.0 | 13.6 | 361.1 | 3.6 | 162.0 | 576.6 | 21.9 | 7.7 | 190.7 | 3.8 | 22.0 | 86.4 | 20.3 | 2.9 | 36.6 | 7.2 |
| 1965 | 176.6 | 1138.1 | 13.4 | 13.4 | 369.2 | 3.5 | 155.4 | 579.6 | 21.1 | 7.7 | 189.2 | 3.9 | 21.7 | 92.7 | 19.0 | 2.9 | 33.9 | 7.9 |
| 1964 | 156.0 | 1102.0 | 12.4 | 12.7 | 355.1 | 3.5 | 135.6 | 563.2 | 19.4 | 7.7 | 183.8 | 4.0 | 19.1 | 87.4 | 17.9 | 3.3 | 32.3 | 9.3 |
| 1963 | 134.9 | 1044.3 | 11.4 | 10.9 | 342.5 | 3.1 | 117.6 | 529.8 | 18.2 | 6.3 | 171.9 | 3.5 | 18.7 | 90.9 | 17.1 | 2.4 | 28.7 | 7.8 |
| 1962 | 134.0 | 1040.5 | 11.4 | 11.9 | 342.7 | 3.4 | 115.5 | 530.8 | 17.9 | 6.6 | 167.0 | 3.8 | 16.7 | 87.4 | 16.0 | 2.5 | 28.8 | 8.1 |
| 1961 | 112.3 | 1002.9 | 10.1 | 10.9 | 349.3 | 3.0 | 96.0 | 502.3 | 16.0 | 5.5 | 151.3 | 3.5 | 16.1 | 89.7 | 15.2 | 2.4 | 27.3 | 7.8 |
| 1960 | 101.9 | 961.3 | 9.6 | 9.3 | 324.7 | 2.8 | 87.3 | 487.4 | 15.2 | 5.4 | 149.2 | 3.5 | 14.7 | 87.9 | 14.4 | 2.3 | 26.3 | 8.2 |

[a]The formula for computing the % female contribution to total arrest rates is $\dfrac{\text{female rate}}{(\text{male} \pm \text{female rate})} \times 100$. This statistic is computed for each offense and the combined property index.

45

There was, however, little change in the percent female contribution for stolen property, from 8.2 to 9.9.

The answer to the second question is clear-cut. Except for stolen property, the relative gap between males and females in rates of property crime has been narrowing since 1960. A closer inspection of Table 1 reveals that while the percent female contribution has doubled since 1960 for burglary, auto theft, larceny, and fraud/embezzlement, the most dramatic increases occurred for the last two. Women now comprise almost one-third of those arrested for both these offenses whereas in 1960 they made up less than one-sixth.

On the other hand, burglary and auto theft remain predominantly male offenses. The finding that females now contribute 5 percent and 6 percent to the total arrest rates for burglary and auto theft, respectively, rather than 3 percent and 3.5 percent as in 1960, can hardly be taken as convincing evidence that females are catching up with males. Given the relatively small base of female arrest rates for these two offenses, only limited significance can be attributed to the finding that the percent female contribution has doubled since 1960 for both these offenses. Data for burglary and auto theft may be the most unreliable because reported female levels are so low to begin with that minor reporting changes could be largely responsible for observed variations.

But in contrast to these increases in rate of property crime for females an examination of absolute differences between males and females presents the opposite picture. Whereas the examination of relative differences shows that females are catching up with males in the category of larceny-theft, the *absolute* difference in arrest rates was greater in 1975 (534.2) than it was in 1960 (400.1). The absolute differences between the sexes in burglary and stolen property were also greater in 1975 than they were in 1960 while those for fraud and auto theft were negligible. Examining absolute differences between males and females in terms of the average annual rate of change[9] reveals larger changes for males than females, especially for burglary. The differences between males and females in the average annual rate of change were: 16.13 for burglary, 8.94 for larceny, .04 for auto theft, .13 for fraud/embezzlement, 5.81 for stolen property, and 25.10 for the combined property index. Obviously, the interpretation of trends in female crime levels depends on the statistical procedure that is used. We contend that relative differences give a more accurate and less misleading picture than absolute differences of convergence in crime levels.[10]

Another issue that we examined with the data in Table 1 was the impact of the women's movement. The data indicate that the changes we observed began before the late 1960s when the women's movement could be expected to have its greatest impact on levels of property crime. The size of increases in the percent female contribution for the various offenses are virtually the same when comparisons are made between the time periods 1960–67 and 1968–75. In general, differences in increases from year to year, or from one decade to the next, reflect random fluctuations around a common upward trend.

Visual inspection of the data in Table 1 suggests that the women's movement has not had a unique effect on levels of female property crime, and regression analysis provides additional support for this conclusion. Table 2 displays two multiple correlation coefficients for each of the property offenses. The equation used to compute the basic $R^2$ for each property offense includes the variables of year, sex, and period as well as the interactions of sex and year, and period and year. The equation used to compute the elaborated $R^2$ adds to the basic equation two more interactive terms, $S$-$P$ and $S$-$P$-$Y$, that represent the effects of the women's movement on female arrest rates. A comparison of the multiple correlation coefficients for the basic and elaborated equations reveals that the coefficients are so high (97.8 and higher) for the basic equation that there is little variation left to be explained and the two terms used to represent the impact of the women's movement have a negligible effect on the amount of variation explained.[11] This analysis, then, offers little support for the position linking the women's movement to observed increases in levels of female property crime.

The third question asks whether, *within* the arrested population, there has been a change in the type of crime for which females are arrested. The data in Table 3 show the percentage of females (and males) arrested for property offenses among females (and males) arrested for UCR Index crimes. The findings are mixed: of the females arrested for serious or index crimes, the percentage of women arrested increased for larceny-theft but has decreased for burglary and auto theft. The combined property index shows an increase from 79.3 percent in 1960 to 89.6 percent in 1975. The latter increase, of course, is due to the increase in larceny-theft arrests. In contrast to these increases for the female arrest population, there is a small decline from 80.2 percent to 78.1 percent for the combined property crime index among the male arrest population. It is often claimed (Wilson and Rigsby; *U.S. News & World Report)* that (1) larceny-theft has been the major area of women's liberation in criminal activity; and (2) that the proportion of women arrested for serious crimes has increased dramatically and that the increase in arrests for serious crimes has been greater for females than males. The first claim has merit, for this offense category does show the largest increases but as we shall point out later, the cause of the increase probably lies elsewhere than women's liberation. The second claim is more sensational than substantive. The data indicate that the increase in

**Table 2.** *Multiple Correlation Coefficients for Basic and Elaborated Equations*

| OFFENSE | $R^2$ FOR BASIC EQUATION* | $R^2$ FOR ELABORATED EQUATION† |
|---------|---------------------------|--------------------------------|
| 3-property index | 99.4 | 99.4 |
| Burglary | 99.3 | 99.5 |
| Larceny | 98.7 | 98.7 |
| Auto-theft | 98.9 | 99.8 |
| Fraud-embezzlement | 98.0 | 98.2 |
| Stolen property | 97.8 | 98.8 |

$$*R^2 = b_0 + b_1{}^Y + b_2{}^S + b_3{}^P + b_4{}^{S-Y} + b_5{}^{P-Y}$$

$$†R^2 = b_0 + b_1{}^Y + b_2{}^S + b_3{}^P + b_4{}^{S-Y} + b_5{}^{P-Y} + b_6{}^{S-P} + b_7{}^{S-P-Y}$$

Where $R$ = arrest rate for specific offenses

$\quad\quad Y$ = year (1960, 1961 . . . 1975)

$\quad\quad S$ = Sex (0 = males, 1 = females)

$\quad\quad P$ = Period (0 = 1960–1967, 1 = 1968–1975)

serious crime arrests for women is for the most part simply an increase in larceny-theft since women constitute a small proportion of arrests for other serious crimes. This increase in larceny, moreover, is probably due to increases in arrests for shoplifting. It is estimated that 70 to 80 percent of female larceny arrests are for shoplifting, usually of items of small monetary value (Allen and Simonsen; Cameron; Pollak). The petty theft value involved in most shoplifting, as well as in many other arrests for larceny (see note 2), and the fact that shoplifting is judged a relatively nonserious offense (Rossi et al.; Steffensmeier and Terry) further underscores the sciolism of declarations of purposed increases of female involvement in serious crimes.

When the foregoing analysis is expanded from serious crimes to arrests for all crimes, property crime trends follow a similar pattern. Data in Table 4 show the percent of females (and males) arrested for *property* offenses out of *all* females (and males) arrested in the U.S. The combined property index reveals a gradual upward trend since 1960 in the percent of women arrested for property crimes which is mostly accounted for by the increase in the percent of women arrested for larceny-theft. While there have been small increases in percent of women arrested for burglary, auto theft, fraud/embezzlement, and stolen property, the largest increase has occurred in the larceny-theft category.

**Table 3.** *Females and Males Arrested for Property Crimes as a Percent of Their Respective Sex Cohorts Arrested for Serious (Index) Crimes, 1960–75*

| | 3 PROPERTY-CRIME INDEX | | BURGLARY | | LARCENY THEFT | | AUTO THEFT | |
|------|---------|-------|---------|-------|---------|-------|---------|-------|
| | Females | Males | Females | Males | Females | Males | Females | Males |
| 1975 | 89.6 | 78.1 | 6.6 | 27.7 | 80.7 | 43.1 | 2.3 | 7.3 |
| 1974 | 89.1 | 77.7 | 6.6 | 27.0 | 80.0 | 42.3 | 2.5 | 8.4 |
| 1973 | 88.4 | 76.4 | 6.6 | 26.8 | 79.0 | 40.0 | 2.7 | 10.0 |
| 1972 | 88.1 | 76.6 | 6.4 | 25.7 | 79.0 | 41.1 | 2.7 | 9.9 |
| 1971 | 88.5 | 78.5 | 6.4 | 25.9 | 78.8 | 42.0 | 3.2 | 10.7 |
| 1970 | 89.4 | 79.1 | 5.4 | 24.4 | 81.2 | 43.2 | 2.8 | 11.5 |
| 1969 | 87.8 | 78.9 | 6.4 | 26.1 | 77.6 | 40.1 | 3.8 | 12.7 |
| 1968 | 87.2 | 79.7 | 7.2 | 27.3 | 75.9 | 39.1 | 4.1 | 13.3 |
| 1967 | 86.7 | 79.7 | 6.9 | 26.8 | 76.2 | 39.7 | 3.6 | 13.2 |
| 1966 | 86.0 | 79.9 | 6.4 | 25.6 | 76.0 | 40.8 | 3.6 | 13.5 |
| 1965 | 86.3 | 81.2 | 6.6 | 26.3 | 75.9 | 41.4 | 3.8 | 13.5 |
| 1964 | 85.4 | 82.0 | 7.0 | 26.4 | 74.2 | 41.9 | 4.2 | 13.7 |
| 1963 | 84.1 | 81.8 | 6.8 | 26.8 | 73.4 | 41.5 | 3.9 | 13.5 |
| 1962 | 83.1 | 80.8 | 7.4 | 26.6 | 71.6 | 41.2 | 4.1 | 13.0 |
| 1961 | 80.9 | 80.4 | 7.8 | 28.0 | 69.1 | 40.3 | 4.0 | 12.1 |
| 1960 | 79.3 | 80.2 | 7.2 | 27.1 | 67.9 | 40.7 | 4.2 | 12.4 |

Moreover, it is only in the categories of larceny-theft and fraud/embezzlement that the increases for females exceed those for males.

In many respects, Table 3 and 4 provide us with a fundamental insight into existing patterns of female criminality in the U.S. First, as reflected in arrest statistics, it is clear that larceny-theft comprises a sizeable proportion of female crime. It accounts for four-fifths of female arrests for serious crimes and one-fourth of female arrests for all crimes. Second, it is the large increase in female arrests for larceny-theft that provides the most convincing evidence for the argument that male and female levels of crime are converging. In addition, the data in Tables 3 and 4 show that the upward trend in levels of property crime for females is gradual and evenly distributed from 1960 to 1975 which thus lends additional support to our contention that the contemporary woman's movement has not had a discernible impact on property crime levels, above and beyond the changes in the status of American women that have been going on for the past two decades.

## CONCLUSIONS AND DISCUSSION

Owing partly to the women's liberation movement, the question is increasingly raised as to whether the role of women in crime might not

**Table 4.** Females and Males Arrested for Property Crimes as a Percent of All Arrests in Their Respective Sex Cohorts, 1960–75

| | 3 PROPERTY-CRIME INDEX | | BURGLARY | | LARCENY-THEFT | | AUTO THEFT | | FRAUD-EMBEZZLEMENT | | STOLEN PROPERTY | |
|------|---------|-------|---------|-------|---------|-------|---------|-------|---------|-------|---------|-------|
| | Females | Males | Females | Males | Females | Males | Females | Males | Females | Males | Females | Males |
| 1975 | 26.3 | 17.7 | 1.9 | 6.3 | 23.7 | 9.8 | 0.7 | 1.7 | 4.2 | 1.5 | 0.9 | 1.3 |
| 1974 | 25.1 | 17.9 | 1.9 | 6.2 | 22.5 | 9.8 | 0.7 | 1.9 | 3.2 | 1.3 | 0.8 | 1.3 |
| 1973 | 22.8 | 15.5 | 1.7 | 5.4 | 20.4 | 8.0 | 0.7 | 2.0 | 2.8 | 1.2 | 0.7 | 1.1 |
| 1972 | 21.3 | 24.9 | 1.5 | 5.0 | 19.1 | 8.0 | 0.7 | 1.9 | 2.9 | 1.2 | 0.7 | 1.1 |
| 1971 | 20.4 | 15.3 | 1.5 | 5.1 | 18.2 | 8.2 | 0.7 | 2.1 | 2.8 | 1.3 | 0.7 | 1.2 |
| 1970 | 21.2 | 14.8 | 1.3 | 4.6 | 19.3 | 8.1 | 0.7 | 2.1 | 2.0 | 0.9 | 0.6 | 1.0 |
| 1969 | 19.0 | 14.6 | 1.4 | 4.8 | 16.8 | 7.4 | 0.8 | 2.4 | 2.3 | 1.0 | 0.5 | 0.8 |
| 1968 | 18.0 | 14.6 | 1.5 | 5.0 | 15.6 | 7.2 | 0.9 | 2.4 | 2.1 | 1.0 | 0.4 | 0.7 |
| 1967 | 17.6 | 14.1 | 1.4 | 4.8 | 15.5 | 7.0 | 0.7 | 2.3 | 2.2 | 1.0 | 0.3 | 0.5 |
| 1966 | 17.1 | 13.7 | 1.3 | 4.4 | 15.1 | 7.0 | 0.7 | 2.3 | 2.0 | 1.0 | 0.3 | 0.4 |
| 1965 | 16.1 | 13.2 | 1.2 | 4.3 | 14.2 | 6.7 | 0.7 | 2.2 | 2.0 | 1.0 | 0.3 | 0.4 |
| 1964 | 15.4 | 13.6 | 1.3 | 4.4 | 13.3 | 6.9 | 0.8 | 2.3 | 1.9 | 1.1 | 0.3 | 0.4 |
| 1963 | 13.3 | 12.6 | 1.1 | 4.1 | 11.6 | 6.4 | 0.6 | 2.1 | 1.9 | 1.1 | 0.2 | 0.3 |
| 1962 | 12.1 | 11.2 | 1.1 | 3.7 | 10.4 | 5.7 | 0.6 | 1.8 | 1.5 | 0.9 | 0.2 | 0.3 |
| 1961 | 10.9 | 11.4 | 1.1 | 4.0 | 9.3 | 5.7 | 0.5 | 1.7 | 1.6 | 1.0 | 0.2 | 0.3 |
| 1960 | 9.9 | 10.7 | 0.9 | 3.6 | 8.5 | 5.4 | 0.5 | 1.7 | 1.4 | 1.0 | 0.2 | 0.3 |

be changing along with other role changes of women in our society. Are women becoming more involved in crime in general and certain types of crime in particular? Gross arrest figures reported on in the Uniform Crime Reports and percentage changes based on these figures show that more women are arrested for property crimes today than in the past. The crucial issues, however, are whether the increase in female arrests is greater than the increase in the female population during the same period, and whether the increase in female arrests is equal to or greater than the increase in male arrests.

Several major findings emerged from our analysis. (1) Levels of female property crime have increased substantially since 1960, with increases occurring for each of the property crimes examined. However, when the relatively low size of the initial base rate is taken into account, it is clear that the largest increase occurred in female arrests for larceny-theft. (2) Comparison of male and female levels of property crime revealed that, with the exception of stolen property, the relative gap between the sexes has been narrowing since 1960. This closing of the gap, however, does not necessarily mean that females are catching up with males in propensities to commit property crimes. While females have made relative gains, absolute differences are still large and have generally increased so that female property crime levels continue to lag far behind those of males. Catching up appears to be the case only for the offenses of larceny and fraud/embezzlement. Nonetheless, even if current trends for these offenses continue, female rates will not match male rates in the forseeable future. (3) The examination of changes within the female arrest population showed mixed results: among females arrested for serious or UCR Index crimes, the percentage of women arrested for larceny-theft increased but decreased for burglary and auto-theft; among all arrested females, there was a large increase in the percent of women arrested for larceny-theft but small increases in the percent arrested for burglary, auto-theft, fraud/embezzlement and stolen property.

By considering these findings along with the results of our previous study of female violent crime (Steffensmeier et al.) we can evaluate the hypothesis that functional changes in a society will be reflected far less in personal than in property crimes. According to this hypothesis, the movement toward greater equality for the sexes should lead to a convergence between the sexes in levels of property crime but not in levels of violent crime. As to property crime, the convergence was far greater for larceny-theft and fraud/embezzlement than for other property crimes. Burglary, auto theft, and stolen property were just as much male dominated offenses in 1975 as they were in 1960. Burglary, in particular, involves skills that are usually acquired within a criminal subculture and women have lacked ties with such networks (Klockars). Their opportunities for acquiring such skills are thus much more limited. Unfortunately, however, because burglary is a somewhat sensational crime, slight increases that have little predictive or theoretical meaning are apt to attract much attention. Overall the findings on sex differences in levels of property crime arrest rates indicate that is only partly true that women are sharing increasingly with men in both legal and illegal economic pursuits.

About levels of violent crime, we found that the gap between males and females has widened or remains the same as it was sixteen years ago, rather than diminishing as men and women move toward greater equality in their rights and privileges. Notwithstanding the existence of such atypical offenders as Lynette Fromm and Emily Harris, levels of female violence have not been rising as rapidly as male levels. The data on female violent crime and property crime tend to demonstrate the simplicity of the hypothesis commonly set forth in criminology writings (Nettler, Sutherland and Cressey) that as men and women approach equality in their cultural roles, the more similar they become in their criminality. But the same data clearly suggest that property crime levels have been more influenced by functional changes in society than have personal crime levels.

Some analysts of female crime have attributed the upward trend in female property crime to changing patterns of women's roles and to the women's movement. But our data suggest that, although there may be general changes in the female role, there is little evidence for the unique influence of the women's movement on changes in women's propensities for crime. Assuming that the women's movement begins in the late 1960s, we found little or no change in the magnitude of increase in female arrest rates relative to male arrest rates before, during and after the initial rise of the women's movement. Female increases occurred uniformly during the 1960 to 1975 time period, suggesting that other forces in society already were providing an impetus for changing patterns of female crime well before the initial rise of the women's movement.

We suggest that increases in arrests of females for larceny and fraud/embezzlement represent extensions of traditional female role activities rather than new role patterns. The increase in larceny probably reflects greater female participation in the traditional female crime of shoplifting, together with recent changes in opportunities for, and surveillance of, shoplifting. This offense, which accounts for a large share of female arrests for larceny (Allen and Simonsen; Cameron), is well suited to traditional sex-linked behaviors since it is not unusual or suspicious for women to shop at various stores throughout the day and the clothing styles of women aid in the concealment of merchandise. The ever-increasing reliance on self-service marketing and continual growth of shopping centers makes shoplifting more possible and probable among those who are the primary consumers. Also, in recent years there have been improvements in store surveillance methods and greater willingness on the part of store officials to prosecute apprehended shoplifters.[12] Both these factors would tend to increase female rates more than male because males are likely to be involved in other kinds of larceny-theft.

Increases in arrests for fraud/embezzlement have also been attributed to changing female roles (Allen and Simonsen; Simon, a). It is argued that as more women enter the labor force, largely in white-collar jobs, they have more opportunities to embezzle and defraud. Linking the rise in fraud/embezzlement to the women's movement and to increased white-collar employment opportunities for women suggests that female criminals are becoming more cunning, more skillful—in short, more manlike—in their criminal activities. (Simon especially argues in this manner.) The image of the modern female criminal as bank embezzler, corporate or white-collar swindler, or as perpetrator of sophisticated business frauds is attractive to many because it shatters conventional stereotypes about female criminality. The image, however, is a highly dubious inference from existing arrest data and to some extent appears to reflect wishful thinking that women are indeed making inroads into traditional male dominated white-collar and corporate criminal endeavors.[13]

Rather than link the increase in fraud/embezzlement arrests to the women's movement, there is another explanation. Earlier attitudinal and behavioral changes have produced shifts in the traditional male-female division of labor, one effect of which has been an increase in certain kinds of fraudulent activities, in particular, that of passing bad checks. Education and increased employment of women in the labor force since World War II have tended to undermine the traditional sex-linked division of labor. Increasingly, women are managers of the pocketbook and are handling a larger proportion of the family's financial and marketplace activities. In addition, both rising divorce rates and an increased proportion of families headed by women (Ross and MacIntosh) suggest that the opportunities and temptations for the fraudulent activities of passing bad checks and welfare fraud have greatly expanded. Morever, these traditional female offenses are most apt to be committed by lower-class and minority group women, those least likely to be affected by the women's movement.

In sum, our analysis of UCR arrest statistics suggests that the new female criminal is more a social invention than an empirical reality and that the proposed relationship between the women's movement and crime is, indeed, tenuous and even vacuous. Women are still typically nonviolent, petty property offenders. Increases in female crime have come primarily in larceny (viz. shoplifting) and secondarily in fraud (viz. bad checks and welfare fraud). These traditionally female offenses reflect traditional sex-determined roles in legal and illegal marketplaces; from shopper to shoplifter, from cashing good checks to passing bad ones, from being a welfare mother to being accused of welfare fraud, and so on.

Finally, what can we expect in the future? What effects will the changing nature of women's position in the workplace and in the family have on women's participation in property crimes? Our findings lead us to conclude that we can expect increases, both relatively and absolutely, in the rate of traditional female property crimes—shoplifting, bad check writing, as well as serving as accomplices with males for other property crimes (e.g., burglary). At least, we should expect a maintenance at present levels. This may also mean, for instance, that if male levels of property crime began to decline (as well they may), then female levels may continue to catch up with those of males even though the rise in female levels is quite small. This possibility aside, the participation of women in big time property crime is likely to be as rare an event in the 1980s as it is in 1976 and as it was in 1960.

## NOTES

1. The beginning date for the women's movement is usually set at 1968 to 1969 (Mason and Czajka; Simon, b.). Support for this starting date comes from a recent study by Cancian. Cancian investigated publicity for topics related to the women's movement by counting the proportion of listings devoted to "women" in the *New York Times Index* and the *Reader's Guide to Periodical Literature* between 1965 and 1974. She reports that these listings were constant between 1965 and 1968, and rose dramatically between 1969 and 1970. These results confirm the impression that the activities and ideas of the women's movement were not operative for most women in the U.S. until very late in the 1960s or early in the 1970s.

2. Criminologists have generally been in error concerning the definition of larceny-theft as used in UCR arrest statistics. The error has been to assume that, at least until 1973, the Crime Index *offense* definition of "larceny $50 and over" was the definition of larceny used in the reporting of *arrest* data as well. Thus, there exists the distinction between petty (under $50) and grand theft ($50 and

over), with only the latter supposedly included in UCR arrest data. The UCR arrest statistics on larceny-theft, however, have always included the combined total of arrests both of "larceny $50 and over" and of "larceny under $50." Clarification of these definitional distinctions was obtained from personal communication with Paul A. Zolbe, Chief, Uniform Crime Reports. "Larceny $50 and over in value was included as a Crime Index offense until January 1973, at which time total larceny-theft was included in the Crime Index. This move was prompted by inflation factors and problems dealing with evaluation of stolen property. Those tables prepared for "Crime in the United States" from 1973 to date where data is presented for 1960 forward reflect adjustments made to depict the concept of total larceny as a Crime Index offense. *The data regarding arrests for the offense of larceny has (sic) always included arrests for all larcenies.*" The implications of this error become apparent when factors such as inflation are used to explain recent increases in larceny among certain population segments. For example, the high rate of increase from 1960–70 in larceny arrests among those under 15 years of age is explained by Daniel Glaser as largely due to "inflation and affluence; there were more portable things to steal each year during the prosperous fifties and sixties, and many more items were priced over $50 when each of these decades ended than when they began." (35) Throughout the remainder of his discussion of arrest trends, Glaser refers to "arrestees for grand theft," erroneously assuming that arrests for petty larceny (under $50) are not included in the UCR arrest tables. Simon makes a similar error in her analysis of female crime trends.

3. Since the UCR did not treat fraud and embezzlement as separate offenses until 1964, it is necessary for purposes of trend analysis to combine the two offenses into fraud/embezzlement. Fraud is defined in the UCR as the "fraudulent conversion and obtaining money or property by false pretenses. Includes bad checks except forgeries and counterfeiting." Embezzlement is defined as "misappropriation or misapplication of money or property entrusted to one's care, custody, or control." In any given year, roughly 90 to 95 percent of arrests for fraud/embezzlement are for fraud.

4. Stolen property refers to "buying, receiving, and possessing stolen property and attempts" (Uniform Crime Reports).

5. The major drawback is that the percentage change tabulations reported in the UCR reflect both an increase in the number of people living within the jurisdiction of the agencies reporting in 1960 and the addition of population covered by agencies reporting for the first time since 1960. (For example, the population coverage is 106 million in 1960 and 179 million in 1975, an increase of over 50 percent over this time period).

6. Simon's analysis, which is the most systematic to date, is primarily limited to examining changes in the kinds of crimes committed by females. Simon correctly concludes that female levels of violence have not increased relative to male levels but overlooks rising levels of female violence over the past decade or so. Unlike our analysis, Simon did not calculate arrest rates which take into account changes in population size and distribution and which facilitate trend comparisons in absolute and relative levels of crime of males and

females. Moreover, Simon's analysis is only up to 1972 and thus does not allow for a sufficient time period to assess the effects of the women's movement on female crime trends. In fairness to Simon, her concern is more with the general status of women in the United States and with the overall handling and treatment of the female offender than with female criminal behavior. Only 14 pages of her 98-page monograph are devoted to female crime.

7. The exogenous factors most commonly associated with measurement error in crime statistics, such as police officers per capita (Wheeler), inconsistencies and changes in police practices and recordkeeping procedures (President's Commission on Law Enforcement and Administration of Justice), and the relation of the suspect to the complainant (Black) are variables for which there is no strong a priori reason for positing a nonrandom distribution across the sexes. While it is plausible to assume that the police and citizenry are becoming less "chivalrous" to women suspects and are beginning to treat women more like equals, the effects of this on arrest data are very likely minimal and are yet to be realized (Simon). To the extent that a change has been occurring, arrest statistics in recent years will tend to over-estimate levels of female property crime vis-à-vis previous years.

8. The sharp rise in arrest rates from 1973 to 1974 and the apparent leveling off of crime from 1974 to 1975 very likely reflects extreme sampling fluctuations in the UCR. In 1973, the population coverage was 155 million, in 1974 it was 134 million, and in 1975 it was 179 million. The loss of about 20 million in the size of the population covered in the 1974 UCR arrest tables was largely from suburban and rural areas (ca. 12 million). Since the latter have lower crime levels than urban areas, the 1974 estimate is generally biased in the direction of overstating the true volume of crime in 1974 relative to previous years and relative to 1975.

9. The difference between males and females in the average annual rate of change is computed as follows:

$$\begin{array}{c} \text{Difference} \\ \text{between sexes} \\ \text{in average} \\ \text{annual rate} \end{array} = \dfrac{\overset{1975}{\text{male rate}} - \overset{1960}{\text{male rate}}}{\text{Number of years} - 1} - \dfrac{\overset{1975}{\text{female rate}} - \overset{1960}{\text{female rate}}}{\text{Number of years} - 1}$$

Using burglary as an example, the computations would be:

$$\frac{588.4 - 324.7}{15} - \frac{31.0 - 9.3}{15} = 17.58 - 1.45 = 16.13$$

10. Our reliance on relative differences follows the precedence of other research on sex differentials in crime levels (see, e.g., Pollak; Reckless; Reckless and Kay; Ward et al.), and research on sex and race differentials in income (see, e.g., Farley and Hermalin; Featherman and Hauser). Relative differences are theoretically more appropriate than absolute differences because of the grossly unequal initial base rates.

11. Statistical tests of significance are inappropriate for this data because we are using the entire population of arrest figures.

12. This "social control" change with its probable differential effect on male
and female arrests for shoplifting represents an exception to our earlier assumption (see note 7) of random distribution of measurement error between the sexes
in arrest data over a given time period.

Granting the changes in control measures toward shoplifting, it seems plausible that arrest statistics in recent years tend to overestimate levels of female
involvement in larceny-theft relative to previous years.

13. With respect to embezzlement, for instance, an analysis of arrest rates
since 1964 (when the UCR commenced giving arrest figures separately for
embezzlement) reveals a small increase in the female arrest rate for this offense:
2.8 in 1964 vs. 3.7 in 1975.

---

# REFERENCES

Adler, Freda. 1975 *Sisters in Crime*. New York: McGraw-Hill.
Allen, Harry, and Clifford Simonsen. 1975. *Corrections in America*. New York:
  Glencoe.
Black, D. 1970. "Production of Crime Rates." *American Sociological Review*
  35:733ε48.
Bruck, C. 1975. "Women Against the Law." *Human Behavior* 4(December):
  24ε33.
Cameron, Mary Owen. 1964. *The Booster and the Switch*. New York: Free Press.
Cancian, Francesca. 1975. "Mass Media Coverage of Women: Changes from
  1965–74." Stanford: Stanford University, Department of Sociology, unpub-
  lished manuscript.
Clinard, M. 1942. "The Process of Urbanization and Criminal Behavior."
  *American Journal of Sociology* 48(September):202ε13.
Farley, R., and A. Hermalin. 1972. "The 1960s: A Decade of Progress for Blacks?"
  Demography 9(August):353ε70.
Featherman, D., and R. Hauser. 1976. "Changes in the Socioeconomic Strati-
  fication of the Races, 1962ε1973." *American Journal of Sociology*
  82:621ε51.
Glaser, D. 1970. "Violence and the City." In Daniel Glaser (ed.), *Crime in the
  City*. New York: Harper & Row.
Jacobson, A. 1975. "Crime Trends in Southern and Nonsouthern Cities: A
  Twenty-Year Perspective." *Social Forces* 54(September):226ε47.
Klockars, Carl. 1974. *The Professional Fence*. New York: Free Press.
Mason, K. Oppenheim, and J. Czajka. 1976. "Change in U.S. Women's Sex-
  Role Attitudes, 1964ε1974." *American Sociological Review* 41:573ε96.
National Commission on the Causes and Prevention of Violence. 1969. *Crimes
  of Violence*. Vol. II. Washington: Government Printing Office.
Nettler, Gwynn. 1974. *Explaining Crime*. New York: McGraw-Hill.

Pollak, Otto. 1950. *The Criminology of Women*. Philadelphia: University of Pennsylvania Press.

President's Commission on Law Enforcement and Administration of Justice. 1967. *Task Force Report: Crime and Its Impact*. Washington: Government Printing Office.

Reckless, Walter. 1940. *Criminal Behavior*. New York: McGraw-Hill.

———, and B.A. Kay. 1967. *The Female Offenders*. Washington: President's Commission on Law Enforcement and Administration of Justice.

Rosenblatt, E., and C. Greenland. 1974. "Female Crimes of Violence." *Canadian Journal of Criminology and Corrections* 16(April):1973-80.

Rosenthal, Alvin, and Darrell Steffensmeier. 1978. "A Method for Converting UCR Arrest Statistics into Refined Arrest Rates." Paper presented at 1978 annual meeting of the Eastern Sociological Association.

Ross, H., and A. MacIntosh. 1973. "The Emergence of Households Headed by Women." Working Paper 776-01. Washington: The Urban Institute.

Rossi, P.E. Warte, C. Bose, and R. Berk. 1974. "The Seriousness of Crime: Normative Structure and Individual Differences," *American Sociological Review* 39:244-37.

Simon, Rita James. a:1975. The Contemporary Woman and Crime. National Institute of Mental Health. Washington: Government Printing Office.

———. b: 1975. "American Women and Crime." *Annals* AAPSS 423(January): 31-46.

Steffensmeier, D., and R. M. Terry. 1973. "Deviance and Respectability: An Observational Study of Reactions to Shoplifting." *Social Forces* 51(June): 417-27.

———, Renee Hoffman Steffensmeier, and Alvin Rosenthal. 1977. "Violence and the Contemporary Woman: An Analysis of Changing Levels of Female Violence, 1960-1974." Paper presented at annual meeting of the American Sociological Association.

Sutherland, Edwin, and Donald Cressey. 1973. *Criminology*. New York: Lippincott.

U.S. Bureau of the Census. a: 1974. *Population Reports: Estimates of the Population of the United States by Age, Sex, and Race: April 1, 1960 to July 1, 1973*. Current Population Reports, Series p-25, No. 519. Washington: Government Printing Office.

———. b:1975. *Population Reports: Estimates of the Population of the United States by Age, Sex, and Race: 1970 to 1975*. Current Population Reports, Series p-25, No. 614. Washington: Government Printing Office.

U.S. Department of Justice, Federal Bureau of Investigation. 1960-75. *Uniform Crime Reports*. Washington: Government Printing Office.

*U.S. News and World Report*. 1975. "Crimes by Women Are on the Rise All Over the World." 79,25(December 22):49-51.

Ward, David, Maurice Jackson, and Renee Ward. 1969. "Crimes of Violence by Women." In Donald Mulvihill and Melvin Tumin (eds.), *Crimes of Violence: A Staff Report Submitted to the National Commission on the Causes and Prevention of Violence*. Washington: Government Printing Office.

Webb, D. 1972. "Crime and the Division of Labor." *American Journal of Sociology* 78:643-56.

Wheeler, S. 1967. "Criminal Statistics: A Reformulation of the Problem." *Journal of Criminal Law, Criminology, and Police Science* 58:317-24.

Wilson, N., and C. Rigsby. 1975. "Is Crime a Man's World? Issues in the Exploration of Criminality." *Journal of Criminal Justice* 3:131-40.

Wolfgang, M. 1963. "Uniform Crime Reports: A Critical Appraisal." *University of Pennsylvania Law Review* 3:708-38.

FOUR

# Patterns of Female Property Crime 1960-1978: A Postscript

DARRELL J. STEFFENSMEIER

The purpose of this "postscript" is to update and elaborate on the findings presented in the preceding article on sex differences in property crime trends, 1960-75. The discussion that follows takes advantage of additional evidence on female criminality, much of which is discussed in greater detail elsewhere (see Steffensmeier, 1979b; Steffensmeier, 1980; Steffensmeier and Steffensmeier, 1980).

The analysis here goes beyond the article is several ways. First, the offense category of forgery is included as a petty property crime in the present analysis. Second, fraud and embezzlement are treated here as separate offense categories rather than as a single, combined category of fraud/embezzlement. For this, our analysis extends back only to 1964 when the Uniform Crime Reports (UCR) first listed these as separate categories. Third, a distinction is made here between petty-property and masculine-property crimes. The latter include the offenses of burglary, robbery, auto theft, and stolen property, as well as arson and vandalism. Arrest data on arson and vandalism are provided for the first time in 1964.

## MASCULINE PROPERTY CRIMES

Masculine crimes are defined as offenses involving physical strength, elements of coercion and confrontation with victim, and/or specialized skills. As reported in Table 1, the major findings are that for both males and females the rates have tended to rise *but* that sex differences have held fairly constant. On the one hand, there are small female gains in each of the masculine-property crimes. On the other hand, absolute differences in arrest rates for these offenses have become greater—that is, females have lost ground compared to males. Table 1 also provides a comparison of the percentage which arrests for masculine-property crimes comprise of all male arrests and all female arrests. For both sexes there are small increases in these percentages, which are nearly identical for males and females. We conclude from this analysis that for masculine-property crimes, females have not gained ground on males, nor has there been a shift toward greater commission of these offenses on the part of females.

## PETTY PROPERTY CRIMES

We designate the offense categories of larceny, fraud, forgery, and embezzlement as petty property crimes. As shown in Table 1 females have made substantial gains on males in the categories of larceny, fraud, and, to a lesser extent, in forgery. Not only are there large increases in the percent of female contribution, but also an increasingly larger share of all female arrests are for larceny and fraud. Arrests of males have increased as well in these categories and comprise a larger share of all male arrests now than in 1960, but the increases are not nearly as dramatic as they are for females.

This classification of larceny, fraud, forgery, and embezzlement as petty property crimes is different from that of some analysts (e.g., Simon) who label these as white-collar or occupational crimes and then use female arrest gains in these categories to support the position linking female crime to changes in labor market opportunities of women. The differences in interpretation stem in large part from the manner which the *broad* or *summary* offense categories of the Uniform Crime Reports are used to infer changes in female crime. Specifically, a variety of specific offenses covering a wide range of seriousness are included within the same UCR category. The category of larceny includes shoplifting a $3.00 item and cargo theft amounting to thousands of dollars. Fraud includes passing worthless checks, usually of small amounts, and stock frauds involving large sums of money. The matter of which position is correct can only be resolved by examining evidence from other sources on the specific kinds of crimes for which persons are arrested within the broad categories.

**Table 1.** *Arrest Rates per 100,000 Males and Females for Petty-Property Crimes and for Masculine-Property Crimes, 1960(64) and 1977. Percentage of Female Contribution (% FC) and Absolute Difference (AD) and Percentage of Each Offense Comprises of All Female and Male Arrests.[a]*

| TYPE OF CRIME | FEMALE RATE | MALE RATE | % FC | AD | % OF ALL FEMALE ARRESTS | % OF ALL MALE ARRESTS |
|---|---|---|---|---|---|---|
| *Petty Property* | | | | | | |
| Larceny | | | | | | |
| 1960 | 87.3 | 487.4 | 15.2 | 400.1 | 8.5 | 5.4 |
| 1978 | 376.2 | 870.4 | 30.2 | 494.2 | 9.0 | 22.2 |
| Fraud | | | | | | |
| 1964 | 16.3 | 73.4 | 18.2 | 57.1 | 1.6 | 0.9 |
| 1978 | 100.3 | 185.3 | 35.1 | 85.0 | 5.9 | 1.9 |
| Forgery | | | | | | |
| 1960 | 9.2 | 52.0 | 15.0 | 42.8 | 0.9 | 0.6 |
| 1978 | 23.8 | 60.6 | 28.2 | 36.8 | 1.4 | 0.6 |
| Embezzlement | | | | | | |
| 1964 | 2.8 | 14.1 | 16.5 | 11.3 | 0.3 | 0.2 |
| 1978 | 2.1 | 6.8 | 23.6 | 4.7 | 0.1 | 0.1 |
| *Masculine* | | | | | | |
| Robbery | | | | | | |
| 1960 | 3.5 | 76.5 | 4.4 | 73.0 | 0.3 | 0.9 |
| 1978 | 10.9 | 154.7 | 6.6 | 143.8 | 0.6 | 1.6 |
| Burglary | | | | | | |
| 1960 | 9.3 | 324.7 | 2.8 | 315.4 | 0.9 | 3.6 |
| 1978 | 32.7 | 536.1 | 5.7 | 503.4 | 1.9 | 5.5 |
| Auto Theft | | | | | | |
| 1960 | 5.4 | 149.2 | 3.5 | 143.8 | 0.5 | 1.7 |
| 1978 | 14.0 | 165.2 | 7.8 | 151.2 | 0.8 | 1.7 |
| Arson | | | | | | |
| 1964 | 0.9 | 9.4 | 8.7 | 8.5 | 0.1 | 0.1 |
| 1978 | 2.4 | 18.7 | 11.4 | 16.3 | 0.1 | 0.2 |
| Vandalism | | | | | | |
| 1964 | 8.6 | 142.3 | 5.7 | 133.7 | 0.8 | 1.7 |
| 1978 | 20.5 | 240.6 | 7.9 | 220.1 | 1.2 | 2.5 |
| Stolen Property | | | | | | |
| 1960 | 2.3 | 26.3 | 8.2 | 24.0 | 0.2 | 0.3 |
| 1978 | 13.5 | 177.5 | 10.3 | 104.0 | 0.8 | 1.2 |

[a]In some cases 1964 data were used because this was the earliest year for which data were reported separately for these categories.

The available evidence is fairly clear on this and we know of no evidence to the contrary. With few exceptions, women arrested for larceny, fraud, and forgery *do not* qualify as white-collar criminals either when that term is used restrictively to refer to crimes committed by persons of high socioeconomic status in the course of their occupation or when it is used to refer to crimes committed by any employee. The evidence indicates that most arrests of women in these categories are for shoplifting, check fraud, forging credit cards, and the like. A similar pattern holds for males, but the value of thefts committed by males tends to be greater.

Further, contrary to what is sometimes assumed, the person *arrested* for embezzlement is usually more a petty thief than a white-collar offender. Most arrestees for embezzlement are *not* persons of high social standing and responsibility who commit a crime in the course of their occupation which involves large sums of money. Rather, the typical embezzler is the club treasurer, trusted clerk, or cashier, who takes his or her employer's money, the amount of which is usually small.

More importantly, while the sex differential has narrowed for embezzlement, the percentage of female contribution increased from 16.5 in 1964 to 23.6 in 1978. Ths offense accounts for a *very small* proportion of all female arrests; the female arrest rate for embezzlement is in fact *smaller* in 1978 than in 1964. The same is true of males. Table 1 shows that the female embezzlement rate was 2.8 per 100,000 in 1964, dropping to 2.1 in 1978. Also, in both 1964 and 1978, less than .3 percent of all female arrests were for embezzlement. We conclude, therefore, that embezzlement is relatively insignificant in terms of over-all female arrest trends.

This analysis of petty property and masculine property crimes clearly indicates that to the extent that females have made arrest gains on males, they have done so in petty thefts and frauds. More women are being arrested for traditional kinds of female crime. Stability rather than change in sex differences in patterns of crimes is the overwhelmingly important observation. The changes in female criminality of both sexes run parallel and appear linked to broader legal, technological, and economic changes than to specific changes in sex roles.

## INTERPRETATIONS AND CONCLUSIONS

On *theoretical* grounds, there are several reasons for *not* linking increases in arrests of females for property crimes to changes in labor market opportunities. Some of these reasons were already suggested in the preceding article. First, even if increasing numbers of women went to work, crimes of employee theft and occupational fraud are unlikely to be reported and prosecuted, and therefore would not contribute to *official* arrest statistics, such as those of the Uniform Crime Reports. Second, the new occupational roles have not feed women from traditional domestic ones. Women have retained the roles of homemaker, childrearer, nurse of the sick, and so on. The time and energy involved in these roles, along with the assumption of new economic roles, means it is unlikely that their opportunities for crime have undergone very much change. Third, work may lessen female temptations toward crime by assuring a steady income which enables them to satisfy material needs in a legal manner. Fourth, occupations vary in terms of criminal liability: Women are making *few* gains in traditional male occupations such as truck driver, dockworker, mechanic, and so on that are facilitative of criminal opportunities and the learning of crime skills. Fifth, to the extent that women have made inroads into traditional male occupations, they continue to have little access to the "old boy system" and the "male buddy network." The former is important in terms of potential participation in organized white-collar and corporate crime activities. The latter, because of time spent after work by males in "drinking, gambling, and carousing," is often an important contingency for many crime-related activities.

What then accounts for the arrest gains of females in the petty property crime categories? As we suggest in the preceding article, *two major factors* appear to be operating: changes in *opportunities* for petty thefts-/fraud and changes in *social control* and law enforcement. The greater reliance on self-service marketing and the purchasing of credit means that women, being the primary consumers, are faced with expanding opportunities for shoplifting, passing worthless checks, and so on. Increases in opportunities for these kinds of thefts and frauds will have a greater effect on female than male crime because males are more likely to commit other kinds of larcenies and frauds. Similarly, the greater willingness of business officials to prosecute, the trend toward computerized records, and improvements in the detection of offenses such as shoplifting, bad checks, credit card fraud, and forged prescriptions would also tend to increase female, more than male, arrests for larceny, fraud, and forgery. An additional factor, but probably of lesser casual significance, is that poverty has become more and more of a female problem and may have pushed more women into petty thievery to support themselves and their families. In sum, the most crucial point, perhaps, is that trends in female criminality, as is true of male crime, appear *linked to broader economic, legal, technological,* and *law enforcement changes than to specific changes in sex roles.*

While females have made gains during the past two decades in petty-property crimes, this does not mean that females will catch up with males in arrests for fraud, embezzlement, and larceny by the 1990s and for forgery by the year 2010 as Simon predicts (Simon, 1975:41,46). If arrest rates for the entire 1960–1978 period are used to project future male and female rates, the results show a widening of the absolute gap and a narrowing of the relative gap which becomes smaller with each passing decade. Nevertheless, the narrowing of the relative gap is small, so that at the turn of the century females will still have a long way to go before catching up with males. These projections of arrest rates also serve to demonstrate the point, made in the preceding article, that arrest gains of females are in part a statistical artifact of low female starting points and rising arrest rates for both sexes. Of special significance in this regard is that female arrest gains, even in the petty-property crime categories, have been levelling off in recent years, and it is reasonable to assume that crime will be as much a male-oriented phenomenon in the year 2,000 as it is in 1978.

We conclude with several observations regarding trends in female criminality. First, in extending the present analysis to include *all* offense categories of the Uniform Crime Reports, we find that arrest trends in fraud, and especially in larceny, are largely responsible for changes in patterns of female crime in general and not confined to changes in property crime patterns (see Steffensmeier, 1980). The available evidence provides very little support for the position that women are catching up with males in the commission of violent, masculine, white-collar, and, as we reviewed above, in serious-property crimes such as burglary and robbery. What is observed is that changes in female crime are minimal and are matched in large part by parallel changes in male crime.

Second, it is significant perhaps that whatever the arrest gains of females were over the entire 1960–78 period, these occurred mostly from 1965 to 1970. During the late sixties, arrest rates of both sexes were rising in many UCR offense categories, while from 1971 to 1978 the arrest rates of both males and females have been levelling off. Sex differences in arrest rates generally have been stable. The arrest patterns in the seventies further suggest the extent to which the early arrest gains of females are due to low female starting points and rising rates for both sexes.

## REFERENCES

Simon, Rita James. *The contemporary woman and crime.* National Institute of Mental Health. Washington, D.C.: U.S. Government Printing Office, 1975.

Steffensmeier, Darrell. Trends in female crime: It's still a man's world. *USA Today*, September 1979, *108*, 44–48.

————.Sex differences in patterns of adult crime, 1965–77: A review and assessment. *Social Forces*, in press.

————, and Steffensmeier, Renee Hoffman. Trends in female delinquency: A review of arrest, juvenile court, self-report, and field data." *Criminology*, in press.

FIVE

# The Economics of Female Criminality: An Analysis of Police Blotters, 1890–1975*†

## PEGGY C. GIORDANO, SANDRA KERBEL, AND SANDRA DUDLEY

The recent interest in female criminality has generated several important questions: (1) Is there "really" an increase in the number of females who commit crimes? (2) Are females becoming more versatile in the kinds of crimes they commit? (3) What factors account for these changing patterns, if indeed they are found? Here these questions will be addressed through analysis of data from the actual police blotters of the city of Toledo. This type of analysis serves as an alternative to Uniform Crime Report statistics, the major data source that has been used to answer such questions in the past.

We are particularly concerned with Simon's (1975) use of official statistics and the explanation that has emerged from this analysis. She indicates from an examination of the years 1953–1972 that the major

---

*Revision of a paper presented at the annual meeting of the Society for the Study of Social Problems, San Francisco, 1976.

†We would like to express our appreciation to the eight undergraduate students whose tireless help in collecting this data made possible the completion of this study within our lifetime.

increases for females have been in the area of property crimes, particularly larceny and embezzlement. To explain these increases, Simon accords significance to women's increased participation in the labor force. She suggests an opportunity model—that as women take on more and different occupational roles, their opportunities for crimes also increase (e.g., one cannot embezzle funds unless one is in a position of trust).

Steffensmeier (1978a) critiques Simon's use of official statistics and utilizes a more methodologically elegant analysis of these same figures, which takes into account population shifts. He reaches conclusions that are not inconsistent with Simon's; however, he attributes the large increases in larceny arrests to increased shoplifting. Since shoplifting has traditionally been considered a female crime and there were no large increases around the time the women's movement began to be visible (late 1960s), he concludes that the female crime picture has *not* changed significantly.

The continued use of UCR statistics as our only data source inhibits our ability to solve these apparent contradictions of evidence/interpretation. The problems in these statistics have, of course, always plagued analyses of male crime patterns but are particularly frustrating as we attempt to understand areas of change (if any) in women's behavior.

There are at least three limitations of Uniform Crime Report statistics which the present research has attempted to overcome, even though it also relies on officially reported crime. First, most analyses only examine a relatively short span of time. The Uniform Crime Reports were not established until the early thirties, and most of the current work looks at change from the years 1960–1975 (Steffensmeier, 1978a), 1953–1972 (Simon, 1975), or 1960–1970 (Noblit and Burcart, 1976). It is our position that the changes in women's roles in society have been incremental, and that it is important to place their participation in a wider historical context than is provided by an examination of a 10- or 20-year time span. Thus, Steffensmeier (1978a) does not see dramatic shifts around the time the women's movement became increasingly visible (late 1960's)—hence, little change is said to have occurred. If the women's movement is equated with its more visible antennae, such an inference is warranted. If women's changing roles are linked instead to more broadly based social and economic forces, we would expect evidence of change to emerge over the long run.

Second, the use of the Uniform Crime Report statistics severely restricts analysis to a few broad offense categories. This is particularly frustrating as we attempt to understand the changing nature of crimes by women. Thus, for example, Simon emphasizes the increases occurring in the broad category of embezzlement and builds a quite plausible theory around these statistics. Unfortunately, we are unable to break down embezzlement into specific offenses to determine whether those offenses actually represent cases of embezzlement or other occupational offenses or, instead, such offenses as passing bad checks or misuse of credit cards. Similarly, Steffensmeier asserts that increased shoplifting is accounting for increases in larceny among women; however, we cannot ascertain this from UCR statistics.

Third, the use of UCR statistics makes it impossible to ascertain much about particular characteristics of the women who make up these arrest figures. We would stress the importance of obtaining such information if we are to further specify the process through which broad structural factors have an impact. Thus, if we juxtapose increased female employment statistics over time with increased female arrest statistics over the same period (Simon, 1975), there is the strong inference that as women move into the employment world, their opportunities for crime increases. While it is quite logical that one cannot embezzle funds unless one is in a position of financial trust, we do not at this point know whether the women who are making up the current arrest statistics are employed at all or at what levels they participate in the labor force. It is our position that changing labor force characteristics of women may indeed be an important variable, but not in the way that has generally been depicted.

While there are problems inherent in the alternative strategy used here, a detailed examination of the police blotters of a single city hopefully overcomes some of the difficulties inherent in attempts to analyze female crime over a short span of years using only a few UCR categories. In addition, it also allows us to make some inferences based on knowing more about characteristics of the individuals who actually make up the arrest statistics. It should be noted that there are other studies which have attempted to analyze longer term change in arrest patterns. Like this one, they also examine a single city. Ferdinand (1967) studjed Boston police annual arrest reports from 1849 to 1951 to follow increases/decreases in selected offenses, although he did not include attention to females. Powell (1966) also examined arrests in a single city—Buffalo—and did mention females but only to indicate that in Buffalo the peak period of criminal activity for women was 1860–1870, after which time it declined—contrary, he states to the "common belief that the emancipation of women must have lead to greater criminality." As in the previous studies, he was only interested in a few broad categories of offenses.

## METHODOLOGY

The present research analyzes the actual police blotters for the city of
Toledo as a source of information about all offenses committed by men
and women of the city over an 86-year time span, as well as to find out
more about basic characteristics of individual offenders. The blotters
were donated by the police to the Center for Archival Collections at
Bowling Green State University. The blotters began in the year 1871 and
ended in 1971. Because it would have been physically impossible to hand
tabulate data from each year, 20-year interval "target" years were
selected, beginning in 1890. Blotters from the early years were often
sketchy; 1890 was the first census year in which fairly complete data
were available. Census years were chosen in order to establish the most
accurate sex and age-specific population bases on which rates could be
calculated. The year 1910 was partially destroyed; hence, for that period
1909 was utilized. The following years were thus targeted: 1890, 1909,
1930, 1950, and 1970. Annual police reports also donated to the archives
were examined for the years immediately before and after each target
year. A comparison of these summary statistics with our tabulated data
gave us increased confidence that there were no unique or dramatic
shifts during that 3-year period (e.g., the very low rates we see in 1890
are similar to the figures for 1889 and 1901).

Even though we expected change to be incremental, we were interested in any possible escalation of women's participation in crime after
1970. We were able to obtain a temporary loan of the 1976 blotters from
the Toledo police in order to examine more recent trends. Population
estimates for that year were obtained from the Toledo Bureau of Vital
Statistics, which indicated a decline in population of some 20,000 since
1970. But since they could not provide age- and sex-specific estimates,
1970 population statistics were utilized in the calculation of rates. This
should provide a conservative index, then, if any change occurred
between 1970 and 1976.

Before discussing the specific use of the blotters, we should note that
while any analysis of a single city or geographic location limits generalizations, we are convinced that Toledo is at least not completely unique
demographically; for example, the median income for all SMSAs in the
United States in 1970 was $10,474, while Toledo's median income was
$10,823. The percentage of blacks in Toledo was 11.1, as compared to
11.3 nationally. The percentage of unemployed workers nationally was
4.3; for Toledo it was 4.2. Nevertheless, the limitations of analyzing a
specific city must always be taken into account.

The process of analyzing the blotters involved two stages. For each of the target years the offense of each male and female arrested was classified according to one of 291 offense types. This offense classification scheme is the one currently utilized by the Toledo police, to which were added all the other offense categories that occur in earlier blotters. Thus, we tallied each offense in the exact way in which it was recorded in the blotter—from violating a dance ordinance or possession of numbers slips to aggravated menacing or attempted robbery. If the individual was arrested for multiple offenses, this was kept as a separate entry. We then had a record of the number of individuals arrested, as well as the number of individual offenses committed for each year. This was a much more time-consuming process than simply using the annual arrest reports made by the police, but it enabled us to be absolutely certain about the *specific* offenses in which females were involved across the target years. But because the blotters were handwritten, some inferences were made. For example, in 1890 the male and female arrests were recorded in the same blotter, but sex was not noted; hence sex was inferred from the first name, or if there was some doubt, from the entry denoting "property removed"—e.g., a necklace or purse. In addition, we found that in 1970 and 1976 the recorder listed the store name if the offense was shoplifting, even though it was officially designated as larceny. Thus, for those years we were able to separate out the percentage of larceny arrests which we inferred were actually shoplifting arrests. Traffic offenses other than driving under the influence were omitted, as well as entries referring to warrants in another state.

The second state involved a selection of a random sample of offenders about whom a more complete set of characteristics in addition to offense was coded. The size of the samples was determined by the number of females arrested in 1890—320. For subsequent years this number was divided into the total number found in each blotter to obtain the sampling fraction. The following information was coded: father's nativity, mother's nativity, employment status, citizenship status, educational level, occupational status, industry, sex, race, age, marital status, and offense. (If more than one offense was committed, up to five were coded: No individual in the sample was arrested for more than five offenses.) The specific occupation was also recorded, as was the street address of the individual. While this sampling procedure allowed us to obtain some basic information on males and females arrested in the target years, unfortunately not all the information was available for every year, or the form in which it was recorded sometimes changed. One of the most frustrating changes was that while the earlier years

recorded the specific occupation of the individual, in 1950 the police
began to record only *place* of employment. At the same time, in this
year they began to record whether the individual was employed or unemployed.

## FINDINGS

The Volume of Female Crime

Tables 1 through 3 present the actual rates of arrest of females and
males in Toledo for each year, as well as male to female ratios. The
population figures used to establish rates are sex specific and based on
all individuals 20 years or older (except in 1890 where the only figure
available was the number of males and females 10 years or older).
Although each offense was tallied according to one of 291 offense types,
these categories have been collapsed somewhat in order to present them
in tabular form. Furthermore, we have arranged and divided these
offense categories into three types of crimes: personal, property, and
public order.

Table 1 presents personal crime rates and male-to-female ratios for
homicide, felony-assaults, other assaults, and all weapon offenses. An
examination of the homicide rates shows no dramatic increases over
these years, a finding that is consistent with the work of others who have
analyzed rates of violence by females (Simon, 1975; Steffensmeier,
1978a).

The area of felony assaults does reveal a generally decreasing male-
to-female ratio, although it is the category of "other assaults" that shows
more obvious change. The male-to-female ratio decreases from 26.7 to 1
in 1890 to 6.1 to 1 in 1976. Within this classification, arrest-related
assaults increase, particularly in 1970 and 1976. (Of course, this offense
would appear to depend heavily on police perceptions as much as on
actual behavior.) Table 1 also indicates increases in females arrested for
weapon offenses. The ratio declines from 38.3 to 1 in 1909 to 7.1 to 1 in
1976, while the female rate increases from zero in 1890 to 47.8 in 1976.

Table 2 presents property crime rates and ratios for the target years,
including robbery, burglary, theft, auto theft, forgery and counterfeiting,
embezzlement and fraud, stolen property offenses, and malicious destruction of property. In analyzing robbery and burglary offenses, it is
apparent that more males are arrested than females. However, the wide
gulf between male and female involvement appears to be narrowing. The
burglary ratio declined from 44 to 1 in 1930 to 17.9 to 1 in 1976. (However, in actual numbers the 1976 figure represents only 25 burglaries
committed by females.)

**Table 1:** *Personal Crime Rate per 100,000 for Toledo, Ohio—1890-1976*

| | 1980 | | | 1909 | | | 1930 | | | 1950 | | | 1970 | | | 1976 | | |
|---|---|---|---|---|---|---|---|---|---|---|---|---|---|---|---|---|---|---|
| | Males | Females | Ratio | Males | Females | Ratio | Males | Females | Ratio | Males | Females | Ratio | Males | Females | Ratio | Males | Females | Ratio |
| Homicide | 12.8 | 3.2 | 4.0 | 3.7 | 00.0 | — | 20.9 | 3.1 | 6.7 | 7.6 | .9 | 8.4 | 24.2 | 5.4 | 4.5 | 45.8 | 10.0 | 4.6 |
| Assaults-Felony (Aggravated, "Intent to kill") | 60.7 | — | — | 66.3 | 3.8 | 17.4 | 136.2 | 23.1 | 5.9 | 38.8 | 15.3 | 2.5 | 59.3 | 10.0 | 5.9 | 122.1 | 12.3 | 9.9 |
| Other Assaults | 597.3 | 22.4 | 26.7 | 627.9 | 26.3 | 23.9 | 842.0 | 89.0 | 9.5 | 730.1 | 75.4 | 9.7 | 1388.5 | 230.0 | 6.0 | 1339.9 | 218.4 | 6.1 |
| A & B/Assault | 463.2 | 22.4 | 20.7 | 578.2 | 22.5 | 25.7 | 700.0 | 73.3 | 9.5 | 633.5 | 67.3 | 9.4 | 684.3 | 72.5 | 9.4 | 625.9 | 81.8 | 7.6 |
| Menacing | 00.0 | — | — | 00.0 | 00.0 | — | 69.6 | 6.3 | 11.0 | 58.7 | — | — | 31.4 | 6.2 | 5.1 | 66.5 | 3.1 | 21.4 |
| Aggravated Menacing | 00.0 | — | — | 00.0 | 00.0 | — | 00.0 | — | — | .9 | — | — | 2.7 | .8 | 3.4 | 85.3 | 7.1 | 12.0 |
| Arrest Assaults (A & B on a police officer) | 124.6 | — | — | 49.7 | 3.8 | 13.1 | 72.6 | 9.4 | 7.7 | 36.9 | 8.1 | 4.6 | 647.5 | 130.0 | 5.0 | 551.4 | 125.8 | 4.4 |
| Other Assaults | 9.5 | — | — | 00.0 | 00.0 | — | 00.0 | — | — | — | — | — | 22.6 | 20.5 | 1.1 | 10.8 | .6 | 18.0 |
| Weapon Offenses | 76.7 | — | — | 145.5 | 3.8 | 38.3 | 122.3 | 4.2 | 29.1 | 41.7 | 2.7 | 15.4 | 214.6 | 17.1 | 12.5 | 339.5 | 47.8 | 7.1 |

**Table 2:** *Property Crime Rate per 100,000 for Toledo, Ohio—1890–1976*

| | 1890 | | | 1909 | | | 1930 | | | 1950 | | | 1970 | | | 1976 | | |
|---|---|---|---|---|---|---|---|---|---|---|---|---|---|---|---|---|---|---|
| | Males | Females | Ratio | Males | Females | Ratio | Males | Females | Ratio | Males | Females | Ratio | Males | Females | Ratio | Males | Females | Ratio |
| Robbery | 31.9 | 6.4 | 5.0 | 70.0 | 1.9 | 36.8 | 173.0 | 11.5 | 15.0 | 36.0 | — | — | 81.7 | 8.5 | 9.6 | 206.6 | 29.3 | 7.0 |
| Burglary | 83.0 | — | — | 167.6 | — | — | 228.6 | 5.2 | 44.0 | 31.2 | .9 | 34.7 | 159.8 | 1.5 | 106.5 | 345.8 | 19.3 | 17.9 |
| Theft | 670.8 | 28.8 | 23.3 | 681.3 | 67.6 | 10.1 | 679.9 | 101.6 | 6.7 | 272.7 | 70.0 | 3.9 | 504.7 | 402.0 | 1.2 | 891.8 | 581.8 | 1.5 |
| Petit Larceny | 559.0 | 22.4 | 25.0 | 502.7 | 35.7 | 14.1 | 478.1 | 57.6 | 8.3 | 182.8 | 52.0 | 3.5 | 90.7 | 38.6 | 2.4 | 290.1 | 67.1 | 4.3 |
| Grand Larceny | 41.5 | 3.2 | 13.0 | 101.3 | 3.8 | 26.6 | 130.2 | 10.5 | 12.4 | 52.1 | 10.8 | 4.8 | 48.5 | 7.7 | 6.3 | 200.3 | 47.8 | 4.2 |
| Petit Shoplift | — | — | — | 3.7 | 7.5 | .5 | — | — | — | — | — | — | 282.1 | 332.1 | .8 | 348.4 | 414.4 | .8 |
| Grand Shoplift | — | — | — | — | — | — | — | — | — | — | — | — | 8.1 | 6.9 | 1.2 | 39.5 | 50.9 | .7 |
| Other | 70.3 | 3.2 | 22.0 | 73.6 | 20.6 | 3.6 | 71.6 | 33.5 | 2.1 | 37.8 | 7.2 | 5.2 | 75.3 | 16.7 | 4.5 | 13.5 | 1.6 | 8.4 |
| Auto Theft (and horse) | 12.8 | — | — | 11.0 | — | — | 98.4 | — | — | 25.6 | — | — | 51.2 | 4.6 | 11.1 | 16.2 | 1.5 | 10.8 |
| Forgery and Counterfeiting | 25.6 | 6.4 | 4.0 | 27.6 | — | — | 23.8 | 2.1 | 11.3 | 12.3 | — | — | 47.6 | 5.4 | 8.8 | 63.8 | 31.6 | 2.0 |
| Embezzlement and Fraud | 76.7 | 3.2 | 24.0 | 180.4 | 1.9 | 94.9 | 340.0 | 26.2 | 13.0 | 69.1 | 12.6 | 5.5 | 175.1 | 82.6 | 2.1 | 382.6 | 202.9 | 1.9 |
| Stolen Property | 16.0 | — | — | 31.3 | — | — | 39.8 | 3.1 | 12.8 | 4.7 | 1.8 | 2.6 | 48.5 | 10.0 | 4.8 | 228.1 | 50.2 | 4.5 |
| Malicious Destruction of Property | 89.4 | 6.4 | 14.0 | 110.5 | 16.9 | 6.5 | 146.1 | 16.8 | 8.7 | 72.0 | 7.2 | 10.0 | 76.3 | 10.8 | 7.1 | 61.1 | 23.9 | 2.6 |

The category of theft is more clear cut. Here we see a ratio of male-to-female involvement in 1890 of 23 to 1, where in 1970 and 1976 the ratios are 1.2 to 1 and 1.5 to 1, respectively. This is an indication of clear increases not only in a diminishing male-female difference, but in a steadily accelerating rate of female involvement—from 28.8 in 1890 to 581.8 in 1976. We have been able to further subdivide theft in 1970 and 1976 to determine what percentage of these larceny arrests is attributable to shoplifting. These figures indicate that there is indeed a high percentage of larcenies accounted for by shoplifting (79 percent of female arrests versus 40 percent of male arrests in 1976). However, if we examine female arrests for grand and petit larceny *other* than shoplifting in 1976, the rates of female involvement (47.8 and 67.1, respectively) are still larger than in any of the other years (where shoplifting and larceny are combined).

While auto theft remains a male-dominated offense, the categories of forgery/counterfeiting and embezzlement/fraud show large increases in female arrests. Forgery is the type of offense category where there are not large numbers of either males or females arrested, but we do see increases in the extent to which females are involved. Embezzlement and fraud show large increases, from a ratio of 24 to 1 in 1890 to 1.9 to 1 in 1976. While these figures denote change, it is erroneous to assume that the arrests are necessarily for embezzlement from the person's place of employment (important in delineating Simon's labor-force participation argument). Instead, for example, in 1970, 75 percent of the females in this category were actually arrested for passing bad checks. (The figure was 58 percent for males in that year.) In 1976, 57 percent of the females in the fraud category represent those passing bad checks, versus 60 percent of the males. There were only five women arrested for the category of "embezzlement" in 1970, and none in 1976. The rest of the women making up this overall category were actually arrested for misuse of credit cards, defrauding an innkeeper or taxi driver, or falsification to obtain aid (e.g., welfare). These offenses hardly indicate a surge in white-collar or other occupational crimes.

Offenses related to stolen property also showed increases as of 1976 when compared with the very low participation of females in the earlier years. The same is true of "malicious destruction of property," where there are increases, but not dramatic ones. Overall, Table 3 presents a picture of increased participation of females in property offenses, with the most significant increases occurring in the larceny category as well as in embezzlement/fraud. The difference between 1909 and 1930 is particularly interesting, as are the increases represented within the 1970 and 1976 blotters.

**Table 3:** *Public Order Crime Rate per 100,000 for Toledo, Ohio—1890–1976*

| | 1890 | | | 1909 | | | 1930 | | | 1950 | | | 1970 | | | 1976 | | |
|---|---|---|---|---|---|---|---|---|---|---|---|---|---|---|---|---|---|---|
| | Males | Females | Ratio | Males | Females | Ratio | Males | Females | Ratio | Males | Females | Ratio | Males | Females | Ratio | Males | Females | Ratio |
| Prostitution | 56.2 | 422.3 | .13 | 5.5 | 18.8 | .3 | 172.0 | 956.5 | .2 | 38.8 | 51.2 | .8 | 22.4 | 148.2 | .2 | 44.0 | 192.9 | .2 |
| Sex Offenses | 124.6 | 9.6 | 13.0 | 31.3 | 5.6 | 5.6 | 111.3 | 31.4 | 3.5 | 88.1 | 18.0 | 4.9 | 87.1 | .8 | 108.9 | 76.3 | 1.5 | 50.9 |
| Offenses Against Family & Children | 345.0 | 9.6 | 36.0 | 49.7 | 1.9 | 26.2 | 332.0 | 21.0 | 15.8 | 319.1 | 32.3 | 9.9 | 415.8 | 15.4 | 27.0 | 304.4 | 7.7 | 40.8 |
| All Drugs | — | — | — | 11.0 | 1.9 | 5.8 | 3.4 | 2.1 | 1.6 | — | — | — | 194.9 | 49.4 | 3.9 | 672.6 | 164.4 | 4.1 |
| Sale | — | — | — | 1.8 | 1.9 | .9 | — | — | — | — | — | — | 18.0 | 0.0 | — | 115.0 | 27.0 | 4.3 |
| Liquor (Drunkenness) | 2980.3 | 108.8 | 27.4 | 31.3 | 46.9 | .7 | 1171.0 | 347.8 | 3.4 | 35.0 | 7.2 | 4.9 | 69.2 | 124.2 | .6 | 41.3 | 7.7 | 5.4 |
| Drunk and Disorderly | 1082.9 | 112.0 | 9.7 | 44.2 | 9.4 | 4.7 | 2184.9 | 188.6 | 11.6 | 1413.7 | 332.1 | 4.3 | 4485.0 | 325.6 | 13.8 | 1650.7 | 227.8 | 5.9 |

| | | | | | | | | | | | | | | | | | |
|---|---|---|---|---|---|---|---|---|---|---|---|---|---|---|---|---|---|
| Disorderly Conduct (Disturbance, etc) | 2159.3 | 233.5 | 9.2 | 975.9 | 139.0 | 7.0 | 333.0 | 109.0 | 3.1 | 280.3 | 118.5 | 2.4 | 302.6 | 111.9 | 2.7 | 521.8 | 159.7 | 3.3 |
| Vagrancy | 185.3 | — | — | 95.8 | 48.8 | 2.0 | 288.3 | 128.9 | 2.2 | 315.3 | 21.5 | 14.7 | 260.4 | 19.3 | 13.5 | .9 | — | — |
| Gambling | 22.4 | — | — | 7.4 | — | — | 356.9 | 3.1 | 115.1 | 190.3 | 3.6 | 52.9 | 165.2 | 20.8 | 7.9 | 92.5 | 2.3 | 40.2 |
| DWI | — | — | — | — | — | — | 304.2 | 2.1 | 144.8 | 271.8 | 9.0 | 30.2 | 1120.0 | 69.4 | 16.1 | 1130.7 | 85.6 | 13.2 |
| Public Order Violations | 565.4 | 16.0 | 35.3 | 119.7 | 7.5 | 16.0 | 56.6 | 3.1 | 18.3 | 39.7 | 3.6 | 11.0 | 51.2 | 12.3 | 4.2 | 48.5 | 13.1 | 3.7 |
| Nonoffense Arrests | 1392.7 | 67.2 | 20.7 | 4956.9 | 762.5 | 6.5 | 2181.9 | 420.1 | 5.2 | 412.8 | 184.9 | 2.2 | 159.0 | 104.2 | 1.5 | 91.6 | 68.7 | 1.3 |
| Safe-keeping | 357.8 | 38.4 | 9.3 | 3294.2 | 520.2 | 6.3 | 281.3 | 56.6 | 5.0 | 147.7 | 3.6 | 41.0 | — | — | — | 1.8 | 13.9 | .1 |
| Safekeep for Doctor | — | — | — | — | 11.3 | — | 373.8 | 236.8 | 1.6 | 72.0 | 79.0 | .9 | 144.6 | 102.6 | 1.4 | 89.8 | 54.0 | 1.7 |
| Suspicion | 862.4 | 25.6 | 33.7 | 1657.2 | 225.4 | 7.4 | 973.2 | 73.3 | 13.3 | 156.2 | 61.9 | 2.5 | — | — | — | — | — | — |
| Other | 172.5 | 3.2 | 53.9 | 5.5 | 5.6 | 1.0 | 553.6 | 53.4 | 10.4 | 36.9 | 40.4 | .9 | 14.4 | 1.6 | 9.0 | — | .8 | — |

Table 3 details the total arrests for public order offenses in the years studied. While we are perhaps more concerned about the participation of females in so-called masculine crimes, this set of data gives added credence—particularly in the case of these offenses—to the importance of taking into account police behavior and attitudes. Thus, for example, it appears that prostitution took a sharp decline in 1909. However, a closer examination of the police blotters reveals that police began to use the category of "safekeeping" as a substitute for prostitution arrests. But beyond the rather obvious use of discretion by the police in these moral areas, several interesting observations can be made. First, it is important to note that offenses related to drinking are the most common offense category for which males are arrested; however, they are also the most common offense category for which females are arrested. This would appear to contradict recent inferences by Steffensmeier (1978) that "drunk and disorderly" is not a female crime. This is not true of the recent years, nor has it been the case as far back as 1890 (at least in Toledo).

Second, as expected, there is a dramatic increase in drug arrests in 1970 and 1976. To determine whether female arrests were more likely to be for simple possession, while selling was more exclusively the province of males, those arrested for sale were separated out. While no females (and few males) were arrested for "sale" in 1970, the approximately 4:1 overall drug ratio in 1976 is similarly reflected in a 4.3:1 male-female ratio specifically for selling.


Versatility of Female Crime

Prostitution is, of course, a female-dominated offense as rape is a male-dominated offense. Even though Table 3 shows high arrest rates in this category, it no longer looms as large in the context of the total volume of crimes women commit. Table 4 presents the actual percentage of the total volume of female arrests that is attributable to prostitution over the years studied.

Clearly, conceiving of female crimes as relating to moral areas alone offers an inadequate portrayal of the character and versatility of women's involvement in a wide range of offenses. While it has been shown that females commit fewer crimes than men, our data suggest a similarity in the patterning of their offense involvement. To examine this statistically, Spearman Rank Order Correlation coefficients were computed comparing the relative participation of males and females in fourteen major offense categories.

**Table 4.** *Percentage of All Arrests of Females for Prostitution or Prostitution-Related Offenses (e.g., safekeeping)*

| 1890 | 40 percent |
|------|------------|
| 1909 | 45 percent |
| 1930 | 36 percent |
| 1950 | 4 percent |
| 1970 | 8 percent |
| 1976 | 8 percent |

**Table 5.** *Spearman's RHO: A Comparison of the Relative Participation of Males and Females in Major Offense Categories[a]*

| 1890 | .66 |
|------|-----|
| 1909 | .75 |
| 1930 | .90 |
| 1950 | .83 |
| 1970 | .81 |
| 1976 | .89 |

[a]The offenses included were homicide, assault, other types of assault, weapons offenses, robbery, burglary theft, auto theft, stolen property offenses, forgery, fraud/embezzlement, drug offenses, all liquor offenses, malicious destruction of property. (Prostitution and rape were not included because they are so totally sex linked.)

An examination of these correlation coefficients suggests a similarity in the relative distribution of male and female participation in given offenses; that is, both males and females are most likely to be arrested for liquor-related offenses, followed generally by arrests for minor assaults, arrest for simple larceny, and so on. There is a greater congruence over time, but it is interesting that in 1930 we find the highest correlation.

In summary, Tables 2-5 illustrate that, at least at the arrest levels, the nature and versatility of female involvement is changing. Though males still comprise the majority of arrests, our statistics indicate that: (1) females are now being arrested for offenses that are similar to those for which males are arrested, (2) females' rates of arrests are increasing more rapidly than males', and (3) the male-to-female ratios are declining for many offenses.

It is not only through Tables 2-5, however, that we observed a change in the character of female crime. Our analysis of the thousands of entries in these blotters over the years provides further impressionistic evidence. In 1890 a high percentage of the total number of women arrested was somehow tied to "houses of ill fame." There were some instances of more aggressive assaults, but these appeared to be primarily

disputes among family and/or neighbors. There were not *any* instances
of females involved in some of the more serious kinds of offenses.

The gentle quality of the offenses in these early years is particularly
well reflected in the 1909 blotters: The individual who made all the
entries had a penchant for including some of the details of the case.
(Concerning a 49-year-old domestic picked up for safekeeping, the individual wrote, "Sent in from a drug store where she was making a show
of herself." Recording another woman picked up on suspicion, it was
noted that "she ran on the street, is being kept by a man, so that she will
not sport. She has a child—she took slippers from the shoe maker." The
following details of an assault and battery were entered in the blotter:
"Man tried to take her cook stove away from her because she failed to
make last month's payment. He accused her of attacking him." The
point is that as we moved to the 1930 blotters, there began to be a more
active, independent-from-hearth-and-home (as well as from-the-house-
of-prostitution) quality of the offenses. As the 1930 figures reflect, this
period, itself characterized by great economic and social changes,
reflects changes in the quality, and to some extent the volume, of
females' participation in criminality. But the contrast is particularly
marked as we moved to the 1970 and 1976 blotters. One indication of
this is provided by an examination simply of the increase in females
arrested on multiple charges over the target years. Table 6 presents the
rates of males and females arrested for multiple offenses per 100,000
population.

Of course this may at least in part reflect different police attitudes
over time, but a comparison of the *types* of multiple arrests also reflects
change. A typical combination of offenses in the early years was "resid-
ing in a house of ill fame and disturbance," or from as late as 1950,
"using a room for immoral purposes and hold for health." In the 1970
and 1976 blotters multiple charges such as the following appeared:

- Disturbance, soliciting, resisting arrest, aggravated robbery, and
  attempted aggravated murder.

**Table 6.** *Rate of Arrests for Multiple Charges per 100,000 Population*

|      | MALES  | FEMALES |
|------|--------|---------|
| 1890 | 559.0  | 3.2     |
| 1909 | 244.9  | 96.5    |
| 1930 | 686.9  | 36.7    |
| 1950 | 190.3  | 108.6   |
| 1970 | 1443.2 | 250.8   |
| 1976 | 1855.4 | 422.1   |

- Arson, aggravated robbery, petit theft.
- Five counts of aggravated burglary.
- Soliciting for prostitution, possession of hypodermic needle, robbery.

## UNDERSTANDING THE INCREASES

The preceding statistics present a somewhat complicated picture of females' participation in crime, but we have proceeded from a time (1890) in which virtually no female in Toledo was arrested for burglary, a major assault, carrying a weapon, (officially) resisting arrest, or receiving stolen property—to a time when increases are observed in most categories, particularly those relating to property. We do not feel that such increases can be explained by "women's liberation" as it is narrowly defined (Adler, 1975). As we have demonstrated empirically (Giordano and Cernkovich, 1979), "liberation" as an individually held set of attitudes has little or no predictive value in understanding females' involvement (or lack of it) in criminality.

The notion that greater labor-force participation of women simply increases one's chances to engage in crimes is more plausible, but it is not substantiated by the finding that women are not often arrested for occupational or white-collar crimes such as embezzlement. There is further doubt about the utility of this explanation when one examines a profile of characteristics of the same of women arrested in the target years. As Table 7 clearly indicates, for the years in which employment status was recorded in the blotters, a high percentage of the women arrested were unemployed. Even those who were employed in the samples were likely to be working at the lowest levels according to anyone's occupational status ranking (Warner, et al., 1949).

**Table 7.** *Characteristics of Sample Offenders in Toledo, 1890–1976*

|                        | 1890 | | 1909 | | 1930 | |
|------------------------|---------|-------|---------|-------|---------|-------|
|                        | Females | Males | Females | Males | Females | Males |
| Percent U.S. Born      | 70.3    | 70.8  | 38.8    | 80.1  | 91.3    | 83.9  |
| Percent Unemployed     | —       | —     | —       | —     | —       | —     |
| Percent Housewife      | 40.2    | —     | 31.8    | —     | 26.6    | —     |
| Percent Non-White      | 12.2    | 3.4   | 18.2    | 6.6   | 28.2    | 18.6  |
| Percent Married        | —       | —     | —       | —     | —       | —     |
| Mean Age               | 32.71   | 33.68 | 32.02   | 36.49 | 31.27   | 35.9  |

Table 7. *Characteristics of Sample Offenders in Toledo, 1890–1976 (continued)*

|                      | 1950 | | 1970 | | 1976 | |
|----------------------|---------|-------|---------|-------|---------|-------|
|                      | Females | Males | Females | Males | Females | Males |
| Percent U.S. Born    | 96.9    | 94.0  | 97.4    | 96.4  | 96.7    | 96.1  |
| Percent Unemployed   | 76.0    | 38.5  | 64.5    | 40.5  | 77.3    | 50.1  |
| Percent Housewife    | 22.7    | —     | 19.9    | —     | 13.6    | —     |
| Percent Non-White    | 31.5    | 26.9  | 39.2    | 35.6  | 50.3    | 43.2  |
| Percent Married      | 42.9    | 44.3  | 35.5    | 41.4  | 20.9    | 23.8  |
| Mean Age             | 35.43   | 39.48 | 33.46   | 36.17 | 29.41   | 31.48 |

We would suggest that the crimes of women can and should be understood in the context of structural and economic forces in society (as those of men have always been). Labor-force participation is an important variable; however, we would suggest that the process through which it has an effect is not as Simon has outlined. To understand the direction of its influence, the findings from more general analyses of labor-market changes must be juxtaposed against the personal characteristics of the women who are actually represented by the police blotter statistics. According to most studies, the critical changes with respect to women have been in the influx of *older married* workers into the labor market. This is contrasted with an earlier pattern of young and unmarried women making up the critical mass of female workers. Oppenheimer (1976) examines in detail the changing supply-and-demand structures which precipitated this change and locates the time of the greatest increase at 1940–1960. Chafe's (1972) historical account of the changing economic role of women similarly stresses the post-World War II period and the role of married women:

> At the turn of the century the young, the single and the poor had dominated the female labor force. Fifty years later, the majority of women workers were married and middle-aged, and a substantial minority came from the middle class. In the story of that dramatic change, World War II represented a watershed event. (1972:195)

In view of this changing labor market structure for females, one must thus begin to look at the women who make up the arrest statistics and the kinds of crimes they commit from the perspective of *economic marginality* rather than simply "new opportunities." These women would be considered economically marginal not only in comparison to men but also when compared to the types of women (e.g., married, thus enjoying a combined income) who are swelling the ranks of the female labor force. As Table 7 shows, for the years in which marital status is recorded there has also been an increase in the percentage of women arrested who are single, divorced, or separated.

The depression year that is part of this study, 1930, provides a further example of the impact of economic forces on patterns of female crime. While the earlier years, 1890 and 1909, are marked by a relative lack of participation by women in crime, 1930 shows significant increases, particularly in such property offenses as robbery, burglary, theft, and embezzlement. Analyses of the depression years suggest that similar to more recent labor market shifts, a major increase occurred during the depression in the number of married women who returned to work, "not because they sought liberation from the burdens of domesticity or enjoyed a new equality with men in the job market but so that their families could survive economically" (Chafe, 1972).[2]

This would have the effect of placing single women in an even more precarious economic position, given that married men often had the top priority of jobs. In his study of public welfare in Toledo during the depression, for example, Sobczak (1975) notes that "men with families found it much easier to become certified for W.P.A. work, while an increasingly large number of single men and women lost their W.P.A. jobs and went on direct relief" (1975:68). It is not unreasonable to hypothesize that at least some of these women (and men) included criminality in the range of adaptations they developed for "getting by."

We thus see it as significant that the major, consistent increases have been documented in the area of property crimes. With Simon we would highlight the importance of the greater labor-force participation of women. However, this analysis of offense types as well as the characteristics of women arrested suggests that the increases may reflect the fact that certain categories of women (e.g., young, single, minority) are now in an even more unfavorable position in the labor market at the same time that they are increasingly expected to function independently.

Future research should be directed to an analysis of female criminality apart from the definitions made by the police or other criminal justice agents. Particularly in "moral" areas, official statistics cannot offer a complete accounting of the scope of female crime, and this continues to cloud our understanding of any increases.

Our analysis of the police blotters allowed us to go further back in time and to examine offenses in greater detail than would be possible using Uniform Crime Report statistics; however, there are many questions which still need to be addressed: What is the meaning of particular criminal acts from the perspective of the women themselves? At what point do criminal options come into play in the context of a women's employment/unemployment career? What factors, other than economic

factors, affect patterns of female crime? Are there differences in the etiology of adult versus juvenile female criminality?

## REFERENCES

Adler, Freda. *Sisters in crime.* New York: McGraw-Hill Book Company, 1975.
Chafe, William H. *The american woman: Her changing social, economic and
    political role, 1920-1970.* New York: Oxford University Press, 1972.
Ferdinand, Theodore N. The criminal patterns of Boston since 1849. *American
    Journal of Sociology,* 1967, *73*(1), 85-99.
Giordano, Peggy C., and Cernkovich, Stephen A. On complicating the relation-
    ship between liberation and delinquency. *Social Problems,* 1979, *26* (4),
    467-481.
Noblit, George W., and Burcart, Janie M. Women and crime: 1960-1970. *Social
    Science Quarterly,* March 1976, *56,* 651-657.
Powell, Elwin H. Crime as a function of anomie. *The Journal of Criminal Law,
    Criminology and Police Science,* 1966, *57*(2) 161-171.
Simon, Rita James. *The contemporary woman and crime.* National Institute of
    Mental Health, Washington, D.C.: U.S. Government Printing Office, 1975.
Sobczak, John N. The inadequacies of localism: The collapse of relief in Toledo,
    1929-1939. Unpublished M.A. Thesis, Bowling Green State University,
    1975.
Steffensmeier, Darrell. Crime and the contemporary woman: An analysis of
    changing levels of female property crime, 1960-1975. *Social Forces,* 1978a,
    *57,* 566-584.
Warner, W. Lloyd, Meeker, Marcia, and Eells, Kenneth. *Social class in america.*
    Chicago: Science Research Associates, 1949.

SIX

# Gender Differences in Delinquency: Quantity and Quality

WILLIAM FEYERHERM

Sociologists, criminologists, and others concerned with aspects of criminal and delinquent activity traditionally have accepted the proposition
that there are substantial differences between the deviant behavior of

male and female adolescents. These differences are ofte
examination of police arrest records, which typically sh
5 to 1 ratio of male to female arrests in the age group u
addition to the presumption that the general level of fer
is substantially lower than that of males, there is another presumption,
also drawn from an examination of official records maintained by the
criminal justice system, that the characters of male and female delinquency are substantially different. Female delinquency is often perceived
as centering around sexual prohibitions, running away from home, and
other "status" offenses. Male delinquency, on the other hand, is often
seen as involving theft or violent behavior. Following these descriptions,
female delinquency has been characterized as specialized (i.e., concentrated in status offenses), while male delinquency has been viewed as
diversified (i.e., less likely to specialize in a single form of delinquent
behavior) (Hindelang 1971).

With the advent of alternatives to the dependence on arrest records
as a source of information, particularly self-reported delinquency studies, these perceptions become open to reexamination. This reexamination often served to change the perceptions of male-female differences.
In one study, for example, Hindelang (1971) found that the ratio of male
to female delinquency was approximately 2.6 to 1, only half the difference found in arrest records. Further, female delinquency was distributed in a fashion similar to male delinquency, raising questions about
the presumption that male and female delinquency differ in character.
Results similar to those of Hindelang have been found in the work of
other investigators using the self-report methodology (Gold, 1970; Williams
and Gold, 1972).

The differences between the findings of those studies based on self-
reported delinquency and those based upon arrest records generate a
variety of problems. Such differences require explanation. Of course the
easiest way of reconciling differences such as these is to argue that one
or the other measurement technique is erroneous. Thus, considerable
rhetoric has been expended in attacking and defending both the self-
report methodology and the methods used in compiling arrest records.
While there is not room in this article to replay all of these arguments, a
few points may be noted in summary. Arrest data are subject to criticism
on the grounds that they represent only a small fraction (perhaps 3 to 5
percent of less) of offenses committed by juveniles and are the result of a
procedure that involves substantial discretion, thus creating the potential
for bias of one form or another. Self-reported measures have been critic-
ized as depending too greatly on the cooperation and veracity of subjects, emphasizing relatively trivial items (e.g., smoking in school or

talking back to parents) and measuring merely the proportion of juveniles who have committed an offense, not the frequency of offending. A more detailed accounting of these arguments may be found in Nettler (1974) or Hood and Sparks (1970). As the use of self-reported delinquency measures has increased, attention has been given to demonstrations of the reliability and validity of the technique (Erickson, 1972; Clark and Tifft, 1966; Feyerherm, 1977; Gold, 1970). While both arrest measures and self-report measures have proven to have some difficulties as measurement devices, neither has been discredited sufficiently to resolve the differences that they display concerning male/female delinquency.

An alternative method of resolving the differences between the methods may be presented by the use of the concept of a "self-fulfilling prophecy." In the abstract, the concept of a self-fulfilling prophecy refers to a condition in which the belief in a statement causes us to act in ways that bring about the apparent proof of the statement. This concept may be applied in two ways to offer an explanation for the differing results regarding male/female differences in delinquency. If one starts with the assumption, or prophecy, that females are less delinquent, then it may follow that the general populace and law enforcement officials will be less likely to expect delinquent behavior from females than from male adolescents. If this is true, then it may follow that fewer suspicions and a correspondingly lower degree of surveillance will be accorded to female adolescents. Since most offenses and offenders come to the attention of the police through citizen reports, it may be likely that a lower proportion of offenses committed by females will be brought to the attention of the police, particularly those in which a suspect is known. Since fewer females will have come to the attention of the police, the prophecy is confirmed—not necessarily because it is true, but because the social processes leading to police knowledge of offenders operate as if the prophecy were true. Indeed, even if the prophecy is to some degree accurate, this process could act to amplify the differences between male and female rates of delinquency. Additionally, since females are expected to "specialize" in certain types of activities, they may be more carefully watched for evidences of those activities, which might produce or amplify the perceptions of differences in the quality of female delinquency.

A second application of this concept of the self-fulfilling prophecy revolves around the behavior of police once they have reason to suspect that a particular juvenile has committed an offense. It is quite clear from studies involving observation of police behavior that much discretion is exercised by police officers in deciding which individuals to arrest (Goldman, 1963; Piliavin and Briar, 1964). Much of the research examining this use of discretion has focused upon the effects of such factors as race or social status, with mixed results depending upon the jurisdiction studied and other factors. One reasonable expectation from this research is that law enforcement officers may engage in some informal estimation of the likelihood of future delinquency. Thus, it is plausible to expect that those juveniles who, in the opinion of law enforcement officers, are less likely to pose a threat of future illegal behavior may be released with a warning or to the custody of parents or with some other disposition short of arrest. Those who are considered more likely to engage in future illegal behavior may be considered to be more suitable candidates for formal intervention (arrest and juvenile court processing). Since the likelihood of future delinquency from females may be perceived as lower than that of males, it may be that the likelihood of arrest is correspondingly lower for females. It may therefore be the case that the apparent differences between male and female delinquency, as indicated by arrest statistics, may be a function of the social processes by which these measurements are created, as well as of the "real" differences in the rate of illegal behavior.

The current article is concerned then with two issues: the extent to which male and female delinquency differ from each other in both qualitative and quantitative ways, and the extent to which a "self-fulfilling prophecy" regarding female delinquency may be used to explain the differences between self-reported and arrest descriptions of male/female differences in delinquency.

The data to be used in these analyses were collected in an industrial community that is part of a large Northeastern metropolitan area. Through the cooperation of the local high school, questionnaire responses were obtained from a sample of 1,119 students (562 males and 557 females). Among the sets of items on the questionnaire were 19 illegal behaviors, for which the students indicated the number of times in the past year they had engaged in each activity, the number of times they had been contacted or questioned by police, and the number of times they had been arrested for each activity. An inquiry with the local police department confirmed that, with the exception of traffic offenses and truancy, the 19 items included all activities for which juveniles had been arrested in the preceding year.

Table 1 presents the results of the self-reported delinquency items. Included in the table are the mean (average) number of acts reported in the preceding year, as well as the percentage of respondents who indicated that they had been involved in the activity at least once in the preceding year. Each of these is presented separately for males and females. Finally, a ratio is presented which was formed by dividing the mean number of acts reported by females into the mean number of acts reported by males.

This ratio may be perceived as an index of the extent to which the rate of delinquent activity for males is greater than that for females for each of the offense categories.

Overall, a vast majority of both males and females (92.0 percent and 78.3 percent, respectively) indicated engaging in at least one form of illegal behavior in the preceding year. Moreover, the mean number of activities is relatively high for both males (90.26) and females (53.12). The ratio of male to female averages is 1.70 across all of the forms of delinquent behavior, which reflects an even smaller male-female differential than the figure of 2.6 reported by Hindelang (1971) in his self-reported data. Thus, while these total scores do show a greater likelihood of male delinquency than female delinquency, the differences are smaller than appear in many earlier analyses. Over three-quarters of the females admitted to at least one delinquent act, and the average number of delinquent acts indicate a quite substantial volume of female delinquency.

This overall conclusion is not replicated in each of the specific types of offenses, however. First, it may be noted that in the last six questions —all related to the use of illegal substances—the average rate of use and percentage of respondents indicating use are very similar for males and females. Tests of significance (t-tests) indicate that these differences are not statistically significant (p greater than .05), while the differences in male and female mean scores are significant in the remaining 13 items and the total scores. Indeed, in two instances (use of pills and use of heroin) the average for the females in the sample was higher than the average for the males (although not significantly higher). Second, at the other extreme there are several offense categories for which the ratio of male to female average scores is quite high. Most extreme are the categories of theft over $50 (ratio = 22.00) and having been in a fight using weapons (ratio = 24.67). Not quite so extreme are the categories involving property damage, both of low value (ratio = 11.36) and valued at more than $10 (ratio = 11.94). For these four offenses, the rate of male delinquency is over 10 times greater than the rate of female delinquency. It must be noted that these four offenses account for a relatively small percentage of the total number of offenses admitted by respondents (8 percent for males and 1 percent for females).

There appears to be some evidence that as the seriousness of the event increases, the difference between male and female participation increases. For instance, three levels of theft behavior are presented. In the lowest level, under $10, the ratio of male to female delinquency is relatively low (1.80). As the value of the stolen item increases to between

**Table 1.** *Self-Reported Delinquent Behavior*

| QUESTION | MALES ($N = 562$) | | FEMALES ($N = 557$) | | RATIO |
|---|---|---|---|---|---|
| | Mean | Percentage | Mean | Percentage | |
| Stolen something worth less than $10 | 6.14 | 55.9 | 3.41 | 36.1 | 1.80 |
| Stolen something worth $10 to $50 | 1.87 | 26.7 | .41 | 8.3 | 4.56 |
| Stolen something worth more than $50 | 1.54 | 21.1 | .07 | 2.5 | 22.00 |
| Destroyed property (less than $10 damage) | 3.18 | 42.0 | .28 | 9.5 | 11.36 |
| Destroyed property (more than $10 damage) | 1.91 | 27.4 | .16 | 5.3 | 11.94 |
| Gotten drunk | 24.81 | 82.1 | 13.83 | 72.9 | 1.79 |
| Been in fist fights | 4.98 | 64.6 | .77 | 20.3 | 6.47 |
| Carried a dangerous weapon | 7.99 | 30.2 | 1.55 | 6.4 | 5.15 |
| Been in a weapon fight | .74 | 15.5 | .03 | 2.9 | 24.67 |
| Obtained valuables by using force | .29 | 5.6 | .09 | 1.3 | 3.22 |
| Broken and entered | .96 | 13.4 | .12 | 5.8 | 8.00 |
| Driven under the influence | 2.62 | 22.2 | 1.36 | 12.4 | 1.93 |
| Taken a car without permission | 1.72 | 17.0 | .36 | 6.9 | 4.78 |
| Used pills to get high | 5.51 | 28.0 | 7.38 | 36.8 | .75 |
| Used marijuana | 23.56 | 57.8 | 20.41 | 54.2 | 1.15 |
| Sniffed glue | .59 | 9.3 | .46 | 9.2 | 1.28 |
| Used LSD, methedrine or mescaline | 1.38 | 13.6 | 1.38 | 13.5 | 1.00 |
| Used heroin | .03 | 2.0 | .13 | 2.0 | .23 |
| Sold drugs | 1.79 | 17.8 | 1.19 | 15.1 | 1.50 |
| Total | 90.26 | 92.2 | 53.12 | 78.3 | 1.70 |

$10 and $50, the ratio of male to female participation increases to 4.56. Finally, as the value of the theft increases to over $50, the ratio increases to 22.00. One can similarly distinguish between fist fighting (ratio = 6.47) and fighting with weapons (ratio = 24.67). The form in which the present data were collected does not permit a more systematic assessment of these differences, but the examples do indicate a shift in the ratio of male to female involvement with increases in the seriousness of the delinquent conduct. Since the sets of arrest statistics most often examined are designed to deal primarily with serious offenses, this tendency may explain why arrest information is more likely to show strong male-female differences. Finally, it should be recognized that two offense categories account for a majority of both male and female delinquent behaviors: getting drunk and using marijuana. Both of these behaviors show a relatively low ratio of male to female delinquency. Thus, the relatively low ratio of male to female delinquency exhibited by the total delinquency scores may be primarily a product of these two offenses.

In addition to the issue of differences in the degree of involvement, we are concerned with the extent to which there are qualitative differences in the patterns of delinquency of males and females. Table 2 provides this analysis. It presents each offense category as a percentage of the total number of delinquent acts admitted by either males or females. A comparison of these percentages addresses the degree to which patterns of delinquency are similar, even though the level of conduct may be somewhat lower among females. The percentage of delinquent acts which fall into many of the offense categories is very similar for males and females; for example, just over one-quarter of the acts of both males and females are in the category "gotten drunk." Males and females likewise show nearly the same concentration of theft of low value (under $10). However, substantial differences occur with regard to marijuana use. This category accounts for approximately one-quarter of male delinquency but more than one-third of female delinquency (38 percent). Taken in combination with the other five drug-related items, these constitute 37 percent of male delinquent acts, but 58 percent of female delinquent acts. When further combined with the category of getting drunk—which may be considered another form of substance abuse—this set of items includes 84 percent of the delinquent acts reported by females, but only 64 percent of the acts reported by males. The difference appears to be accounted for among males by higher proportions of offenses involving property damage and fighting behaviors.

An alternate method of examining patterns of behavior is also presented in Table 2. This is provided by the columns in which the offenses are ranked in order by the mean number of delinquent acts reported.

**Table 2.** *Self-Reported Offenses as Percentage of Total Offenses and Ranked by Frequency and Sex*

| QUESTION | MALES | | FEMALES | |
|---|---|---|---|---|
| | Rank | Percentage | Rank | Percentage |
| Stolen something worth less than $10 | 4 | 7 | 4 | 6 |
| Stolen something worth $10 to $50 | 10 | 2 | 11 | 1 |
| Stolen something worth more than $50 | 13 | 2 | 18 | 0 |
| Destroyed property (less than $10 damage) | 7 | 4 | 13 | 1 |
| Destroyed property (more than $10 damage) | 9 | 2 | 14 | 0 |
| Gotten drunk | 1 | 27 | 2 | 26 |
| Been in fist fights | 6 | 6 | 9 | 1 |
| Carried a dangerous weapon | 3 | 9 | 5 | 3 |
| Been in a weapon fight | 16 | 1 | 19 | 0 |
| Obtained valuables by using force | 18 | 0 | 17 | 0 |
| Broken and entered | 15 | 1 | 16 | 0 |
| Driven under the influence | 8 | 3 | 7 | 3 |
| Taken a car without permission | 12 | 2 | 12 | 1 |
| Used pills to get high | 5 | 6 | 3 | 14 |
| Used marijuana | 2 | 26 | 1 | 38 |
| Sniffed glue | 17 | 1 | 10 | 1 |
| Used LSD, methedrine or mescaline | 14 | 2 | 6 | 3 |
| Used heroin | 19 | 0 | 15 | 0 |
| Sold drugs | 10 | 2 | 8 | 2 |

For males, the most frequent activity is getting drunk, while marijuana use is second. For females this ranking is reversed. An examination of the rankings shows that they are generally similar. The greatest difference in rankings is for the activity represented by the use of LSD, methedrine, or mescaline, which ranks sixth among the offenses for females but fourteenth among the offense for males. It is interesting to note that males and females in this sample have exactly the same average frequency for this category (average = 1.38). A rank order correlation coefficient (Spearman's rho) calculated between the two sets of rankings is .78, a statistically significant value indicating a substantial degree of agreement between the two rankings.

The evidence presented in Table 2 seems to indicate that there is a substantial similarity in the patterns of delinquent behavior of males and females. Both groups tend to engage most often in activities involving getting drunk and the use of marijuana. Both groups tend to engage least often in activities such as fighting with weapons, use of force in obtaining valuables, breaking and entering, and the use of heroin. However, despite these similarities, there remains a substantially greater concentration of female delinquency in the area of substance abuse (including alcohol) and a higher concentration of male offenses in activities involving fighting, property damage, and theft of more valuable items.

Having examined the extent of differences in the quantity and quality of self-reported delinquent behaviors of male and female adolescents, there remains the problem of explaining differences between the portrayals found in the self-reported measures and the measures of delinquency based upon arrests. A possible explanation for these differences was advanced earlier in this chapter in the hypothesis of a self-fulfilling prophecy. In the current study this hypothesis may be indirectly tested through the development of what are termed "transition probabilities." These figures present the probability of transition from one condition to another, subsequent condition. In the current study three transition probabilities have been calculated and are displayed in Table 3. These are the probability of a delinquent act resulting in a police contact, the probability of a police contact resulting in an arrest, and the combination of the two: the probability of a delinquent act resulting in an arrest. Given the relatively small number of arrests for all subjects (247) and the relatively low number of police contacts reported by females (446), it was not possible to calculate transition probabilities on an offense-specific level with any degree of confidence in their statistical stability. Table 3 therefore presents the aggregate of all offenses.

Table 3. *Transition Probabilities from Self-Reported Incident to Police Contact and Arrest*

| TRANSITION | MALE | FEMALE |
|---|---|---|
| Self-Reported Delinquency to Police Contact | .022 | .015 |
| Police Contact to Arrest | .185 | .118 |
| Self-Reported Delinquency to Arrest | .004 | .002 |

One of the most striking features about Table 3 is the low probability of transition from delinquent activity to arrest. Indeed, even for those juveniles who were the subject of police inquiries, the probability of an arrest is low (under 20 percent). Moreover, as predicted earlier, the probabilities of females progressing through the entry stages of the juvenile justice system are lower than for males. At the first stage, which represents the likelihood of an individual coming to the attention of police, the probabilities are quite low: .022 for males and .015 for females. At the second stage, the probabilities are higher than an individual will be arrested once contacted by the police, but still the difference between males and females is maintained, with males having a higher likelihood of arrest once contacted. When these two stages are combined, it is clear that although any delinquent activity has a very low probability of resulting if an arrest, this probability is more than doubled if the individual is a male. Thus, the transition process which leads from delinquency to arrest will tend to amplify the apparent differences between males and females. In the current study the ratio of male to female delinquency was found to be 1.70 to 1. When examined at the point of arrest, this ratio has increased to 3.88 to 1, more than doubling the apparent difference between males and females.

At least two possible explanations may be suggested for this amplification process. First, it is possible that a social process, termed here a "self-fulfilling prophecy," may have influenced the perceptions about females and, therefore, the process by which a delinquent act is discovered and leads to an arrest. A second explanation concerns the differences in types of activities between males and females. It was noted that a greater proportion of the offenses of the female subjects tended to occur in the categories of substance abuse, while a somewhat higher proportion of the offenses of males tended to occur in the areas of property damage, fighting activities, and thefts valued at over $10. To the extent that these offense categories have different transition probabilities, it may be argued that the tendency of males to commit activities which are more serious and have a higher probability of arrest will result in the appearance of greater male-female differences in delinquency. To test such a proposition would require offense-specific analyses of the differences between transition probabilities for males and females. Given the limited number of arrests in the current data set, such analysis does not appear feasible. However, it should be noted that the two explanations advanced here are not mutually exclusive; that is, it is possible to envision the simultaneous operation of both processes. Whichever is operative—or even if both are operative—it is clear that the social processes that move adolescents from the point of commission of a delinquent deed to the point of arrest tend to operate in ways that increase the likelihood of arrest for males rather than females. This process thus serves to accentuate the social perceptions of differences in the quantity and quality and female misconduct.

## REFERENCES

Clark, John, and Tifft, Larry. Polygraph and interview validation of self-reported deviant behavior. *American Sociological Review,* 1966, *31,* 516–523.

Gold, Martin. *Delinquent behavior in an american city.* Belmont, California: Brooks/Cole Publishing Company, 1970.

Goldman, Nathan. *Differential selection of juvenile offenders for court appearance.* New York: National Council on Crime and Delinquency, 1963.

Feyerherm, William. *The interrelationship of various indicators of crime.* Unpublished doctoral dissertation, State University of New York at Albany, 1977.

Hindelang, Michael. Age, sex and the versatility of delinquent involvements. *Social Problems,* 1971, *18,* 522–535.

Hood, Roger, and Sparks, Richard. *Key issues in criminology.* New York: McGraw-Hill Book Company, 1970.

Nettler, Gwynn. *Explaining crime.* New York: McGraw-Hill Book Company, 1974.

Piliavin, Irving, and Briar, Scott. Police encounters with juveniles. *American Journal of Sociology,* 1967, *70,* 206–214.

Williams, Jay R., and Gold, Martin. From delinquent behavior to official delinquency. *Social Problems,* 1972, *20,* 209–229.

# STUDIES OF SPECIFIC CRIMES COMMITTED BY WOMEN

The authors of most studies of specific crimes either included only males in their samples or included both genders and failed to break down any of their findings by sex of offender. As a result, there are relatively few studies of female crimes except for prostitution. Reading the literature on specific female crimes leaves one with the impression that most female criminals are prostitutes. This over-sexualization of female crime is misleading, for most female crime (like most male crime) is property crime, not sex or violent crime. A second distortion in the literature is the emphasis on unusual or spectacular female crimes such as pyromania (Greenberg, 1966) or infanticide (Deadman, 1964). It is hoped that the current surge of interest in female crime will result in future studies of female economic crimes such as fraud, forgery, counterfeiting, burglary, and embezzlement.

## 1. ROBBERY

Normandeau's (1968) pioneering study of robbery in Philadelphia includes a considerable amount of material on gender differences in crimes of robbery. Only one recorded Philadelphia robbery in every 20 was committed by a woman, a proportion that was not increased greatly in the last decade, judging from the FBI's Uniform Crime Reports. Female robbers were overrepresented in robberies on private premises and in robberies that developed after a preliminary association of short duration between victim and offender, and underrepresented in robberies committed in the open following a sudden attack. Female robbers were much more likely to use firearms as a threat than male robbers, but less likely to use sharp or blunt instruments or physical violence without weapons. Despite their heavy use of firearms, these women were less likely than male robbers to harm their victims. Convicted female robbers were also less likely to be sentenced to imprisonment than their male counterparts. This is not necessarily an indication of judicial favoritism, for women were less likely to have a record of previous arrests (63 percent as compared with 85 percent for men) and, as we have already mentioned, had a lower probability of injuring their victims.

In a recent investigation of female robbers, Spears et al. (1977) found that there were two basic types of offender: the situational offender and the career robber. The situational offender responded to social pressures and cues in deciding to participate in a robbery. Personal crises, economic need, peer pressure, and the use of intoxicants are examples of the factors leading to a situational offense. Although not fully professional criminals, the career robbers have been heavily involved in crime since adolescence. Some of them were actively involved in committing robberies, typically in groups of four or more criminals, while others limited their participation to planning, facilitating the escape, or concealing stolen items. Some of the career robbers were opportunistic in that they committed nonrobbery crimes more frequently than robberies, using whatever crime seemed easiest at the moment as a way of obtaining money which was often spent on heroin or other drugs.

## 2. MARITAL MURDER

There have been many popular sensationalistic publications on female murderers over the years (see, for example, Sparrow's *Women Who Murder),* but few research studies. The existing scientific studies reveal that husbands and wives are approximately equally likely to kill each other, but that women are much more likely than men to restrict their killing to those who are close to them. Men kill more often than women, killing strangers and acquaintances in addition to lovers and family members (Bowker, 1978). The popular literature notwithstanding, stealth, cunning, and the use of poison are not major components of female murders. Instead, women who murder men usually cope with the men's greater strength by catching them off guard. Many cases of marital homicide result from the continued beating of wives over a long period of time. These women are sometimes beaten to death and other times kill their husbands in self-defense or out of the despair that they will never be free to live normal lives.

## 3. PROPERTY CRIME

Shoplifting has been studied more than all other female property crimes combined. One reason for this is that shoplifting by middle-aged females was considered to be a clinical entity in which menopausal women responded to uncontrollable neurotic needs. This stereotype, altogether without a shred of empirical support, has survived into the 1970s in the social science literature (Brady and Mitchell, 1971). More objective research has been accumulating since the early 1960s, and it shows that women are not much more likely than men to shoplift (Mayhew, 1977), that very few female shoplifters have been previously apprehended for shoplifting (Cameron, 1964), and that the shoplifters' physical appearance and the value of the stolen items are more important determinants of the decision to prosecute than the gender of the offender (Steffensmeier and Terry, 1973; Cohen and Stark, 1974). Exposure is also important, with women stealing only more than men in stores that are predominantly entered by women.

Two articles related to female property crime are reprinted in this text. The first is a study by Block (1977) of female participation in organized crime in New York during the early 1900s. There are very few women in organized crime today, and we tend to think that this has always been so, or perhaps even that it is due to something fundamental about the female personality. Block's account shows us that women can be full participants in underworld activities and suggests the possibility that women are are effectively excluded from participation in organized crime today than they were in the past.

The second reprinted article shows how women's involvement in crime can be overestimated as well as underestimated. When Miller (1969) carefully examined the records of 437 women committed to the Women's Detention Center after the Washington, D.C., riot of April 1968, he found that many more arrests were for curfew violation (271) than for the highly publicized property crime of looting (75). Even among the looters, few were seriously criminal, for only three of them had prior criminal records.


# 4. PROSTITUTION


Prostitution has undoubtedly suffered a serious historical decline in the United States starting around the time of the First World War. Until that time, there were large red light districts in the major American cities. Closing down these districts forced prostitution underground, where it has remained ever since. Some houses of prostitution (now generally apartments) are still in operation, but most prostitutes are either streetwalkers or call girls. In general, call girls serve the highest status clientele and earn the highest income. Streetwalkers serve the lowest status clientele and earn the least after expenses. House prostitutes fall in between.

Many prostitutes enter the field in their mid-teens, as Gray (1973) has described in her Seattle study. Her subjects began prostituting themselves between the ages of 12 and 18, with an average age of 14.7. They were not generally promiscuous before beginning prostitution, and nearly all of them began without any specific training. Few young women became prostitutes without first knowing someone in the life who served as a role model.

A higher percentage of streetwalkers and a somewhat lower proportion of call girls and house prostitutes have pimps, men who control their lives and take their money in return for giving them protection and a feeling of security and love. James (1975) asked a sample of prostitutes about the advantages and disadvantages of working for a pimp. The major advantages they mentioned were the pimp's taking care of the prostitute's business affairs, giving them protection from other pimps and status in the hustler's world, and caring about them as persons. The disadvantages most commonly mentioned were losing one's earnings, individuality, and independence, along with being beaten. Not all pimps assault their prostitutes. Some are quite loving most of the time, while others are brutal and sadistic on occasion. Pimps who push their prostitutes too far will usually lose them to other pimps who are kinder.

Aside from those call girls who have address books full of steady customers who pay them well for their services, prostitutes do not generally achieve a high level of independence through their earnings. Pimps, lawyers, customers, and vice squad officers—all men—take their toll. Expenses for streetwalkers are so high that many of them cannot build up a savings account to fund a different lifestyle when they decide to retire from prostitution. With the closing of most houses of prostitution, there are few madams (proprietors of houses of prostitution) left, so there is little opportunity for upward mobility within the profession.

If the picture is so dismal, then why do prostitutes who are not doing well economically stay in the trade? The answer is that their lower-class background and limited job skills do not qualify them for more than the most menial low-paying labor in the legitimate world. They live at a much higher level than this while prostituting, even if they can't save much for the future. In addition, they are accorded higher status in their neighborhoods than they could otherwise hope to achieve, and they successfully fight the boredom of poverty by their involvement in the fast life. There are other reasons for entering into and continuing in prostitution in specific cases, such as needing money to support a narcotics habit, but these do not explain the phenomenon of participation in prostitution as well as the general effects of poverty and limited opportunity structures open to women in the lower classes.

Prostitution, like other crimes without victims, is often suggested as a candidate for decriminalization. Proposals usually include continued regulation through the State Health Department and city ordinances, with fines rather than incarceration used as a penalty for noncompliance. When the decriminalization argument is applied to drugs, the proponents cite historical examples from the United States and policies from other countries, while the opposition claims that these examples do not apply to contemporary America. This stalemate need not occur in discussions about decriminalizing prostitution, for the profession is practiced legally in most Nevada towns outside of the Las Vegas, Lake Tahoe, and Reno urban areas. A recent comprehensive treatment of Nevada prostitution has been written by Symanski (1974). Judging from his and earlier accounts, noncriminal regulation of prostitution in Nevada is extremely successful in protecting the interests of the government and society at large and also has substantial advantages for the prostitutes themselves. The main problem with the Nevada system seems to be that it controls the movements of prostitutes so tightly that it constitutes an infringement on their rights as citizens. Students tho think that prostitution works better in Nevada only because of the unique characteristics of the state should take a look at Las Vegas, where keeping prostitution illegal has caused the same problems for law enforcement officers and citizens in general that we find in other parts of the country.

# REFERENCES

Block, Alan. Aw! Your mother's in the mafia: Women criminals in progressive New York. *Contemporary Crises*, 1977, *1*, 5–22.

Bowker, Lee H. *Women, crime, and the criminal justice system*. Lexington, MA: D. C. Heath, 1978.

Brady, J. F., and Mitchell, J. G. Shoplifting in Melbourne. *Australia and New Zealand Journal of Criminology*, September 1971, *4*, 154–162.

Cameron, Mary O. *The booster and the switch*. New York: Free Press, 1964.

Cohen, L. E., and Stark, R. Discriminatory labeling and the five finger discount. *Journal of Research in Crime and Delinquency*, January 1974, *11*, 25–39.

Deadman, William J. Infanticide. *Canadian Medical Association Journal*, September 5, 1964, *91*, 558–560.

Gray, Diana. Turning-out: A study of teenage prostitution. *Urban Life and Culture*, January 1973, *1*, 401–425.

Greenberg, Harvey. Pyromania in a woman. *Psychoanalytic Quarterly*, 1966, *35*, 256–262.

James, Jennifer. Prostitute-Pimp Relationships. *Medical Aspects of Human Sexuality*, November 1973, *7*, 147–163.

Mayhew, Pat. Crime in a man's world. *New Society*, June 16, 1977, *41*, 60.

Miller, E. Eugene. The woman participant in Washington's riots. *Federal Probation*, June 1969, *33*, 30–34.

Normandeau, Andre. *Trends and patterns in crimes of robbery*. Unpublished doctoral dissertation, University of Pennsylvania, 1968.

Sparrow, G. *Women who murder*. London: Barker, 1970.

Spears, Eddyth, Vega, Manuel, and Silverman, Ira J. *The female robber*. Paper given at the annual meeting of the American Society of Criminology, Atlanta, Georgia, 1977.

Steffensmeier, Darrell J., and Terry, Robert M. Deviance and respectability: An observational study of reactions to shoplifting. *Social Forces*, 1973, *51*, 417–426.

Symanski, Richard. Prostitution in Nevada. *Annals of the Association of American Geographers*, September 1974, *64*, 357–377.

SEVEN

# Aw! Your Mother's in the Mafia: Women Criminals in Progressive New York*

ALAN BLOCK

The criminal justice system in New York during the 1930s was an ethnic meeting ground: Irish, Jew and Italian were all part of a "social system held together by friendships and favors" and marked by a vision of the whole world as a racket and of themselves as "the smart guys who recognized how the world operated." Significantly, among the Jewish "smart guys" who functioned as more-or-less corrupt intermediaries within the system, were a number of women.[1] The examples were unique and suggestive enough to signal an area within the generally neglected topic of kinship patterns in organized crime that needed attention. This paper will deal, therefore, with women in organized crime. More specifically, it will focus on female criminals who operated primarily in the Jewish underworld in New York's Lower East Side during part of the Progressive Era. There are several reasons to center an inquiry on female criminals during the heyday of Progressivism. The most important one is that it was the period in which public attention was most intensely centered on female criminality and during which a particular and long-lasting image of the female criminal reached its malign apotheosis.

The only female criminal role discussed during the Progressive period is that of prostitute. And that literature, whether a study of the reformers who moved to eradicate the social evil, or the enterprise itself, depicted women as passive victims of social disequilibrium and the venality and brutality of men. Equally as striking, the image of the prostitute, especially as developed by Progressive-Era reformers, was of a lonely, detached and confused female. Nowhere was it suggested that prostitutes or madams consciously and aggressively chose their activities as a positive adaptation to urban life, their class position in society or as an escape from male oppression and economic exploitation.[2]

Along with this particular view of the "dynamics" of prostitution, Progressive reformers concentrated their energies upon female deviance

*Contemporary Crises, 1 (1977) 5–22.

© Elsevier Scientific Publishing Company, Amsterdam. Printed in the Netherlands.

in the burgeoning immigrant neighborhoods of selected American cities. The controlling metaphor for prostitution during this period was "white slavery" and while there was compassion and concern for the rootless, uneducated immigrant prostitute, there was only hatred and contempt for the white slavers. It was a Progressive discovery or invention that the slavers were also members of the immigrant communities—in New York, especially, it was claimed that the leaders of supposedly vast vice operations were Russian and Polish Jews. It was undoubtedly of some solace to Progressive moralists that sexual slavery was an alien phenomenon.[3]

Perhaps the classic example of this vision of prostitution was broadcast by *McClure's Magazine* in a famous series of articles published in 1909. One of the essays, written by the editor of the magazine, S.S. McClure, begins with praise for the "Germanic races" as the architects of Western civilization. In contrast to this achievement, McClure holds that the

> great masses of primitive peoples from the farms of Europe, transported to this country as laborers, together with a considerable proportion of Negro slaves liberated by the Civil War, have struggled to degrade the standards and guaranties of civilization in America.

For proof, McClure turns to a description of the white slave traffic in New York linking it to Tammany Hall and the East Side immigrant Jews. McClure writes: "There has grown up, as an adjunct of this herd of female wretchedness, a fraternity of fetid male vermin (nearly all of them being Russian or Polish Jews), who are unmatchable for impudence and bestiality."[4]

Another of the essays was George Kibbe Turner's "The Daughters of the Poor." Turner's concern was the "transfer of a vast empire of prostitution from its European base to the East Side of New York." He notes that around 25 years before, during the "third great flush of immigration," which consisted of Hungarian, Austrian and Russian Jews, "a large number of criminals settled in New York." In fact, Turner writes, it was the "Jewish district" which opened "the eyes of the minor politician of the slums to the tremendous enterprise, the business of procuring and the traffic in women offered him." It is also stated that the largest number of prostitutes came from immigrant Jewish families. Turner adds, finally, that the East Side Jewish pimps, along with Jewish prostitutes, were transferring their activities to other American cities.[5]

Clearly enough, as Arthur A. Goren point out, these writers "played upon the widely shared anxieties of the times: the fear of organized conspiracy by amoral business and political interests," and the degradation of the immigrants who now appeared to control a number of American cities.[6] Actually, Egal Feldman reports in his excellent essay "Prostitution, the Alien Woman and the Progressive Imagination, 1910–1915," there were a couple of distinct campaigns or approaches to the issue of immigrants and crime during those years. First was "a nativistic attack on prostitution with all its ugly xenophobic overtones"; this was "paralleled by an anti-nativist outburst." The nativist simply blamed the immigrant communities for prostitution, while the anti-nativist not only attempted to uncover the causes and devise cures for the problem of prostitution, but also tried "at the same time to disassociate the reputation of the immigrant from commercialized vice.[7] For all of its decency of purpose, however, the anti-nativist position was weak. Obviously, it was logically unsound as the premise of immigrant innocence precluded discussion of immigrant venality. More importantly, it subsumed female crime under the single heading of prostitution. And concomitantly it undermined any consideration of female criminality outside the Progressive formula of weak women and brutal, exploitative men. The somewhat remarkable staying power of this sort of imagery can be seen in the following passage from Moses Rischin's *The Promised City*, one of the finest historical studies of New York Jewry and published in 1962:

> The Bowery, way-station of derelicts, transients, and unsuspecting immigrants, attracted the less stable and wary of the immigrant girls. The dancing academies that sprang to popularity in the first decade of the twentieth century snared impetuous, friendless young women. Lured by promises of marriage, they soon were trapped by procurers for the notorious Max Hochstim Association and other white slavers who preyed upon the innocent and unsuspecting.[8]

But surely, it is past time to question the adequacy of the description of Progressive-Era prostitution in the Lower East Side as represented by innocent, unsuspecting, impetuous and friendless young women being lured, snared and trapped by white slavers. Unsettling as it may be, women could have rationally and consciously chosen criminal careers (even prostitution) as a path of upward mobility. Indeed, there is no necessary and obvious correlation between female criminality, including prostitution, and female weakness compounded by the brutal domination of men. Simply put, just as other Progressive formulations have been junked, it is time to cast off these early notions about female criminality.

The analysis of women in organized crime (organized crime in this essay covers those women who were career criminals, as well as those connected to bands, rings, syndicates, and combinations formed to conduct and/or aid illegal enterprises) which follows is based on information contained in the reports of a unique organization known as the Bureau of Social Morals which was part of a Jewish "self-defense" association called the Kehillah.[9] The New York Kehillah's considerable influence was routed through its annual conventions and scientific bureaus which by the late summer of 1912 included the Bureau of Social Morals formed in the aftermath of the infamous Rosenthal murder. More generally, the Kehillah and the Bureau were part of the Jewish community's response to accusations of Jewish criminality—that aspect of the nativist outburst discussed above. The Kehillah maintained the anti-crime Bureau of Social Morals for five years. Staffed by a number of private investigators, the Bureau focused on the First Inspection District, the 6 police precincts of the Lower East Side. The Bureau's most imporant communal contribution was the supplying of "detailed information that led to gambling raids, revocation of licenses, and the arraignment of individual criminals."[10] For the historian of crime the significance of this information is obvious.

Unfortunately, there is no summary or final comprehensive report on organized crime, and there is no particular organizational scheme to the material. The investigators' function was to document Jewish involvement in crime and then presumably to turn their evidence over to law enforcement agencies. But within the mass of material there are some data concerning ethnicity, criminal occupations, kinship, past criminal records, the geography of illegal enterprises, membership in particular gangs or vice rings, and so on for some of the 311 female criminals identified by the Bureau. There are several things to be said about the data, however. They are much more complete when discussing male criminals; for example, the investigators were more careful to include ethnicity when discussing male drug dealers than in their reports on female thieves. Even more significant is the nature of the evidence—all of it is positive. For almost every variable the value is either yes or unknown. This reflects the fact that while we positively know that a certain number of prostitutes in the sample were married, it cannot be assumed that all the others were not. In certain cases, of course, the absence of evidence has a special meaning. Given what is known about the Progressive imagination and the purposes of the New York Kehillah—the defense of the immigrant Jewish community from accusations of criminality—it is meaningful to note the virtual lack of information on either white slavery or the coercion of female criminals.

There were 5 fairly distinct groups of female criminals haphazardly described in the hundreds of Bureau reports: those involved solely in prostitution (prostitute); those who achieved a management position usually in a vice operation or displayed special business skills such as fencing stolen goods or corrupt bail bonding (entrepreneur); those whose criminality was exclusively some form of stealing (thief); an exceptionally small group who were both whores and thieves (whore-thief); and those who worked a combination of vice, gambling and drug dealing (narc). After careful scrutiny, the 311 women criminals have been distributed in the five categories in the following numbers: Prostitute (149); Entrepreneur (78); Thief (56); Whore-Thief (4); Narc (24). The data have then been analyzed to determine the differences and similarities of the various groups according to such variables as age and recruitment patterns. Another part of the investigation focuses on the issue of organization in the illegal enterprises and the influence such variables as kinship had on structure. More importantly, however, this paper will suggest new parameters for female roles in organized crime during the Progressive Era in which willfulness, independence, and assertiveness (stereotypically masculine not feminine qualities) are central to an understanding of women in crime.

## THE MARRIED LADIES

The first area to be discussed is personal background, and it begins with an admission of partial failure. It is impossible to determine with any degree of accuracy the question of ethnicity. Out of over 300 criminals in the sample, the Bureau's investigators only positively identified four as members of a particular ethnic group (the four were Jewish prostitutes). Clearly though, there is a strong likelihood that a substantial number of the sample were Jewish given the preponderance of Jewish surnames and Yiddish aliases. But for all the Cohens, Solomons and Yettas, Beckies and Minnies, there are also Ryans, Kellys and Martins along with such aliases as Spanish Mary, Toothpick Mollie and Sadie Africaner which cloud the ethnic picture. Ethnic variability seems to hold for all groups with a majority having Jewish names and the remainder Irish, German and Anglo names.

The information concerning age is more substantial as the investigators reported on the age of 82 of the women. The topic of age is of some importance because of its role as one of the implicit postulates in the stereotype of prostitution. Whores were "girls" whose youthfulness, impetuousness and inexperience with the world betrayed them. A natural corollary to this was the belief that prostitutes were quickly burned-out, becoming diseased "hags" at an exceptionally early age. That this was shown to be false as early as 1913 does not seem to have shaken the belief. George J. Kneeland's masterful study, *Commercialized Prostitution in New York City,* published under the auspices of the Bureau of Social Hygiene in 1913, notes that "the life of the professional prostitute has been [erroneously] estimated at 5 years, on the ground that she dies, withdraws, or is incapacitated" in that time. Kneeland goes on to state that according to his study of more than a thousand prostitutes the view is wrong. He writes: "The majority of these girls, though entering the life before 18 are at 24 still active and aggressive in seeking trade." Kneeland computes the average age of prostitutes at 25 years.[11] The Kehillah's figures are somewhat higher than Kneeland's, although the same is much smaller, and, therefore, probably not as reliable when dealing only with prostitutes.

The average age for the 82 women in the Bureau of Social Morals reports is almost 31 years. The sample is composed of 60 prostitutes, thirteen entrepreneurs, four thieves, and five narcs. Figuring the groups separately the averages of 28.6 for prostitutes, almost 41 years old for the entrepreneurs, almost 31 for the four thieves, and 22 for the narcs. The most pronounced age cluster for the entire group is in the 24 through 30 year old bracket with 41 women represented. Between the ages of 40 and 50 years, the Bureau notes that 16 women are still active. For the same group Kneeland counts 17 women, although in his study they only comprised 1.5 percent of the women investigated. In the Bureau of Social Morals' reports this elderly group is almost 20 percent of the total. The extremes of age range from a 17 year old prostitute to four 50 year old criminals made up of three enterpreneurs and one prostitute. Unlike the Kneeland study, the Kehillah's investigators gave no starting point for the criminal careers and, therefore, the duration of the illicit activities cannot be computed. But it does seem that most of the women had been criminals for a substantial number of years except for the narcs. Certainly there is no indication of any rapid deterioration or early termination of activities for the women.

One of the significant and unappreciated topics of female criminality is marital status. As noted earlier, it is part of the Progressive litany that prostitutes were lonely, detached and friendless. When marriages of prostitutes or madams were discussed, the context typically has been, "Strange as it may seem, some men marry these women and find them devoted wives." Even stranger still, commentators have written, "year after year, through adversity and prosperity they have followed their masters and obeyed their will. Beaten, exploited, infected, jailed, they still remain steadfast.[12] The language of these accounts, obviously, implies that these are marriages in name only—legalized equivalents of master-slave pimp-whore relationships.

With this viewpoint in mind, consider the data of marriage furnished by the Bureau of Social Morals. The reports contain information on 87 married women criminals distributed as shown in Table 1.

The percentages for each group are naturally the minimum possible, but even these exceptionally conservative figures indicate the importance of marriage and female criminality. What needs to be explored, of course, is the nature of these marriages—do they fit the Progressive model or not? To begin an answer Table 2 was constructed.

There are several things that could be said about these rather minimal figures. First, they may suggest that marriage for prostitutes and whore-thieves approximates the Progressive formula. On the other hand, the lack of information for 3 of the groups coupled with the 10 thieves who were partners with their husbands indicate the opposite. Clearly, the Bureau's descriptions of the married criminals must be scrutinized for a more definitive answer.

Concerning the married entrepreneurs, the reports are extremely telling. For example, Sadie Chink, whose husband was Sam Schimil,

**Table 1.** *Female Criminals Known to be Married*

| CRIMINAL CLASS | NUMBER MARRIED | PERCENTAGE OF KNOWN MARRIED IN EACH CLASS |
|---|---|---|
| Prostitute | 20 | 13.4 |
| Entrepreneur | 22 | 28.2 |
| Thief | 35 | 62.5 |
| Whore-thief | 2 | 50.0 |
| Narc | 8 | 33.3 |

**Table 2.** *Business Relationships Among Married Criminals*

| | WORK FOR SPOUSE | PARTNERS WITH SPOUSE |
|---|---|---|
| Prostitute | 12 | — |
| Entrepreneur | — | 1 |
| Thief | 1 | 10 |
| Whore-thief | 2 | — |
| Narc | 1 | — |

was co-owner with Jennie Morris (Jennie the Factory), wife of Harry Morris, of a disorderly house that employed at the very least 3 prostitutes. Sadie and Jennie also employed Freda Martin, whose husband was Harry Martin, as a manager. Mrs. Martin was also a cocaine dealer. Ray Treibetz, married to Abe Treibetz, owned a hairdressing parlor frequented by prostitutes which was additionally a gambling and opium parlor. Her husband was a professional fence and bail bondsman. Another of the married entrepreneurs was Rosie Barth who, like Ray Treibetz, ran a hairdressing parlor which catered to prostitutes. Her husband, Bernard Barth, was a bail bondsman, fixer and steerer (corrupt intermediary between criminals and members of the criminal justice bureaucracies), and loanshark. The Barths (who had 5 daughters) invested their money in real estate and reportedly owned several tenements.

Several of the other married enterpreneurs included one whose husband started her in the disorderly-house trade, another whose husband was an ex-policeman (Hannah Bernstein), one who was both an owner and madam in several whore houses employing a fairly large number of prostitutes, and a Mrs. Cooper who owned a building used or rented by drug dealers. One of the more interesting cases concerns a Mrs. Bowles who leased various properties and then moved in with a crew of both prostitutes and panhandlers. Also living with Mrs. Bowles were her daughter Freda and a grandson. Mr. Bowles, the investigators found, held a respectable position with the Zimmerman Provision Company.

The final example in this particular category was gathered from a series of reports filed by the Bureau in August 1912. This extensive investigation centered on a disorderly house owned by the Hertz family and located at 7 East First Street. The building was known as the Columbia Hotel and was owned by Rose Hertz, her husband Jacob Hertz and Max and David Rosenbach, brothers to Rosie Hertz. Also working there were two of Rose Hertz's cousins, Hyman and Morris Goldman, the latter being the manager. The family were Hungarian Jews and supposedly ran some of the most famous whore houses in New York City. The Bureau notes that Rosie Hertz had made a great deal of money and owned "a few tenement houses on 5th Street, and also the house she occupies in Borough Park, Brooklyn." Concerning her past, the Bureau states "from an authentic source . . . that Rosie's mother Gittel was the first Jewish madam in New York, if not in the entire United States." Rosie's career began when she went from "one coal cellar to another—from one shoe-making basement to another." By living modestly, the Hertz's had succeeded in becoming "bosses in the disorderly house graft"; to protect their interests they "contributed $1,000

every year to both the Democratic and Republican organizations."
Other interests that the Hertz family included were the fencing of stolen
goods and a small bail bond business: Rosie would "very often sign
bonds for gambling houses," although in those cases she supposedly
never charged anything. The Bureau also notes that Rosie broke in such
other female criminals as Hannah Bernstein, Slavish Anna, and Rosie
Cheesecake among others.

Again, it is important to consider the implications in marital relationships between those who are married and either work independently
of their husbands or are partners with them, and those who are
employed by their spouses. In the cases of the entrepreneurs discussed
above, all our examples with the exception of Rosie Hertz appear to
have worked independently of their husbands. And the Hertz family,
which technically a partnership, was run by Rosie not Jacob, according
to the Bureau's investigators. Independence in the other examples does
not, of course, mean that the husbands were either criminally innocent
or of minimal importance in the lives of the female entrepreneurs.
Except for Mrs. Bowles' arrangement, these seem to be complementary
criminal enterprises some under the leadership of wives, others led by
husbands.

These points are further developed by an examination of the category "thief." As was noted earlier out of 35 married thieves, 10 were
partners with their husbands while only 1 was employed by hers. The
term partnership and employee, however, are not always clear and definitive. For instance, the one thief described by the Bureau as working for
her husband is Rosie Stahl. But a careful reading of the investigators'
reports suggests little substantive difference between working for, or
with, in this case. The strong probability is of a series of criminal partnerships with no indication of either overt or covert coercion on the part
of husbands. Of equal interest is the appearance of not only husband
and wife criminal equality, but of a number of partnerships linked
together by a variety of marital styles.

One of these confederations is composed of four of the married
thieves including Rosie Stahl. The apparent leader or center of this
group is Bessie London (Bessie Solomon) the wife of Meyer Solomon
alias Meyer Boston. Bessie was reportedly a master thief and pickpocket
responsible for training such other female criminals as Tillie Finkelstein
the wife of Candy Kid Phil, Rosie Stahl and Skinny Mollie the wife of a
thief known as Itschky. Another Bureau report also notes that Bessie
Solomon trained her brother-in-law's wife and that the two women were
so successful as thieves that their husbands (who were also brothers)
were able to abandon stealing in order to specialize in gambling, loan

sharking and the fencing of stolen goods. Other stealing combinations dominated by kinship relations involve a Mrs. Lubitz whose husband was "Lubitz the Pickpocket" and whose sister, Mrs. Greene Zindel worked with her husband. Dave Hoffman, Little Carl, and the husband and wife team of Harry and Toothless Kitty Davis also were members of this combination.

It is apparent that sexually-integrated teams far removed from the master-slave model of the Progressive imagination abounded among thieves. Consider Spanish Mary and her husband Earle Williams known as the "King of the Panhandlers" who worked ferry boats, elevated trains and subways. In the same category are Sarah and Jacob Glucksman, May and Joe Hess and the pickpocket team of Taube and Aaron Goldsbard. Another interesting case is that of Katt Schoenberg the wife of Joe Feldman alias Joe English. The Schoenberg family along with the already discussed Hertz and Solomon groups furnish one of the best examples of the familial dimensions of organized crime and the importance of aggressive female participation. The Schoenberg's criminality began in the "old country" when Katt's mother and father started their illegal careers. Following in their parent's footsteps were two of their sons (one from a previous marriage), of one Katt's brothers-in-law and her first husband. At the time of the investigation, the Schoenberg-Feldman entourage seem to have concentrated their stealing in the fish markets under the Williamsburg Bridge. One final perhaps revealing instance of the nature of the marriage relationships among our thieves deals with Mrs. Rose Segal and her husband Louie Segal. The Bureau reports that Mrs. Segal was a thief and also co-owner of a restaurant with a pimp named Joe Bernstein. There is no evidence that Mr. Segal was involved in any criminal activities.

Information about the marital styles of the smallest group "whore-thief" is insufficient for any generalizations. There are, however, some things to be noted about those women in the category "narc." Eight out of 24 women in this group are known to have been married. For one of them the information about both her career and marriage is hopelessly confused. Another, Mary Lesser, was reportedly married to Hymie Lesser a "dope fiend and pimp" and a relative of some minor East Side politician. For unknown reasons Mary left her husband first to live with a pimp known as "Jack the Wop" and then finally to move in with another pimp, Edward Land. The Bureau adds that Mary not only solicits, but also smokes opium and plays poker in Ray Treibetz's hairdressing parlor. Another married prostitute and gambler the Bureau reports on is Annie Sullivan (Sloppy Annie) who lives with her "Irish pimp husband." The remaining five married women in this group also present a complicated picture. For three of them there is the decided possibility that they are another extended criminal family. The women are: Rose Newburger a prostitute and narcotic dealer married to Fred Newburger; Annie Newburger a co-owner of a cocaine joint with her husband, Joe Newburger; and Dolly Newburger who kept narcotics for Annie's husband, Joe. The last two married women in this classification might more accurately be placed in the entrepreneurial group. One owned and managed apartments used by prostitutes and drug dealers, the other was a prostitute, cocaine and opium user, and landlady who probably ran various vice and drug establishments. Aside from noting that they were married, the Bureau gives no information about their husbands.

The last criminal class tabulated in Table 2 to be discussed is that of "prostitute." According to the breakdowns, 20 of the 149 prostitutes were known to have been married and 12 of the 20 worked for their husbands. Based on the Bureau's all too meager reports there are some indicators that the relationships of 7 of them could fit the traditional model. Of the 5 remaining women there is no evidence on the marital/ working relationships of 3 of them. For the fourth member of this group there is solid information that her husband (Andy Collins) was a pick-pocket. It is possible, therefore, that Mrs. Collins' whoring was an independent venture (presumably encouraged by her husband) while at the same time the 2 of them were pick-pocket partners. The last example is difficult of interpret although intriguing. The prostitute's name was Elsie Sonnenschein and although married and the mother of a child she lived with her mother. Apparently, Elsie's husband had attempted to make her a prostitute which so enraged her that she had him arrested and committed to jail. Subsequently, however, Elsie became a prostitute.

For the small group of 8 prostitutes known to have been married, but who were not employed by their husbands, there are a number of intriguing relationships. Sadie Gluck, the wife of Maxie Gluck, and the mother of 2 children, worked for one of the Lower East Side's most famous all-round criminals, "Dollar John." Then, there is Mrs. Friend, who had 3 children and both lived with and worked for a succession of men named Spinetti, Fisher and Louis Boston. The next woman is known only as Martha. She allegedly had several husbands, was rather elderly and appears to have been independently employed. The last prostitute in this category for whom there is much information is a Mrs. Greenberg who worked with another prostitute known only as Carrie who was employed by a Mrs. Klein. The most plausible explanation is that Mrs. Greenberg's marriage had little to do with her professional life, at least in a managerial sense.

The questions about marital relationships and styles is exceptionally complex and perhaps ultimately insoluble given the kinds of evidence needed. With this clearly in mind, however, certain speculations and tentative conclusions are warranted. For instance, given what is known about the nearly 28% of the 311 female criminals who were married, there is simply no reason to retain the Progressive notion of masters and slaves. The evidence on this particular point is especially persuasive when discussing the neglected area of female criminality—stealing and management. Even for the relatively small group of known married prostitutes there is enough variability to call for a search for more accurate terms.

## SIDELINES AND DIVERSIONS

Other evidence pointing to the same conclusion—the need for new terms and concepts in dealing with the history of female crime—are the findings of collateral criminal occupations. These are illegal activities engaged in by members of the sample besides or in addition to their primary criminal occupations. We have already discussed a number of women whose primary occupations were in stealing or in prostitution, and who also were engaged in various other criminal sidelines. The total of women involved in one or more collateral criminal occupations is 269 out of 311. However, there is some confusion on this point in both the investigators' reports and in the open-minded nature of the criminal class designated entrepreneur to make the total questionable. Nevertheless, it is evident that female criminals were not only members of stealing rings, prostitutes, entrepreneurs, and narcotic dealers, but were involved in a multiplicity of illegal enterprises at the same time. The ability to create and take advantage of changing criminal opportunities seems to demand individuals who were aggressive, willful and adaptive. Quite the opposite of the dominated and helpless creatures traditionally portrayed.

## DOES MARRIAGE PAY?

So far the analysis has dealt primarily with the known married criminals leaving virtually undiscussed the bulk of the sample (72%) whose marital status is unknown. There is nothing to add on the topics of age distribution, ethnicity and collateral criminal occupations as these examples were not cross-tabulated with marital status. The first area to examine is

methods of recruitment concentrating on those women who were recruited by pimps and what the Bureau calls "boyfriends." As with ethnicity, however, the evidence on the point is meager. Out of 224 women
only 13 are positively stated to have been recruited by pimps. As might
be expected, all but 1 of the 13 was a prostitute. The exception was
Jennie Feldman, a prostitute and opium dealer—"narc"—recruited by a
pimp named Meyer, the Special. The number of women recruited by
boyfriends was only 16—they were all prostitutes. A more telling indication of the quality of relationships among male and female criminals
might have come from the variable indicating employers' position, part
of which, at an earlier stage, was displayed in Table 2. The values for
employers' position are pimp, boyfriend, and spouse. Leaving out the
value spouse, the frequently distribution shows that 28 women worked
for pimps and 14 for boyfriends. But the sample consulted in this case
includes all 311 women. The reason for not dropping the known married
women is, as we have seen, that married female criminals were at times
employed by both spouses and pimps or, while married, worked for
pimps who were not their husbands, etc. Another difficulty in drawing
conclusions between pimps and boyfriends is that the Bureau's investigators often used both terms in different reports concerning the same criminals. Rae the Muskateer a gambler and prostitute lived with an Italian
pimp in some reports and an Italian boyfriend in others. In such cases it
is impossible to know whether Rae's consort was her pimp in the traditional sense or whether they were lovers who shared in some equitable
fashion Rae's illegal earnings as a prostitute and gambler.

A more fruitful comparison in determining female roles than the
above is one related to female independence and female-male equality in
organized crime, as reported by the Bureau's investigators [Table 3]. The
criminal classes to be discussed are "prostitute" and "entrepreneur." Out
of the 6 whores who work independently, there are 2 who are reportedly
married. Of the 7 prostitutes who have partners none are reportedly
married. Two of them are sisters (Sarah and Bessie Winters), and 2 others are partners with unrelated women. But, while partners in some
instances, it also appears that 4 of these women are employees of pimps
and madams at the same time. The unanswerable question is whether
this complex group represents women who were basically partners and
occasionally worked for others of the converse. More definitive answers
can be made about the last category of prostitutes—those who were
members of rings. None of them was reportedly married. The 7 women
appear to have formed 14 separate rings. One was composed of Lizzie
Articles, Mary the Bum and Hungarian Mary; another was formed by
Lena, Jennie and Susie. Interestingly, it appears that Jennie and Susie

joined a different ring with a whore known as Dutch Lilly which excluded Lena. It is unclear whether these last 2 combinations were contemporaneous. One other ring alluded to in the Bureau's reports includes 4 women 2 of whom are identified as Miss Marshall and Miss Wilson. (Obviously there are more than 7 women mentioned; those who were not identified by some type of name were not counted.)

Turning from the prostitutes to the "entrepreneurs" the meaning of female independence and equality becomes clearer. There are 18 women reliably described by the Bureau as both entrepreneurs and employers. As might be expected this is the only group found to contain bosses. The first thing to note about them is that 6 were married. While insignificant in itself, a comparison between the married entrepreneurs and the 12 others is revealing. With only 1 exception the married ones are property owners: 4 of them owned whore houses, 1 leased a series of disorderly houses, owning 1 of them. It is also important that these owners were involved in a multitude of criminal activities outside of owning and renting rooms in their establishments to criminals. When comparing this group with the 12 women entrepreneurs left in the boss category not identified as married, the difference in property-ownership is striking. Only 3 out of the 12 owned property described by the Bureau. And these 3 women either had male partners or were involved in several different criminal activities at the same time. One conclusion concerning ownership for this particular class—"enterpreneur"—seems inescapable: marriage and involvement in a variety of criminal enterprises probably meant the accumulation of enough capital to transform these criminals into property owners—surely some sort of ideal for members of the underworld.

If one thing should by now be clear, it is that women were as interested as men in extending their expertise, influence, power, and capital in the underworld, at least New York's Jewish underworld in the Lower

**Table 3.** *Roles in Illegal Enterprises*

| CRIMINAL CLASS | INDEPENDENT | PARTNER | BOSS | MEMBER OF A RING |
|---|---|---|---|---|
| Prostitute | 6 | 7 | — | 7 |
| Entrepreneur | — | 3 | 18 | — |
| Thief | 3 | — | — | — |
| Whore-thief | — | — | — | — |
| Narc | 1 | — | — | 1 |

East Side. There is certainly enough evidence to establish aggressive, purposeful, willful, behavior on the part of female organized criminals. But perhaps the most startling of all the evidence is that which points to marriage as a primary building block for successful criminal careers for both men and women. Attention, therefore, might best be focused on criminal families, characterized by husband and wife partnerships and by the effects of capital accumulation gathered by husbands and wives pursuing related but often semi-independent criminal careers.

In order to devise a meaningful correlation about property ownership and marriage patterns, a list of those women known to have been either managers or owners of criminal establishments was compiled and then compared with two variables: (1) those women from this list known to have been married, and (2) the number of establishments owned or managed by them. It is important to remember that all these womeen were part of the "entrepreneurial" class. As Table 4 shows 57 individuals controlled 83 establishments. Significantly, the married female criminals in this group while comprising only 30% of the group controlled over 45% of the places. And it is crucial to remember that these are the minimum figures: undoubtedly some of the women whose marital status was unknown were married.

While it seems clear from Table 4 that marriage and the control of criminal establishments are significantly related it is important to differentiate between ownership and management which up until now have been included in the notion of control. Unfortunately, there are not enough hard data to compute these differences, or the monetary value of the properties described. Nevertheless, the Bureau's reports do contain descriptive material relative to these points and the 4 married women who controlled 3 or more places. Sadie Chink owned outright 5 disorderly houses and was a partial owner of another along with Jennie Morris. Bertha Hitz owned 3 disorderly houses 1 of which was located in Baltimore, Maryland. And Rosie Hertz owned 2 disorderly houses, managed 4 other ones, and was also the manager of a gambling house. The last example is Freda Martin who spent her professional career managing 3 of Sadie Chink's houses.

In compiling the above figures it also seems pertinent to discuss those establishments with the largest reported clientele, to see if their owners or managers were likely to have been married. There are 13 places where the reported number of habitues were 4 or more (the highest figure was 29 for a hairdressing parlor frequented by almost the whole range of female criminals). Out of the 13 places, 3 were owned by women, 2 of whom were married, 3 were managed by married women, 4 were owned by men, and 3 are unclassifiable. The 1 unmarried women in this group is Lena Hoberg whose apparent criminal affluence was probably based on her "romantic" relationship with an unidentified Police Captain.

**Table 4.** *Distribution of Property Control by Female Criminals*

| | NUMBER OF ESTABLISHMENTS[a] | | | | | | |
|---|---|---|---|---|---|---|---|
| Marital | 1 | 2 | 3 | 4 | 5 | 6 | 7 |
| Status | | | | | | | |
| Married | 7 | 6 | 2 | — | — | 1 | 1 |
| Unknown | 35 | 5 | — | — | — | — | — |

[a]Criminal establishments refer to places where the female criminals lived, met and congregated, worked, managed, and owned. From the Bureau's reports 233 different places were identified including hotels, restaurants, saloons, disorderly houses, gambling places, hairdressing parlors, candy stores, etc. But, only 102 of the 233 addresses given by the investigators could be specifically identified as one of the above. Out of the 102 places there were 47 disorderly houses, 12 restaurants, 9 hotels, 9 saloons, 5 gambling places, and so on in descending order. The number of women identified as users of the different types of places is also interesting. For instance, although there were 5 gambling places only 5 women were reported as users; however, 45 women were found to meet and congregate, etc., at the 3 hairdressing parlors indentified by the Bureau. It should also be pointed out that the places had multiple criminal and non-criminal uses and that their ultimate designation is somewhat arbitrary. Saloons were found in hotels, restaurants were also gambling dens, and hairdressing parlors were used to distribute narcotics.

# CONCLUSION

The subject of female involvement in organized crime is, as we have seen, dominated by a series of sentimental conceptions dealing especially with prostitution and cast principally by Progressive reformers and their immediate forebearers as they grappled with the enormity of urban culture. Once firmly established, these notions left little room for any understanding of female criminality, including prostitution, as a rational method of adaptation to class structure and urban institutions. Indeed, the sentimentality of the approach fixed concern upon the single question of cause—what could have led girls to so degrade themselves, ultimately destroy themselves—was the reigning issue. This meant that female criminality would really become a part of the general field of juvenile delinquency, that area of criminology devoted to seeking reasons for the transformation of young people from potential citizens to criminals. Adult female criminality had seemingly been settled as a separate topic by that part of the Progressive formula which went inexorably from juvenile female crime to degradation, disease and death. Under this formulation, mobility in organized crime for females was an explicit one-way street, leading rapidly downward. As long as this is maintained, there is little sense in considering adult female criminals as more than the victims of brutal male criminals; used by them until they reach some disgusting level of disease which renders them criminally useless and then abandoned. The marriage of female criminals is, therefore, only another aspect of male domination confirming the gullibility of female criminals by tying them to their masters in a kind of a masochistic frenzy.

Naturally, within this traditional litany of causes and concerns there is no room for female independence and equality in the world of adult crime. Women such as Rosie Hertz, Bessie Solomon, Sadie Chink, Katt Schoenberg, Sarah and Bessie Winters, etc., make little sense. Indeed, the criminal class called entrepreneurs is either a gross misinterpretation or, at best, a historical oddity with no general significance. Without some serious re-thinking, therefore, the indisputable facts that female criminals pumped money into local real estate and legitimate businesses, as well as providing often unique goods and services to a variety of urban customers, lie dormant. Also unappreciated is the importance of female support (and sometimes ownership) of saloons, candy stores, hotels, disorderly houses, hairdressing parlors, pool rooms and gambling dens which materially contributed to the quality of urban life.[13] Once female criminality is taken seriously, of course, the list of important topics is only limited by the researcher's imagination. For instance, a searching look into female roles and their changes over time as intermediaries between the underworld and upperworld of the criminal justice systems in municipal America is needed.[14] Finally, while the subject of mobility in organized crime has long been posited,[15] the relationship between criminal mobility and marriage among criminals demands recognition and study.

Organized crime has been a functional part of urban America providing goods and services for a variety of patrons and clients and potential money and power for criminals both male and female. Contrary to many popular accounts organized crime is not the unique creation of any particular immigrant community, but flourished in a variety of urban ethnic communities. And as it was not ethnically unique, neither was it sexually segregated.

## NOTES

1. Alan Block (1975). "Lepke, Kid Twist and the Combination: Organized Crime in New York City, 1930-1944," (unpublished Ph.D. dissertation, (UCLA). Especially chapter five.

2. See Howard B. Woolston (1969). *Prostitution in the United States: Prior to the Entrance of the United States into the World War.* Montclair, New Jersey: Patterson Smith; Edwin R. A. Seligman (ed.) (1912). *The Social Evil With Special Reference to Conditions Existing in the City of New York,* New York: G.P. Putnam's Sons, chapters 1 and 6; Harry Benjamin and R.E.L. Masters (1964). *Prostitution and Morality: A Definitive Report on the Prostitute in Contemporary Society and an Analysis of the Causes and Effects of the Suppression of Prostitution,* New York: The Julian Press, Inc., chapters 3 and 4; Willoughby Cyrus Waterman (1932). *Prostitution and its Repression in New York City, 1900-1931.* New York: Columbia University Press; Helene Feldman King (1956). "The Banishment of Prudery: A Study of the Issue of Prostitution in the Progressive Era," unpublished Ph.D. dissertation, Columbia University; David J. Pivar (1973), *Purity Crusade: Sexual Morality and Social Control, 1868-1900.* Westport, Conn.: Greenwood Press, Inc., chapter 5; Roy Lubove (1963). *The Progressives and the Slums: Tenement House Reform in New York City, 1890-1917.* Pittsburgh: University of Pittsburgh Press, pp. 49-80, 132-149, and 187-215; Egal Feldman (1967). "Prostitution, the Alien Woman and the Progressive Imagination, 1910--1915," *American Quarterly,* XI, (Summer). For some of the legislation dealing with prostitution including tenement house prostitution see *Digest of State and Federal Laws Dealing with Prostitution and other Sex Offenses, with Notes on the Control of the Sale of Alcoholic Beverages as it Relates to Prostitution Activities* (1942). New York: The American Social Hygiene Association, Inc. pp. 263-275.

3. In addition to the works cited above, one should also consult U.S., Congress, House, *White Slave Traffic,* H.R. 47, 61st Cong. 2d sess., where it is noted that "there are few who really understand the true significance of the term 'white-slave trade' . . . the inmates of many houses of ill fame are made up largely of women and girls whose original entry into a life of immorality was brought about by men . . . who by means of force and restraint, compel their victims to practice prostitution." p. 10. Much the same view is found in U.S. Congress, Senate, *Importing Women for Immoral Purposes,* S.D. 196, 61st Cong. 2d sess.

The reported connections between New York's immigrant Jewish population and prostitution moved several residents of New York's Lower East Side to petition President William H. Taft protesting communal innocence. See U.S., Congress, Senate, *Petition of Citizens of Orchard, Rivington, and East Houston Streets, New York City, Relative to the Reports of Officials and the Conditions of Immigrants,* S.D. 785, 62nd Cong., 2d sess.

A brilliant discussion of the whole issue of Jewish criminality during the Progressive Era is Arthur A. Goren's (1970). *New York Jews and the Quest for*

*Community: The Kehillah Experiment, 1908–1922,* New York: Columbia University Press.

4. S.S. McClure (1909). "The Tammanyizing of a Civilization," *McClure's Magazine.* XXXIV, (November). (1909). pp. 117–118.

5. George Kibbe Turner, "The Daughters of the Poor," Ibid., pp. 47, 49–52.

6. Goren, op. cit., pp. 138–144.

7. Feldman, op. cit., p. 197.

8. Moses Rischin (1962). *The Promised City: New York's Jews, 1870–1914.* New York: Harper & Row, pp. 77–78.

9. Information on the New York Kehillah was obtained from the Judah L. Magnes Archives. The Central Archives for the History of the Jewish People, Jerusalem, Israel. I first became acquainted with the material in the Magnes Archives through Goren's study noted above. In Goren's note on sources he states that the Magnes Archives in Jerusalem "contain an outstanding collection of sources for the study of Jewish life in New York and Jewish communal politics in America from 1908 to 1922 . . . . The largest part of this material consists of the Kehillah's records which contain a wealth of sources on Jewish education, religious life, philanthropic organization, industrial conditions, and crime." Using Goren's citation for the specific material on crime—MA (SP/125–139)—I wrote to the Central Archives for the History of the Jewish People, Jerusalem, Israel, and requested a microfilm copy of the almost 2,000 "case histories of Jewish criminals prepared by the Kehillah's chief investigator and based on information supplied by his informers and agents." Ms. Hadassah Assouline of the Central Archives was kind enough to fulfill my request.

In his book on the Kehillah, Goren notes that the "first meeting of the executive committee" of the Kehillah set up "standing committees on religious organization, on Jewish education, on finance, on social and philanthropic work, and on propaganda and organization." It was the job of the committees to establish "permanent bureaus in their fields." The first bureau which dealt with Jewish education was formed in 1910. This was followed by the Bureau of Social Morals in 1912, and so on. Goren, op. cit., pp. 59–63.

10. Ibid., pp. 159–170.

11. George J. Kneeland (1913). *Commercialized Prostitution in New York City.* New York: The Century Co. p. 107. Kneeland's study is the definitive effort to investigate prostitution during the Progressive period. While extraordinarily inclusive and insightful, it suffers from a complete emphasis on prostitution, a system of documentation designed to protect identities, and a style that is characteristically male chauvinist.

12. Ibid., pp. 92–93.

13. Henry Miller (1955). *Nights of Love and Laughter.* New York: New American Library.

14. One might profitably consider the historical evidence gathered by Paul Blanshard head of the New York City Department of Investigations and Accounts in an investigation of bail-bond rackets in the mid-1930s. Blanshard identified 53 bail-bond racketeers 21 of whom were women. A breakdown of the

ethnicity of the identified women racketeers reveals that 7 were Jewish, 7 Italian, 2 Hispanic, and 5 unidentifiable. See Department of Investigation and Accounts, *Investigating City Government in the La Guardia Administration: A Report of the Activities of the Department of Investigation and Accounts, 1934–1937.* Another important source for female involvement in bail-bonding rackets and loan sharking in the 1930s and 1940s is John Harlan Amen, *Report of the Kings County Investigation, 1938–1942.*

    15. Daniel Bell (1962). "Crime as an American Way of Life: A Queer Ladder of Social Mobility," *The End of Ideology: On the Exhaustion of Political Ideas in the Fifties.* New York: Free Press. pp. 127–150.

------

## EIGHT
# The Woman Participant in Washington's Riots*

### E. EUGENE MILLER

The brief period of April 4 to 6, 1968, brought untold grief to the Nation and a tragedy to Washington, D.C. Dr. Martin Luther King, Jr., was slain and thousands in the Nation's Capital reacted with fire and wanton looting. It must be recognized that the death of Dr. King was only the precipitating cause of the riot. Those involved did so for various reasons, including retaliation for the death of Dr. King, pent-up hostilities against whites, resentment against merchants who were alleged to be cheating ghetto residents, a general Roman holiday contagion, a ready opportunity to steal groceries, clothing, appliances, liquor, and many other similar reasons. Most of the Negro community, on the other hand, was greatly distressed by the disturbances and did not participate in them.

    Now that we have had a chance to reflect on the April riots, what had gone on before, and the events since, some conclusions may be formulated in an attempt to understand the underlying causes for riot behavior and the prevention of similar occurrences in the future. Specifically this article will focus attention on women participants in the disorders who, in general, have gone unnoticed. It will attempt to present a

------

*Reprinted with permission from *Federal Probation*, June 1969.

profile of the women arrested during the disorders and discuss their motivation and degree of participation.

## FACTORS WHICH PRECIPITATED THE RIOT

In order to place our analysis in its proper perspective it may be helpful to examine some of the background factors which preceded the riots.

Washington (also known as the District of Columbia) is a unique city. It is a city of many contrasts with many problems. Traditionally, it has been ruled by The Congress, a body in which it has no formal representation. The city is scarred by slums of which the rest of the country is unaware. At the same time the Supreme Court was deciding *Brown* v. *Topeka Board of Education* (1954), the District of Columbia school system for all intents and purposes was still segregated.

Unlike all other major cities, Washington is almost totally devoid of heavy industry. Large numbers of unskilled or semiskilled jobs simply do not exist. The major employer is the Government and virtually all of its jobs require passing a written examination and a fair amount of formal academic training. This factor becomes increasingly important in view of the migration from the rural South to Washington by large numbers of undereducated and unskilled people. What these people find on arrival is an area with a high cost of living index and few available jobs. For those who decide to stay, life becomes the same struggle as in the homes they left, but intensified by a complex and cold urban milieu. Faced with continued unemployment, higher living costs, and housing shortages, they quickly become despondent. The initial hope with which they migrated turns to frustration. They become depersonalized members of a voiceless society. At home there was at least some security in the fact that everyone knows each other. Their fellowship provided an escape from their mutual plight of poverty.

A highly transient life style has developed in some areas of the city and there is little opportunity to develop camaraderie. This further adds to the already present feelings of insecurity. The government agencies confronted with such large-scale problems must deal with the mass and are unable to resolve problems on an individual basis.

Corresponding to the mass immigration to Washington was a large-scale exodus of the established Washington middle class to suburban Maryland and Virginia. Between 1950 and 1960 the population of the District of Columbia declined by 38,222 from 802,178 in 1950 to 763,956 in 1960. By 1967, however, the population had risen to 809,000. In the corresponding decade, suburban Maryland and Virginia had an increase of 563,510 in population.[1] The racial composition of the District of Columbia's population flow can best be shown by the fact that in 1950 the nonwhite enrollment in the District's public schools was 50.7 percent of the total, in 1960 it was 79.7 percent, and by 1966 it had grown to 90.8 percent.[2] With the white middle class went the tax base with which meaningful programs for the immigrants to the City might have been established and maintained.

It should also be pointed out that when the middle class left so did a traditional social control. Since the burghers of the Middle Ages, the middle class has been relied upon to provide a steadying influence on the community. Among other sociological advantages, the existence of a large middle-class population provided the poor with an observable opportunity for reasonable upward mobility. For persons without jobs, education, and the perspective which education brings, reasonable opportunities for advancement must be present and readily apparent in order for hope to be kept alive.

In the District of Columbia some slums exist geographically close to Georgetown, an exclusive, and wealthy urban living area. However, the actual distance between these contrastingly squalid and luxurious areas in terms of possible attainment is indeed formidable. Only the extremes exist and these extremes are unfortunately polarized by the lack of any existential middle ground.

Within this framework, frustration is inevitable. When the toleration level is exceeded, steps are taken to ease the frustration. Washington had become an angry community filled with hate. By some miracle, it had escaped serious blowups in the past. The murder of Dr. King was cited by many as igniting the existing powder keg; and the riot was the result.

Contrary to the reports of many throughout the Nation, the riots were confined largely to two streets (14th and 7th) in the Northwest part of the city and to H Street in the Northeast. The majority of the burning and looting took place in those areas.

The participants in the riots probably could not pinpoint their true motivations. After a time, the reasons for the initial outburst and behavior are forgotten, yet an unreasoning and somewhat undirected hate remains. Youths growing up in such an environment cannot "cool it," for they find little encouragement or reinforcement to do so in their immediate surroundings. The April riots were the result of long-smouldering situations and circumstances which were forcefully brought to the attention of the Nation and the world at the time of the riots.

## THE WOMEN'S DETENTION CENTER AND THE RIOTS

Under normal circumstances, any adult woman arrested in the District of Columbia is brought to the Women's Detention Center, a facility of the District of Columbia Department of Corrections. The institution is located on a main thoroughfare in Washington. Its immediate environs during the riots were plagued by arson and looting.

Once a woman is received at the Center, she is fingerprinted, photographed, and searched. If court is still in session, she is taken before a judge or United States commissioner. If court is closed, she is given the opportunity to post bond or collateral. Failing that, she is held until the following day (2 days if arrested on a Saturday night) when she is taken to court.

The Center is also responsible for women awaiting various types of court action, sentenced misdemeanants, and felons awaiting transfer to the Federal Reformatory for Women at Alderson, West Virginia. The Center's normal housing capacity is 80 persons. It provides a full program of education, counseling, job training, work release, and similar activities designed to help people become productive, responsible, and law-abiding members of the community. On a typical day there would be 85 women confined at the Center. For the fiscal year ending on June 30, 1968, the Center had 5,935 admissions and 5,892 releases.

During the April riots, the Women's Detention Center received 437 commitments. The highest count in the facility at any one time during that period was 157. Most of the 437 commitments were for curfew violations. The women were usually issued a summons, given a court date, and released as soon as the curfew was lifted the following morning.

The large volume of commitments and the fires and disorder in the immediate areas placed heavy pressures on the Center. A male security force was arranged for the predawn hours of April 5 in case the Center should be placed in danger of arsonists. Additional bedding was brought in on short notice from other departmental institutions. Additional film and fingerprint cards were obtained from central supply within an hour. Temporary in-house sleeping arrangements were made for some of the staff. The switchboard (four outside lines) was lighted continuously, with hundreds of calls from panicky husbands, parents, and friends inquiring as to the whereabouts of family members and friends.

The Center's population was calm. Many were most helpful and felt sorry for the correctional officers who had to work difficult and long hours. With but few exceptions, they were on their best behavior. It was necessary to maintain calm and a sense of humor, for no one knew what to expect next.

A temporary arrangement was made with the Youth Aid Division of the Metropolitan Police Department to provide emergency assistance to children whose mothers had been arrested.

To provide assistance to the Women's Detention Center and other institutions as well, should help be needed there, the Director of Corrections Office functioned as a 24-hour command post, coordinating with other institutions and agencies and aprising each of any change in community conditions. The central supply unit also was in operation around the clock to provide additional bedding, food, paper goods, and the like.

Inasmuch as four of the six Department of Corrections institutions are located at a 3,500-acre reservation at Lorton, Virginia, the various supportive services and distribution of supplies are administered there by the Office of the Associate Director for Institutions. The office is not only responsible for the coordination of all activities at the reservation, but also at the two institutions in the District of Columbia. Every effort was made by that office to provide prompt assistance on short notice in as simple and direct a manner as possible.

Moral support and help also came from the Department headquarters in the Distict. They kept in close touch with the Detention Center, offering encouragement, guidance, and direction as well as services.

The dedicated Center staff proved equal to the challenge, working long hours as a team (three women worked 24 hours consecutively) to accomplish a most difficult task.

## THE FEMALE RIOT PARTICIPANTS

Of the 437 commitments, 276 were for curfew violation, 75 for burglary II (looting), 36 for drunk, 27 for disorderly, and 23 for a variety of other offenses ranging from homicide to traffic violations.

Three hundred eighty-nine of the 437 female commitments were Negro. The typical female participant was in her early twenties (266). She was either single or not living with her husband (245). She was unemployed (198) or employed in a low-paying service occupation (119), and lived in the Northwest or Northeast quadrant[3] of the city (306). She had not been committed to the Center prior to the disturbance. (As of April 15, 1969, less than 5 percent have been returned to the Center for violation of law.) With few exceptions those committed were very cooperative with the institutional personnel.

There were exceptions, however. For example, a recently married 24-year-old accountant had, unknown to the police, taken LSD just before she was arrested on a curfew violation. The drug took effect shortly after her commitment. She took a "nightmare" trip and became hysterical as she was being "attacked" by the fiendish creatures of her own subconscious imagination. It took seven people to put her in an ambulance and take her to a hospital for emergency treatment. She awoke in an apparently normal state and went to work the next morning.

A vociferous and obviously pregnant woman was brought to the Center with only a blanket draped about her. She had been asleep when a girl friend banged on her door and screamed: "Come on, they just knocked over the liquor store on the corner." Off the expectant mother ran. In the excitement she forgot to dress! When the police arrested her, she was clutching four fifths of scotch taken from the store's display window. The police had provided the blanket.

One woman had become so distraught about her sick youngster that she was found at a liquor store window 47 blocks from home "looking for asthma medicine"! In cruel reality, the boy indeed needed medicine which he had not received for 2 weeks because he mother had not been home during that period.

These illustrations suggest that during the riots there were never any dull moments at the Center and in the community.

## VIOLATOR TYPES

The following descriptions of violator types give some insight as to how and why the women at the Center became involved in the disorders.

### The Curfew Violator

The typical woman charged with violation of curfew was in her early twenties, single or not living with her husband. She was employed in a service occupation and lived in the Northwest and Northeast quadrant of the city.

By and large, the curfew violator violated for one of three reasons.

First, she did not know that a curfew was in effect. Despite the accounts presented by various news media, many persons were unaware that there were any problems in the city. Many had heard the term "curfew" broadcast but did not fully realize what it meant.

Second, she was fully cognizant of the existence of the curfew but had adopted a "they wouldn't arrest me for it" attitude. Typical of this attitude was the woman who said: "I always walk my dog after dinner, my neighborhood appeared alright, and I could see no reason to change my routine."

Third, her curiosity got the better of her and she decided to go to the riot area to watch the looting. Some may well have had a little larceny in mind if the circumstances were right.

The latter two categories probably explain the motivations of the majority of those arrested for curfew violations. The curfew violators were, in general, not directly involved in arson and looting but were peripheral bystanders who apparently were apprehended by the police who believed that by clearing the streets, further serious problems could be averted or at least a lesser degree of involvement.

Those Arrested for Looting

The women charged with burglary II present a markedly different picture than the curfew violators. Burglary II suspects were in their twenties, were or had been married, were unemployed or employed on a day-by-day basis, and lived in the Northwest and Northeast sections of the city. Several lived in other cities and came to Washington on the second or third day of the trouble specifically to steal merchandise to sell back home. Their occupational status gives a clue as to the probable motivation for their eventual participation.

In talking with them, many apparently had no intent to steal but were caught up, instead, in the contagion of the excitement, became involved, and were acting as mindless members of a crowd. One woman, for example, always did her weekend shopping after work on Friday at the only large grocery store in her neighborhood. The store was being looted when she arrived. She explained that she was faced with the choice of not looting and not having any food for the weekend or taking what she ordinarily would have purchased.

Others living in neighborhoods serious affected by the disturbance could not sleep, went into the streets, saw a friend in a crowd, and joined in. Several woman expressed that if everybody does something, then it is all right! That this justification prevailed is further substantiated by the fact that only three of the women had prior criminal records.


### Those Arrested for Being Drunk or Disorderly

For all intents and purposes these two offender categories can be combined. During the riots the charges of drunk and disorderly were used interchangeably. These women were in the 45 and over age range, married, employed in low-paying service occupations, and lived in the Northwest part of the city. Most of them were on the streets after curfew and just as easily could have been charged with curfew violations. Some were not aware that there was any trouble in the city. Others were the type that ordinarily would have been ignored by the police or assisted home, but were arrested, instead, as much for their own protection as to clear the streets. A few "disorderly" commitments could have been involved in the lootings. The drunks seemed to be relatively harmless.


## SIGNIFICANCE OF RESIDENCE

As mentioned earlier, the major areas of serious trouble during the riots were 14th and 7th Streets in the Northwest section and H Street in the Northeast section. If the majority of offenders came from these two areas, it would seem to imply that the citizens from other areas of the city stayed home or at least made no attempts to become involved. An analysis of the quadrants of residence might also support the contagion theory of participation. As can be noted from the foregoing offender composites, only in those instances where burglary II offenses were alleged did the women come in any substantial numbers from other parts of the city. In this category, 30 percent of those arrested lived in the Southeast section. Nonetheless it can be asserted that the large majority of female participants lived in the immediate areas where the "action was" and that Southeast and especially Southwest residents remained away from actual involvement. Thus it would appear that a contagion or "Roman holiday" explanation for participation accounts, in part, for the unusual pattern of behavior of citizens who normally are law-abiding persons.

## CONCLUSION

The offender profiles in this article would tend to point out that female participation was foremost among the youthful unemployed or marginally employed. Participation was also, in large part, determined by the situation and circumstances in the individual's immediate environment—large hordes of outsiders were not especially apparent. The probability of participation of a person living in an area directly affected by the riot was substantially greater than if she resided in a peaceful neighborhood.

It should be pointed out that this article deals only with women and it not meant to imply that the same findings would apply to male participants. It is also important to remember that in any study of the phenomenon of the urban riot we must focus our attention on human behavior in general. Anyone familiar with American history or cognizant of contemporary events both on college campuses here at home and in many foreign countries will recognize that violent disturbances are not characteristic of any racial, national, or religious group. Disorders are an unfortunate expression of human behavior.

The facts presented herein tend to show that civil disorders arise from an extremely complex matrix of social problems which have very deep roots. Prevention of similar incidents can be accomplished only through careful study, communication, and realistic planning. There are no simple and immediate solutions. From a law enforcement and correctional viewpoint we must prepare ourselves to deal effectively with disorders while at the same time utilizing the positive resources in our local communities to effect meaningful and lasting prevention.

## NOTES

1. Annual Report, Metropolitan Police Department, Washington, D.C. 1967, p. 16.

2. *Ibid.,* p. 17.

3. For those unfamiliar with the District of Columbia, it is divided into four sections or quadrants. As of July 1960 the city's population by qaudrant was as follows: Northeast 197,536; Northwest, 374,165; Southeast 173,988; and Southwest, 18,267. The riot-torn 14th and 7th Streets are in the Northwest quadrant and H Street in the Northeast quadrant.

NINE

# Prostitution in Nevada*†

RICHARD SYMANSKI

Nevada is one of the few states in puritan American where prostitution is either legal or openly tolerated. This thriving and infamous legacy of early western individualism and the Gold Rush days is a model for what some believe should exist elsewhere in the United States, and almost by definition, is a part of any polemic on the subject. The number of brothels and prostitutes in Nevada is small and legally limited to rural areas and small towns, and most of the population accepts or is positively inclined toward brothel prostitution.[1] This acceptance can be accounted for in large measure by the manner in which brothels, madams, and girls are restricted by legal and quasi-legal means, and by the perceived positive benefits that accrue. My purpose is to describe the legal, locational, and ecological aspects of brothel prostitution in Nevada.

## HISTORICAL BACKGROUND

Brothels with their madams and harlots were as much a part of the early West as were miners, cowboys, town preachers, and small merchants. From Denver to San Francisco, and north to south in between, boom towns had few women. Prostitution was inevitable on this isolating frontier where the lust for a woman may have been as great as that for a gold nugget. In myth and fact, it gave impetus to the fanciful Julie Bulette of Virginia City, the cribs of Goldfield, Eureka, and innumerable

*Reproduced by permission from the *Annals of the Association of American Geographers,* Volume 64, 1974, pp. 357–377, R. Symanski.

†Field work was carried out in the summer of 1973, and on an occasional basis prior to 1969. I wish to thank Nancy Burley and Pat Burnett who provided valuable advice on a draft of this paper, Margaret Day who did the cartography, James Root who assisted in the early phases of the 1973 field work, and the numerous law enforcement people, attorneys, townspeople, madams, and brothel maids for their willingness to talk with me about prostitution. Most of all, I wish to thank the many prostitutes who unknowingly gave me insights into prostitution in Nevada for little more than the price of a drink. I owe them an apology for deceiving them as to my true intentions and, in some cases, of depriving them of time with a prospective client.

other boom towns, and the huge establishments in the larger cities known as "cow yards."[2]

Then, perhaps more than now, there were notable geographical and class distinctions. In the 1860s the prostitutes of Virginia City had D Street to themselves. There were "two rows of white-washed cottages at the head of the street, the cheaper women in cribs below, farther down the Chinese, and at the bottom of the slope the Indian mahalies."[3] Denver in the 1880s was notable for its cribs which, as elsewhere, were adjacent to one another. They had both "dollar and four-bit whores—a dollar if white and four bits if black."[4] There was a wide gap between crib women and those in brothels or parlor houses, who were of higher class and were higher priced. Above prostitutes were hurdy girls, who worked in bars and dance halls. At the lowest end of the scale were the "hog ranches," the cheapest houses on the frontier. The Army permitted these to operate at a distance of five miles from a post.[5]

Moral rectitude had to wait until enough women arrived to bring gentility to a male population and to change the supply and demand function, until the frenzied atmosphere of discovery, despair, and fortune-making slowed, and until churches were firmly established. Prostitution was outlawed in numerous states in the twentieth century, and had to go underground. In Nevada it was only circumscribed. It was made illegal and the law was strictly enforced where opposing groups were strong, it was tolerated elsewhere in spite of church and book illegality because "it had been there as long as anyone could remember and seemed all right," and it was occasionally regulated or temporarily suppressed when the objecting party was the federal government. As an example, Storey County approved by ordinance a red-light district for Virginia City in 1878. This district existed continuously until it was closed during World War II upon request from the Federal Security Agency to protect military personnel in the area.[6] Virginia City no longer had a red-light district in 1973, but the county had the state's largest and most famous brothel. Elsewhere in Nevada prostitution was also doing well, though increasingly in the last decade it has been formalized in state statute, local ordinances, and quasi-official regulations.

## LAW PROHIBITING PROSTITUTION

The location of brothels and the activity spaces of prostitutes cannot be understood apart from legal, quasi-legal, and brothel-owner regulations. Statutes or ordinances at the state, county, or city levels define the legal context. Madams and girls also obey written and unwritten rules of

questionable legal validity formulated by city councils and law enforcement officials. Madams make rules which regulate the girls and control
house and community behavior.

The combined effect of these regulations on the location and activity
of houses and girls is impressive. The brothels literally become prisons
or, depending on one's point of view, noxious or acceptable equilibrat-
ing spatial nodes. Occasionally even prostitutes describe themselves as
"prisoners," although they emphasize the voluntary nature of their confinement. They are there, so they claim, for pecuniary profit, because
they like what they are doing, or because of the number of different
people they meet. It is, however, not only prostitutes who explicitly recognize the peculiar nature of their activity spaces. Legislators and those
who write authoritatively about prostitution refer to them as "inmates."[7]

The Nevada Revised Statutes of 1971 provide that a county with a
population of 200,000 or more at the last national census cannot grant a
license for the purpose of operating a house of "ill fame or repute" or
any other business employing a prostitute.[8] Only Clark County (which
includes Las Vegas), with a 1970 population of 273,288, is excluded by
this statute. The second largest county, Washoe, which includes Reno
and Sparks, had a population of 121,068. State statute grants the board
of county commissioners the power to license, tax, regulate, or prohibit
brothels in cities and unincorporated towns.[9] Four Nevada counties,
Storey, Lincoln, Lyon, and Esmeralda, license brothels by ordinance;
others, where brothels may be illegal outside towns, license them not as
brothels, but as bars and boarding houses which are specifically regulated by prostitution ordinances.[10] Washoe (Reno), Ormsby (Carson
City), Churchill, and Douglas counties prohibits brothels (Fig. 1).[11]

The four counties which license brothels do so to avoid any possibility of brothels being defined as common-law nuisances and thereby subject to abatement. In 1948, in *Cunningham* vs. *Washoe County,* the
Nevada Supreme Court held that an unlicensed brothel in Reno was a
common-law nuisance, and that this aspect of the common law could
not be changed by statute. The counties which now license brothels take
the position that the court case involved an unlicensed brothel, and
licensing precludes them from being defined as a common-law nuisance.[12]

Counties and cities take different and sometimes complex approaches
to exclusion. Churchill County flatly prohibits pandering, prostitution,
and the keeping of brothels.[13] A Carson City Municipal Code (Carson
City accounts for the entire population of Ormsby County) places
emphasis on the prostitute, a person defined as one having an "evil reputation" and thereby engaging in "prohibited conduct."[14] The City of Fallon, within Churchill County and thereby prohibited from having

FIG. 1. Legal and illegal prostitution in Nevada. Data were compiled from state statutes and city and county ordinances.

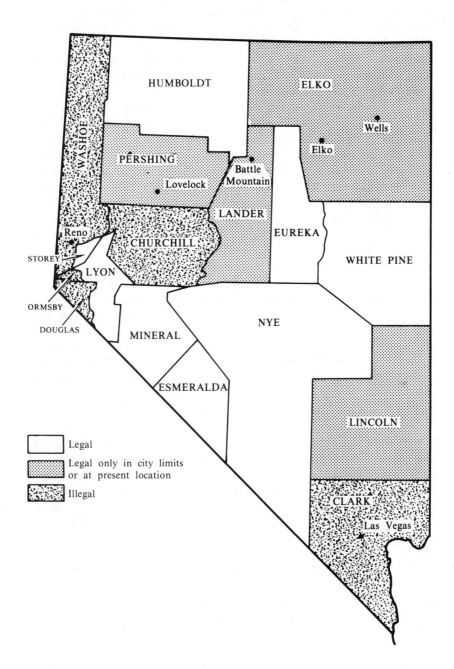

prostitution, nevertheless maintains a number of sections in its City Code under miscellaneous offenses or acts affecting public decency. Included are loitering in or near any thoroughfare or public place for the purpose of procuring one to engage in prostitution, entering or remaining in a place for the purpose of prostitution or "the commission of any lewd or indecent act," allowing any place to be used for prostitution or a "lewd purpose," directing or transporting any person to a brothel, procuring prostitutes, and engaging in prostitution or "any lewd or indecent act." All that is required in Fallon to support a charge of pimping or prostitution is the "common repute" of a person; there need be no proof of an act of sexual intercourse or payment.[16]

Clark County, where brothels are illegal by State statute, has a 1973 ordinance which defines prostitution as an act of vagrancy.[17] The ordinance excludes law enforcement officers working in their official capacity, presumably to avoid legal problems when they pose as pimps, prostitutes, or clients for purposes of entrapment. Other approaches to prostitution include illegality under nuisance provisions rather than a specific prostitution ordinance (Douglas County), and de facto legality through absence of applicable ordinances in spite of the presence of brothels (Humboldt and Eureka counties).[18]

The two counties containing Nevada's major population centers and two others near Reno and Lake Tahoe have prohibited prostitution. The poor image of gambling and its importance to these areas and to total state revenues have apparently been major factors in the minds of gambling magnates and legislators when considering the desirability of prostitution. Gambing is a "family activity," at least to the extent that both husband and wife can participate. Prostitution would impair business and possibly give gambling a worse name than it already possesses.

The legal suppression of prostitution in these counties has an ironic aspect. Both Reno and Las Vegas have problems with streetwalkers and call girls, who are not registered and cannot be regulated or examined for venereal disease as they would be elsewhere in the state. Proportionately they may be more important in spreading such disease than brothel girls, who receive a monthly blood test (serology) and a weekly examination for venereal disease. The weekly checkup may include a pelvic examination and an endocervical culture for gonorrhea. Only one reactive blood test for syphilis came from a regulated brothel in the years 1970 to 1972.[19] All local evidence seems to suggest that "independents" are usually responsible for the spread of venereal disease.[20] Prostitutes tend to be very careful in accepting clients, to protect themselves. A girl will carefully inspect a man's penis before there is sexual activity. She will have another house girl inspect him, if she is uncertain about his health, and he will be refused if they decide that he is diseased. Additionally, the man's penis is washed in warm soapy water before and after sexual activities, and some houses have the girls apply tincture of methylate in an attempt to protect the client.[21]

There are no streetwalkers or call girls in any of the casinos or bars in areas where prostitution is legal in the state. They could not compete, as the prices in brothels are cheaper.[22] Brothel prostitutes gain in volume what they lose in not charging high prices to a few customers.

## ORDINANCES CONFINING PROSTITUTION

At least three counties allow prostitution in towns or unincorporated areas, but exclude it from rural areas (Fig. 1), and Lincoln County restricts it to the specific plots of land where its two rural brothels are located.[23] Prostitution in Elko County is limited to the incorporated towns of Elko, Wells, and Carlin. This ordinance prohibits brothels in the unincorporated border town of Wendover which, because of heavy truck and tourist traffic and relative proximity to Salt Lake City, could support at least a couple of houses. Although the new county ordinance permits prostitution in Carlin, which is twenty-three miles west of Elko, the town enforces a 1925 ordinance defining a prostitute as a vagrant punishable by imprisonment and a fine.[24] Prostitution is excluded from rural areas in Lander County indirectly by limiting the number of brothels to two in the county; both are in Battle Mountain. The reason given by law enforcement officers for restricting prostitution to population centers is the difficulty of policing or controlling houses at great distances or in rural areas.

Winnemucca's detailed Municipal Code prohibits the practice of prostitution, pimping, transportation of prostitutes, and indirect involvement such as directing customers to houses.[25] Ely also specifically states that prostitution is not allowed within the City.[26] In both towns, however, subsequent sections of the ordinances make an exception if the brothels are in a specified section of the city, namely, where they are placed at present.[27]

The City Code of Ely is among the most detailed. It specifies that brothels are only allowed "on High Street between Second and first Street and on the west side of First Street, being lots 16–20 inclusive of Block T, 1–5 in Block U, 11 and 12 in Block W, and 9 and 10 in Block X."[28] This description suggests that more than the two brothels are currently operating in the area. One was closed in July, 1973, because the owner was charged and convicted of beating one of the girls. In addition to this areal delimitation, the City also reserves the right to limit the number of houses.

The state statutes make a brothel illegal within 400 yards of a school or building erected for religious services, or on a principal business street.[29] The latter is elaborated to exclude the possibility of a brothel entrance or exit on a major street in the state. Many counties do not license prostitution as such, but rather bars and rooming houses, and they may take a similar approach to these establishments in their ordinances. White Pine County will not grant a license for the sale of alcohol or drugs to any place which is within 500 feet of a school or church.[30]

A further provision of the Ely ordinances is that "operators and inmates" are subject to rules which may be promulgated from time to time by the city council and carried out by the police department.[31] Such rules, often not referred to in city or county ordinances, are common in most of the towns and unincorporated places having prostitution. They provide that prostitutes be at least twenty-one (eighteen in a few counties), obtain a work permit, and be fingerprinted, photographed, and examined by a physician before commencing work. In some counties they must register their automobiles and notify the police when terminating employment. They are also required to obtain weekly and monthly medical examination at their own expense. These regulations, not always adhered to, are designed to protect customers and community alike from venereal disease and from girls who have criminal records or are addicted to drugs. These "rules and regulations" provide some of the strongest arguments for legalized prostitution. The brothel operators accept them without question, despite their questionable legal status, because it would jeopardize the existence of the brothels to challenge them. It is these rules that most rigidly and specifically define the activity spaces of prostitutes.

The ordinances of Lyon (four brothels) and Esmeralda (one brothel) counties provide a striking contrast in the extent to which rural brothels are regulated. Esmeralda County requires brothels to have permits designating the areas where they may be located. They must be in uninhabited areas at least five miles from a city, town, mobile home park, or place where people normally dwell.[32] No gambling or narcotics are permitted on the premises, and prostitutes must have weekly and monthly medical examinations.[33]

In contrast, the eighteen-page 1972 ordinance for Lyon County is perhaps the most comprehensive in the state. Because of its concern over the legality of brothels, it states that they do not constitute a public nuisance nor an offense of public decency.[34] To insure that they will not be a nuisance, elaborate sections require data on the financial condition of the owner, addresses of the owner and prostitutes during the previous ten years, and complete information on previous convictions of the owner. A prostitute who has ever been convicted of any felony cannot be employed.[35] The sheriff can limit the hours-per-day or days-per-week that a brothel is open, the number of prostitutes that a house can have, and the size of the building. He is to receive weekly reports on the health of the girls, and they must have regular examinations. The houses may employ males only for the maintenance and repair of the brothel premises, and no male is permitted to live on the property occupied by the brothel.[36]

Brothels in Lyon County must be at least three miles from incorporated and unincorporated towns, and they must be more than 300 yards from any public street, road, highway, private residence, or business establishment, although they may be closer to a business establishment if they receive the written consent of the owner. Brothels are prohibited from advertising, and can only have three-foot by five-foot signs which must read "Guest Ranch—Men Only." Signs on public roads may give only the name oif the operation, approximate distance to the brothel, a single arrow pointing in the direction of the operation, and others where the road divides. Finally, the brothels must be enclosed by a fence at least six feet high with an entrance that can be opened only from the inside.[37]

## LEGAL CONTROVERSIES

During World War II the Federal Security Agency exerted considerable pressure on a number of Nevada's tows to close their brothels.[38] In Tonopah alone, according to Bobby, the town's only remaining madam, twelve houses were closed.[39] The townspeople of Beatty objected to the government's demands and in the introduction to a petition declared that "after all, there isn't much to do at Beatty, we haven't television, we don't have a radio station.[40] In Wells, the city council enacted an emergency ordinance in October, 1943, as elaborate as that described for Fallon.[41] The introduction to the ordinance stated that it had been enacted because[42]

> it had been made to appear to this Board that the absence of such an ordinance results in the spread of venereal disease, to the detriment of members of the armed forces of the United States sojourning in said city or in the neighborhood . . . and this ordinance [is] for the protection of [their] health and safety.

This ordinance remained in effect until three months after the end of World War II.

Most brothels in the State were apparently closed in spite of opposition, and some remain off-limits to the present day, yet there were other economic benefits in legalized gambling and easy liquor sales.[43] Elko and Ely outdrew Salt Lake City as overnight destinations for soldiers stationed at the Wendover Air Base on the Nevada-Utah border.[44] Prostitution may simply have been driven into cheap hotels, rooming houses, or the outskirts of town.[45]

In recent years conflict has arisen between branches of the federal government and individual brothel owners. One of the brothels in Lovelock is located where a section of Interstate 80 will be placed, and the government does not know how it can pay for displacing something which it does not recognize. The Bureau of Land Management (BLM) ordered that a brothel be moved from federal lands in a rural section of western Mineral County.[46] The brothel was renamed and relocated at a better site in 1973, nearer the California border on the Los Angeles—Bishop—Tonopah route. Another rural brothel in Esmeralda County, the "Cottontail Ranch," was told to move since it was leasing five acres of virtually unusable land from the BLM at $100 a year, with an option to purchase the land at a nominal sum.[47] The land was obtained under the Small Tract Act of 1938 which makes land available for residential and commercial use. Although the 1938 federal law does not specifically exclude brothels, the BLM contends that it is illegal to use federal land for a brothel. The order was contested in court and in September 1973, the brothel had not been relocated.[48]

One nationally publicized dispute in the 1950s involved the *Territorial Enterprise,* the newspaper on which Mark Twain served his apprenticeship, which took up the cause for prostitution in a way that was undoubtedly offensive to many. The controversy involved the Nevada State Highway Department and a brothel in Searchlight. The Highway Department complained that heavy traffic to the house had ruined the road surface and that, in addition, the brothel was close to one of the village's one-room school houses, which was a violation of state law. The paper advocated the "Searchlight Plan," in which the school rather than the brothel would be moved.[49]

In counties where prostitution is legal there are occasional attempts by legislators and especially by newly arrived fundamentalist preachers to have prostitution outlawed or to limit the number of houses. In early 1973, the County Commissioner of Storey County issued a statement against legalized prostitution, claiming that he was receiving complaints from people within and without the state.[50] Storey County has Nevada's largest and most publicized brothel, the Joe Conforte "Mustang Bridge Ranch."[51] Other counties generally have small license fees for liquor and for running a "boarding house," and a moderate fee for running a brothel, but Storey county, with a population of 695, receives approximately ten percent of its income from its single brothel.[52] Nevertheless, the County has refused to issue a license for another house on the grounds that having houses too close together can create problems.[53]

Humboldt, Lander, Elko, White Pine, and Lyon counties are likewise opposed to increasing the number of houses. Lyon County in 1971 had five brothels, all of which the district attorney attempted to close.[54] After his attempt aborted, in 1972 the county legalized four houses, the present number, and instituted the most comprehensive ordinance regulating prostitution in the state.

## LOCATION OF BROTHELS

Thirty-three brothels were open for business in Nevada in July, 1973 (Fig. 2).[55] Twenty-two, or sixty-seven percent, were in places with a 1970 population of 500 or more, and the remaining eleven were in rural areas. Four were thirty miles or more from a place of at least 2,000. The largest town with brothels was Elko, with a 1970 population of 7,621. Elko ranks only tenth in the state in population size, an indication of the extent to which prostitution is excluded from Nevada's larger urban places Between 225 and 250 prostitutes were working in these brothels, divided about half-and-half between town and rural houses.[56] This is an average of five girls per town brothel and, excluding the very large "Mustang Bridge Ranch," seven per rural brothel. The "Mustang Bridge Ranch" has over fifty prostitutes.

The brothels are town-oriented in the northern and west central part of the state, and rural brothels are confined to the west and south (Fig. 2). The rural brothels are newer and more tied to trucking, airplanes, impermanency, and the hurried, harassing industrial age than to cowboys, miners, and provincial locals. Six of the eleven rural houses are in mobile homes, and others have mobile home additions, but only three of twenty-two town brothels are in mobile homes. Three of the rural houses have landing strips to attract customers from Las Vegas and Los Angeles, an amenity indicative of isolation and a special type of client.

The cluster of five rural brothels around Reno and Carson City has an accentuated "assembly line approach" of such notoriety that prostitutes in other houses have pejorative names for the brothels and may express displeasure at having worked in them. A customer is expected

FIG. 2. Nevada's brothels.

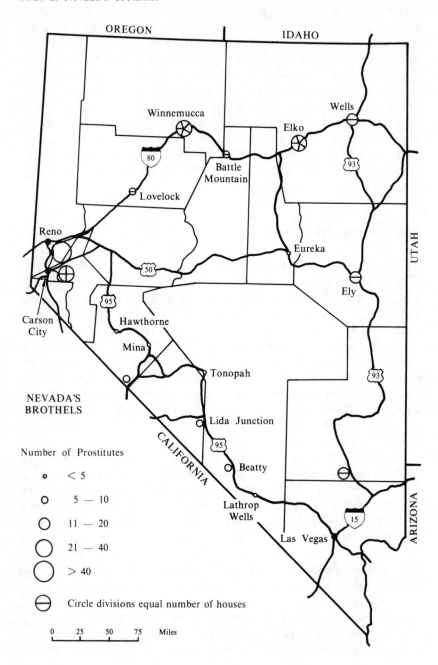

not to ask for a drink upon entering a house, but only to choose a girl quickly, make payment and receive the services requested, and then leave immediately.[57] Although common to many of the brothels, the approach is generally more muted in the population centers. Drinking before buying is a traditional and integral part of the house atmosphere, a way to relax or briefly know a girl before buying her services.

The town brothels are usually near the railroad tracks, on the "wrong side," in lower class or declining areas. These characteristics suggest how long they have existed, more than fifty years in a few cases. Brothels are also near the edge of town, and even exceptions in Elko and Hawthorne have adjacent unoccupied lands. A further commonality is the strong clustering tendency. The brothels in Winnemucca, Elko, Wells, and Ely are adjacent to one another, and the houses in Battle Mountain and Lovelock are no more than a few blocks apart.

## SIZE OF BROTHELS

Nevada's brothels can be classified by number of girls in a brothel or in a cluster (Fig. 2). The largest houses are closest to major cities (Reno, Carson City, and Las Vegas), to major feeder regions (the San Francisco–Oakland area and Los Angeles), or are in the largest towns permitting prostitution. The brothels near Las Vegas are farther from Las Vegas than the brothels near Carson City are from their respective urban centers. Los Angeles, which feeds the brothels near Las Vegas, is farther from the houses than the Bay Area is from Nevada's largest brothels near Reno and Carson City. Brothels of intermediate size are on the major tourist and truck route traversing the state, Interstate 80. The smallest brothels are in the small places, at some distance from large cities, or in inaccessible rural areas.

The variety increases as the number of girls increases. Better (often larger) houses have services not available in smaller houses. Two or more girls can provide a "party," which includes movies, or a large house may have a bedroom which is built entirely of mirrors. The smallest brothels are unable to offer these amenities and, in addition, they occasionally have only a single girl on hand. The better brothels have younger and more attractive girls, although even this rule has exceptions. A small house may have only a single girl, and she may be young and quite attractive.

The larger brothels have the most attractive facades and interior settings. Bars and parlors are comfortable and have a nice atmosphere. Parlors are spacious and often resemble modern middle-class living rooms, and in a few cases, there is a gaming room or swimming pool. In one brothel, a room adjoining the bar had a large color television set that girls watched while waiting for business. The lowest-order houses tend to be small and have sparsely decorated bars, have a dirty and unkempt appearance, and are without other amenities.

It is difficult to generalize about prices, but in the larger brothels the girls get more business, know they can demand better prices, and do so. In the lowest-order houses business is often slack, and a client is in a much better position to bargain. Girls can do this rather easily since they determine the prices themselves except for some basic house prices.

Places on Interstate 80 generally had a smaller 1970 population per girl than other places. The ratios ranged from 108 to 464 persons per girl for the five places along the Interstate, whereas the other places had ratios of 161 to 780 (excluding a high of 1,769). The places on Interstate 80 had more transient traffic, and the brothels there had more out-of-town business.

## PROSTITUTES

Data on the homes or current residences of prostitutes are difficult to obtain. Prostitutes either reside in or presently identify large and usually nearby urban places as home. Eight girls indicated they previously had been streetwalkers or call girls in Las Vegas, Los Angeles, or San Francisco. Others had worked as waitresses, secretaries, in sales, or had been at a university before coming to the brothels.

Where it was possible to discuss reasons for entering the houses, money or quick financial gain was often expressed as the main motive. Some simply said they liked what they were doing or that they could not hold a steady job in the "straight world," a fact attested to by high turnover in the houses. Prostitutes may have heard about the brothels while working as streetwalkers, from bartenders and cab drivers who mentioned that it was a job and a way of making good money, or through a friend. A few got into prostitution by turning tricks for extra money in their home towns. The money was very attractive in comparison with a low-paid job as a secretary or waitress. Although there is variability by girls, house, and season, a prostitute can make upwards of $350 a week after the house takes its percentage and payment is made from room and board.[58]

In both rural and town brothels blacks constitute at least twenty-five to thirty percent of the prostitute population. An equally high percentage of house or bar maids is also black. Only two Oriental girls and one

Chicana were noted. This high proportion of black prostitutes, well above black representation in the total population, is not surprising when compared to their incidence in the total prostitute population.[59] Although information on background is not always reliable, a number of black prostitutes, in contrast to whites, indicated that they previously had been streetwalkers in a major urban area.

The reasons such a large number of black women enter prostitution may be obvious, but the extent to which or why they are apparently systematically functional is not so clear. Perhaps they are an important element in a "diversity mix" of services which brothels offer. Outside a brothel a white male is unlikely to have an opportunity to pursue sexual activities with a black. In a house, the desire to "try something different" can be pursued without reproach from peer group or community members. In fact, in brothels one may gain insight into what some whites want or, more important, the role of diversity in accounting for their behavior. Both white and black girls have told me that one of a pair of white males entering a brothel may be inclined toward an available black girl, yet he will either supress his wishes or seek the approval of his friend before choosing her. This principle of diversity would seem to explain the large number of black girls in brothels in which black male customers are virtually absent. It is also supported by the commonly expressed statement by prostitutes that diversity is a principal reason men go to prostitutes.[60]

Most prostitutes have considerable knowledge of the characteristics and rules of at least a few of the brothels in the state. Some girls have extensive knowledge of a half-dozen houses or more. Madams also seem to know the existence, location, and madams of other houses. They acquired this information by working in the business for a decade or more, and because of the relatively small number of like entrepreneurs.

Prostitutes acquire and disseminate information differently. Many have worked in two or more houses in Nevada, and some report having worked in as many as eight. They are free agents and may change jobs as frequently as they desire. Information about other houses and activities comes from a number of sources, principally through personal acquaintance and co-workers. Some information may also be acquired from travelling merchants who visit the brothels selling clothing, lingerie, cosmetics, and shoes.

Madams and girls in conversation speak of frequent, variable, and seasonal turnover and mobility. Law enforcement records for seventy-seven girls show that twenty (more than a quarter) worked ten days or less before quitting, and forty-five (nearly sixty percent) worked less than a month, yet some girls have worked as long as four years in a single house.[61]

Different classes of prostitutes seem to have different mobility potentials and patterns, and they may even be immobile near the end of their careers. Houses which clearly have lower-class girls, as judged by age and appearance, appear to receive girls from similar houses. The same holds for higher-class houses, although there is always the inevitability of moving downward in the system. Girls move horizontally between houses at Mina, Eureka, and Battle Mountain, where brothels are among the least desirable in the state. On the other hand, movement by higher-class or more attractive prostitutes is found between houses in Winnemucca, Elko, and Wells. These houses receive more customers because of the general quality and range of girls offered, the reputation of these red-light districts, the physical cleanliness of the brothels, their accessibility, and the greater size of the local population which provides demand for the girls.

The most notable seasonal movement of girls occurs during deer season, from approximately the middle of September to the middle of November. Deer hunters come from the West Coast to hunt in Nevada, Utah, and Colorado. The most affected brothels are those along Interstate 80 from Winnemucca to Wells, and south to Ely. Other seasonal peaks occur during the National Basque Festival (which is held in July on different dates in Elko and Ely), local rodeos, automobile races, and, according to some madams, New Year's Eve. In addition, brothels have more business in summer because of the heavy east-west tourist traffic. The houses receive less business during heavy snowfalls in the winter, especially those which are on access roads. Most of these seasonal variations to do appear to affect the movement of girls from one house to another. Prostitutes do not move seasonally or yearly among a given set of brothels on a regular basis.

Reasons given by girls for movement were usually limited to three or four principal factors. The most important was house atmosphere, a general rubric which included the nature of house rules, approach to clients (some girls expressed great distaste for the very mechanical "in and out" approach), and the number and kinds of girls in the house. Particularly in the small houses there was often mention of how easy it is for a girl to ignite a social fire in the confined atmosphere. Other reasons for moving were boredom, the opportunity to make more money elsewhere, particularly during deer season, and the presence or absence of a friend.

The rapid turnover in brothels is functional in at least four principal ways. First, in the small and legally restricted activity space of the town, and given the usual house requirements that a girl must work three weeks without a day off before taking a week's vacation, new faces and personalities reduce the potential if not actual amount of social friction. Second, moving gives the prostitutes variety in the customers they service and in the madam, girls, and rules they must live with. Third, it provides variety for customers, an element that may help to account for the very existence and viability of prostitution. Fourth, there is less likelihood of a regular client forming an emotional attachment to a prostitute, thereby avoiding problems with spouse, community, and the girl. Some girls have mentioned that they receive frequent proposals of marriage.

## RESTRICTIONS ON PROSTITUTES

Brothel prostitutes are required to observe a number of regulations established by local authorities.[62] A few are necessary, nearly universal, and relate directly to their work; others are of questionable value, are found primarily in urban areas, and place restrictions on personal relationships and mobility only occasionally related to work. The latter restrictions define prostitutes as people of questionable social standing who cannot be trusted. The legal or quasi-legal limitations placed on mobility result in socially sanctioned restricted activity spaces.

Activity spaces, or those locations with which individuals have direct association at frequent intervals, are of two basic types: open and restricted. In open activity spaces an individual may and often does move as money, time, or predilection permit. There are, to be sure, few completely open activity spaces since, for example, personal or state property rights or regulations prohibit or restrict movement to certain locations within one's normal range. With these exceptions, most of us are not confined in the way we define our activity spaces. Those who operate brothels, and prostitutes even more so, are clear examples of individuals who have peculiar kinds of restricted activity spaces.

Restricted activity spaces are off-limits during certain times. Prohibited spaces are either permanently off-limits, or off-limits as long as one remains a member of a particular class. When a member leaves a class, temporarily or permanently, or gives the impression of having left, prohibited and restricted activity spaces no longer exist for that person, or they are redefined. For example, when a girl leaves prostitution, changes houses from one county to another, or permits herself to be "bought" out of a house for a day or more (commonly known as an "outdate"), the nature of her activity space may be redefined. Prostitution in Nevada provides examples of these concepts.

Prostitutes are permitted outside the brothels, with a few exceptions, only between the hours of 10 A.M. and 5 or 6 P.M. In Wells, the hours are from 1 PM. to 4 P.M. Winnemucca allows girls in town after 4 A.M. and until 7 A.M. if the brothel is closed and the police department is notified of intentions and areas to be visited. Lander County also prohibits leaving the brothels on Sunday. Activity within these permitted hours is confined to visiting certain establishments or sections of the town, and to particular interactions. Places which can be visited include doctors' and dentists' offices, beauty parlors, shopping areas, and, perhaps, a movie theater. Girls are explicitly prohibited from going to bars, gaming houses, and residential areas; they are not permitted to rent rooms in town. The present sheriff of Wells makes an uncommon exception by permitting a girl to go to a hotel with a "bottle" and a customer. Ely allows girls to eat in restaurants with bars during shopping hours if they are unaccompanied by a male escort. Until recently there was an additional provision that the restaurant had to have a side entrance.

The rule that no girl may solicit business outside the house is rigidly enforced. Written regulations usually state that a girl may not be accompanied by a male escort in town. The twenty-three point list in Winnemucca goes farther: prostitutes are not allowed to have friends within the town, including pimps, boyfriends, husbands, and others defined by the police department. Girls in three different counties report that they cannot talk to anyone when out of the brothel, or, at most, can only exchange salutations. One reason, in addition to the obvious desire to confine prostitution, was given by a prostitute. "Imagine me beginning a conversation with one of my married customers in the presence of his wife. It doesn't matter if she knows her husband goes to one of the houses." To obviate problems after a girl's official status changes, Ely now requires that girls who have terminated or been fired must leave town on the first available transportation.

There are exceptions and house variations in the way activity spaces are defined. If a girl has a birthday, or on a special occasion such as Thanksgiving, the madam may obtain permission to escort the girls as a group to a bar in town. Wells permits only three girls to accompany the madam. One brothel in Winnemucca with six or seven girls avoids problems by permitting each girl to shop and attend to medical needs on a different day of the week. In rural areas, where most of these issues do not arise, the prostitutes often go for their medical checkups in a group, accompanied by the madam.

Local rules and regulations also place restrictions on family proximity, outdates, and employment changes. A prostitute cannot be employed in a brothel in Winnemucca or Battle Mountain if a member of her family lives in the same county. The rule on outdates varies. Some towns require that a client meet a girl at the town limits or date her beyond the town limits. Others stipulate that girl and client must leave the county. In either case, the intent is the same—to avoid embarrassment for those in the community. If a girl quits or is fired from a house, she usually has to leave the county for a period ranging from fifteen days to three months before she can be hired by another house in that county. Violation of these or other rules results in revocation of the work permit and perhaps banishment from the county.

Most brothels permit their girls to leave for a week once every three or four weeks. Bogus Christian names by which clients know girls and equally bogus surnames on police records are temporarily shelved while they return to previous identities as "respectable" mother, daughter, student, or vacationer. Likewise, the names of cities, towns, and even states are discarded for real places and remembered neighborhoods. One can only speculate on the effect of constant shifting between real and work-designated identities, or between restricted and open activity spaces on those who remain long in prostitution.

The madams place other restrictions on activity, especially during work hours. They may limit the number of telephone calls a girl can make, or specify that there will be no calls at all during certain hours.[63] Many houses permit girls to drink only sugar water, tea, or nonalcoholic beverages during work hours.

In general, there are fewer restrictions on madams, and certainly nothing approaching those placed on prostitutes. Madams are respected entrepreneurs simply making a living. Restrictions on their spatial activities seem to be limited to the entry of bars. They are, of course, prevented from hiring pimps, pimping themselves, permitting pimps, ex-felons, or felons on the premises, and, in most places, hiring males. Male prostitution does not exist in the brothels nor does, to my knowledge, lesbianism; women other than the madam, maids, and prostitutes are not permitted in brothels.

## CLIENTS

Data on clients are even more difficult to obtain than data on prostitutes. Truck drivers, locals, tourists, traveling salesmen, sportsmen, and high school and college students appear to be the major sources of business. Locals include ranchers, farmers, and cowboys. Long-distance or cross-country truck drivers and locals, married as well as unmarried, seem to be the largest groups. There are strong differences of opinion on how important locals are to town brothels. Some girls and madams insist they are no more important than other groups; others state that the brothels could not exist without the local married men. In the rural areas it seems certain that locals are less important.

The most obvious sources of client information about Nevada's brothels are friends, truck drivers telling other truck drivers, hunters or fishermen telling aficionados, and so on. A guide book first published in 1970 is a recent and possibly significant information source.[64] Available primarily in adult literature stores, this guide with accurate hour minimum prices and questionable brothel ratings is already in its seventh printing. It is a favorite holiday and special-occasion gift, with one store reporting a single order for 5,000 copies from a distributor on the East coast. In addition to introducing Nevada's brothels to many who never knew they existed, the publication and a newer rival undoubtedly have diversified and expanded the activity of those who frequent brothels.[65] They have also probably created new business for houses that are inaccessible or less well known.

Clients or prospective clients get information about houses or girls by telephone, for three reasons. First, a stranger has heard that there is a brothel, but is unable to locate it, and is unwilling to ask townspeople for directions. Second, a regular client has a "steady" girl in the house and wants to make certain that she is available. Third, regular clients want to know if new girls are available. For these, and one cannot be certain of their numbers, variety or "something different" is clearly the drawing power of the brothels.

Information about Nevada's brothels also circulates among university and high school students within the state and, perhaps more importantly for trade, among students in Oakland, San Francisco, Los Angeles, Salt Lake City, and the smaller cities of southern Idaho. Students differ from other clients. Many are as interested in the psychologic-philosophic side of their visit as they are in sex. One madam said that "you can always tell a university student by the fact that he is long on time and psychology and short on money, more interested in talking about it than in doing it."

Most brothels in Nevada are in relatively inconspicuous locations, and it is easy for a client to enter and leave without being noticed, but many customers do not follow minimum distance or time paths to a house. Some towns circumscribe the desire to follow circuitous pathways by local regulations which prohibit "back door customers." Most houses in western and southern Nevada are outside population centers, and there is little reason for not parking at the front door. In towns a high proportion of trade parks away from the houses. Long-distance truck drivers are less concerned, though they frequently park at a truck stop or on a side street within walking distance. None of the houses today offers the advantage that Lovelock locals used to enjoy: they could enter a hotel, exit through a back door, cross an alley into one of the brothels, and innocently exit from the hotel after an alleged game of cards or round of drinks with friends. Most town brothels can only offer their customers peripheral locations, a high wooden fence, a side entrance, or truck-trailer parking lots.

## PARLOR DYNAMICS

In the parlor a client meets the girls that are available and makes an immediate choice, usually from the lineup called by the madam. If an immediate choice is not required by the house, he can relax, drink, inspect one or more girls, or talk before making a decision. Physical contact is rarely permissible in the parlor. If a client is not initially attracted to a prostitute, then it is the task of the madam and girls to make a sale as quickly as possible.

Madam and girls waste little time in making explicit the nature of their business, especially after 6 P.M. and on Friday and Saturday nights, when business is brisk. They tell anyone who seems unfamiliar with brothels that they are not selling love, companionship, and not even really drinks, although most brothels have a liquor license. In extreme cases, if it is clear to the madam that someone is only interested in drinking and conversing with the girls, he will not be permitted to enter. Prostitutes will frequently leave the parlor and return to their rooms when they sense that a client is not interested in buying their services. An obvious reason for demanding a quick purchase is that idling clients reduce the turnover rate, which directly affects the girls, since they only get a percentage of what they make. Also, with rate exceptions, prostitutes only have a financial interest in their clients. To place as few financially unrewarding demands as possible on prostitutes, services are paid for on the basis of what is requested and the amount of time spent with a girl.[66]

Even the process of entering a brothel is indicative of the parlor atmosphere. After ringing a bell on a front door or an outside locked gate, the client usually hears the madam calling the girls to prepare for the lineup. Upon entry of a client, the prostitutes are ready to present themselves in the parlor, and do so when called by the madam. Once the lineup is formed, the prostitutes introduce themselves in succession by Christian name, and then the madam asks the client if he would like to make a choice, or whether he would prefer to have a girl join him at the bar. This pattern changes only in the late morning or early afternoon hours when business is slack, and girls as well as madam may be rising (they frequently work until 4 or 5 A.M.). Only a few, if any, of the prostitutes are available, and they filter in as they become ready for business. The "hustle" is usually more relaxed because there is neither as much competition from other girls, who are in town or sleeping, nor as many clients to deal with hurriedly on a "pay or leave" basis.

Variations from house to house are based on the different philosophies of madams regarding the most effective presale activities of prostitutes. Some feel that neither alcohol nor relaxed conversation is good for business; they prohibit interaction between girls and clients, and pressure the client to make his choice of girl immediately upon entering. Other madams think that alcohol and conversation are necessary to relax the client or "get him in the mood," but even in their parlors relaxation time is relatively short, no more than ten minutes or the duration of a drink. Aggression in most houses is greater at night or on the weekend than during slacker hours.

I encountered physical contact from the girls in only two houses. The overwhelming pattern is a cold or distant atmosphere, and the house policy is "pay before you play." Only a few houses used the "rotational approach," with a bar but no lineups. The girl who initially joined a client at the bar excused herself if she felt unsuccessful, and she was immediately replaced by another. The process continued until a purchase was made, the client left, or the girls ignored him. The "group conversational approach" may not have a lineup. The client sits in the parlor, with or without a drink and converses with a number of girls. Although there are both overt and covert attempts to force a quick choice, the client is given the opportunity to choose from a number of girls rather than from just a few. Finally, madams fall into two categories: those who only serve drinks and often leave the bar area or parlor, and those who continually prod the client and remind him of the house business in the girls' presence.

The parlors along the line in Winnemucca are unique in the state. Located at the end of Baud Street (townspeople will occasionally speak of "bawdy" women or "that bawdy place"), the five brothels form an elongated circle. This gives them a privacy not found elsewhere in town, and not even in many rural areas. Three of the five houses have large bay windows near which the girls sit facing Baud Street to beckon passing clients or to be inspected by them. When business is slow or when girls sense that those at the bar are present to socialize but not to buy, they often return to their window seats to watch for others or, if bored, read a novel or newspaper. Elko, where girls today can only be seen inside the brothel, had the same setting in the 1870s. The girls would sit by red-lighted windows along Piety and Adobe Rows, the latter a block of low adobe houses, "beckoning to cowboys, miners, woodchoppers, teamsters, and gamblers."[67]

The drinking age in Nevada is twenty-one which would suggest that younger males would be excluded, since most of the brothels are licensed to sell alcohol. Included in the local rules often is that no one under twenty-one will be permitted on house premises, but minors are permitted in the houses in at least a half-dozen brothels in eastern Nevada, in spite of rules to the contrary in one town. They are excluded from the bar, however, and must meet with prostitutes in a separate room. Lyon County, with four houses and an extensive ordinance regulating prostitution, only prohibits those under eighteen.[68] Three of these brothels have no bars, so there is no problem with drinking by minors.

In Battle Mountain this arrangement has worked without incident over the years and for the good of the community, according to law enforcement officers and locals. They say the brothels have provided a "place to learn," and help to keep the town's teenage girls from getting pregnant. Knowledgeable residents estimate that eighty percent or more of male high school graduates have been to the town's two houses. In Ely those under twenty-one formerly were permitted to enter the houses, but rules are being instituted to prohibit them.


## VISIBILITY

The visible impact of brothels in Nevada is small, not only because of their small numbers, generally low-visibility locations, and numerous restrictions placed on prostitutes, but also because none has a conspicuous sign giving directions to its location. The state statutes provide that it is unlawful to advertise in a public theater, on public streets of any town or city, or on the highway, any "resort where females congregate for the purposes of illicit intercourse."[69] A few ordinances, such as the detailed one for Lyon County, also prohibit advertising.[70] In addition to the legal restrictions, however, brothel owners are aware that their continuing existence is a function of local image, and they try to maintain at least an acceptable facade. They donate freely to Little League, school, and other fund-raising activities.[71]

Although the red-light districts are patrolled frequently and a county ordinance may include a "consent to search" if reason is given, there are relatively few problems with the brothels. Some law enforcement officers claim that there are many fewer disorder complaints related to brothels than to other bars or gaming houses. There is almost a paranoia regarding narcotics in brothels, to the extent that some houses refuse to permit the entry of "long hairs" or hippies. The fear of being closed for even a minor infraction of the law is real. When a girl was caught selling marijuana in one of Ely's houses recently, the house was closed for thirty days and the girl was banished from the county.

Prostitutes must be fingerprinted and registered with the police upon beginning work. They must carry a work card at all times. An attempt is made to discover if they have police records, until recently through the Federal Bureau of Investigation. A bad record or any violation of local rules by a prostitute could result in her permanent expulsion from a county.

In smaller towns residents claim that they know who the prostitutes are, and that they are distinguishable on the streets. This is a function of town size, familiarity with residents, and dress and grooming. Prostitutes who have been permitted to attend local events, such as rodeos or auto racing, have caused indignation because of their scanty or suggestive dress. Battle Mountain in its written rules specifies that "no girl shall be allowed uptown in bikinis, bathing suits, etc.," costumes which are common dress in all of the state's brothels during working hours. Some girls claim the problem comes in the interpretation of "etc." No short skirts may be worn, and on occasion they have been told to wear pants. In Winnemucca the Chief of Police has refused to issue work permits to girls "improperly" dressed.

At a smaller scale, the visible impact from signs and brothel names is greater. Nearly half of the houses have suggestive names, such as "Cottontail Ranch," "Coyote Springs Ranch," "Players Club," "Villa Joy," "Valley of Love," and "Moonlight Ranch." At a still smaller scale the calling cards and the interiors of bars are even more explicit. "Donna's Bar" in Wells makes an ecological pun is noting that it is a "Sportsman's Paradise," for the deer hunters and fishermen who frequent the area and houses. Bar walls are frequently decorated with nude pictures or posters and signs with sexual puns.

## ATTITUDES TOWARD PROSTITUTION

An overwhelming majority of those who live with open or legalized prostitution in Nevada favor its presence. This positive attitude is expressed in the news media and by law enforcement officers and people of all socioeconomic classes. In a 1972 newspaper poll in Yerington, where prostitution is illegal, twenty-nine of thirty people interviewed wanted it legalized.[72] In 1967 the sheriff owned the two brothels of Battle Mountain.[73] The challenger, who is currently in office, privately polled a large proportion of the community regarding their views on prostitution, with the idea that he would run on a platform opposing it. Less than ten percent of the community were against it; most favored it. The issue was not raised in his campaign. The major opposition comes from fundamentalist church groups, and especially new ministers who have not previously encountered open prostitution. Legislators occasionally express the apparent indignation of a small, active constituency.[74]

A variety of reasons is given in support of prostitution. Three clusters of responses in decreasing order of importance are: 1) the control factor; 2) the historical factor; and 3) the image. The reasons given may not always conform to fact, but discrepancies between belief and reality are largely irrelevant, since it is perceived and not demonstrated fact that determines the viability of prostitution.

The principal argument in favor of prostitution is control; this can be divided into spatial and nonspatial sets of reasons. Among the spatial reasons is the frequently encountered belief that it is better to restrict prostitution to one area of town than to have it everywhere. Since it is assumed that prostitution will exist whether or not it is wanted, it is preferable to confine it, to keep it off the streets and out of the casinos. A related view is expressed by law enforcement people, who often claim they have fewer complaints of disorderly conduct from the houses than from other establishments which serve alcohol and are thought to be comparable. Seen in this light, brothels are not so much good in and of themselves as they are better than alternative institutions.

One common attitude is that controlled prostitution is responsible for diminishing the incidence of rape and other violent crimes. Over a six-year period there have been no proven cases of rape in Battle Mountain and only one may have occurred, but in nearby Austin, which is one-fourth the size of Battle Mountain, two or three cases have been proven.[75] A police officer in Winnemucca was less certain about this supposed relationship, however, stating that there had been recent cases of rape in Winnemucca, and that in his mind rape has little to do with the presence of brothels.

Parents sometimes state that prostitution keeps their sons from being forced into an early marriage, from getting venereal disease, or that it keeps their daughters "out of trouble." A few even argue that brothels are educational for their sons. Lastly, control of venereal disease is seen as a commendable aspect of the brothels. Townspeople know that the prostitutes are required to have frequent medical examinations, and they will state that outbreaks of venereal disease usually do not come from brothels.

The historical factor is perhaps the most fundamental. Many towns have had brothels as long as most people can remember, and they are as much a part of the town as the drugstore, the post office, and the railroad station. Townspeople may say they only tolerate prostitution, yet they have no strong feelings against it, and may go on to say that they can remember the brothels as children. One suspects that they are prepared to defend the continuance of controlled prostitution if only because it has been present for so long.

The third attitude supporting prostitution is the brothels' image. Madams make a good livelihood, and are keenly aware that they are subject to the changing attitudes of the city council and the community. Madams are respected citizens. They place restrictions on their girls to avoid problems, and they give generously to community activities. These facts are common knowledge, and are important in the local image of brothels. Image, history, and the perceived importance of control thus combine to provide widespread public support for open and legal prostitution. The basic question about prostitution is not whether it will exist, but what form it will take. I am convinced that the "Nevada approach" has considerable merit. The people of Nevada think so too.

## NOTES

1. I have used a standard set of terms. "Brothel" and "house" (short for house of prostitution) are used by the Nevada State Department of Health, Welfare, are Rehabilitation. When grouped together, brothels are referred to as "the line" or the red-light district. "The line" was commonly used in the nineteenth century to refer to the row or line of "cribs," an imitation of the crib streets of New Orleans. A crib was a small confining shack with a bed, coal stove, small dresser, and wash bowl. A prostitute would put her name over the door, a feature which still exists in the sense that nearly half of Nevada's brothels have the Christian name of the madam. "Prostitute" is in common use in statute and ordinances, although other terms such as "entertainer" may be encountered. "Girl" is frequently used in quasi-legal city and county regulations and in brothels. In brothels the girls are addressed by spurious Christian names both by madams and by customers. I have used "girl" and "prostitute" interchangeably, no special meaning being attached to either. It is relatively rare for a girl to refer to herself as a prostitute, and she will refer to another girl as a prostitute in a disparaging way; Charles Winick and Paul M. Kinsie, *The Lively Commerce: Prostitution in the United States* (New York: New American Library, 1971), p. 44. "Madam" is a general rubric for brothel owner, bartender, and brothel maid unless otherwise noted. These three terms are not synonymous, although brothel owner, bartender, and madam are often the same person. A maid or bartender often acts as the madam while the madam, who is often the owner, is busy,

especially during the day when business is slow. In some cases the owner is a male who employs a madam to run the house, and does little more than take care of finances. In a few cases, the owner is a male who tends bar, encourages customers to choose a girl, and thereby acts as house "madam." Some of the owner-madams resent being referred to as madam, and prefer to be called either by their Christian name or their full name. In law, and in community and self-perception, madams are more respectable than prostitutes, even though they may once have been prostitutes. Prostitution in Las Vegas and Reno not only is illegal, but may involve a different kind of girl, higher paying clients, a pimp stratum, a lack of police protection, and none of the explicit spatial and other regulations imposed on brothels. The places of interest in this paper vary in size from 500 to 8,000, and "town" will refer to any population center within this size range.

2. Reno had its stockade or "Bull-pen;" Ronald D. Miller, *Shady Ladies of the West* (Los Angeles: Westernlore, 1964), p. 152.

3. Harry S. Drago, *Notorious Ladies of the Frontier* (New York: Dodd, 1969), p. 72.

4. Drago, op. cit., footnote 3, p. 129.

5. Drago, op. cit., footnote 3, p. 219.

6. Letter from Virgil A. Bucchianeri, District Attorney, Storey County.

7. Winick and Kinsie, op. cit., footnote 1, pp. 47, 69, and 97; and *Ely City Ordinance*, Sec. 15.27.

8. *Nevada Revised Statutes, 1971*, Vol. 7, Title 20, Ch. 244.345.

9. *Nevada Revised Statutes*, op. cit., footnote 8, Ch. 269.175.

10. *Lincoln County Ordinance No. 1971-4 and No. 1973-6; Lyon County Ordinance No. 77; Esmeralda County Ordinance No. 124; Lander County Ordinance LC 6-72; Winnemucca Municipal Code, 1973;* and *White Pine County Code, 1971.*

11. *Washoe County Ordinance No. 137; Carson City Municipal Code, 1973; Churchill County Ordinance No. 25;* and *Douglas County Ordinances.*

12. This interpretation is from Virgil A. Bucchianeri, District Attorney of Storey County.

13. *Churchill County Ordinance No. 25,* op. cit., footnote 11.

14. *Carson City Municipal Code,* op. cit., footnote 11.

15. *Fallon City Ordinance*, Sec.s 18.6 to 18.16.

16. *Fallon City Ordinance,* op. cit., footnote 15.

17. *Clark County Ordinance No. 408.*

18. *Letters from Earnhart W. Thran, Douglas County Clerk and Treasurer; Grace Bell, Humboldt County Clerk;* and *Joan Shangle, City Clerk, Eureka.*

19. *Letter from William M. Edwards, Chief Community Health Services, Division of Health, Department of Health, Welfare, and Rehabilitation, State of Nevada, to Lander County Commissioners, September 1972.*

20. *Nevada State Journal,* April 13, 1972; a longtime state sanitation engineer who had knowledge of the brothels over a long period of time knew of no epidemic which originated in them; W. Wallace White, *Caring for the Environment: My Work with Public Health and Reclamation in Nevada* (Reno: University of Nevada, 1970), p. 177. Venereal disease may be largely eliminated within

brothels; Harry Benjamin and R.E.L. Masters, *Prostitution and Morality* (New York: The Julian Press, 1964), p. 240.

21. Bill Erickson, *Nevada Playmates: A Guide to the Cathouses,* 4th edition (San Francisco: Bangkok, 1973), p. 30.

22. The minimum price in a brothel is ten to fifteen dollars for fifteen minutes of simple intercourse timed on an alarm clock. Higher prices depend on what a client requests and how much time he wishes to spend with a girl. Call girls are usually much more expensive; Winick and Kinsie, op. cit., footnote 1, p. 158.

23. *Lander County Ordinance LC 6-72,* op. cit., footnote 10; *Pershing County Ordinance No. 53; Elko County Ordinance 1971-G;* and *Lincoln County Ordinance No. 1972-6,* op. cit., footnote 10.

24. *Carlin Town Ordinance No. 1.*

25. *Winnemucca Municipal Code, 1973,* op. cit., footnote 10, Sec. 20.210.

26. *Ely City Ordinance,* op. cit., footnote 7, Sec. 15.10.

27. *Winnemucca Municipal Code, 1973,* op. cit., footnote 10; and *Ely City Ordinance,* op. cit., footnote 7, Sec. 15.26.

28. *Ely City Ordinance,* op. cit., footnote 7.

29. *Nevada Revised Statutes,* op. cit., footnote 8, Chs. 201.380, 201.390.

30. *White Pine County Code, 1971,* op. cit., footnote 10, Sec. 4.12.120.

31. *Ely City Ordinance,* op. cit., footnote 7, Sec. 15.27.

32. *Esmeralda County Ordinance No. 124,* op. cit., footnote 10, Secs. 2, 3.

33. *Esmeralda County Ordinance No. 124,* op. cit., footnote 10, Secs. 8, 10.

34. *Lyon County Ordinance No. 77,* op. cit., footnote 10, Sec. 2.

35. *Lyon County Ordinance No. 77,* op. cit., footnote 10, Secs. 6 and 12.

36. *Lyon County Ordinance No. 77,* op. cit., footnote 10, Secs. 9, 13, and 14.

37. *Lyon County Ordinance No. 77,* op. cit., footnote 10, Sec. 8.

38. Bucchianeri, op. cit., footnote 6; *Wells Emergency Ordinance No. 24;* and Russell R. Elliott, *History of Nevada* (Lincoln: University of Nebraska, 1973), pp. 313 ff.

39. Interview with Bobby, madam of "Bobby's Buckeye Bar," Tonopah, Nevada, July 20, 1973.

40. White, op. cit., footnote 20, p. 175.

41. *Wells Emergency Ordinance No. 24,* op. cit., footnote 38.

42. *Wells Emergency Ordinance No. 24,* op. cit., footnote 38.

43. Bell, op. cit., footnote 18.

44. Elliott, op. cit., footnote 38, p. 313.

45. Elliott, op. cit., footnote 38; and Edna B. Patterson, Louise A. Ulph, and Victor Goodwin, *Nevada's Northeast Frontier* (Sparks, Nevada: Western Printing, 1969), p. 565.

46. *Reno Evening Gazette,* October 9, 1971.

47. *Reno Evening Gazette,* August 30, 1971.

48. *Las Vegas Review-Journal,* September 2, 1973.

49. Lucius Morris Beebe, "Sincere Sinning of the One Sound State," *Saturday Review,* October 20, 1962, pp. 48-49 and 63.

50. *Nevada State Journal,* March 22, 1973.

51. *Look,* June 29, 1971, pp. 34–36; and "Joe Conforte, Crusading Pimp," *Rolling Stone,* No. 122 (November 23, 1972), pp. 26–32.

52. In Esmeralda County, the license fee for running a brothel is $100 a year; *Esmeralda County Ordinance No. 124,* op. cit., footnote 10 Sec. 1. Lyon County charges a minimum fee of $6,000 a year; if a brothel has more than six prostitutes the fee is $12,000; *Lyon County Ordinance No. 77,* op. cit., footnote 10 Sec. 11. In Storey County a brothel pays a license fee of between $20,000 and $25,000 a year; Bucchianeri, op. cit., footnote 6; *Nevada State Journal,* March 22, 1973; and *Reno Evening Gazette,* May 20, 1972.

53. *Reno Evening Gazette,* May 20, 1972.

54. Erickson, op. cit., footnote 21, p. 35.

55. I visited every brothel in the state thought to be operating as of July, 1973. Field work was facilitated by *The Official Guide to the "Legalized" Brothels in the State of Nevada* (Las Vegas: The Ivy House, 1972); and the more widely distributed Erickson, op. cit., footnote 21.

56. I entered all but two of the brothels in 1973, and determined the number of girls in a house by discussion with a madam or girl; by observation, especially at night; by counting the number of alarm clocks which were occasionally visible—each girl has one to determine time spent with a client; and where necessary, by using or comparing the figures in Erickson, op. cit., footnote 21, which were quite reliable. The number of prostitutes in a house at any given time varies as much as 200 to 300 percent, since turnover is high and some girls are usually on vacation.

57. One facet of brothels which flusters many customers when they enter for the first time is that services are paid for on the basis of time spent with a girl. In one of the larger houses in this group, unlike elsewhere, time begins to run when the money exchanges hands, not when the services begin.

58. *Rolling Stone,* op. cit., footnote 51, p. 32.

59. Winick and Kinsie, op. cit., footnote 1, p. 43.

60. See, for example, Winick and Kinsie, op. cit., footnote 1, pp. 17, 22, 53, and 246; and Kate Millett, *The Prostitution Papers: A Candid Dialogue* (New York: Avon, 1973). pp. 55 and 127. Even popular sources of questionable value make the same point; Xaveria Hollander, *The Happy Hooker* (New York: Dell, 1972), p. 176. Winick and Kinsie, pp. 42 and 247, note that black prostitutes usually seek white customers, and that until recently prostitution has been the major source of interracial sex.

61. The law enforcement officer who gave me access to these data had doubts concerning my right to see them, and I agreed not to reveal the town where they were obtained.

62. The discussion which follows is based on a number of written rules and regulations, and interviews with sheriffs, chiefs of police, madams, and prostitutes.

63. *Rolling Stone,* op. cit., footnote 51, p. 30.

64. Erickson, op. cit., footnote 21.

65. *The Official Guide . . . ,* op. cit., footnote 55.

66. The house usually receives less than fifty percent of what the girls charge, and the girls receive the rest.

67. Patterson et al., op. cit., footnote 45, p. 544.

68. *Lyon County Ordinance No. 77,* op. cit., footnote 10, Sec. 14.

69. *Nevada Revised Statutes,* op. cit., footnote 8, Chs. 201.430 and 201.440.

70. *Lyon County Ordinance No. 77,* op. cit., footnote 10.

71. White, op. cit., footnote 20, p. 174.

72. *Reno Evening Gazette,* March 18, 1972.

73. Interview with George E. Schwin, Sheriff of Lander County, July 28, 1973.

74. *Nevada State Journal,* March 22, 1973; and *Reno Evening Gazette,* May 20, 1972.

75. Schwin, op. cit., footnote 73; and T. David Horton, attorney, Battle Mountain, July 28, 1973.

# WOMEN
# AS VICTIMS
# OF CRIME

---

# PART TWO

# VICTIMIZING WOMEN

Studies about the victimization of women have been as rarely conducted as studies of the criminality of women. Only in the last decade has substantial attention been given to the crime of heterosexual rape, and wife beating is not yet fully understood. Robbery, theft, and other crimes committed against women are hardly ever mentioned in the research literature. Instead, descriptions of these crimes usually depend upon the victimization of men, and the authors then state their conclusions as if they apply to both genders. We do not yet know to what extent this is true.

The first systematic collection of data on the victimization of women was carried out as part of the National Crime Survey Program performed under the sponsorship of the Law Enforcement Assistance Administration. These studies, conducted nationally on an annual basis and in 26 selected cities less frequently, allow us to compare male and female victimization with respect to all major crimes except homicide. Although these survey data do not permit us to understand the way in which crimes against women are carried out (the phenomenology of female victimization), they do give us supporting information that is very useful. For example, they tell us what proportion of the offenders in the crime were strangers to the victim, what protective measures the victim took, and the degree of injury sustained by the victim.

In the following article, Bowker surveys the results of the National Crime Survey Program as they apply to women. It is clear from these surveys that women are less likely to be victimized than men, overall. The only two major crimes for which they are more likely to be victimized than men are rape and crimes of theft with contact (of which purse snatching is a good example). In general, the female-male difference in victimization is smaller for property crimes than for crimes of violence.

It would be misleading to think of women as uniformly safer from criminal victimization than men, for certain categories of women are much more likely to be victimized than other categories of men. For example, young women between the ages of 12 and 19 are much more likely to suffer property and violent crime victimization than men age 65 and over. It is also true that women who have been separated or divorced may suffer higher rates of certain crimes than men who are married, and that black women living in high crime areas will suffer higher rates of almost all crimes than white men living in low crime areas. Considering these facts, we should be very careful in applying the generalization that men suffer higher levels of criminal victimization than women to any specific group of women in the United States.

The reason that generalizations about the victimization of women cannot be uniformly applied to all women is that there are substantial differences in the rates of victimization among different groups of women. The National Crime Surveys show that young women are much more likely to be victimized than older women, with the victimization rate generally declining throughout the life span. Black women are more likely to suffer crimes of violence than white women or women of Spanish origin, but white women are more likely to suffer crimes of theft than women of other ethnic or racial groups. Victimization rates are higher in urban areas than in rural areas. Finally, women who have been separated or divorced are much more likely to suffer all categories of criminal victimization that women who are currently married or widowed.

The supporting data collected by the National Crime Surveys undermine many of the stereotypes about female victimization that are current in the literature. Although it is true that women are more likely to be victimized by friends, relatives, neighbors, and acquaintances than men, it is not true that they protect these offenders more than men do. The truth of the matter is that women are more likely than men to report victimization by nonstrangers to the police.

Another stereotype is that women are much less likely to protect themselves than men. Again, the facts fail to support the stereotype. The National Crime Survey reports that 68 percent of the women and 66 percent of the men who suffered a violent criminal victimization in 1976 took measures to protect themselves. They differed in the methods used, but not in their willingness to resist the aggressor in the crime.

It is fair to say that we cannot afford to accept any generalizations about the victimization of women without sufficient objective evidence. There are far too many sexist stereotypes about women for us to even trust our own judgment about this subject. The article in this section gives us a scientific basis for understanding of the victimization of women.

TEN

# Women as Victims: An Examination of the Results of L.E.A.A.'s National Crime Survey Program*

LEE H. BOWKER

The Law Enforcement Assistance Administration has been collecting victimization data since 1972 in selected cities and since 1973 for the nation as a whole. Two dozen reports have been issued to date on these self-report victimization surveys, all of which include at least a few breakdowns of victimization data by gender of victim. What do these reports tell us about the victimization of women in America? This article summarizes descriptive data on female victimization from these reports and analyzes trends from the earliest to the most recent surveys. Differences between male and female victimization experiences are highlighted. Propositions derived from 172 National Crime survey city data by Hindelang, Gottfredson, and Garofalo are found to be consistent with data from the 1973-76 National Crime Survey national samples. The article concludes with a comment on the implications of the patterns of female victimization for the criminal justice system.

After a series of pretests, the National Crime Survey program began with interviews of samples of citizens in Atlanta, Baltimore, Cleveland, Dallas, Denver, Newark, Portland (Oregon), and St. Louis in July 1972, covering the period from mid-1971 to approximately mid-1972. Chicago, Detroit, Los Angeles, New York, and Philadelphia were surveyed in 1973 to yield statistics for a period roughly corresponding to 1972. Thirteen other major American cities were surveyed in 1974, and then the first 13 cities were resurveyed during the first half of 1975 to provide comparative data on criminal victimization over a 2- or 3-year interval. When the city studies were under way, the Law Enforcement Assistance Administration turned to an annual series of national studies of criminal victimization. The national samples were selected separately from the city samples and used a somewhat different methodological design. The first national sample yielded victimization data for 1973. By mid-1979, 4

*Revision of a paper delivered at the annual meeting of the Academy of Criminal Justice Sciences, 1979.

years of detailed victimization data had been published (United States, Law Enforcement Assistance Administration, 1976b, 1977b, 1977c, 1979). A number of other reports derived from the National Crime Survey program were published in 1977, among which were two on public opinions and attitudes about crime and the police (Garofalo, 1977a, 1977b). Although the early NCS reports had only a single table that listed women separately from men, they rapidly improved, with the most recent annual report containing 18 tables displaying specific victimization information for women.

## METHODOLOGY OF THE NATIONAL CRIME SURVEY[1]

In each of the 26 cities surveyed, housing units were randomly selected using data from the 1970 census and a complex stratified sampling design. The exact sample sizes varied from city to city, the average being about 10,000 households, which yielded approximately 22,000 eligible respondents. In Milwaukee, for example, the sampling design produced interviews with 23,495 residents age 12 and over, living in 10,734 housing units (United States, Law Enforcement Assistance Administration, 1977i). A larger number of housing units (12,069) had originally been selected for inclusion in the sample, but 1,119 were vacant, demolished, unoccupied, or otherwise inappropriate for the survey. Of the remaining housing units, 216 did not result in interviews because of subject unavailability or unwillingness to cooperate, which means that 98 percent of the eligible housing units produced at least one interview. A total of 23,688 eligible individuals were identified in the 10,734 housing units, of which 99 percent (23,495) contributed completed interviews to the survey—an amazingly high response rate. Although Milwaukee, like the other 25 and the national samples, also included a survey of businesses, these surveys are excluded from the present discussion because they are not broken down by gender of victim.

The national surveys use multi-stage random samples that ultimately select clusters of approximately four housing units, so that each housing unit in America has an equal probability of being included in the sample. Because many types of crime occur infrequently and because the statistics derived from the survey are analyzed using several control variables at once, it is necessary to secure a very large national sample—nothing like the small samples that habitually predict correctly the winners in presidential elections. The sampling design used in the national surveys yields a sample of approximately 60,000 households and 136,000 individuals. As with the city surveys, the national surveys have been blessed with extremely high response rates. Approximately 96 percent of all eligible housing units produce at least one interview, and 98 percent of all eligible residents within the selected housing units cooperate fully with the survey.

Interviewing 136,000 individuals at the same time would require a huge staff, which would then have nothing to do between surveys. This problem and others are solved in the national surveys by interviewing the individuals in 10,000 housing units each month for 6 months, by which time the entire sample has been completed. Since the same housing units are revisited every 6 months, this results in a continuous flow of approximately 23,000 interviews per month. Each housing unit is visited seven times over a 3-year period, and is then replaced. Because pretests revealed a tendency for victims to telescope victimizations that occurred before the reporting period into the current reporting period, thus artificially inflating victimization rates, the first of the seven interviews does not count in the victimization data. Instead, it is used in a bounding procedure wherein any crimes reported in the second interview that were already reported in the first interview are eliminated from the official count of victimization incidents. This procedure is also used with each successive interview in the series. Unfortunately, since the sample is technically composed of households rather than individuals, subjects leaving their household are not reinterviewed, and new subjects moving into a household in the sample during the 3-year panel period cannot be subjected to the bounding procedure.

## THE VICTIMIZATION OF WOMEN IN AMERICA

Table 1 presents data on the basic categories of criminal victimization for men and women in 1973, 1974, 1975, and 1976. Crimes of violence against women slowly rose during 1973–1976, while crimes of violence against men declined slightly. Personal crimes of theft peaked for men in 1974 and declined slowly, but the personal theft rate continued to rise for women throughout this period. These figures, like other statistics discussed in this paper, cover too short a period to be taken as indicative of any major trends in victimization phenomena over time.

Men are subject to personal crimes of theft at a rate about 25 percent higher than women and to violent crimes at nearly twice the rate suffered by women. The only exceptions to this general pattern are that crimes of theft with contact are slightly more likely to be committed against women and that rape victimization statistics are dominated by

**Table 1.** *Personal Crime Victimization Rates[a] for Persons Age 12 and Over, by Sex of Victims, 1973–1976*

| TYPE OF CRIME | FEMALE | | | | MALE | | | |
|---|---|---|---|---|---|---|---|---|
| | 1973 | 1974 | 1975 | 1976 | 1973 | 1974 | 1975 | 1976 |
| Crimes of violence | 21.6 | 21.7 | 23.0 | 23.1 | 44.1 | 45.1 | 43.6 | 42.9 |
| Rape | 1.8 | 1.8 | 1.7 | 1.4 | 0.1 | 0.0 | 0.1 | 0.2 |
| Robbery | 3.8 | 4.3 | 4.0 | 4.0 | 9.9 | 10.3 | 9.8 | 9.1 |
| with injury | 1.5 | 1.4 | 1.3 | 1.6 | 3.3 | 3.3 | 3.0 | 2.6 |
| without injury | 2.3 | 2.8 | 2.7 | 2.4 | 6.7 | 7.0 | 6.7 | 6.5 |
| Assault | 16.1 | 15.6 | 17.3 | 17.6 | 34.1 | 34.8 | 33.7 | 33.6 |
| Aggravated | 5.2 | 5.2 | 5.4 | 5.7 | 15.2 | 16.0 | 14.2 | 14.4 |
| Simple | 10.9 | 10.4 | 11.9 | 11.9 | 19.0 | 18.8 | 19.6 | 19.2 |
| Crimes of theft | 80.3 | 82.3 | 84.9 | 86.8 | 102.9 | 108.7 | 108.1 | 106.2 |
| with contact | 3.4 | 3.2 | 3.3 | 3.2 | 2.6 | 3.0 | 2.9 | 2.5 |
| without contact | 76.8 | 79.1 | 81.7 | 83.6 | 100.2 | 105.7 | 105.2 | 103.7 |
| Total personal crimes | 101.9 | 104.0 | 107.9 | 109.9 | 147.0 | 153.8 | 151.7 | 149.1 |

Sources: *Criminal Victimization in the United States, A Comparison of 1975 and 1976 Findings* (Washington, D.C.: U.S. Government Printing Office, 1977; *Criminal Victimization in the United States, A Comparison of 1973 and 1974 Findings* (Washington, D.C.: U.S. Government Printing Office, 1976).

[a]Rates are per 1,000 persons age 12 and over.

women. The crimes in which the absolute male-female difference is largest are robbery without injury and aggravated assault. The rates for these two crimes in 1976 were 6.5 and 14.4 per 1,000 for men and 2.4 and 5.7 per 1,000 for women. Although male victimization is quite a bit higher than female victimization, there are numerous categories of women (for example, black women and women age 16–19) for which victimization rates for some crimes are higher than they are for men in general.

Some women are much more likely to be victimized than others. In Tables 2, 3, and 4, female victimization is successively broken down by age, race/ethnicity, and marital status. Women age 16–24 are much more likely to suffer a violent crime victimization than women age 25 and over or women age 12–15. For crimes of theft, women age 12–15 are the prime targets, and the victimization rates are inversely proportional to age of victim. Looking at the four years presented in Table 2, we can see a considerable amount of variation from year to year in the age category suffering the highest victimization rates for each type of crime. Only robbery is completely consistent, with women age 20–24 experiencing the highest rate of any age groups appearing in four years. Despite these inconsistencies, a number of clear trends can be observed in the data. Violent crimes are up for women age 16–19, which is due to a considerable increase in the assault rate for these young women. Personal crimes of theft are down sharply for women age 12–15, inconsistent for age 16–19, and increasing for women age 20 and over. The age group experiencing the sharpest rise is 25–34, for which the personal theft rate rose from 86.6 in 1973 to 90.1 in 1974, 95.2 in 1975, and 104.7 in 1976.

As Table 3 shows, blacks are consistently more likely to be victimized than whites for rape, robbery, and assault, and therefore for crimes of violence in general. They are also generally more heavily subject to

**Table 2.** *Personal Crime Victimization Rates$^a$ for Women Age 12 and Over, by Age of Victims, 1973–76.*

| AGE | 1973 | 1974 | 1975 | 1976 |
|---|---|---|---|---|
| Rape | | | | |
| 12–15 | 1.3 | 2.7 | 1.6 | 2.1 |
| 16–19 | 4.6 | 4.9 | 4.7 | 4.0 |
| 20–24 | 6.2 | 4.0 | 4.7 | 4.2 |
| 25–34 | 2.4 | 2.5 | 2.3 | 2.2 |
| 35–49 | 0.4$^b$ | 0.4$^b$ | 0.4$^2$ | 0.1$^b$ |
| 50–64 | 0.1$^b$ | 0.6 | 0.4$^2$ | 0.1$^b$ |
| 65 and over | 0.2$^b$ | 0.1$^b$ | 0.1$^2$ | 0.0$^b$ |
| Robbery | | | | |
| 12–15 | 3.3 | 5.2 | 5.2 | 3.3 |
| 16–19 | 4.5 | 5.5 | 4.5 | 5.6 |
| 20–24 | 5.9 | 6.4 | 7.3 | 8.0 |
| 25–34 | 4.0 | 5.2 | 3.7 | 4.5 |
| 35–49 | 3.2 | 3.5 | 3.5 | 3.5 |
| 50–64 | 2.6 | 3.0 | 2.5 | 3.2 |
| 65 and over | 4.3 | 3.0 | 3.4 | 1.7 |
| Assault | | | | |
| 12–15 | 31.3 | 27.7 | 34.1 | 31.2 |
| 16–19 | 30.1 | 32.7 | 32.7 | 37.9 |
| 20–24 | 33.5 | 26.6 | 31.4 | 32.9 |
| 25–34 | 17.1 | 20.4 | 20.9 | 22.0 |
| 35–49 | 12.5 | 11.0 | 11.9 | 12.0 |
| 50–64 | 5.2 | 4.5 | 6.7 | 5.6 |
| 65 and over | 2.4 | 3.7 | 3.0 | 2.5 |
| Crime of violence | | | | |
| 12–15 | 35.8 | 35.6 | 40.9 | 36.6 |
| 16–19 | 39.2 | 43.0 | 41.9 | 47.5 |
| 20–24 | 45.6 | 37.0 | 43.5 | 45.1 |

violent-crime victimization than residents of Spanish origin (mostly
Puerto Ricans and Mexican-Americans). When it comes to personal
property crimes, whites are more heavily victimized, with blacks and
those of Spanish origin suffering approximately 15 percent fewer victimizations. In the period from 1973 to 1976, the only steadily declining
statistic is for rapes of white women. General increases appear among
blacks for rape, robbery, total crimes of violence, total personal crimes
of theft, and total personal crimes; among Spanish-Americans for rape;
and among whites for crimes of theft and total personal crimes. In general, black and white women are continuing to experience rising crime
rates, with crime against Spanish-American women showing a rise up to

**Table 2.** *Personal Crime Victimization Rates[a] for Women Age 12 and Over, by Age of Victims, 1973-76. (continued)*

| AGE | 1973 | 1974 | 1975 | 1976 |
|---|---|---|---|---|
| 25–34 | 23.4 | 27.9 | 26.8 | 28.7 |
| 35–49 | 16.1 | 14.9 | 15.9 | 15.5 |
| 50–64 | 7.8 | 8.2 | 9.6 | 9.0 |
| 65 and over | 6.9 | 7.0 | 6.5 | 4.2 |
| Crimes of theft | | | | |
| 12–15 | 158.3 | 155.8 | 143.8 | 138.7 |
| 16–19 | 139.1 | 136.7 | 145.7 | 137.7 |
| 20–24 | 113.6 | 121.5 | 125.6 | 128.9 |
| 25–34 | 86.6 | 90.1 | 95.2 | 104.7 |
| 35–49 | 69.4 | 74.6 | 77.9 | 79.4 |
| 50–64 | 45.5 | 44.6 | 47.7 | 52.5 |
| 65 and over | 18.1 | 20.2 | 22.7 | 22.3 |
| Total personal crimes | | | | |
| 12–15 | 194.1 | 191.4 | 184.7 | 175.3 |
| 16–19 | 178.3 | 179.7 | 187.6 | 185.2 |
| 20–24 | 159.2 | 158.5 | 169.1 | 174.0 |
| 25–34 | 110.0 | 118.0 | 111.1 | 133.4 |
| 35–49 | 85.5 | 89.5 | 93.8 | 94.9 |
| 50–64 | 53.3 | 52.8 | 57.3 | 61.5 |
| 65 and over | 25.0 | 27.2 | 29.2 | 26.5 |

Sources: *Criminal Victimization in the United States, A Comparison of 1975 and 1976 Findings* (Washington, D.C.: U.S. Government Printing Office, 1977); *Criminal Victimization in the United States, A Comparison of 1973 and 1974 Findings* (Washington, D.C.: U.S. Government Printing Office, 1976).

[a]Rates are per 1,000 women.
[b]Estimates based on about 10 or less sample cases are statistically unreliable.

1975 and then a decline. White and black women are equally victimized, but the nature of the victimization varies, with blacks being higher on violent crime and whites suffering more personal property crime.

Much has been written about the difficulties of divorce or separation for women. Most women are aware of the loss of income and social contacts that accompany a divorce. How many of them are equally aware that as compared with married women, separated or divorced

**Table 3.** *Personal Crime Victimization Rates[a] for Women Age 12 and Over, by Race/Ethnicity, 1973–1976.*

| RACE/ETHNICITY | 1973 | 1974 | 1975 | 1976 |
|---|---|---|---|---|
| Rape | | | | |
| White | 1.7 | 1.6 | 1.6 | 1.2 |
| Black | 2.6 | 3.7 | 1.8 | 3.2 |
| Spanish origin | 1.2[b] | 0.9[b] | 2.1[b] | 2.4 |
| Robbery | | | | |
| White | 3.3 | 3.7 | 3.5 | 3.4 |
| Black | 7.1 | 8.8 | 7.6 | 8.2 |
| Spanish origin | 3.4 | 4.3 | 5.3 | 4.1 |
| Assault | | | | |
| White | 15.4 | 15.2 | 16.3 | 16.7 |
| Black | 22.0 | 16.4 | 24.8 | 24.2 |
| Spanish origin | 17.1 | 14.7 | 22.5 | 16.2 |
| Crimes of violence | | | | |
| White | 20.4 | 20.5 | 21.5 | 21.4 |
| Black | 31.7 | 28.9 | 34.2 | 35.7 |
| Spanish origin | 21.7 | 19.9 | 29.9 | 22.7 |
| Crimes of theft | | | | |
| White | 81.8 | 83.9 | 87.0 | 88.4 |
| Black | 70.4 | 66.9 | 73.3 | 75.4 |
| Spanish origin | 69.6 | 75.2 | 69.1 | 73.2 |
| Total personal crimes | | | | |
| White | 102.2 | 106.4 | 108.5 | 109.8 |
| Black | 102.1 | 95.8 | 107.5 | 111.1 |
| Spanish origin | 91.3 | 95.1 | 99.0 | 95.9 |

Sources: *Criminal Victimization in the United States, A Comparison of 1975 and 1976 Findings* (Washington, D.C.: U.S. Government Printing Office, 1977); *Criminal Victimization in the United States, A Comparison of 1973 and 1974 Findings* (Washington, D.C.: U.S. Government Printing Office, 1976).

[a] Rates are per 1,000 women.
[b] Estimates are based on 10 or less sample cases are statistically unreliable.

women are about six times as likely to be raped or robbed, five times as likely to be assaulted, and 60 percent more likely to suffer personal crimes of theft? Women who have never married are also much more likely to be victimized than married women, but they exceeded the victimization level among divorced or separated women only for rape in 1976 and for personal crimes of theft in 1973–1976. Widowed women have the lowest rates for all crimes. Although marital status exerts an independent effect upon victimization, part of the pattern shown in Table 4 is an indirect effect of differential age-specific crime rates, since women who have never married tend to be young (where victimization is high) and widowed women tend to be elderly (where victimization is low). Overall, crimes against married women and separated or divorced women are rising, while crimes against women who have never married or widowed women are holding steady.

**Table 4.** *Personal Crime Victimization Rates[a] for Women Age 12 and Over, by Marital Status, 1973–1976.*

| MARITAL STATUS | 1973 | 1974 | 1975 | 1976 |
|---|---|---|---|---|
| Rape | | | | |
| Never married | 3.8 | 3.6 | 3.1 | 3.5 |
| Married | 0.6 | 0.7 | 0.8 | 0.5 |
| Separated or divorced | 5.5 | 5.4 | 4.7 | 3.1 |
| Widowed | 0.6[b] | 1.0[b] | 0.5[b] | 0.3[b] |
| Robbery | | | | |
| Never married | 4.9 | 5.8 | 5.9 | 5.7 |
| Married | 2.5 | 2.7 | 2.3 | 2.3 |
| Separated or divorced | 9.8 | 10.9 | 9.9 | 14.1 |
| Widowed | 4.1 | 4.5 | 3.9 | 1.9 |
| Assault | | | | |
| Never married | 28.7 | 25.6 | 29.3 | 30.9 |
| Married | 8.3 | 9.1 | 9.5 | 9.5 |
| Separated or divorced | 50.0 | 45.6 | 50.2 | 49.1 |
| Widowed | 6.6 | 5.9 | 6.8 | 5.3 |
| Crimes of violence | | | | |
| Never married | 37.3 | 35.0 | 38.3 | 40.1 |
| Married | 11.4 | 12.5 | 12.6 | 12.2 |
| Separated or divorced | 65.3 | 61.9 | 64.8 | 66.3 |
| Widowed | 11.3 | 11.4 | 11.1 | 7.4 |
| Crimes of theft | | | | |
| Never married | 133.4 | 132.8 | 131.3 | 130.3 |
| Married | 63.7 | 67.9 | 70.2 | 72.4 |
| Separated or divorced | 100.0 | 97.7 | 107.7 | 117.5 |
| Widowed | 31.6 | 29.4 | 34.6 | 34.9 |

**Table 4.** *Personal Crime Victimization Rates[a] for Persons Age 12 and Over, by Marital Status, 1973–1976 (continued)*

| MARITAL STATUS | 1973 | 1974 | 1975 | 1976 |
|---|---|---|---|---|
| Total personal crimes | | | | |
| Never married | 170.7 | 167.8 | 169.6 | 170.1 |
| Married | 75.1 | 80.4 | 82.8 | 84.6 |
| Separated or divorced | 165.3 | 159.6 | 172.5 | 183.8 |
| Widowed | 42.9 | 40.8 | 45.7 | 42.3 |

Sources: *Criminal Victimization in the United States, A Comparison of 1975 and 1976 Findings* (Washington, D.C.: U.S. Government Printing Office, 1977); *Criminal Victimization in the United States, A Comparison of 1973 and 1974 Findings* (Washington, D.C.: U.S. Government Printing Office, 1976).

[a]Rates per 1,000 women.
[b]Estimates based on about 10 or less sample cases are statistically unreliable.

Tables 4 through 8 deal with four important characteristics of crime: the involvement of strangers in crimes, the use of self-protective measures, criminal injuries resulting in hospital care, and the proportion of crimes reported to the police. The percentage of violent crimes committed by strangers is presented in Table 5. As compared with violent crimes against men, a considerably higher proportion of violent crimes against women are committed by nonstrangers such as friends, co-workers, acquaintances, and family members. The difference is primarily due to assault, for differences in robbery victimizations are smaller and there are too few cases of rapes of males to make a meaningful comparison on that crime. Among women, robbery is the most likely violent crime to be committed by a stranger and assault is the least likely, with rape falling in between. For all 4 years reported, approximately half of all assaults on women were carried out by people they knew.

In Table 6, we see that women are about as likely as men to take self-protective measures during the commission of a crime against them. Approximately two-thirds of both sexes took measures to protect themselves against violent crimes. Men were more likely than women to use physical force to protect themselves (35 vs. 20 percent in 1976), and women were more likely than men to try to get help or to frighten off the offender (21 vs. 8 percent in 1976). These figures indicate that women are no more passive than men when confronted with a crime. Their smaller size and lower level of self-defense training means that they often use less violent resistance techniques than men do, not that they do nothing at all about the crime.

**Table 5.** *Percent of Violent Crime Victimizations Involving Strangers, by Sex of Victims, 1973-1976.*

| SEX | 1973 | 1974 | 1975 | 1976 |
|---|---|---|---|---|
| Rape | | | | |
| Female | 77 | 74 | 69 | 75 |
| Male | 20[a] | 100[a] | 100[a] | 100[a] |
| Robbery | | | | |
| Female | 78 | 78 | 82 | 68 |
| Male | 88 | 88 | 86 | 83 |
| Assault | | | | |
| Female | 48 | 48 | 47 | 51 |
| Male | 66 | 67 | 66 | 65 |
| Crimes of violence-total | | | | |
| Female | 55 | 56 | 55 | 56 |
| Male | 71 | 72 | 71 | 69 |

Sources: *Criminal Victimization in the United States* (Washington, D.C.: U.S. Government Printing Ofice, 1973, 1974, 1975, and 1976 editions).

[a]Estimates based on about 10 or less sample cases are statistically unreliable.

Are women more chivalrously treated by criminals than men? There is little reason to think so based on the data presented in Table 7. Women were quite a bit more likely than men to be physically injured in a robbery and equally likely to be injured in an assault in 1976. Men were more likely to be hospitalized from assault injuries, and the sexes were about equally likely to be hospitalized as a result of robbery injuries.

The final table in this series on characteristics of crimes shows the proportion of crimes reported to the police for five different crimes (plus a summary statistic for violent crime), broken down by gender, year, and whether the offender was known to the victim or a stranger. Women are more likely than men to report crimes to the police. Men and women are both more likely to report crimes involving strangers than crimes by people they know. The fable that women are much more likely than men to protect friends by not reporting them to the police is resoundingly refuted in Table 8. In fact, there is a slight tendency for just the reverse to be true.

The amount of information on crimes against women in the national surveys is rather limited. It is much more difficult to talk about data from the city surveys, for there are 26 separate data sets, 13 of which have an entire book of tables devoted to them. Table 9 presents city

**Table 6.** *Percent of Violent Crime Victimizations in which Victims Took Self-Protective Measures, and Specific Measures Taken, by Sex of Victim, 1974-1976.*

|  | FEMALE | | | MALE | | |
|---|---|---|---|---|---|---|
|  | 1974 | 1975 | 1976 | 1974 | 1975 | 1976 |
| Took any protective measure against: |  |  |  |  |  |  |
| Rape | 85 | 80 | 83 | 67[a] | 76 | 92 |
| Robbery | 52 | 54 | 56 | 55 | 48 | 56 |
| Assault | 67 | 65 | 70 | 70 | 70 | 68 |
| All violent crime | 65 | 64 | 68 | 67 | 65 | 66 |
| Specific protective measures: |  |  |  |  |  |  |
| Used or brandished firearm or knife | 2 | 2 | 1 | 3 | 3 | 3 |
| Used physical force or other weapon | 20 | 20 | 20 | 33 | 34 | 35 |
| Tried to get help or frighten offender | 23 | 22 | 21 | 7 | 7 | 8 |
| Threatened or reasoned with offender | 17 | 17 | 17 | 20 | 19 | 19 |
| Nonviolent resistance including evasion | 28 | 28 | 29 | 24 | 27 | 24 |
| Other | 10 | 11 | 11 | 13 | 11 | 11 |

Sources: *Criminal Victimization in the United States* (Washington, D.C.: U.S. Government Printing Office, 1974, 1975, and 1976 editions).

[a]Estimates based on about 10 or fewer sample cases are statistically unreliable.

**Table 7.** *Percent of Robberies and Assaults in which Victims Sustained Physical Injury and Received Emergency Room or Inpatient Hospital Care, by Sex of Victim, 1973-1976.*

|  | FEMALE | | | | MALE | | | |
|---|---|---|---|---|---|---|---|---|
|  | 1973 | 1974 | 1975 | 1976 | 1973 | 1974 | 1975 | 1976 |
| Sustained physical injury |  |  |  |  |  |  |  |  |
| Robbery | 38 | 34 | 33 | 40 | 33 | 32 | 31 | 29 |
| Assault | 31 | 29 | 30 | 30 | 26 | 27 | 29 | 29 |
| Received emergency room care |  |  |  |  |  |  |  |  |
| Robbery | 6 | 7 | 6 | 9 | 6 | 7 | 8 | 9 |
| Assault | 5 | 6 | 6 | 4 | 5 | 6 | 6 | 6 |

**Table 7.** *Percent of Robberies and Assaults in which Victims Sustained Physical Injury and Received Emergency Room or Inpatient Hospital Care, by Sex of Victim, 1973–1976 (continued).*

|  | FEMALE | | | | MALE | | | |
|---|---|---|---|---|---|---|---|---|
|  | 1973 | 1974 | 1975 | 1976 | 1973 | 1974 | 1975 | 1976 |
| Received inpatient care | | | | | | | | |
| Robbery | 2 | 0 | 0 | 2 | 3 | 3 | 4 | 1 |
| Assault | 1 | 1 | 1 | 1 | 2 | 2 | 2 | 2 |
| Received any hospital care | | | | | | | | |
| Robbery | 8 | 7 | 6 | 11 | 9 | 10 | 12 | 10 |
| Assault | 6 | 7 | 7 | 5 | 7 | 8 | 8 | 8 |

Sources: *Criminal Victimization in the United States* (Washington, D.C.: U.S. Government Printing Office, 1973, 1974, 1975, and 1976 editions).

**Table 8.** *Percent of Personal Crime Victimizations Reported to the Police, by Sex of Victim and Victim-Offender Relationship, 1973–1976.*

|  | FEMALE | | | | MALE | | | |
|---|---|---|---|---|---|---|---|---|
|  | 1973 | 1974 | 1975 | 1976 | 1973 | 1974 | 1975 | 1976 |
| Rape | | | | | | | | |
| Involving strangers | 48 | 57 | 62 | 55 | 100[a] | 70 | 18 | 68[a] |
| Involving nonstrangers | 29 | 36 | 50 | 46 | 48[a] | 0[a] | 0[a] | 38[a] |
| Robbery | | | | | | | | |
| Involving strangers | 66 | 73 | 61 | 66 | 49 | 47 | 51 | 48 |
| Involving nonstrangers | 53 | 54 | 60 | 59 | 32 | 42 | 43 | 46 |
| Aggravated assault | | | | | | | | |
| Involving strangers | 57 | 56 | 57 | 65 | 51 | 53 | 55 | 60 |
| Involving nonstrangers | 56 | 61 | 58 | 60 | 48 | 46 | 53 | 50 |
| Simple assault | | | | | | | | |
| Involving strangers | 43 | 40 | 44 | 44 | 37 | 39 | 41 | 40 |
| Involving nonstrangers | 42 | 44 | 41 | 48 | 29 | 31 | 29 | 31 |
| Crimes of violence—total | | | | | | | | |
| Involving strangers | 52 | 55 | 53 | 55 | 45 | 46 | 48 | 49 |
| Involving nonstrangers | 47 | 50 | 47 | 52 | 36 | 38 | 38 | 39 |
| Personal larceny with contact | | | | | | | | |
| Involving strangers | 33 | 42 | 40 | 44 | 32 | 24 | 28 | 28 |
| Involving nonstrangers | 16[a] | 0[a] | 16[a] | 12[a] | 29[a] | 25[a] | 30[a] | 18[a] |

Sources: *Criminal Victimization in the United States* (Washington, D.C.: U.S. Government Printing Office, 1973, 1974, 1975, and 1976 editions).

[a]Estimates based on about 10 or fewer sample cases are statistically unreliable.

victimization rates for the most recent year available. The variability in victimization rates is considerable. Total crime victimization rates for women range from 68 (Miami) to 183 per 1,000 (Portland, Oregon); personal property crime rates from 41 (Miami) to 132 (Portland); and violent crime rates from 17 (Miami) to 59 (Minneapolis). Rates for specific crimes show similar variations, from 1 (New York) to 7 (Minneapolis and Portland) for rape; 6 (Miami and Dallas) to 24 (Detroit) for robbery; and 9 (Miami) to 37 (Minnneapolis) for assault. These differences among cities are surprisingly large, and women faced with the possibility of moving into the more dangerous cities should think of the move as constituting a serious danger to their well-being. The odds of suffering a victimization in Boston, Minneapolis, San Francisco, and Portland are so high that it would be fair for women to consider them as being in a state of plague—enter at your own risk and take extreme precautions to protect yourself. This dictum takes on special meaning when one realizes that even the safest of the 26 cities has a higher violent crime rate than the national average. That is to say, life in all of these cities is extremely dangerous to life and limb, but some cities are far worse than others.

In an earlier publication (Bowker, 1978), male and female victimization rates in the 26 cities were compared in some detail. Although male victimization rates generally parallel but are higher than female victimization rates, it is also true that women in some cities are more likely to have crimes committed against them than men in other cities. For example, in New York (1972) and Newark (1971–72 and 1974–75), women reported proportionately more property crimes than men living in these same cities.

## ADDITIONAL DATA ON RAPE

Because a very high proportion of self-reported rapes are of females, we can take crime survey rape data as applying to women with little risk of error. As one of the standard set of violent crimes, rape is included in many more crime survey tables than sex of victim. We will use the 1975 national report (Law Enforcement Assistance Administration, 1977c) as an example of the quantitative data that can be abstracted from crime survey reports to complement the more qualitative rape data being produced by researchers such as Bart (1975) and Burgess and Holmstrom (1976).

**Table 9.** *Female Personal Crime Victimization Rates[a] for Persons Age 12 and Over in Major American Cities.*

|  | RAPE | ROBBERY | ASSAULT | VIOLENT CRIME | PROPERTY CRIME | TOTAL CRIME |
|---|---|---|---|---|---|---|
| **1973** | | | | | | |
| Boston | 3 | 20 | 24 | 47 | 127 | 174 |
| Buffalo | 3 | 11 | 23 | 37 | 69 | 116 |
| Cincinnati | 3 | 8 | 28 | 39 | 100 | 139 |
| Houston | 5 | 11 | 20 | 35 | 115 | 150 |
| Miami | 2 | 6 | 9 | 17 | 41 | 68 |
| Milwaukee | 4 | 13 | 31 | 48 | 90 | 138 |
| Minneapolis | 7 | 15 | 37 | 59 | 113 | 172 |
| New Orleans | 4 | 10 | 18 | 32 | 87 | 119 |
| Oakland | 5 | 15 | 27 | 47 | 93 | 140 |
| Pittsburgh | 3 | 9 | 21 | 33 | 78 | 111 |
| San Diego | 4 | 7 | 24 | 35 | 127 | 162 |
| San Francisco | 5 | 20 | 32 | 57 | 123 | 180 |
| Washington, D.C. | 2 | 10 | 11 | 23 | 66 | 89 |
| **1974** | | | | | | |
| Chicago | 4 | 18 | 20 | 43 | 85 | 128 |
| Detroit | 3 | 24 | 26 | 53 | 76 | 129 |
| Los Angeles | 4 | 10 | 28 | 42 | 110 | 152 |
| New York | 1 | 15 | 15 | 32 | 62 | 94 |
| Philadelphia | 2 | 12 | 16 | 30 | 79 | 109 |
| **1974/5** | | | | | | |
| Atlanta | 4 | 10 | 17 | 31 | 86 | 117 |
| Baltimore | 4 | 19 | 27 | 51 | 102 | 153 |
| Cleveland | 4 | 19 | 26 | 50 | 73 | 123 |
| Dallas | 3 | 6 | 22 | 31 | 106 | 137 |
| Denver | 5 | 10 | 33 | 48 | 116 | 164 |
| Newark | 3 | 15 | 10 | 27 | 47 | 74 |
| Portland, Oregon | 7 | 10 | 35 | 51 | 132 | 183 |
| St. Louis | 2 | 14 | 19 | 35 | 83 | 118 |

Sources: *Criminal Victimization Surveys,* editions for Boston, Buffalo, Cincinnati, Houston, Miami, Milwaukee, Minneapolis, New Orleans, Oakland, Pittsburgh, San Diego, San Francisco, and Washington, D.C. (Washington, D.C.: U.S. Government Printing Office, 1977); *Criminal Victimization Surveys in Chicago, Detroit, Los Angeles, New York, and Philadelphia: A Comparison of 1972 and 1974 Findings* (Washington, D.C.: Government Printing Office, 1976): and *Criminal Victimization Surveys in Eight American Cities: A Comparison of 1971/72 and 1974/75 Findings* (Washington, D.C.: Government Printing Office, 1976).

[a]Rates are per 1,000 women.

In 1975, the national rape rate was 1.7 per 1,000 women age 12 and over and .1 for males. The 1.7 per 1,000 females rate was composed of .7 per 1,000 completed rapes and 1.0 per 1,000 attempted rapes. The likelihood of a woman's experiencing rape rose from 1.6 per 1,000 at ages 12–15 to 4.7 at age 20–24, and then rapidly declined. Black women were slightly more likely to be raped than white women, 1.8 to 1.6 per 1,000. Divorced or separated women were much more likely to be raped than women who have never married, 4.7 to 3.1, with married women trailing far behind at .8 and widowed women at .5 (an unstable estimate because of a small number of sample cases). For both blacks and whites the rape rate was more than three times as high for those having an annual family income of less than $3,000 a year as it was for those with an income of $15,000 or more.

Women living in households where they were not family members were seven times as likely to be raped as wives, and women living without husbands were *less* likely to be raped than if they headed households of two or more people meaning that they had one or more children living with them in most cases. Unemployed women were nearly five times as likely to be raped as employed women. Private household workers were more likely to be raped than clerical workers and service workers, who were, in turn, much more likely to be raped than other workers. Those living in the central cities in metropolitan areas were more likely to be raped than those living in the suburbs or entirely outside of metropolitan areas.

About one-third of all attempted rapes were completed, with nonstrangers having a higher completion rate than strangers. The proportion of rapes by nonstrangers was highest at ages 12–15 and 25–34, and higher among white women (34 percent) than black women (13 percent) Rape by nonstrangers was particularly common among women from families with incomes between $3,000 and $10,000 and women who were separated, divorced, or never married.

Nearly four-fifths of all rapes were interracial. Blacks were about as likely to rape whites as whites were to rape blacks in the limited proportion of rapes that were interracial. Black offenders were more likely than white offenders to appear in multiple-offender rapes than in rapes by a single offender. One in every 20 rape incidents involved more than one victim, and multiple-victim rapes were somewhat more likely to be committed by strangers than single-victim rapes.

Slightly more than a quarter of the rapes were committed during the daytime. The nighttime rapes generally occured between 6 P.M. and midnight, although a considerable number of rapes also occurred between midnight and 6 A.M. Rape by nonstrangers was less likely to occur between 6 P.M. and midnight, and more likely to occur between midnight and 6 A.M. than rape by strangers. Twenty-two percent of the rapes occurred inside the victim's own home, but most rapes (54 percent) were committed on streets or in other public places such as parks, playgrounds, schoolgrounds, or parking lots. As might be expected, rapes by nonstrangers occurred in the victim's home more than any other place, while rapes by strangers were much more likely to occur in public places. Weapons were used to subdue the victims by the offenders in 29 percent of the rapes by strangers but few of the rapes by nonstrangers. Slightly less than a third of the weapons used were firearms, and just over a third were knives. Four of every five rape victims took self-protective measures. It is interesting to note, in view of common stereotypes about female passivity, that the few male rape victims in the sample were slightly less likely than female rape victims to take self-protective measures (76 vs. 80 percent). Twenty-two percent of the female rape victims tried to get help or frighten the offender, 26 percent resisted with physical force or a weapon, 17 percent threatened or reasoned with the offender, and 28 percent practiced evasion or some other form of nonviolent resistance.

Rape incidents were accompanied by proper damage in 29 percent of the cases and by theft in 13 percent of the cases. Only one rape victim in every nine reported losing time from work because of the crime, but when they did lose time at work, it was longer than the time lost because of other types of criminal victimizations. Unfortunately, data on hospitalization and medical expenses are not separately provided for rape, but from what data are presented it is possible to infer that rape victims were more likely than female victims of robbery or assault to receive hospital care and that of those female victims receiving hospital care, rape victims were more likely to require inpatient care as opposed to emergency room treatments.

Only 56 percent of the rape victims reported the crime to the police. However, this was higher than the proportion of robbery, assault, personal larceny, or burglary crimes that were reported. When we look only at female victims, the same pattern holds, except that robbery and rape were about equally likely to be reported (61 and 58 percent, respectively). Women reported 62 percent of the rapes by strangers and 50 percent of the rapes by nonstrangers. White rape victims were much more likely to report the crime to the police (59 percent) than black rape victims (36 percent). The number of black rape cases in the sample was too small to provide a statistically reliable estimate, but the cases that did appear in the sample suggest the possibility that this racial difference is due to a lower black propensity to report rapes by strangers. Rape victimizations were slightly more likely to be reported by those age 20–24 than by victims under age 20. The most common reasons given for not reporting rapes were that it was a private or personal matter (20 percent), that nothing could be done, perhaps because of lack of proof (15 percent), and that there was a fear of reprisal (11 percent). The private matter and reprisal reasons were emphasized in cases of rape by nonstrangers, while lack of proof was the most commonly mentioned reason for not reporting a rape by a stranger.

## WOMEN'S OPINIONS ABOUT CRIME AND THE POLICE

Half of the households in the L.E.A.A. samples selected in 13 major American cities for victimization interviews in early 1975 also were randomly selected into a subsample that received a series of questions about attitudes toward the police and crime. These questions became the basis for two reports in the Applications of the National Crime Survey Series published by L.E.A.A. From one of these reports (Garofalo, 1977b), we learn that women evaluated the police in almost exactly the same way as men did. Forty percent of both groups believed that the police did a good job, as compared with 13 percent of the men and 11 percent of the women who felt that the police did a poor job. Rape victims were substantially more negative, 31 percent of them giving the police the lowest rating possible on the 4-point scale used in the questionnaire.

The other attitude report (Garofalo, 1977a) covers citizen attitudes and opinions about crime in America. In the eight impact cities (Atlanta, Balitmore, Cleveland, Dallas, Denver, Newark, Portland, and St. Louis), 83 percent of the women and 81 percent of the men thought that U.S. crime was increasing. In contrast, only 41 percent of the women and 40 percent of the men thought that crime was increasing in their own neighborhood. Very few members of either sex thought that the newspapers and television made crime look more serious than it was in reality. In fact, about 40 percent of both sexes believed just the reverse. Two-thirds of the women felt that the chances of their being attacked or robbed were increasing, with women age 35–49 being slightly more likely to hold this opinion than either younger or older women. By age, women were much more likely than men to see the changes of their being attacked or robbed as going up at age 16–19, but this difference steadily declined until age 65 and over, when the sexes were essentially equal.

Women were more likely than men to be afraid of going to some parts of the metropolitan area during the day (23 vs. 17 percent) and at night (38 vs. 33 percent) and to feel personally unsafe when out alone in their own neighborhood during the day (13 vs. 5 percent) and at night (59 vs. 27 percent). Women's feeling of unsafeness increased directly with age for daytime and nighttime figures. Women were much more likely than men to report limiting or changing their activities in the past few years because of crime (52 vs. 37 percent). Results from the five largest American cities (Chicago, Detroit, Los Angeles, New York, and Philadelphia), which are presented separately in Garofalo's report, are the same as the results from the eight impact cities, except that the figures are slightly more negative.

## DISCUSSION

There are many methodological problems with the National Crime Survey Program, but dealing with them is beyond the scope of this paper. Interested readers should consult publications such as *Surveying Crime,* a volume issued by the National Research Council of the National Academy of Sciences (Penick and Owens, 1976). For our purposes here, the most important point is that NCS data are far superior to other known sources of information on the victimization of women. The recent increase of interest in women's studies has produced a large number of publications in a short period of time, most of which are personal commentaries or ideological pieces disguised in pseudoscientific dress. When field research is reported, it is almost always of an exploratory nature, and utilizes only small, nonrepresentative samples. The fact that this was due more to funding limitations (up until about 1975) than to researchers' preferences does not make it any easier to get a handle on female victimization phenomena nationally. The exploratory studies have yielded many theoretical insights. What is now needed is to test these insights (as well as ideological assumptions) using larger, randomly selected samples.

An example of the use of NCS data for theory building is *Victims of Personal Crime,* by Hindelang, Gottfredson, and Garofalo (1978), which analyzes 1972 victimization data from Atlanta, Baltimore, Cleveland, Dallas, Denver, Newark, Portland, and St. Louis. The result of these researchers' analysis is a set of eight propositions that relate victimization to lifestyle. Among these propositions are the following:

1. The probability of suffering a personal victimization is directly related to the amount of time that a person spends in public places (e.g., on the street, in parks, etc.), and particularly in public places at night.

2. An individual's chances of personal victimization are dependent upon the extent to which the individual shares demographic characteristics with offenders.

3. The probability of person victimization, particularly personal theft, increases as a function of the proportion of time that an individual spends among nonfamily members.

4. Variations in lifestyle are associated with variations in the convenience, the desirability, and vincibility of the person as a target for personal victimizations (Hindelang, Gottfredson, and Garofalo, 1978, 251–264).

The data discussed in earlier sections of this paper can be used to make an informal test of these propositions.

The first proposition is supported by the fact that women, who spend less time in public places than men, are less likely to be victimized than men. Similarly, the breakdowns of victimization statistics by race/ ethnicity, marital status, and age show that in every case, criminal victimization rises directly with the amount of time spent in public places. The statistics on victimization by marital status are supportive of proposition 3, that victimization rates are directly related to the amount of time spent among nonfamily members. There are two contrary statistics, which are the higher victimization rates for rape and personal property crime with contact among women than among men. However, these are consistent with proposition 4, in that women's higher victimization rates for these crimes are related to their higher desirability (relatively few men desire to commit a homosexual rape) and lower vincibility (which can be raised through courses in self-defense). Proposition 2 is upheld in that black women are more likely to be raped by blacks than whites, and so forth, but challenged by the point that women are much more likely to be victimized by men than by members of their own gender. The reason behind this is that the demographic similarity between offenders and victims is based on propinquity—ecological segregation in housing, education, occupation, and informal socializing. Women are not ecologically segregated from men. Quite to the contrary, once married they tend to be isolated from other women to a surprising degree.

The general point that lifestyle is related to victimization is also supported by the observation that male-female differences in victimization rates are smallest where lifestyle differences between the sexes are minimized, such as among adolescents, the elderly, and divorcees. This and numerous other points drawn from Hindelang, Gottfredson, and Garofalo's analysis are supported by the national victimization survey data. Indeed, practically any conclusions drawn from the 1972 city data sets

will hold for the 1973–1976 national data sets because of the considerable degree of consistency in the victimization statistics produced since
the beginning of the National Crime Survey. Hindelang, Gottfredson,
and Garofalo do predict one change between 1972 and later victimization data sets, saying that

> as sex role expectations become increasingly less differentiated and
> sex-linked structural barriers become less rigid, with a correspond-
> ing convergence of the adaptations and lifestyles of males and
> females, rates of victimization for males and females will tend to
> converge. (1978: 269)

They point out two main reasons for this. First, decreasing gender differentiation is likely to increase women's exposure to nonfamily members.
The second reason is that as women heighten their own level of criminal
behavior, the sex ratio among criminals will more nearly approximate
the sex ratio of potential victims in the general population; and conversely, according to the second proposition, increasing similarity of the
characteristics of women to those of offenders is associated with increasing victimization.

This prediction is supported by a series of small, cumulative changes
in the national survey data between 1973 and 1976. In Table 1, we can
see that the gender differential has narrowed for every crime on the list.
For crimes of violence, the narrowing is from 22.5 in 1973 to 19.8 in
1976; for personal crimes of theft, the differential narrows from 22.6 to
19.4. These statistics constitute modest support for Hindelang, Gottfredson, and Garofalo's prediction that the convergence of male and female
lifestyles will be associated with a similar convergence of criminal victimization rates.

## CONCLUSION

This article has summarized a variety of victimization data on women
from the National Crime Survey Program and has related these data to
the propositions and predictions made by Hindelang, Gottfredson, and
Garofalo in their recent book, *Victims of Pesonal Crime.* These propositions and predictions are generally supported by 1973–1976 NCS data.
The analysis points up one crucial difference between women and other
groups of victims. While others are more likely to be victimized by
offenders who are demographically similar to themselves, women are
more likely to be victimized by men than other women. In this respect,
the situation of women in the United States today resembles the classical

state of minority-group oppression, one that no longer fully applies to racial and ethnic minorities in America. Criminal justice system administrators have learned that it is advisable to use minority police officers as much as possible when dealing with minority group members. They have begun to do this for women only in the case of special rape investigation units. In view of the fact that men are the main source of general female oppression as well as criminal victimization, it is particularly important that the entire criminal justice system not be staffed and dominated by men. Because it *is* currently staffed and dominated by men, women are in the same position that blacks were in the Deep South before the Civil War and later after the failure of the Reconstruction. As the women's movement progresses, increasing attention will be given to this problem by movement spokespeople. Criminal justice system administrators would do well to choose action over reaction and to begin to radically increase female representation in law enforcement and other criminal justice areas now instead of waiting until a grass-roots popular movement forces them to do so through a massive publicity and mobilization campaign.

## NOTES

1. Much of the material in this section is derived from James Garofalo and Michael Hindelang, *An Introduction to the National Crime Surveys* (Washington, D.C.: U.S. Government Printing Office, 1977).

---

## REFERENCES

Bart, Pauline. *Rape doesn't end with a kiss.* Unpublished manuscript, University of Illinois, 1975 (Summarized in *Viva,* June 1975).

Bowker, Lee H. *Women, crime, and the criminal justice system.* Lexington, MA: D. C. Heath, 1978.

Burgess, Ann W., and Holmstrom, Lynda L. Coping behavior of the rape victim. *American Journal of Psychiatry,* 1976, *133,* 413–418.

Garofalo, James. *Public opinion about crime: The attitudes of victims and non-victims in selected cities.* Washington, D.C.: U.S. Government Printing Office, 1977a.

———. *The police and public opinion: An analysis of victimization and attitude data from 13 American cities.* Washington, D.C.: U.S. Government Printing Office, 1977b.

————, and Hindelang, Michael J. *An introduction to the national crime survey.* Washington D.C.: U.S. Government Printing Office, 1977.

Hindelang, Michael J., Gottfredson, Michael A., and Garofalo, James. *Victims of personal crime: an empirical foundation for a theory of personal victimization.* Cambridge, MA: Ballinger, 1978.

Penick, Bettye K., and Owens, Maurice E.B., *Surveying crime.* Washington, D.C.: National Academy of Sciences, 1976.

United States, Law Enforcement Assistance Administration. *Criminal Victimization in the United States: A comparison of 1973 and 1974 findings.* Washington, D.C.: U.S. Government Printing Office, 1976a.

————. *Criminal Victimization in the United States, 1973.* Washington, D.C.: U.S. Government Printing Office 1976b.

————. *Criminal victimization surveys in eight American cities: A comparison of 1971/72 and 1974/75 Findings.* Washington, D.C.: U.S. Government Printing Office, 1976c.

————. *Criminal victimization surveys in Chicago, Detroit, Los Angeles, New York, and Philadelphia: A comparison of 1972 and 1974 findings.* Washington, D.C.: U.S. Government Printing Office, 1976d.

————. *Criminal victimization in the United States: A comparison of 1975 and 1976 findings.* Washington, D.C.: U.S. Government Printing Office, 1977a.

————. *Criminal victimization in the United States, 1974.* Washington, D.C.: U.S. Government Printing Office, 1977b.

————. *Criminal victimization in the United States, 1975.* Washington, D.C.: U.S. Government Printing Office, 1977c.

————. *Criminal victimization surveys,* editions for Boston, Buffalo, Cincinnati, Houston, Miami, Milwaukee, Minneapolis, New Orleans, Oakland, Pittsburgh, San Diego, San Francisco, and Washington, D.C. Washington, D.C.: U.S. Government Printing Office, 1977d through 1977p.

————. *Criminal victimization in the United States, 1976.* Washington, D.C.: U.S. Government Printing Office, 1979.

# RAPE AND OTHER
# SEXUAL ASSAULTS

## 1. WHAT IS RAPE?

A recent survey of prosecutors' offices in the United States found that more than three-fourths of the respondents identified four elements that had to be present in order to file a complaint of forcible rape. These were penetration, lack of victim consent, the threat of force, and having the victim be a female (David, Schram, and Ulberg, 1977). Actual physical force, as contrasted with only threat of physical force, was required in 38 percent of the prosecutors' offices, and physical evidence of resistance by the victim was required in 25 percent. Penetration as used in this context presumably includes anal and oral intercourse as well as genital intercourse. Although males can be homosexually raped, as is demonstrated by the literature on prison violence, such an act could not be charged as a rape in three-fourths of the jurisdictions. If rape is limited to genital intercourse, then it is appropriate to exclude males as possible victims of the crime, but as soon as one includes oral and anal intercourse under the definition of forcible rape, then it is inconsistent systematically to exclude males since they also can be forced to participate in these acts against their will. We recognize that rape may be either homosexual or heterosexual, and that it may have either male or female victims. However, the rape of adult males outside of correctional institutions is not common enough to be considered a major social problem, while the rape of females is a major element in the human condition of American women. For this reason, we limit our discussion in this text to rape and other sexual assaults of females by males.

What if the rapist uses the threat of force to attempt to coerce sexual intercourse against the victim's will, but she is successful in avoiding physical penetration? In this case, what we have is attempted rape, which may be prosecuted as a nonsexual assault, if it is prosecuted at all. Although these events are not technically forcible rapes, they are clearly sexual assaults, and they may be as terrifying for the victim as forcible rape itself. Perhaps the best definition of sexual assault is any attempted or completed sexual act that is forced on an individual against his or her will. This includes the elements of lack of consent and the use of force or the threat of force from the accepted legal definition of rape, but it excludes the necessity for penetration or the limiting of victims to females.

Under our definition of sexual assault, a female college student who engages in genital petting with her date because he has been physically aggressive with her rather than because she wishes to engage in the behavior is a victim of a sexual assault. Coerced genital petting and forcible rape differ from each other in degree but not in kind. They are both examples of male sexual aggression against females in which the needs and preferences of the females are disregarded and they are forced to engage in behavior which they find undesirable, offensive, or, at the very least, inappropriate. The first of the three articles included in this section is a study of sexual aggression directed toward college females by Kanin and Parcell (1977). In this study, which was carried out at a large midwestern state university, they found that college coeds were offended by a wide range of sexually aggressive behavior, including kissing, breast fondling, genital fondling, intercourse, and intercourse with violence. Slightly more than half of the young women who completed questionnaires in the study indicated that they had been sexually offended at least once during the 1971–72 academic year, and almost 70 percent had been offended since they entered college. Those young women who had been sexually offended were not offended just once, for the average number of incidents they had suffered was just over five per person, of which slightly more than one incident in every eight involved coerced sexual intercourse.

## 2. THE RAPE VICTIM

Since we have no national data on sexual assault other than forcible rape, we will be talking mostly about forcible rape in the remainder of this section. However, it must be remembered that forcible rape constitutes only a small portion of the total number of acts of sexual aggression carried out against females in American society. Victimization statistics derived from the National Crime Survey and presented earlier in this book indicate that the probability of being raped is between one and two per 1,000 females age 12 and over per year in the United States. Taken by itself, the statistic is misleading, for women age 16 through 24 are nearly three times as likely to be raped as women in general, black women are between two and three times more likely to be raped than white women, and separated and divorced women and women who have never married are six to seven times more likely to be raped than married women. Women from the lower socioeconomic classes are more likely to be raped than women from the middle or upper classes, an increased susceptibility which is also true for other kinds of serious crimes (Katz and Mazur, 1979). Women who are living in poverty are not only less able to protect themselves and their property from the possibility of criminal victimization, but they also live in neighborhoods that experience much higher levels of crime than middle or upper class neighborhoods.

Women in some occupations may be more likely to be sexually victimized than women in other occupations. Although all women are subject to the risk of rape, women in the helping professions may be in particularly great danger. In a recent article in *Psychology Today*, Selkin (1975) found a number of nurses who had been raped. This is probably due both to the late hours that nurses keep because of their work schedules and because of their willingness to get themselves in dangerous situations if called upon to help someone in trouble. A willingness to help is potentially dangerous to all women as the rapist has often been successful with techniques such as asking a woman to let him into her house so that he can make an emergency call because of an accident. The most dangerous of the predominantly female helping professions is almost certainly prostitution, in which women put themselves in positions of great danger as they meet the sexual needs of their clients. Because rapes of prostitutes occur in the context of illegal activity, prostitutes rarely report these crimes to the police. Their profession is outside the law in all states except Nevada, and therefore they are only partially subject to the protection of the law.

## 3. WHO ARE THE RAPISTS?

Anyone can be a rapist, and there is no group of men with whom women should automatically feel safe from the possibility of sexual assault. However, some men are more likely to become rapists than others. After analyzing all the studies on rape and other sexual assaults, Katz and Mazur (1979) concluded that the rapist is most likely to be a young man, age 15 to 24, single, from the lower socioeconomic classes, and of the same race as the victim. Because rape is primarily intraracial rather than interracial, it follows that the higher susceptibility of black women to rape means that a disportionately large proportion of rapists are also black. When an interracial rape occurs today, it is most likely to be a black rapist and a white victim, which is a reversal of the historical situation that existed in the United States during the days of slavery and the decades that followed its termination. During this period, it was black women who were constantly in danger of being sexually assaulted by white men.

According to National Crime Survey data, approximately two-thirds of all rapes are committed by strangers. Although this is consistent with the stereotype of the rapist who leaps out from behind a tree and drags his victim into the bushes to commit the rape, it is important to realize that approximately one-third of all rapes are committed by people who are known to their victims. Nonstranger rapists include social acquaintances, neighbors, friends, boyfriends, dates, and relatives. The younger the rape victim, the more likely she is to be assaulted by someone she knows, including incestuous sexual attacks by family members. Incestuous sexual attacks by fathers, stepfathers, common-law fathers, uncles, grandfathers, and older brothers are probably the least reported of all criminal acts committed in the United States today. There is some evidence that college students are in greater danger of rape from their dates and boyfriends than they are from rape by strangers (Katz and Mazur, 1979). This is even more true of sexual assaults that go beyond the legal definition of forcible rape, as Kanin and Parcell (1977) have shown in their work with college students.

Jackson (1978) has demonstrated the way in which rape grows out of the general sexual scripting of male/female interaction in our culture. One reason that rapists and other sexual assaulters come from all parts of society is that there are broad social forces conducive to rape that condition the interaction between men and women throughout America. Thus, coerced sexual acts are commonly found on college campuses as well as in high-crime center-city neighborhoods and suburban settings.

## 4. WHAT HAPPENS IN A RAPE?

Statistics from scientific studies of rape confirm that the street is the most common meeting place of the rapist and his victim (McDonald, 1971; Amir, 1971). There is also some support for the idea that hitchhiking is an invitation to rape (Nelson and Amir, 1977; Storaska, 1975). What is less commonly understood is that between a quarter (Amir, 1971) and a third (McDonald, 1971) of known rape cases begin in the homes of the rape victims and an even higher percentage of rapes are consumated there. Many contacts that are initiated on the street progress to the homes of either the victim or the aggressor where the rapes take place.

Rapes committed by boyfriends or dates are often preceded by a lower level of consensual sexual activity, while rapes by strangers are, by definition, without previous sexual activity of any kind. Once sexual activity begins in a rape, there is no telling what sexual acts the rapist will require of his victim. Oral and anal intercourse are often added to genital intercourse, and many rapists seem to delight in torturing their victims with unusual sexual acts that appear to be designed to humiliate and degrade them. If the rapist is more interested in degrading his victim than in sexual activity per se, then perhaps we should change our perception of rape as primarily a sexual act. An article that is reprinted in this section gives us convincing evidence on this point. Groth, Burgess, and Holmstrom (1977) analyze the experiences of 92 adult rape victims from the Boston City Hospital to create a typology of the types of rape. They show that sexuality never dominates rape incidents but is rather used to express power and anger in differing proportions. In a power rape, the assaulter wants to show power and control over his victim and uses physical aggression to affect the conquest. When anger is the dominant motive of the sexual assault, he reflects contempt and hatred for women, it is in this type of rape that the victim is forced to engage in the most degrading of all possible acts.

It is striking that the authors were unable to find a single case in which sexuality was the dominant motive in the rape events. The dominance of nonsexual motives in rape events should not be surprising, for many rapists have access to consensual sexual activities through their marriages or other heterosexual relationships. Perhaps their anger or need to demonstrate power over women has something to do with feelings of sexual inadequacy and doubts about their masculinity. Evidence is accumulating about the homosexual activities of rapists (Gebhard et al., 1967; Goldstein et al., 1971) and the fact that many of them experience serious sexual dysfunctions (Groth and Burgess, 1977).

## 5. EFFECTS OF RAPE

Rape has effects that are both psychological and social. Individuals who are raped usually suffer much more after the rape is completed than they do during the event itself. Rape also has social effects that go far beyond the individual victims of these aggressive acts. For example, a series of sexual attacks on a college campus resulted in the following effects: one woman changed her job to reduce her exposure to the risk of rape; other women changed their working hours for the same reason; there was a considerable increase in the amount of fear displayed by female students and staff members about walking around on campus after dark; some female students demonstrated an unwillingness to take night classes; and a WhistleStop campaign was begun to protect women against campus rape.

On the individual level, the damages are physical, psychological, and social. The majority of rapists use physical force to subdue their victims, causing physical injuries in approximately half of these incidents. One student of the effects of rape sums it up by saying, "If a normal, healthy adult is raped, serious injury will be found, not to the genitalia, but to other parts, particularly the face, neck and extremities" (Schiff, 1973: 344). Burgess and Holmstrom (1977) found that the initial, or acute, phase of the victims' psychological reaction to being raped lasted from 2 to 3 weeks, during which they experienced symptoms such as fatigue, insomnia, tension headaches, loss of appetite, nausea, self-blame, hatred, embarrassment, and fear. Following this period of severe personality disorganization, there was a second phase of reorganization of the personality which laste much longer. Even during the reorganization phase, some victims continued to have nightmares, defensive reactions, phobias, and disturbances in their sex lives or in their relations with men in general.

Socially, rape victims tend to be transformed from a person into an object and to lose status. They may feel less close to their friends and family members and may socially withdraw from them even if they do not tell anyone about their experience. On the other hand, if they share the experience with others, they may find these others treating them differently, withdrawing from them, or acting as if it was their fault that they were raped. Goffman's (1963) discussion of stigma can be applied to the problem of whether or not to tell people about one's rape experience. In his conceptualization, a person who has acquired a stigma has to choose between keeping it secret (in which case the person is potentially discreditable should the secret become public) and having the problem of information management, or making the stigma public (in which case the person is discredited) and having the problem of handling the tension that is introduced into social relations with others because of the knowledge of this stigma. The problem of the stigmatization of the rape victim is exacerbated by the procedures of the criminal justice system, which seem to bend over backwards to protect the rights of the rapist but which offer little protection to the rape victim and show almost complete disregard of her immense emotional upset.

Great as the individual negative effects of rape are, the social effects of rape on all women are greater still, for they touch the entire female population rather than only a small percentage of women each year. Women who curtail their activities because of the fear of rape and other sexual assaults are unfairly disadvantaged, both in their social relations and in the economic marketplace. The American ideal of freedom and democracy for all people is undermined when the fear of victimization and its effects is so much higher for women than for men that they must be judged to be less free than men.

Down through history, rape traditionally has been practiced against females from the lower classes and those who have the misfortune to be on the losing side in war. The mass rapes of women and girls by Pakistani troops in Bangladesh during 1971 are a recent addition to this ugly history. In Bangladesh, more than 200,000 women were raped, many of whom were kept as sex slaves in army barracks for extended periods of time. Ray's (1975) report on this tragedy mentions that some of these women were kept naked with their hair cut short because they had been so dishonored by the way in which they were treated that they would use any clothing or even their own hair to hang themselves if they could. The point is that rape, whether set in the context of contemporary America, American history, or world history, has always been an oppressive crime designed to humiliate and degrade women. More than any other crime, it symbolizes the relegation of women to legal second-class citizenship.

## 6. INCEST AND SEXUAL ASSAULTS AGAINST CHILDREN

Sexual assaults against children rarely come to the attention of the authorities, partially because so many of them are carried out by family members. An early hint that the incidence of incest, particularly attacks against women, was much higher than commonly supposed, was found in a study of women in treatment for drug abuse problems at the Odyssey House by Benward and Densen-Gerber (1975). These researchers found that 44 percent of the women they interviewed had been involved in one or more incestuous experiences. The most common partner in the incestuous experience was an uncle or a quasi-family member who was living with the family but was not a blood or legal relative, followed by a cousin, an in-law, a natural father, stepfather, sister, and brother. Of 93 aggressors in these acts, 85 were male, and the 8 females appeared only in the role of assisting males in the incestuous relationship. Those girls who told their mothers were generally not believed and so continued to suffer repeated sexual assaults.

Almost half of the recorded incidents occurred when the girls were 9 years old or younger, and the authors estimate that as many as 5 percent of the women in America may have experienced some sort of incestuous assault at some time during their lives. The fact that all the women seen by Benward and Densen-Gerber were heavy drug users and had emotional problems suggests the possibility that one of the effects of exposure to incestuous activity may be greatly increased psychological problems and social deviance.

Burgess et al. (1978) report on a number of child sexual assault cases with which they are familiar from their research conducted in their Boston area. They describe the fear that keeps so many incest victims from reporting the crime to the police or some other responsible adult. In some cases the victim has been physically threatened, but in others the fear of what will happen if they report the crime is enough to keep them quiet. Most incest victims do not wish to break up their families, and many realize that this is a likely consequence of prosecuting their fathers or other male relatives for sexual attacks they have suffered.

Denial is a major theme in the reactions of fathers or other incest offenders against children. These men often seem unable to see that they have done anything wrong. Most of them have not been violent with their daughters but rather have seduced or coerced them using their status as a parent or an adult in the place of the force that is commonly used in incidents of adult rape. The denial, or perhaps rationalization, of their incestuous behavior means that many of the offenders in incest cases are not prime candidates for rehabilitation. There is a very real danger that they will at some time return to their families and engage in the same sort of incestuous behavior that led to their prosecution. Little is known about treating incestuous offenders because the crime has been ignored for so long. Perhaps the most successful treatment program for incest offenders to date is the Child Sexual Abuse Treatment Program in Santa Clara County, California, in which both offenders and victims are included in extensive programs of group therapy. The Child Sexual Abuse Treatment Program claims that there has been no recidivism in more than 600 families that they have successfully treated and discharged (Giarretto et al., 1978).

Both of the studies that we have discussed in this section were carried out with specialized treatment populations, and there is a danger in generalizing from these treatment populations to the general public. Because treatment populations are such selected groups, they may not be representative of the general public in any way. The reason that it is necessary to generalize from studies of treatment populations when dealing with certain types of sex crimes and other deviant activities is that we have no detailed studies of these subjects that have been carried out with samples drawn from nontreatment population groups. In the case of incest, this deficiency in the research literature has been remedied in the study of sexually victimized children by Finkelhor (1979), which is based on questionnaires administered to college students at six institutions of higher education in New England. Finkelhor's technique was to have the students fill out questionnaires anonymously so that they could be honest about any sexual experiences they might have had as children without having to fear being embarrassed. His results are astounding. Nineteen percent of the females and 9 percent of the males in his sample reported having childhood sexual experiences with adults or with adolescents who were at least 5 years older than themselves. Approximately three-quarters of these experiences were with family members or acquaintances rather than with strangers, and females were between two and three times more likely than males to be offended by a family member. The average age at the time of victimization was 10 years for females and 11 years for males. Slightly over half of the victims reported either the use of force or some sort of threat to induce their cooperation in the sexual act; the rest were seduced and manipulated in one way or another, often by adults for whom they had the greatest respect. The girls were not only much more likely to be sexually victimized than boys, but they also experienced significantly higher levels of trauma as a result of the sexual victimization. Therefore, future discussions of sex crimes against women should not be limited to rape carried out against adults but should also include sexual crimes against children, and it should be recognized that these sexual crimes may not technically conform to the legal definition of forcible rape, even though they are as traumatic for the children as forcible rape is for an adult.

## 7. THE CAUSES OF RAPE

All three of the articles that are reprinted in this section tell us something about the causes of rape in American society. In general, these causes can be classified as social, situational, and psychological. Social causes refer to norms, values, beliefs, and structural arrangements that facilitate the carrying out of sexual assaults on women. For example, American culture is more positive toward violence than many other cultures and also strongly supports the idea of the male as the aggressor in sexual relationships with the female. Furthermore, the double standard of sexual behavior and the myth of the virgin-whore dichotomy tend to legitimate the definition of some women as victims of sexual assaults. Situational factors conducive to sexual assault include the way in which dating is organized, the social use of alcohol and other drugs, and the interaction between males and females that occurs in bars, on dates, and in cross-sex social intercounters that occur in relatively isolated areas.

Much has been said about victim precipitation in sexual assault, and the reprinted article by Kanin and Parcell discusses this issue as it applies to sexual behavior on college campuses. The issue of victim precipitation is perhaps the most inadequately treated aspect of the analysis of rape in the literature. We generally do not hear about victim precipitation with regard to all crimes, but only with regard to crimes against persons, and sexual assaults in particular. Many authors seem to have the impression that women who engage in some levels of sexual behavior with their dates or who accept rides with strangers have precipitated their own sexual victimization. Nothing could be further from the truth. A woman who engages in one level of sexual behavior has in no way committed herself to engage in any other level of sexual behavior. Each progressive level of sexual behavior must be mutually negotiated on a date or in any other situation. The idea that there is a threshold beyond which "anything goes" is based on the myth that males who have reached the threshold of sexual behavior can no longer restrain themselves and must consumate an act of sexual intercourse. The truth of the matter is that many males have never learned to control themselves sexually in these situations, and they often believe that there is no reason to attempt to do so. This is a problem of deficient socialization rather than of biology, and it is correctable in that males can clearly control their sexual urges whenever they choose, just as women can.

The parallel argument to the myth that women who have gone "too far" on a date have to go all the way is that women are not allowed to behave in certain ways, dress in certain ways, or talk in certain ways lest they bring sexual assault upon themselves. In this way of thinking, a woman who is hitchhiking is sexually available, and a woman who wears sexually exciting clothing is fair game for rape. Here we have an example of the use of the threat of rape to restrict the freedom of women to live their own lives as they see fit. The threat of rape and its image as justifiable in certain situations constrains all women to limit their behavior to socially prescribed standards. This is a kind of extralegal social control over women that is the structural equivalent of the beating and lynching of blacks in the South by the Ku Klux Klan and other white supremacist organizations. If there is to be freedom and equality in our society, then we must agree that women have the same hitchhiking privileges and other behavioral freedoms as men. This not to say that every woman should take unnecessary risks in her life, for we must live in a society that is less than perfect, and there is no sense in exposing oneself to risk levels above those that are absolutely necessary. One of the burdens of being a woman in America is that there must be a constant calculation and recalculation of the trade-offs involved in reducing one's freedom on one hand and increasing one's exposure to the possibility of sexual assault and other kinds of criminal victimization on the other hand.

# REFERENCES

Amir, Menachan. *Patterns in forcible rape.* Chicago: University of Chicago Press, 1971.

Benward, Jean, and Densen-Gerber, Judianne. Incest as a causative factor in antisocial behavior: An exploratory study. *Contemporary Drug Problems,* Fall 1975, *4,* 323-340.

Burgess, Ann W., and Holmstrom, Lynda L. Rape trauma syndrome. In Duncan Chappell, Robley Geis, and Gilbert Geis (Eds.), *Forcible rape— The crime, the victim, and the offender.* New York: Columbia University Press, 1977, 315-328.

————, Groth, A. Nicholas, Holmstrom, Lynda L., and Sgroi, Suzanne M. *Sexual assault of children and adolescents.* Lexington, MA: D. C. Heath, 1978.

David, Larry, Schram, Donna, and Ulberg, Cy. *Forcible rape. A national survey of the response by prosecutors.* Washington D.C.: U.S. Government Printing Office, 1977.

Finkelhor, David. *Sexually victimized children.* New York: Free Press, 1979.

Gebhard, Paul H., Gagnon, John H., Pomeroy, Wardell B., and Christenson, Cornelia V. *Sex offenders.* New York: Bantam Books, 1967.

Giarretto, Henry, Giarretto, Anna, and Sgroi, Suzanne M. Coordinated community treatment of incest. In A. Burgess, A. N. Groth, L.L. Holmstrom, and S.M. Sgroi, *Forcible rape—The crime, the victim, and the offender.* New York: Columbia University Press, 1978, 231–240.

Goffman, Erving. *Stigma.* Englewood Cliffs, NJ: Prentice-Hall, 1963.

Goldstein, Michael J., Kant, Harold S., Judd, Lewis L., Rice, Clinton J., and Green, Richard. Exposure to pornography and sexual behavior in deviant and normal groups. In Commission on Obscenity and Pornography (Eds.), *Erotica and antisocial behavior* (Volume VII of the Technical Reports of the Commission). Washington, D.C.: U.S. Government Printing Office, 1971, 1–89.

Groth, A. Nicholas, and Burgess, Ann W. Sexual dysfunction during rape. *New England Journal of Medicine,* October 6, 1977, *297,* 764–766.

————, Burgess, Ann W., and Holmstrom, Lynda L. Rape: Power, anger, and sexuality. *American Journal of Psychiatry,* November 1977, *134,* 1239–1243.

Jackson, Stevi. The social context of rape: Sexual scripts and motivation, *Women's Studies International Quarterly,* 1978, *I,* 27–38.

Kanin, Eugene J., and Parcell, Stanley R. Sexual aggression: A second look at the offended female. *Archives of Sexual Behavior* 1977, *6,* 67–76.

Katz, Sedelle, and Mazur, Mary Ann. *Understanding the rape victim.* New York: John Wiley and Sons, 1979.

MacDonald, J.M. *Rape offenders and their victims.* Springfield, IL: Charles C. Thomas, 1971.

Nelson, Steve, and Amir, Menachen. The hitchhike victim of rape: A research report. In I. Drapkin and E. Viano (Eds.), *Victimology: A new focus,* (Vol. 5). Lexington, MA: D. C. Heath, 1975, 47–64.

Ray, K. K. Feelings and attitudes of raped women of Bangladesh towards military personnel of Pakistan. In I. Drapkin and E. Viano (Eds.), *Victimology: A new focus* (Vol. 5). Lexington, MA: D. C. Heath, 1975, 65–72.

Schiff, Arthur F. Rape in foreign countries. *Medical Trial Technique Quarterly,* 1973, *20,* 66–74.

Selkin, James. Rape: When to fight back. *Psychology Today,* January 1975, *8,* 71–76.

Storaska, Frederic. *How to say no to a rapist . . . . . and survive.* New York: Random House, 1975.

ELEVEN

# The Victim in a Forcible Rape Case: A Feminist View*

PAMELA LAKES WOOD

*Force and consent are the significant issues in rape trials. Many times a female will submit after a lot of talk, liquor, and lunges, and later, for a wide range of reasons, decide that she was really raped. Some girls rape awful easy. So many chicks say no no when there's yes yes in their eyes, and their thighs seem to spread at a mere flick of the finger. The rape law is often used by a woman to "get" a former boyfriend or a hoped-for boyfriend who never materialized.[1]*

The most curious thing about forcible rape[2] cases, despite common misconceptions, is the amount of sympathy which is afforded the offender, and the callousness, or even hostility in some cases, which is felt for the victim. Because of the assumption that jurors are likely to feel sympathy for the victim and convict the assailant without adequate evidence, many states have more stringent proof requirements than would be necessary for other crimes.[3] Nevertheless, many commentators still are obsessed by the fear that innocent men are often convicted of rape due to the malice of "sick" women, who either fabricate stories of forcible rape or "trap" men in situations from which they can reasonably infer consent. These fears are largely groundless. It is more likely that guilty assailants escape due to the reluctance of victims to report the crime, police and district attorneys to prosecute, and jurors to convict. Due to the traumatic experience which a victim must go through in order to attempt to secure the attacker's successful prosecution, it is amazing that any rape cases ever come to trial.

## REQUIREMENTS OF PROOF: TRADITIONAL JUSTIFICATIONS

The law of rape is such that it is highly unlikely to produce an inordinate number of false convictions. Although most jurisdictions still pay lip service to the common law rule which permits a conviction based

---

*From Vol. II, No. 2, 1973, of the *American Criminal Law Review*, the quarterly law review of the Criminal Justice Section of the American Bar Association.

upon the uncorroborated testimony of the complainant, corroboration is usually required whenever the testimony is incredible, contradictory, or improbable.[4] Moreover, several states have, by statute, required corroboration in all rape cases; a number of others have required it in special circumstances; and still others do not require it, but prefer it.[5]

## FEMININE MALICE

One argument raised by commentators to justify more stringent proof requirements for rape accusations is the greater possibility of convicting an innocent man. It is assumed by some writers, that men are often unjustly imprisoned because of accusations brought by malicious women who all too often are afflicted with sexual and emotional problems.[6] These alleged victims, it is argued, are able to take advantage of the irrational sympathy which jurors inevitably feel for a woman who alleges that she has been "wronged."[7] These assumptions are at best questionable. Although Wigmore, for instance, strongly asserted that men are often falsely convicted of rape,[8] he fails to cite even one illustration of this having occurred. What he *does* rely on are five case histories of mentally ill girls who made false sexual accusations against men.[9] In none of these cases was a man convicted of a sexual crime.[10] One author does cite a 1931 case in which nine black men were falsely convicted of raping two white women,[11] but such interracial rape cases are hardly typical as the vast majority of rapes are intraracial.[12] In addition, there is reason to suppose that due to racial conditions in the South at the time of the alleged assault blacks may have been unjustly convicted of other crimes as well.[13]

It would, of course, be foolish to assert that fabricated stories of rape never occur. However, there is no reason to conclude that juries are less able to deal with fabrications in rape than they are in any other type of cases. The "beyond reasonable doubt" standard should be adequate to guard against unjust convictions. A study by Kalven and Zeisel, to be discussed in more detail later, shows that juries, in fact, are more likely to sympathize with the offender than with the victim, whenever there is an indication that her character is less than flawless.[14]

## FEMININE MASOCHISM

Another justification raised in support of stringent proof requirements is the notion that the woman may have really wanted to be raped.[15] In cases in which the victim and assailant are acquainted some authors assert that it is often difficult to tell whether or not the victim did, in fact, consent since it is "customary" for a woman to say "no" when she means "yes."[16] Further, others submit that a woman may have an ambivalent attitude towards intercourse due to fear that her date will have a low opinion of her whether she consents or not. He may consider her a "prude," a "tease," or an "easy lay," depending upon her degree of resistance.[17]

But can one assume that the assailant could reasonably infer consent due to such "social phenomena"? Statistics indicating the amount of violence used upon rape victims tend to negate such a conclusion. A Philadelphia study[18] showed that in 85.1% of the reported rapes some sort of violence—either roughness, beating, or choking—was perpetrated upon the victim.[19] The study further showed that violence was used in 93% of the cases in which the rape was victim precipitated[20] (when the victim placed herself in a "dangerous" position or did not react adversely enough when the assailant's intention to have intercourse was first made clear), but violence was employed only in 83% of the nonvictim precipitated cases.[21] It is difficult to conclude that assailants were misled in this preponderant number of attacks.


Victim Precipitated Forcible Rape


Some authors go further and suggest that in many cases the victim actually sets up the rape either consciously or unconsciously. It is asserted that women are so inherently masochistic that rape may actually be a "pleasurable event" or a "liberating experience."[22] Supposedly this attitude leads women into unconsciously taking unnecessary risks. It has also been suggested that because of a "riddance mechanism" a woman may unconsciously expose herself to dangerous situations. The victim is thought to fear rape so much that she wants to "get it over with."[23] Moreover, in cases in which the prosecutrix attempted to arouse the offender, without the intention to have intercourse, the "assumption of risk" is asserted, even though it would not constitute a valid legal defense. In such cases the defense may allege a "rape trap."[24] The concept of "assumption of risk" is also applied to situations in which the victim agreed to have a drink or go for a ride with a stranger (showing a reckless attitude) or in which she failed to react strongly enough to the advances of the assailant.[25]

All of these situations constitute what Professor Amir calls "victim precipitated forcible rape."[26] What the victim does is less significant than how the assailant interprets her actions.[27] The effect of this theory is to make the victim partly responsible for the crime having occurred thereby mitigating the guilt of the assailant.[28] Such a conclusion is likely to focus the blame on women for having innocently participated in "dangerous" situations. If a woman goes drinking with a man her accusation of rape is weakened "since by drinking she took a chance, made herself vulnerable, and also introduced an element of stimulation for the male."[29] If she allows a man to come to her house, or if she goes to his, she is either indicating a willingness to have sexual intercourse or showing her readiness to assume the risk of attack.[30] If she allows any sexual intimacies, she is playing "the dangerous game of posing as a possible 'bad' girl who in the end turns out to be a 'good' girl."[31] It is dangerous for her to trust her friends or relatives since in 29% of primary relationship cases "gentlemen forfeited their positions of trust and committed the crime of forcible rape."[32] A woman could not remain blameless under such an analysis unless she lived in a constant state of fear that every man she encountered was a potential rapist. This hardly would constitute a healthy attitude, yet it would fail to counter suggestions that unconscious behavior precipitated the rape.

The real danger of this victim precipitation—assumption of risk doctrine, however, is its frequent extension to the point where the offender is freed from guilt.[33] Jurors, in particular, tend to think in terms of assumption of risk and victim precipitation.[34] The extent to which this doctrine is applied can be seen in the results of a study by Kalven and Zeisel. The entire study, which analyzed many crimes in addition to rape, relied upon 3,576 trials which were included in two surveys.[35] For each trial, a questionnaire was sent to the judge which asked him questions concerning the fact pattern, what outcome was reached by the jury, and how he would have decided the case if he were sitting without a jury.[36]

In two cases from the study, the judges thought that the jury had weighed the conduct of the prosecutrix in reaching their result:

---

Case 1:  A 17-year-old girl was raped during a beer drinking party. The jury probably acquitted, according to the judge, because they thought the girl asked for what she got.[37]

Case 2:  The prosecutrix and the defendant were divorced but were considering getting back together. The defendant alleged that they had continued sexual relations, but the prosecutrix denied this. According to the judge, "[T]he jury was of the opinion that if it was in the course of conduct which she had accepted, she was in no position to complain of her leading him on."[38]

In a series of other cases, the judge noted circumstances which Kalven and Zeisel interpret as suggesting assumption of risk:

Case 3: The complainant was raped after she got into a car with the defendant and three of his companions. Prior to the attack she had had several beers. The jury acquitted.

Case 4: The victim, a 33-year-old woman who had been married twice and divorced, met the assailant at a dance, went to a night club with him, and was raped on the way home. The jury acquitted.

Case 5: The complainant met the defendant at a dance and both had been drinking. She was raped in a deserted wooded area on the way home. The jury acquitted.[39]

---

In order to test their hypothesis that juries take factors such as contributory behavior on the part of the complainant into account, Kalven and Zeisel broke up the rapes in the study into two groups—1) aggravated rape—when there was extrinsic violence, more than one assailant, or no prior acquaintance of the defendant and the victim, and 2) simple rape—all other cases. This division was based upon the lesser chance of contributory behavior present in the aggravated rape cases.[40] As expected, it was found that the judge and jury agreed much more frequently as to what the result should be in the aggravated rape cases than in the simple rape cases.[41] In 12% of the aggravated rape cases the jury acquitted when the judge convicted, but the comparable figure for simple rape was 60%.[42] In 9 out of 10 cases of simple rape in which the jury was given the opportunity to convict of a lesser charge, they did so.[43] These figures seem to indicate that in the simple rape cases the jury feels that the assailant is guilty of some crime, but they think rape is too severe a charge.[44] Since the jury lacks the discipline of the judge, it retains a certain amount of discretion and autonomy regardless of what the judge's instructions are.[45] As a result, the jury may take such factors as assumption of risk, victim precipitation, or reputation of the victim into consideration.

## THE VICTIM'S CHARACTER AND MENTAL STATE

The concentration upon the reputation of the prosecutrix, almost as if she were the one whose guilt or innocence were to be determined, is an indication of the bias against the rape victim in the current system.

Police may dismiss a case merely because the victim is suspected of being promiscuous, particularly if she is black.[46] At trial, evidence of bad reputation or unchastity is generally admissible as substantive evidence bearing on the consent of the prosecutrix.[47] In a few jurisdictions, the moral character of the complainant may actually be a defense to the crime under the theory that an unchaste female or one with a bad reputation is likely to have consented.[48] Even when unchastity is not considered a defense, evidence of the parties having engaged in prior sexual relations—or even evidence of prior acquaintance or dating of the parties—may be used to infer a "continuous state of mind" or the "unlikelihood of a serious attitude of opposition."[49]

As has been previously discussed,[50] the jury is more likely to sympathize with the assailant, particularly when there is evidence of the parties having formerly had some sort of interaction. Male jurors are especially likely to be unsympathetic to the prosecution in such situations,[51] presumably because they can more easily identify with the male offender than they can with a female victim. Although prosecutors usually seek out women jurors, they may end up with mostly men, often because women ask to be excused because they feel they would not be objective.[52] Even if the prosecution can get female jurors, however, such jurors may find it difficult to empathize with a victim who has a bad reputation. Consequently, they may be just as harsh as their male counterparts.[53]

It is therefore submitted that jurors of both sexes may allow the reputation of the prosecutrix to influence them on issues other than consent. This would explain the fact that prostitutes stand little chance of obtaining a conviction for rape, even though they are often the victims of gang rapes.[54] It would also provide an explanation for the results in cases such as the following:

1. In a 1970 case, a woman was beaten, raped, and sodomized by four men in an apartment where she had been brought by four men at gunpoint. The defense counsel won the case upon the grounds that both his client, who was the tenant at the apartment where the complainant had been raped, and the prosecutrix were sexual libertines. At the trial he destroyed the victim's reputation, revealing that she was a divorcee whose children were in a foster home, that she had had numerous affairs, and that she was living illicitly with a man at the time of the trial.[55]

2. In another case, three men seized a woman from the street at 1:30 A.M. and took her to an apartment where they brutally raped her. At the trial of one of the assailants it was revealed that the

complainant had two illegitimate children and the defendant alleged that she was a prostitute without offering any evidence to that effect. The jury acquitted.[56]

3. The situation is even more extreme when the victim and the offender have previously had sexual relations since the reputation of the complainant as well as her assumption of risk are considered. In one case of "savage rape," the victim's jaw was fractured in two places. The jury nevertheless acquitted because it found that there may have been sexual relations on previous occasions, and the parties had been drinking on the night of the incident.[57]

Although character evidence is admitted on the issue of consent,[58] its probative value is arguably low since the fact that a woman has consented to sexual relations with men in the past does not show that she has consented to intercourse with a particular man on a particular occasion. The probative value of character evidence on the issue of consent may also be outweighed by its prejudiciality to the victim. Such evidence should, in most cases, be excluded.

In some jurisdictions, the unchastity of the complainant may also be admissible on the question of her veracity.[59] Here again, prejudiciality is high and probative value low. Fortunately, character evidence is not usually admitted for this purpose.

More often it is evidence concerning the victim's psychiatric state which is admitted on the issue of her credibility as a witness.[60] According to Wigmore, the "social history and mental makeup" of the prosecutrix in a sex crime case should be examined before the charge is given to the jury.[61] Fortunately, no court has felt compelled to follow this,[62] although currently the mental stability of the complainant can be put at issue in a rape case.[63]

Since psychiatric evidence is highly prejudicial it should only be admitted when it clearly has bearing upon the issue of veracity. When the evidence is admitted the judge should be careful to instruct on both the purpose to which the evidence is to be put and the weight which it is to be given. When it appears that the alleged purpose of the evidence is merely an excuse for its admission on another issue it should be excluded.

## RESISTANCE

Even if a victim does not precipitate the rape, has a good reputation, and is mentally well-adjusted, her efforts to have her assailant convicted may nevertheless go unrewarded if the jury feels that she has not shown enough resistance. A dramatic illustration of this phenomenon is a recent case in the District of Columbia in which 17-year-old Santionta C. Butler was accused of raping a George Washington University student and forcing her and another female student to commit sodomy.[64] Although Butler conceded that he committed the crimes, his confession was not admitted at trial due to technical reasons.[65] The jury, composed of four men and eight women, acquitted, according to one juror because the women neither resisted enough nor tried to escape.[66] According to testimony at trial, both victims were hysterical after the crime, and one was found by a physician to have at least ten sizeable bruises on her body.[67] One woman, who had been beaten repeatedly on the head, said that she was afraid that Butler had a gun;[68] the other was described by her roommate, who saw her and Butler emerge from the washroom where the assault occurred, as being bruised and disheveled after the incident.[69] One of the complainants, who claimed to feel more like a defendant than a plaintiff, said, "I wasn't on trial. I don't see anything I did wrong. I screamed. I struggled. How could they have decided that he was innocent, that I didn't resist. It's preposterous."[70] Nevertheless, the jury did not find that "consent was induced by physical force, or by threats which put her in reasonable fear of death or grave bodily harm," as required by District of Columbia law.[71]

The victim is thus placed in a very difficult predicament. If she chooses to resist to the extent of her physical capacity, she is likely to incur serious injuries. In one case a 37-year-old woman required 120 stitches on her face and head after having resisted a man who attempted to rape her in Central Park at 7:30 A.M.[72] Detective Al Simon of the Central Park Precinct said of this case:

> We've been looking for this guy for a long time. Two years ago we picked him up for attempted rape, and it was a throw-out in court; no corroboration. Now we have this poor woman, who fought like hell and didn't get raped. The guy has been indicted for assault in the first degree. She's scarred for life. And you know what she says now? She says she wishes she hadn't fought, and maybe he wouldn't have cut her up the horrible way he did.[73]

If the victim does not resist, however, her assailant is likely to escape punishment and, due to the sadistic nature of the act, he may use violence upon her anyway. Furthermore, he may commit the crime again and may set an example for would-be rapists.

## THE COMPLAINANT'S ORDEAL

Reporting the Crime

Because of the bias within the system and the emotional trauma which accompany the crime, victims often fail to report rape. According to the *Uniform Crime Reports,* rape is probably reported to the police less than any other Crime Index offense.[74] It is difficult to estimate the percentage of crimes which are, in fact, reported, but estimates run from a high degree of reportability to as low as 5%.[75]

Some women do not bother reporting rapes because they feel it would be useless. One past victim at the Rape Crisis Center in Washington, D.C. remarked that a woman must be "bruised, bloody, and damned near dead" in order for the activity to be considered not consensual.[76] Others do not report the crime because they do not wish to encounter additional stress and abuse.[77] Many victims feel the process through which they must go in order to even attempt to obtain a conviction may be worse than the crime.[78]

Victims who have received aid the the Rape Crisis Center in Washington, D.C. report a wide range of treatment by the police.[79] Some victims were satisfied with the treatment they received.[80] At the other extreme were complaints about the police having made snide remarks, such as "How many orgasms did you have?", "I know why you got raped," or "Didn't I pick you up last week for prostitution?"[81] Some of the police even harp over sexual details with relish—"How big was he?" and "What were you thinking about while he was doing it?" are questions victims have been asked.[82] One woman said that although the rape was really bad, the police interrogation was six times as horrible.[83]

The police in effect have absolute discretion as to whether or not any action is taken to obtain a conviction.[84] Often they will refuse to accept charges, especially when the victim is alone when she comes to file them[85] and even when the charges are accepted, they may neglect to work on cases which they feel are unsubstantiated.[86] Often the police (and the court) may, due to a common socio-cultural orientation, see the situation from the offender's point of view rather than from the victim's.[87] Hence they may infer consent when none was given or think in terms of victim precipitation. As a result it is often both futile and frustrating for a woman to report the crime.[88]

The Investigatory Process

For those who wish to report rape, the first step in Washington, D.C. is for the complainant to call the police so that they can pick her up and take her to the precinct for questioning by the Sex Squad. Next she is taken to the hospital by the police, who leave her there alone. Since some hospitals are crowded and rape victims are not given priority, women may have to wait up to four hours before obtaining medical aid.[89] This can be extremely unpleasant since victims cannot cleanse themselves of any blood or semen which might be present.[90] The major problem, however, is that no one is concerned with the victim's mental state.[91]

The physical examination is used to prove that intercourse took place since the crime is rarely witnessed. A blood alcohol test may also be taken since, intoxication may be used to imply assumption of risk.[92] The woman is next undressed and her clothing is examined for blood and seminal stains and for any indications of violence. The presence of seminal stains on clothing, however, may merely indicate attempted rape. Tests for semen on clothing are nevertheless valuable since they may be effective even if several months have passed.[93]

The victim is next asked whether she has washed or douched, since either would be likely to destroy any evidence. She is then given a routine gynecological examination and tested for the presence of spermatozoa to see if intercourse did, in fact, occur.[94]

In Washington, D.C., the physician is required to fill out a form concerning the rape. The "mental health evaluation" consists of nine categories: apparently normal, lethargic, crying, agitated, angry, verbose, hysterical, unconscious, and "other."[95] The physician is also asked whether the evidence is most compatible with vaginal intercourse, forced vaginal intercourse, anal sodomy, or forced anal sodomy.[96]

Generally the victim goes home after the physical examination and returns to the Sex Squad the next day to make a complete report. Although after a wait in the emergency room the complainant may not be out until 5 A.M., she may still be told to appear before the Sex Squad at 8:30 A.M.[97] At that time she makes a formal statement and is shown photographs of potential suspects. Then she is sent away, often with the promise that she will hear from a "lawyer."[98] Usually she is not informed as to when there is to be a preliminary hearing, whether the charges have been dropped, or what action is being taken.[99] In order to find out any information, the victim must call the police herself.[100] This uncertainty only adds to the mental pressure which the victim is experiencing.[101]

## The Trial

Even if a woman is able to convince the police and the district attorney that there is some possibility that she has been raped, her ordeal is not over. She must still endure a personal attack during private hearings before a magistrate, grand jury investigations, and a public trial.[102] In fact, an official at the San Francisco Crimes Department stated that one of the functions of police interrogation in a rape case is to prepare the victim for the attack which she can expect from the defense counsel "to make sure the woman is not petrified, embarrassed, or driven to tears on the stand."[103]

The cross-examination in court can be grueling.[104] The accused rapist's attorney often initiates his case by inquiring as to the number of men with whom the victim has had intercourse.[105] He then makes her go over the details of the rape,[106] while insinuating that she is mistaken as to the identity of her assailant or that she consented to the intercourse. Although in the interests of justice a careful cross-examination is warranted in any type of criminal proceeding, the psychological side effects which a victim in a rape case must otherwise endure may justify the limitation of the amount of pressure used by the defense attorney. It should not be forgotten that the prosecutrix is the victim and, as such, should not be subjected to any more duress than necessary.

The victim in a rape case thus may find herself subjected to an ordeal as bad or worse than the crime itself if she does not choose to keep her victimization a secret. According to Pittsburgh Police Superintendent Robert Colville:

> Rape is the only crime in which the victim is doubly violated, first by the attacker, and then by society. It is the only crime in which social, religious, and cultural core attitudes of society turn upon the victim. In rape, society tends to blame or accuse the women.[107]

## ALTERNATIVES

As has been shown, the present system is less than ideal. The best solution, of course, would be to effectuate a change in attitudes—to try to make men see the crime from the victim's point of view and to try to stop the victims from blaming themselves. Hopefully policemen eventually will sympathize with women to the point at which they will be able to refrain from making sarcastic or callous comments. Authors will hopefully stop thinking about such concepts as victim precipitation and assumption of risk and start thinking of the complainant as the helpless victim of an act of hatred and aggression. Jurors, too, will hopefully start following the law rather than their own ideas about sexual property rights and blameworthiness.

Emotional Support

These hopes are unlikely to materialize in the near future. There are, however, present schemes which are being used to alleviate the bias in the current system. The Rape Crisis Center, begun in June, 1972, in Washington, D.C. has been a successful effort. The Center provides information and services for women who have just been raped as well as support for women who have been raped in the past and either are having trouble adjusting emotionally or just would like to talk to someone about their experience. The Center also provides lessons in self-defense. If a woman has just been raped, the Center will provide another woman to go to the police with the victim as "a friend." This often makes members of the police force more careful in their treatment of victims. Sometimes the police assume an actual friend is from the Rape Crisis Center since they do not know all the names of the members.[108] Crisis centers are beginning to be formed in other areas.

Another promising development is the chaplains' counseling service for rape victims—or "Code R"—which was begun at the University of Chicago hospitals and clinics in March, 1972.[109] After a victim arrives at the emergency room, a chaplain is summoned who takes the victim to a private consultation room where he attempts to assuage her anxieties. He then accompanies her while she fills out forms and waits for her gynecological examination, and he may even, if necessary, offer to help the victim break the news to her husband. Apparently this project has also been successful in changing the attitudes of the police. According to Dr. Peter Rosen, medical director of the emergency room at the University of Chicago's Billings Hospital, "They don't come into the emergency room any more and yell, 'I got a rape for ya, Charlie.'"[110]

An increase in the number of women on the police forces would also be helpful. More women would then be available both to take complete reports at the precinct and record the victim's initial complaint. Moreover, those policemen who are assigned to question rape victims should be discouraged by their superiors from making any remarks concerning the incident.

Suggested Legal Changes

Within the legal system itself, several changes should be made in order to obtain more equitable treatment for rape victims. The distinctions between rape victims and victims of other crimes should be abolished. Corroboration should never be required in order to bring a case before the jury since the jury itself is capable of determining whether or not the evidence is sufficient to support a conviction. The notion that the victim's character has an unquestionable bearing on the issue of consent should no longer be adhered to. Evidence of the victim's reputation and psychiatric state should only be admitted when probative value clearly outweighs prejudicial effects and the resistance standard should depend upon whether the victim's resistance was reasonable under the circumstances.

In order to partly compensate for the jury's concentration upon assumption of risk and victim precipitation,[111] the law itself should be changed in all jurisdictions to provide for different degrees of rape. The National Commission on Reform of Federal Criminal Laws has come up with a proposed federal law which would divide rape into different sexual offenses.[112] Such a scheme would prevent jurors from acquitting in situations in which they feel that the crime committed does not justify the punishment and stigma of a rape conviction.

Under the proposed federal statute, the sexual offense known as rape would include situations in which the victim was compelled to submit either by force or "by threat of imminent death, serious bodily injury, or kidnapping, to be inflicted on any human being."[113] It would also include attacks upon victims who were less than 10 years old, or who were drugged or intoxicated by the assailant.[114] Rape would be a Class A felony if serious bodily injury were inflicted upon the victim, if the victim were less than 10 years old, or if the victim was not a voluntary companion of the actor and had not previously permitted him sexual liberties.[115] Otherwise it would be a Class B felony.[116]

The crime of Gross Sexual Imposition, a Class C felony, would consist of intercourse with a woman whom the offender knows to have a mental disease or defect which "renders her incapable of understanding the nature of her conduct,"[117] whom he knows is unaware a sexual act is being performed upon her, who submits due to the mistaken supposition that he is her husband, or who submits because of "any threat that would render a female of reasonable firmness incapable of resisting.[118] The crimes of aggravated involuntary sodomy and involuntary sodomy would be analagous and have analagous penalties, but a person of either sex would be capable of being an offender or a victim.[119] The offense of corruption of minors would consist of intercourse or deviate sexual relations with a person less than 16 years old when the actor is at least 5 years older than the other person.[120] Less severe sexual offenses would be covered by the sexual assault section.[121]

Another plan has been suggested which would provide for Rape in the First Degree, Rape in the Second Degree, and Sexual Intercourse by

Deceit.[122] Under this proposal it is significant that the fact that the victim was not a voluntary social companion of the actor and had not previously permitted him sexual liberties would be irrelevant.[123] Actually such circumstances are, arguably, irrelevant since, from the victim's point of view, it is hardly more desirable to be abused by an acquaintance than by a stranger. To treat such factors as relevant is to adopt Amir's victim precipitation approach. However, from a more practical point of view it would be wise to adopt a distinction between "date rape" and "stranger rape" since jurors are likely to adopt such a distinction on their own. Whether such factors should be taken into consideration in legislative proceedings is beyond the scope of this article.


## CONCLUSION

Temporary measures, such as crisis centers or legislative reforms, may be able to alleviate current atrocities, but until the time when the rape victim is no longer looked upon with suspicion and distrust, most rapists are likely to commit the crime with impunity. The bias against the rape victim in the United States today can only be dispelled if people become aware of the quandary in which she has been placed by a society which tends to adopt a male perspective. Exposing the defects in the present system is the first step in curing them.


## NOTES

1. S. ROSENBLATT, JUSTICE DENIED 36 1971) [hereinafter cited as ROSENBLATT].

2. Although only forcible rape will be considered in this article, some of the discussion is applicable to statutory rape. Since in some states the penalties for statutory and forcible rape are identical, statutory rape is alleged because no force need be proven. J. MACDONALD, PSYCHIATRY AND THE CRIMINAL 235 (2d ed. 1969) [hereinafter cited as MACDONALD.].

3. *See* notes 4 & 5 *infra* and accompanying text.

4. Note, *Criminal Law—Psychiatric Examination of Prosecutrix in Rape Case,* 45 N.C. L. REV. 234 (1966).

5. Note, *Corroborating Charges of Rape,* 67 COLUM. L. REV. 1137 (1967). New York, for instance, previously required corroboration of the assailant's identity, penetration, and the application of force. Now only corroboration of the use of force and an attempt at penetration need be shown. N.Y. PENAL

LAW § 130.15 (McKinney Supp. 1972). In California, corroboration is unnecessary unless the testimony of the prosecutrix is "inherently improbable or unbelievable." 42 CAL. JUR. 2d § 97 at 286 (1965). In Texas, corroboration is required only when there has been a delay in reporting the crime. *E.g.,* White v. State, 478 S.W.2d 506 (Tex. Crim. App. 1972); Thomas v. State. 476 S.W.2d 305 (Tex. Crim. App. 1972).

      6. ROSENBLATT, *supra* note 1, at 37; 3A J. WIGMORE, EVIDENCE 736 (Chadbourne rev. 1970) [hereinafter cited as WIGMORE].

      7. A recent analysis reflects this attitude and comments upon it:

> False accusations of sex crimes in general, and rape in particular, are generally believed to be much more frequent than untrue charges of other crimes. A woman may accuse an innocent man of raping her because she is mentally sick and given to delusions; or because, having consented to intercourse, she is ashamed of herself and bitter at her partner; or because she is pregnant, and prefers a false explanation to the true one; or simply because she hates the man whom she accuses. Since stories of rape are frequently lies or fantasies, it is reasonable to provide that such a story, in itself, should not be enough evidence to convict a man of crime. . . . Normally our law relies on a jury to distinguish truth from falsehood after hearing evidence on both sides and giving weight to the truth that a man must be considered innocent unless proven guilty beyond a reasonable doubt. It is normally assumed, not that false accusations never occur, but that they will not mislead a jury into convicting. When the crime charged is rape, it is unsafe to rely on this assumption.

Note, *Corroborating Charges of Rape,* 67, COLUM. L. REV. 1137, 1138 (1967).

      8. Wigmore states:

> Modern psychiatrists have amply studied the behavior of errant young girls and women coming before the courts in all sorts of cases. Their psychic complexes are multifarious, distorted partly by inherent defects, partly by diseased derangements or abnormal instincts, partly by bad social environments, partly by temporary physiological or emotional conditions. One form taken by these complexes is that of contriving false charges of sexual offenses by men. The unchaste (let us call it) mentality finds incidental but direct expression in the narration of imaginary sex incidents of which the narrator is the heroine or the victim. On the surface the narration is straightforward and convincing. The real victim, however, too often is the innocent man; for the respect and sympathy naturally felt by any tribunal for a wronged female helps to give easy credit to such a plausible tale.

WIGMORE, *supra* note 6, at 736.

      9. *Id.* at 737.

      10. *Id.* Despite the lack of evidentiary support for his conclusions, Wigmore is often quoted to substantiate the contention that fabricated stories may lead to convictions in rape cases. *See* Ballard v. Superior Court, 64 Cal. 2d 159,

171, 410 P.2d 838, 846 (1966); Note, *Corroborating Charges of Rape,* 67 COLUM. L. REV. 1137, 1139 (1967); Note, *Criminal Law—Psychiatric Examination of Prosecutrix in Rape Case,* 45 N.C. L. REV. 234, 235 (1966).

11. ROSENBLATT, *supra note* 1, at 39.

12. According to a Philadelphia study of 646 rapes taking place between January 1, 1958 and December 31, 1958 and between January 1, 1960 and December 31, 1960, less than 7% were interracial. (In 4.2% there were black offenders and white victims and in 2.6% there were white offenders and black victims.) Amir, *Victim Precipitated Forcible Rape,* 58 J. CRIM. L.C. & P.S. 493, 498 (1967) [hereinafter cited as *V.P. Rape.*].

13. Murder of a white woman by a black person also causes much unrest in southern communities. A. TREBACH, THE RATIONING OF JUSTICE 6 (1964). After discussing a case in which 88 blacks were arrested in Odessa following the rape of a 19-year-old white girl, Trebach comments:

> These dragnet operations frequently are ordered in response to crimes that shock the conscience of the community, especially the rape or murder of white women by nonwhite assailants.

*Id.*

14. H. KALVEN & H. ZEISEL, THE AMERICAN JURY 249 (1966) [hereinafter cited as KALVEN & ZEISEL].

15. One girl who had been raped was asked by her assailant why she did not enjoy it. Margolin, *Rape: The Facts,* 3 WOMEN: A JOURNAL OF LIBERATION 9 (1972). Another, whose assailant was convicted, has been approached at parties by men who say, "I'll bet you loved it." Schurr, *Rape: Victim as Criminal* 4, KNOW, INC. reprint of a series of articles published in the Pittsburgh Forum, beginning November 5, 1971 [hereinafter cited as Schurr]. Even a man who attempted rape is still told by other men, "You should have gone ahead and done it. Every chick wants you to do it." Ms., Dec. 1972, at 23.

16. Slovenko, *A Panoramic View: Sexual Behavior and the Law,* in SEXUAL BEHAVIOR AND THE LAW 51 (R. Slovenko ed. 1965) [hereinafter cited as Slovenko].

17. Note, *The Resistance Standard in Rape Legislation,* 18 STAN. L. REV. 680, 682 (1966).

18. The study is discussed in more detail at note 12 *supra.*

19. M. AMIR, PATTERNS IN FORCIBLE RAPE 156 (1971) [hereinafter cited as PATTERNS].

20. *See* notes 23–27 *infra* and accompanying text.

21. *V.P. Rape, supra* note 12, at 501. The explanation for this seeming paradox given by Professor Amir of the Hebrew University is that although the offender might believe the victim to be sexually accessible, he resorts to violence so that he will not have to risk not completing the act in case he is mistaken. *Id.* This explanation does not in any way absolve the assailant from guilt for the crime of rape since it shows his intention to have intercourse even without the consent of the victim.

22. PATTERNS, *supra* note 19, at 254.

23. Note, *The Resistance Standard in Rape Legislation*, 18 STAN. L. REV. 680, 682 (1966).

24. Slovenko, *supra* note 16, at 52.

25. Women who accept a ride home from a casual tavern acquaintance, who walk alone in dark streets late at night, who accept modelling appointments and babysitting jobs in strange homes without prior investigation, or who associate with motorcycle gangs invite trouble. Girls who have a reputation for promiscuity may find that some men will use force when their expectations of compliance are not fulfilled. MACDONALD, *supra* note 2, at 238.

26. *V.P. Rape, supra* note 12, at 493.

27. Professor Amir describes his theory as follows:

In the sexual sphere, a man can interpret verbal and nonverbal behavior on the part of a woman in such a way as being contrary to the expectations of appropriate female behavior or, even as conflicting with the whole image of a woman's propriety. She will be placed, then, in the category of a sexually available female. Thus, wrongly or rightly, a woman's behavior, if passive may be seen as worthy to suit action, and if active it may be taken as an actual promise of her access for one's sexual intentions. The offender then will react as seems appropriate toward such a woman.

*Id.* at 494.

28. This analysis, however, is not without its critics:

It is a vain delusion that rape is the expression of uncontrollable desire or some kind of compulsive response to overwhelming attraction. Any girl who has been bashed and raped can tell you how ludicrous it is when she pleads for a reason and her assailant replies "Because I love you" or "Because you're so beautiful" or some such rubbish. The act is one of murderous aggression, spawned in self-loathing and enacted upon the hated other. Men do not themselves know the depth of their hatred. It is played upon by inflammatory articles in the magazines designed for morons with virility problems which sell for high prices in transport cafes: "Eager Females: How they reveal themselves," writes Alex Austin in *Male* and proceeds to describe a number of harmless mannerisms, like slipping a shoe off, and showing a hearty appetite (for food) which indicate concealed goatishness in women. Barry Jamieson describes the underhand tactics of "The Willing Cheater: Your Wife's Best Friend" in Stag. The object of such articles is to imply that the world is full of liquorish sluts in flimsy disguises, who will welcome the most unceremonious advances despite their prissy denials. Such women are *available, easy, pushovers*. Whatever they get, they have deserved.

G. GREER, THE FEMALE EUNUCH 265-66 (1971).

29. PATTERNS, *supra* note 19, at 22.

30. *V.P. Rape, supra* note 12, at 497.

31. PATTERNS, *supra* note 19, at 252.

32. *Id.* at 235.

33. One author comments:

> Yet, even though the female sometimes unconsciously sets up the rape, the fact remains that she is the victim. The law's purpose is to deal with the act and responsibility of the offender. The victim may seek psychotherapy for masochistic tendencies, but that is a private matter. The law's task is to protect against victimization. The offender, not the victim, is the guilty party. There seems to be, however, more and more attention being given to the contribution that the victim makes to his injury . . . True, individuals are responsible for their affairs, but it is the aggressor who acts out his feelings against an available subject, and he is legally at fault.

Slovenko, *supra* note 16, at 54.

34. The law recognizes only one issue in rape cases other than the fact of intercourse: whether there was consent at the moment of intercourse. The jury, as we come to see it, does not limit itself to this one issue; it goes on to weigh the woman's conduct in the prior history of the affair. It closely, and often harshly, scrutinizes the female complainant and is moved to be lenient with the defendant whenever there are suggestions of contributory behavior on her part.

KALVEN & ZEISEL, *supra* note 14, at 249.

35. *Id.* at 33. Sample I was from 1954 to 1955; sample II was from 1958. *Id.*

36. *Id.* at 45.

> As a matter of both theoretical interest and methodological convenience, we study the performance of the jury measured against the performance of the judge as a baseline. Our material is a massive sample of actual criminal jury trials conducted in the United States in recent years. For each of these trials we have the actual decision of the jury and a communication from the trial judge, telling how he would have disposed of that case had it been tried before him without a jury. In this sense, we have been able to execute the grand experiment of having each case, over the wide universe of contemporary jury business in the criminal law, tried by a jury and also by a judge, thus obtaining matched verdicts for a study. The result is a systematic view of how often the jury disagrees with the judge, of the direction of such disagreement, and an assessment of the reasons for it.

*Id.* at 10.

37. *Id.* at 250.

38. *Id.*

39. *Id.* at 250.

40. *Id.* at 252.

41. *Id.* at 253.

42. *Id.* at 253. A hung jury was counted as ½ an acquittal for the study.

43. *Id.* at 253.

44. *Id.* at 250.

45. *Id.* at 86, 87.

46. PATTERNS, *supra* note 19, at 11. It should also be noted that due to the operation of the "slum sex code," some girls are more likely to be raped than others because of their relationships with boys. *Id.* at 249. This does not mean that they give any sort of consent.

47. *Id.* at 14.

48. *Id.* at 23.

49. *Id.* at 23. Professor Amir uses the Philadelphia study discussed in note 12 to show that there is little truth to the common myth that most rapes are explosive crimes committed by strangers. In 42% of the cases the assailant was a complete stranger, in 10% the victim had some knowledge of him, and in 48% he was an acquaintance or friend. *Id.* at 235. A Detroit study for 1949 showed that 57% of the victims were known to the offender, whereas 43% were strangers. *Id.* at 250. The Philadelphia study also showed that 75% of the rapes had been planned. Amir, *Forcible Rape,* 31 FED. PROBATION 51 (1967).

50. *See* note 34 *supra.*

51. Lear, *Q. If You Rape a Woman and Steal Her TV, What Can They Get You For in New York? A. Stealing Her TV,* N.Y. Times, Jan. 30, 1972 (Magazine) at 11 [hereinafter cited as Lear].

52. *Id.* at 11.

53. Schurr, *supra* note 15, at 4.

54. *Id.* at 4.

55. *Id.* at 5.

56. KALVEN & ZEISEL, *supra* note 14, at 251.

57. *Id.*

58. *See* notes 47 & 48 *supra* and accompanying text.

59. WIGMORE *supra* note 6, at 729.

60. Note, *Corroborating Charges of Rape,* 67 COLUM. L. REV. 1137, 1142 (1967) [hereinafter cited as Note, Corroborating Charges of Rape].

61. WIGMORE, *supra* note 6, at 737.

62. Note, *Criminal Law—Psychiatric Examination of Prosecutrix in Rape Case,* 45 N.C. L. REV. 234, 235 (1966).

63. Note, *Corroborating Charges of Rape, supra* note 60, at 1142.

64. Smith, *The Rape Victim's Dilemma: How to React?,* Washington Post, Dec. 2, 1972, at El, col. 2-3 [hereinafter cited as Smith].

65. *Id.* at El, col. 4-5.

66. Barker, *She Felt Like a Defendant,* Washington Post, Dec. 2, 1972, at El, col. 6 [hereinafter cited as Barker].

67. Smith, *supra* note 64, at El, col. 2-6.

68. Barker, *supra* note 66, at El, col. 7.

69. *Id.* at El, col. 6.

70. *Id.* at El, col. 5.

71. *Id.* at El, col. 6.

72. Lear, *supra* note 51, at 55.

73. *Id.*

74. F.B.I., UNIFORM CRIME REPORTS 14 (1970).

75. PATTERNS, *supra* note 19, at 27.

76. Television program, "Perspective," on WRC, Washington, D.C., Nov. 12, 1972.

77. The woman's shame may be so great that she does not reveal the assault to anyone. Fear of rejection by her husband may seal her lips. Risk of newspaper publicity and embarrassment in the courtroom may deter the victim from informing the police. As many rapists threaten to kill their victims if they go to the police, fear of retaliation may also be a factor. Some victims do not report sexual assaults by close relatives or family friends.
MACDONALD, *supra* note 2, at 238.

Testimony in rape cases can be extremely embarrassing and humiliating, and our courts bend over backward to spare the victims any undue shame or strain. Often they are permitted to testify in secret and their testimony may later be suppressed or sealed. Even in secret testimony, naturally, the woman must speak before the jury and the court personnel, which fact sometimes may cause a woman not to press charges even when they are eminently justified.
ROSENBLATT, *supra* note 1, at 37.

78. MACDONALD, *supra* note 2, at 238. The Michigan Governor's Study Commission on the Deviated Criminal Sex Offender in 1951 recommended that police, district attorneys, defense counsel, and courts handle the victims of sex crimes, and children in particular, more carefully in order to reduce the traumatic effects of the entire experience. *Id.* at 238.

79. Interview with Brenda, member of the Rape Crisis Center, in Washington, D.C., Nov. 20, 1972. This interview was supplemented by a simultaneous interview with Darlene, another member of the Center, and an earlier interview with Karen, also a member, on November 14, 1972. The information obtained in the interview with Karen was verified by the later interviews. Since all three women have worked at the Rape Crisis Center in Washington, D.C., opened in June 1972, they have talked to a large number of rape victims. Currently Darlene is working with other members of the Center on a book about rape. (The last name of these women have been withheld upon their request, due to the fact that they are past rape victims, as are most of the members of the Rape Crisis Center.)

80. Interview with Brenda, member of the Rape Crisis Center, in Washington, D.C., Nov. 20, 1972.

81. Interview with Karen, member of the Rape Crisis Center, in Washington, D.C., Nov. 14, 1972.

82. *Id.*

83. *Id.* Many women at the Rape Crisis Center have complained that the interrogation was worse than the rape. Interview with Darlene, member of the Rape Crisis Center, in Washington, D.C., Nov. 20, 1972.

84. Interview with Karen, member of the Rape Crisis Center, in Washington, D.C., Nov. 14, 1972.

85. KEARON & MEARHOF, *Rape: An Act of Terror,* NOTES FROM THE THIRD YEAR 80 (1971).

86. Interview with Brenda, member of the Rape Crisis Center, in Washington, D.C., Nov. 20, 1972.

87. PATTERNS, *supra* note 19, at 263.

88. [T]he main issue was . . . whether a rape should ever be reported. On one hand, it can be argued that because of the rarity of rape convictions, the haranging questions asked at the police station and in court, and the voyeurism exhibited by many police officers, a woman should be discouraged from reporting a rape—personal considerations aside, it just doesn't do much good. On the other hand if rapes are not reported, or if the rapist is not otherwise dealt with, this would mean that men can rape with full knowledge that nothing will happen to them.

D.C. RAPE CRISIS CENTER, HOW TO START A RAPE CRISIS CENTER 7 (1972).

89. Interview with Darlene, member of Rape Crisis Center, in Washington, D.C., Nov. 20, 1972.

90. In one case a girl had managed to severely scratch the face of her assailant so that blood and flesh were present under her fingernails. She showed the evidence to the police, who told her they would not need it. The next day, after she had taken a bath and destroyed the evidence, they asked her for it, and when she was unable to produce it they claimed they could do nothing since there was no evidence. *Id.*

91. Interview with Darlene, member of Rape Crisis Center, in Washington, D.C., Nov. 20, 1972.

92. Bornstein, *Investigation of Rape: Medicolegal Problems,* 9 MED. TRIAL TECH. Q. 61,63 (1963).

93. *Id.* at 68.

94. Motile spermatozoa are present 12 hours after coitus and nonmotile are present 48 hours afterwards. *Id.* at 65. Although there are no visible marks in a mature woman after normal intercourse, severe lacerations may be produced by violent rape, and there are usually visible lesions after a woman's first intercourse. These lesions are actually produced from a tear in the mucosa of the vulva rather than by the tearing of the hymen, as is commonly believed. *Id.* at 66.

95. "Medical Examination of Allegedly Sexually Assaulted Persons" Form P-4760.

96. *Id.*

97. Interview with Karen, member of the Rape Crisis Center, in Washington, D.C., Nov. 14, 1972.

98. *Id.*

99. *Id.* One woman was not shown a line up until months after the crime occurred. Her assailant had been detained and released shortly after the crime.

100. Interview with Darlene, member of the Rape Crisis Center, in Washington, D.C., Nov. 20, 1972.

101. [T]he following pattern has been noticed from the women who have called the Center: the first few days is a period when the woman feels isolated and alienated from herself and others; the first year is a period when the woman is very much involved with fear—on the streets, at home, and among strangers; after the first year the woman is concerned with the effect the rape has had on interpersonal relationships. D.C. RAPE CRISIS CENTER, HOW TO START A RAPE CRISIS CENTER 7 (1972).

102. Schurr, *supra* note 15, at 5.

103. Margolin, *Rape: The Facts,* 3 WOMEN: A JOURNAL OF LIBERATION 21 (1972).

104. Schurr, *supra* note 15, at 5.

105. *Id.*

106. *Id.*

107. *Id.* at 3.

108. D.C. RAPE CRISIS CENTER, HOW TO START A RAPE CRISIS CENTER 7 (1972).

109. NEWSWEEK, Nov. 13, 1972, at 75.

110. *Id.*

111. *See* note 34 *supra* and accompanying text.

112. NATIONAL COMMISSION ON REFORM OF FEDERAL CRIMINAL LAWS, FINAL REPORT 187 (1971).

113. *Id.*

114. *Id.*

115. *Id.*

116. *Id.*

117. *Id.* at 188.

118. *Id.*

119. *Id.* at 189.

120. *Id.*

121. *Id.* at 191.

122. Note, *The Resistance Standard in Rape Legislation,* 18 STAN. L. REV. 680, 688 (1966).

123. *Id.*

TWELVE

# Rape: Power, Anger, and Sexuality*†
## A. NICHOLAS GROTH, ANN WOLBERT BURGESS, AND LYNDA LYTLE HOLMSTROM

Within the last few years, increasing awareness of and concern for the rape victim has become evident in this country. However, relatively little attention has been directed toward understanding the rapist and the motivations underlying his offense. A major handicap in this regard has been access to offender populations; rapists rarely report voluntarily to mental health clinics, and the conviction rate for rape is extremely low. In commenting on the professional literature on the rapist, Abel and colleagues (1) pointed to the lack of accessibility of offenders for evaluation and treatment and the failure of the professional community to develop effective and efficient models of treatment. Pacht (2) believes that until a sufficient number of controlled research studies are completed, ineffective approaches may be used in efforts to provide appropriate treatment for the rapist.

Research in the field of sexual assault is multi-disciplinary (3). Amir (4), in his survey of several hundred rape cases handled by the Philadelphia Police Department, discussed the role relationship between victim and offender. MacDonald (5) evaluated rape cases in the Denver area on such epidemiological factors as time of day, season, and the relationship of victim and offender. The operational behavior approach to studying deviant sexual behavior has been undertaken by Abel and Blanchard (6), Barlow (7), Evans (8), and Marshall (9). Rada (10) devised a combined social and psychiatric diagnostic classification for use with rapists in a clinical setting. In the psychological literature, the motivational aims and needs of the rapist have been described by Guttmacher and Weilhofen (11), Gebhardt and associates (12), and Cohen and colleagues (13) Sociologists and criminologists have reported on the issue of power and dominance as factors in rape (14) and on rape as social control (15–18)[1]; Gelles examined power, sex, and violence in marital rape (19).

†The authors wish to acknowledge the clinical work of Murray L. Cohen, Ph.D., Boston University, on the psychology of rape, which has contributed to their conceptualization of sexual assault.

To date, few reported comparative data have been available on the phenomenon of rape from the experiential standpoint of both the offender and the victim. This paper examines forcible rape through an analysis of separate offender and victim accounts and suggests a clinical typology of rape derived from these data.

## METHOD

Written into the General Laws of Massachusetts is a statute (Chapter 123A) that provides for diagnostic evaluation of anyone convicted of sexual assault in regard to the probability of repetition and dangerousness. If it is adjudicated likely that the offender will repeat his offense and in so doing jeopardize the physical safety of his victim, he may be civilly committed for an indefinite period of from one day to life (in lieu of or in addition to a prison sentence) to a special maximum security treatment center operated by the state Department of Mental Health. The clinical and statistical data reported in this paper in regard to the offender are derived from a random sample collected by Groth of 133 convicted rapists committed for clinical assessment to the Massachusetts Center for the Diagnosis and Treatment of Sexually Dangerous Persons.

The victim sample population is derived from a one-year counseling and research study conducted at the Boston City Hospital that included all persons admitted to the emergency service with the chief complaint, "I've been raped." Burgess and Holmstrom clinically assessed the 146 victims of sexual assault according to three categories: rape trauma, accessory to sex, and sex-stress situation (20). The 92 adult rape victims from that study comprise the sample for this paper.

The offenses committed by the offender population and those experienced by the victim population were congruent in time, but they were unrelated in that none of the women in the sample were victims of the offenders studied.

The descriptions of the rape assaults given by offenders and victims were analyzed in order to develop a typology of rape. A major intent was to see if the accounts provided by the two groups could be encompassed within one conceptual framework.

## RESULTS

Typology of Rape

One of the most basic observations one can make about rapists is that they are not all alike. Similar acts are performed for different reasons or

different acts serve similar purposes. Our clinical experience with convicted offenders and with victims of reported sexual assault has shown
that in *all* cases of forcible rape three components are present: power,
anger, and sexuality. The hierarchy and interrelationships among these
three factors, together with the relative intensity with which each is
experienced and the variety of ways in which each is expressed, may
vary, but there is sufficient clustering to indicate distinguishable patterns
of rape. We have found that either power or anger dominates and that
rape, rather than being primarily an expression of sexual desire, is, in
fact, the use of sexuality to express issues of power and anger. Rape,
then, is a pseudo-sexual act, a pattern of sexual behavior that is concerned much more with status, aggression, control, and dominance than
with sensual pleasure or sexual satisfaction. It is sexual behavior in the
service of nonsexual needs and, in this sense, is clearly a sexual deviation
(21).

*Power Rape.*   In this type of assault, the offender seeks power and control over his victim through intimidation by means of a weapon, physical force, or threat of bodily harm. Physical aggression is used to
overpower and subdue the victim and is directed toward achieving submission. The aim of the assault usually is to effect sexual intercourse as
evidence of conquest; to accomplish this, often the victim is kidnapped,
tied up, or otherwise rendered helpless.

This type of offender often shows little skill in negotiating interpersonal relationships and feels inadequate in both sexual and nonsexual
areas of his life. Because he has few other avenues of personal expression, sexuality becomes the core of his self-image and self-esteem. Rape
is the means by which he reassures himself of his sexual adequacy and
identity, of his strength and potency.

Since it is a test of his competency, the rape experience for this
offender is one of anxiety, excitement, and anticipated pleasure. The
assault is premeditated and preceded by an obsessional fantasy in which
his victim may initially resist him but, once overpowered, will submit
gratefully to his sexual embrace. She then will be so impressed with his
sexual abilities that she will respond with wild abandon. In reality, this
offender may be handicapped by impotency or premature ejaculation
(22). Even if he is not, he still tends to find little sexual satisfaction in
the rape. The assault is disappointing because it never lives up to his
fantasy.

Often he must convince himself that his victim became "turned on"
to him, really wanted sex but could not admit it, and clearly consented
nonverbally and enjoyed the sexual contact. However, at some level he

realizes that he has not found what he is looking for: something he cannot clearly define is lacking. He does not feel reassured by either his own performance or his victim's response and therefore must go out and find another victim—this time the "right one."

The offenses become repetitive and compulsive. The amount of force used in the assault may vary and there may be an increase in aggression as the offender becomes more desperate to achieve that undefinable experience that continues to elude him. Usually there is no conscious intent on the part of this offender to hurt or degrade his victim. The aim is to have complete control over her so that she has no say in the matter. She will be submissive and gratify his sexual demands.

This rape may be understood as the result of an endogenous developmental psychological crisis precipitated by some perceived challenge from a female or threat from a male that activates the offender's feelings of inadequacy and insecurity (23). Rape is the way in which this type of person asserts his identity, potency, mastery, strength, and dominance and denies his feelings of worthlessness, rejection, helplessness, inadequacy, and vulnerability.

The victim of this assault is typically within the same age group as the offender or younger. Hospital examination generally shows minimum or inconclusive evidence of physical or sexual injury, and clinical evidence of intercourse—presence of motile sperm—may be absent. The victim often reports being questioned by the offender regarding her sexual life, her reaction to his sexual performance, and her identity, with the implication of expected further contact. The victim is fearful that the offender will attempt to return and is upset about the forced conversation and sexual assault. Her coping behavior is often in the service of trying to talk her way out of the rape or resisting intimidation initially by being assertive and confrontational.

Rapists who fall into the power assault category can be subdivided on the basis of whether the major goal in the offense is assertion or reassurance.

The *power-assertive rapist* regards rape as an expression of his virility and mastery and dominance. He feels entitled to "take it" or sees sexual domination as a way of keeping "his" women in line. The rape is a reflection of the inadequacy he experiences in terms of his sense of identity and effectiveness. Case vignettes below illustrate this subtype.

Mr. A, a 20-year-old single man on leave from the Coast Guard, picked up an 18-year-old hitchhiker and drove her to a secluded beach. She begged to be let go, but he grabbed her, saying, "You don't want to get hurt, baby—you want to get laid. You want it as much as I do." He forced her to submit to intercourse and then offered to buy her dinner. While out on bail he committed an identical offense. As an adolescent, he had been involved in a number of sexual incidents involving exhibitionism and sexual play with children and was treated at a local mental health clinic. As an adult he had no steady girlfriends and while in the service was living with and being supported by a 30-year-old man in exchange for sexual favors. However, he does not regard himself as a homosexual. He committed two previous rapes for which he was never apprehended; his only other arrests were for motor vehicle violations. Although he is of above-average intelligence, his academic and vocational accomplishments were mediocre, and the only activity he had pursued with any diligence was body-building.

Ms. B is a 45-year-old divorced woman. A former boyfriend came by her home with a bottle of gin and asked her to share a drink with him. She agreed. Later that evening she refused to have sex with him and her account of what happened follows: "He messed me over the street way. I'm not supposed to tell. He said he'd beat me if I tell and he gave me a sample tonight to show me. They work you over to control you so they can have you sexually any time they want. He hit me on the ear, pulled my hair, hit me in the back by my kidneys—very strategic. But it's not the physical part that's the thing. It's mental—to control you."

The *power-reassurance rapist* commits the offense in an effort to resolve disturbing doubts about his sexual adequacy and masculinity. He wants to place a woman in a helpless, controlled position in which she cannot refuse or reject him, thereby shoring up his failing sense of worth and adequacy.

Mr. C is a 24-year-old married man who pleaded guilty to six charges of rape. In every case he approached the victim with a gun in a shopping mall. His fantasy was that the woman would say, "You don't need a gun. You're just what I've been waiting for," and then "rape" him. He kidnapped the women, tied them up, forced them to submit to intercourse, and then questioned them as to whether he was as good as other sex partners they had had. Mr. C had no criminal history other than the sex offenses. His background was unremarkable, but he had never felt that he did particularly well in any area of his life (academic, social, vocational, marital) with the exception of his military service. He dated actively as a teenager and indulged in pregenital sexual play, stopping short of intercourse. He found intercourse unsatisfying, partly because of premature ejaculation and partly because it never lived up to his expectations, although he could not define what was missing. He saw marriage as a solution, but since he could not be sensitive or attentive to anyone else's needs but his own, his marriage floundered. Mr. C discovered he was sterile and began having disturbing homosexual thoughts before his offense. He described the offense as a compulsion—something he felt he must do. Although he realized the consequences of what he was doing, he could not control himself. The six assaults occurred within a 2-month period.

Ms. D, a 21-year-old single woman, had just stepped off a bus on her way home from work and was walking in a well-lighted area of the city. A man approached her from behind, put a knife to her back, pushed her into some bushes, and pulled her sweater over her head so that he would not see him. He raped her vaginally and kept asking her questions such as: "How does it feel? Am I as good as your boyfriend?" She said, "He seemed as if he needed to be reassured and so I tried to reassure him. I was lying on my back in the gravel . . . he was odd saying those things . . . then I had to bargain with him to get my clothes back. He also wanted my address and to know if he could come and do it again. I felt if I could convince him I was being honest, he would let me go. He had my pocketbook and would know who I was so I told him where I lived but not the right apartment." The medical record indicated abrasions on lower and upper back, with no other signs of bleeding or trauma.

*Anger Rape.*   In this type of sexual assault, the offender expresses anger, rage, contempt, and hatred for his victim by beating her, sexually assaulting her, and forcing her to perform or submit to additional degrading acts. He uses more force than would be necessary simply to subdue his victim. The assault is one of physical violence to all parts of the body: the rapist often approaches his victim by striking and beating her, tears her clothing, and uses profane and abusive language.

The aim of this type of rapist is to vent his rage on his victim and to retaliate for perceived wrongs or rejections he has suffered at the hands of women. Sex becomes a weapon, and rape is the means by which he can use this weapon to hurt and degrade his victim.

This offender displays a great deal of anger and contempt toward women. He sees them as unloving, ungiving "whores and bitches." Sex itself is regarded at some level as base and degrading, and the anger rapist typically finds little or no sexual satisfaction in the rape. He tends to react subjectively to the sexual act with revulsion and disgust, and he may experience difficulty achieving erection or ejaculation during the assault (22).

His relationships to important women in his life are fraught with conflict, irritation, and irrational jealousy, and he is often physically assaultive toward them. His sexual offenses tend to be episodic and sporadic, triggered by conflicts in his relationships to these women (mother, girlfriend, wife), but the anger is often displaced onto other individuals.

The rape experience for this offender is one of conscious anger or sadistic excitement. His intent is to hurt his victim, and his assault is brutal and violent. The motive is revenge and punishment; in extreme cases, homicide may result.

He finds it difficult to explain his assault when he cannot deny it except to rationalize that he was drunk or on drugs. Often the details are lost to his memory because he becomes "blind with rage" during the assault. Satisfaction and relief result from the discharge of anger rather than from sexual gratification. He derives his pleasure from degrading and humiliating his victim.

Older or elderly women are a particular target victim for this type of rapist, although victims may be of any age. Medical examination generally reveals considerable physical trauma to all areas of the victim's body, often requiring X rays and consultation from other medical specialties. Victims report experiencing the rape as life-threatening, and their symptoms after the rape are disruptive to physical, behavioral, social, and sexual lifestyles.

Victims describe a blitz style of attack (20) or a sudden and dramatic switch in the offender's behavior. Having used a confidence ploy to entrap his victim, the offender then exhibits a behavior change in which he assaults her in a fury of anger. Victims may be physically immoblized and unable to use any coping strategies during the rape (24). Abusive and humiliating language may be used, and "perverted" acts are often a major aspect of the assault.

Rapists who fall into the anger-assault category can be subdivided into two groups on the basis of whether or not the degradation of the victim represents conscious rage or pleasure on the part of the offender.

The *anger-retaliation rapist* commits rape as an expression of his hostility and rage towards women. His motive is revenge and his aim is degradation and humiliation.

Mr. E is a 25-year-old married man and father of four. His mother abandoned the family shortly after his birth, and throughout his life his father reminded him that his mother was a "whore and never trust any woman; they are no good." During his adolescence he became acquainted with his mother and once when she was drunk she exposed herself to him and asked him to fondle her. He fled, terrified. In vain efforts to win his father's recognition and approval, he put a premium on physical toughness. In high school he played sports "like a savage." He then entered the Marine Corps and had an outstanding service record. After his discharge he married (against his father's wishes) and attended college. One day he got into a dispute with his female history teacher over the merits of the Viet Nam war and felt she was ridiculing and humiliating him in front of the class. He stormed out of the room, very angry, thinking "women are dirty, rotten bastards" and went to a bar for a few drinks. On his way to his car he spotted a 40-year-old woman (whom he described as looking older) in the parking lot. He grabbed her by the throat and hit her in the mouth; then he ripped off her clothes and raped her. Before this offense, Mr. E's only criminal record consisted of arrests for gambling, loitering, and drunkenness.

Shortly after midnight, Ms. F, a 33-year-old mother of two, was in bed reading and waiting for her husband to return from work. A man known to the family for 10 years knocked at the door and the 14-year-old son let him in. He said he was leaving town the next day and wanted to say goodbye. Ms. F talked to him from the bedroom and wished him well on his trip. Suddenly the man ordered the boy to his room, grabbed Ms. F, and forced her to go outside to another building. He beat her far more than was necessary to subdue her, choked her, and sexually assaulted her. On followup, Ms. F reported considerable physical pain from the beatings. She had pain and swelling of the face, neck, arms, and leg, and she reported loss of appetite, insomnia, nightmares, crying spells, restlessness, and a fear of being followed as she walked home from work. She was unable to carry out usual parenting and household tasks for the first week following the assault. There was tension within the marital relationship, delay in resuming sexual relations, and flashbacks to the assault.

The *anger-excitation rapist* finds pleasure, thrills, and excitation in the suffering of his victim. He is sadistic and his aim is to punish, hurt, and torture his victim. His aggression is eroticized.

Mr. G is a 30-year-old divorced man charged with first-degree murder. His victim, a 20-year-old woman he picked up at a singles bar, was tied to a tree, whipped, raped, sodomized, and slashed to death. Although found to be sane, he claimed he was high on drugs and could not remember what had happened. He had a criminal record that included assault and battery, breaking and entering, nonsupport, and motor vehicle violations. At the age of 17 he had tied a 13-year-old neighbor girl to a bed and assaulted her. He beat his children and burned his wife with cigarettes during intercourse. Shortly after his conviction, Mr. G committed suicide.

Ms. H, a 33-year-old single woman, was returning to her apartment at about 9:00 p.m. when she was suddenly jumped from behind and knocked to the ground. She remembered nothing until she awoke in the assailant's apartment. She was held captive there for 2 days, during which time she reported being continually beaten, raped, and forced to perform fellatio. She said, "He bit me and burned me. He had pictures of rattlesnakes on his wall." The medical exam revealed multiple injuries to her face and eye, multiple bruises and lacerations to her body, and human bite marks and cigarette burns on her chest. Ms. H was hospitalized for several days.

Rape, then, rather than being an expression of sexual desire, in fact is the use of sexuality to express issues of power and anger. In every case of rape all three factors coexist but their relative intensities and interrelationships vary. The incidence of each type of rape assault in our respective samples is presented in table 1.

Overall, power rapes outnumber anger rapes: of the 225 offenses studied, 146 (64.9%) were classified as power rapes and 79 (35.1%) as anger rapes. The anger-retaliation assault was the most frequent type of

**Table 1.** *Incidence of Sexual Assaults Classified According to Typology*

| Type of Assault | SAMPLE | | | | | |
| | Offender $N = 133)^a$ | | Victim ($N = 92)^b$ | | Total ($N = 255$) | |
| | Number | Percent | Number | Percent | Number | Percent |
| Power | | | | | | |
| Assertive | 50 | 37.59 | 48 | 52.17 | 98 | 43.55 |
| Reassurance | 22 | 16.54 | 26 | 28.26 | 48 | 21.33 |
| Anger | | | | | | |
| Retaliation | 53 | 39.84 | 14 | 15.21 | 67 | 29.77 |
| Excitement | 8 | 6.01 | 4 | 4.34 | 12 | 5.33 |

[a] For those convicted offenders who also had a codefendent ($N = 21$) each rapist is categorized separately.

[b] For those victims with more than one assailant ($N = 33$), the rape is categorized for the initial assailant.

offense in the offender sample, but it ranked only third in the victim sample. One possible explanation is that the incidence of anger-retaliation rape is in fact lower than the incidence of power offenses, but since the physical evidence of anger assault is more apparent, the likelihood of conviction is greater. Consequently the anger-retaliation rapist may be overrepresented in the convicted-offender sample. The anger-excitation offender seems to be the least prevalent type among both samples.

## DISCUSSION

The proposed conceptualization of the issues of power, anger, and sexuality in rape has several implications. Clinical work with offenders and victims indicates that the initial impact of rape is not sexual for either group. Although the act is sexual, what is traumatizing to the victim is the life-threatening nature of the assault, her helplessness and loss of control in the situation, and her experience of herself as the object of her assailant's rage. This is important because the etiology of the victim's trauma is the offender's pathology. Rape is more than an illegal act and more than an extreme of cultural role behavior. From a clinical point of view, it is important that rape be defined as a sexual deviation and that the pathology of the offender be recognized.

The clinical typology of offenders we have presented offers one approach to differentiating offenders with regard to identification, disposition, treatment planning, and prognosis. Further research is warranted to determine whether the trauma reaction varies according to the motivation of the rapist and to ascertain whether conviction rates differ for the four types of offenders.

## NOTES

1. An abridged version of Bart's paper (18) was printed in the June 1975 issue of *Viva* magazine.

## REFERENCES

1. Abel G, Blanchard EB, Becker JV: Psychological treatment of rapists, in Sexual Assault: The Victim and the Rapist. Edited by Walker MJ, Brodsky SL. Lexington, Mass. DC Heath Co, 1976, pp 99–115

2. Pacht AR: The rapist in treatment: professional myths and psychological realities, in Sexual Assault: The Victim and the Rapist. Edited by Walker MJ, Brodsky SL. Lexington, Mass, DC Heath Co, 1976, pp 91–97

3. Holmstrom LL, Burgess AW: Rape victimology: past, present and future research. Presented at the annual meeting of the American Association for the Advancement of Science, Boston, Mass, Feb 23, 1976

4. Amir M: Patterns of Forcible Rape. Chicago, University of Chicago Press, 1971

5. MacDonald J: Rape: Offenders and Their Victims. Springfield, Ill, Charles C Thomas Co, 1971

6. Abel GG, Blanchard EB: The role of fantasy in the treatment of sexual deviation. Arch Gen Psychiatry 30:467–475, April 1974

7. Barlow DH: Increasing heterosexual responsiveness in the treatment of sexual deviation: a review of the clinical and experimental evidence. Behavior Therapy 4:655–671, 1973

8. Evans DR: Masturbatory fantasy and sexual deviation. Behav Res Ther 6:17–19, 1968

9. Marshall WL: The modification of sexual fantasies: a combined treatment approach to the reduction of deviant sexual behavior. Behav Res Ther 11:557–564, 1973

10. Rada RT: Treatment of offenders. Presented at the annual meeting of the American Orthopsychiatry Association, Atlanta, Ga, April 4, 1976

11. Guttmacher M, Weihofen H: Psychiatry and the Law. New York. WW Norton Co, 1952

12. Gebhardt P, Gagnon J, Pomeroy W, et al: Sex Offenders. New York, Harper & Row, 1965

13. Cohen ML, Garafalo RF, Boucher R, et al: The psychology of rapists. Semin Psychiatry 3:307–327, 1971

14. Schwendinger JR, Schwendinger H: Rape myths: in legal, theoretical and everyday practice. Crime and Social Justice: A Journal of Radical Criminology 1:18–26, 1974

15. Weis K. Borges SS: Victimology and rape: the case of the legitimate victim. Issues in Criminology 8:71–115, 1973

16. Reynolds JM: Rape as social control. Catalyst 8 (Winter):62–67, 1974

17. Russell DEH: The Politics of Rape: The Victim's Perspective. New York, Stein and Day, 1975

18. Bart PB: Rape doesn't end with a kiss (unpublished paper. Department of Psychiatry. Abraham Lincoln School of Medicine, University of Illinois, Chicago, Ill)

19. Gelles RJ: Power, sex, and violence: the case of marital rape. Presented at the annual meeting of the Western Social Science Association, Phoenix, Ariz, April 30, 1976

20. Burgess AW, Holmstrom LL: Rape: Victims of Crisis. Bowie, Md, Robert J Brady Co, 1974

21. Groth AN, Burgess AW: Rape: a sexual deviation. Am J Orthopsychiatry 47:400–406, 1977

22. Groth AN, Burgess AW: Sexual dysfunction during rape. N Engl J Med
    (in press)
23. Burgess AW, Groth AN, Holmstrom LL, et al: Sexual Assault of Children
    and Adolescents. Lexington, Mass, DC Heath Co, 1977
24. Burgess AW, Holmstrom LL: Coping behavior of the rape victim. Am J
    Psychiatry 133:413–414, 1976

THIRTEEN

# Sexual Aggression: A Second Look at the Offended Female*

EUGENE J. KANIN AND STANLEY R. PARCELL

## INTRODUCTION

This study represents an effort to replicate and extend the 1957 investigation of male sex aggression (Kirkpatrick and Kanin, 1957). Our prime
motive for replication stems from the observation that the intervening
years have evidenced social changes that could prompt one to hypothesize that the 1957 findings are now something of a period piece. Those
findings, it could be argued, were the product of a more sexually repres-
sive era where the male-female subculture was characterized by comparatively greater social distance contributing to intrasex communication
difficulties and sexual exploitation of the female. Since the initial investigation, we have seen something of a sexual revolution, the woman's
liberation movement, and a youth movement asserting that honesty and
candor between the sexes have replaced the older order of sexual exploitation. In short, there exist social indicators that seriously question
whether such conduct as uncovered in the 1950s still persists at *comparable* levels and in *comparable* patternings.

---

*Reprinted by permission of Plenum Publishing Corporation, New York,
1977.

## METHOD

A mimeographed schedule was distributed to the females in 23 varied university classes in a large Midwestern state university, males and married females being excused. Anonymity was guaranteed and, for the most part, cooperation was good. Of the 358 females approached, 76 either refused to cooperate or else submitted incomplete schedules, leaving 282 usable instruments for analysis. Of course, these 282 females cannot be regarded as a representative sample from a defined student universe. Although the 1957 sample was of a comparable nature and drawn from a comparable type of institution, we feel a certain reserve in making time comparisons since both samples were accidental. Only the more exaggerated differences and findings will receive attention in this report.

In an effort to arrive at more insightful interpretations and to shed light on current sexual folkways bearing on our data, 55 females—not necessarily members of the sample—volunteered to provide case histories and/or engage in group sessions to discuss dating-courtship activities. The information obtained proved to be a valuable adjunct to the statistical findings and will be selectively used to interpret the findings.

The schedule was focused on male sex aggression, i.e., aggressively expended male efforts to kiss, attempts to fondle the breasts and genitals, attempts at coitus, and coital attempts in the course of which menacing threats or physical pain were employed. In each of the foregoing levels of intimacy, the female had to perceive the male efforts as offending and displeasing.

A realistic interpretation of the meaning of these levels of intimacy is in order. It does not necessarily follow that merely because a male exerts offensive efforts to kiss or fondle that this conduct constitutes his ultimate sexual goal. A forced kiss could be coitally directed equally as well as an attempt to expose oneself or to attempt to remove the female's garments. Therefore, there is a certain static artificiality imputed to these data. These levels reveal only the female's perception of the immediate objective of the aggressive maneuver. Certainly, however, they do reveal the behavioral dimensions of the aggressive act.

In this article, we will examine the prevalence and the nature of the aggressive episodes, the provocation factors, and the nature of the dyadic relationships of the offender-offended. The traditional personal and social characteristics of the offenders and the offended, e.g., age, social class, and educational level, will not be reported since analysis has shown them to be devoid of significance for these data. This latter point will receive comment in our conclusions.

# INCIDENCE, FREQUENCY, AND NATURE
# OF THE EPISODES

As evidenced in previous studies, the present findings show sexual aggression to be a common experience for college females. Of the 282 university women in this investigation, one-half (50.7%) indicated that they were offended at some level of erotic intimacy during the 1971–1972 academic year (see Table 1). These 143 coeds reported being involved in 725 episodes, approximately 5.1 episodes per offended female.[1] Examining experience with aggressive sex prior to the year studied reveals that 69.2% of all respondents were offended since college entrance and that 63.5% were offended during their high school years. Including *all* previous aggressive experience at the time of the administration of the questionnaire, i.e., from high school entrance to the time of the current study, reveals that sexual aggression at some level of erotic intimacy was encountered by approximately 83%.

Those who reported themselves offended during the year of this study were also more likely to be habitual victims. These persons were involved more frequently and at the more serious levels of aggression, both while in high school and while in college. Of the females reporting being offended during the year of this study, 75.5% also reported an offensive experience during their high school years, in contrast to 51.1% of the nonoffended. In similar fashion, 79% of the offended experienced aggressions during their previous college years while only 59.7% of the nonoffended reported such aggressions. The overall history of the currently offended shows a mean of 22.5 offensive episodes, in contrast to 8.5 for the nonoffended. The offended coed's prior history also amply

**Table 1.** *Offensive Episodes and Level of Erotic Involvement by Episodes and by Maximum Level of Offense*

| PERCEIVED LEVELS OF AGGRESSION | EPISODES (%) | MAXIMUM LEVEL OF AGGRESSION (%) |
|---|---|---|
| Kissing | 35.8 | 22.4 |
| Breast fondling | 34.1 | 20.3 |
| Genital fondling | 17.2 | 30.8 |
| Intercourse | 12.3 | 23.8 |
| Intercourse with violence | 0.5 | 2.7 |
| Total | 100.0 | 100.0 |
| number | 725 episodes | 143 offended females |

demonstrates that she was more apt to be a target at the more serious levels of aggression. Fully 20% of the offended but only 6.5% of the nonoffended experienced coitus-directed aggression while in high school. Furthermore, she was almost twice as likely to experience efforts at genital fondling as her nonoffended peers, 39% and 21%, respectively. A less exaggerated but comparable pattern is maintained during her college years prior to this study. Twenty-seven percent of the offended but only 19% of the nonoffended experienced aggressive efforts for intercourse, while 42% of the offended and 24.5% of the nonoffended reported offensive efforts at genital fondling.

Keeping in mind that for these episodes to be included here certain criteria had to be met, *viz.,* these episodes were offensive and displeasing, there is then the question of the ability of the female to fend off the aggressive overture. In this study, an attempt was made toward obtaining some estimate regarding the success of these male efforts. Our data illustrate that offended females were not always able to successfully rebuff aggressive advances. These respondents reported that 40% of all male aggressions were successful. With respect to the various levels of intimacy, the percentages of successful episodes were as follows: kissing, 36.2%; intercourse, 29.2%; intercourse with violence, 100.0%. However, the meaning of these figures is not at all clear. They do not tell us whether the female was forcibly rendered sexually superable and, subsequently, compliant or whether the entire event was characterized by duress. The only significance that can be attributed to "success" is obviously associated with the level of aggression. To succeed in kissing or sexually touching a refractory female may be a rather fleeting and innocuous type of accomplishment, but success at achieving intercourse, regardless of the brevity of the experience, is indeed a phenomenon of a significantly different caliber, psychologically, socially, and legally. Approximately 32% of the intercourse aggressions were reported to be successful. It is unfortunate that we cannot elaborate further on the character of these episodes so as to possibly reveal something on the order of a rape index.


## PROVOCATION OF AGGRESSIVE EPISODES

It has become customary to speak of many types of victims as provoking or precipitating their own misfortunes. The behavioral phenomenon under discussion here offers a classic example of scrutinizing the behavior of the offended for possible provoking conduct. Our language abounds with sexist admonitions for the female that clearly convey the notion that whatever interactional difficulties she sexually encounters are of her own making. The conduct of the male, it would appear, is strictly dictated by the female's demeanor. Males have given the female little latitude and have been able to impute to her responsibility for most any type of sexual misunderstanding. "She was asking for it" is the archetype from which stems a myriad of verbalizations that not only "explain" but also serve to mitigate the male's role in his enthusiastic pursuit of sexual activity. These may include anything from her manner of dress, speech habits, and drinking customs to her participation in any form of sexual involvement. In this context, several dimensions of the offended female's behavior will be examined in an effort to assess whether some of the more frequently labeled provocative female behaviors are associated with her victimization.

### Antecedent Consensual Sex Play

In the context of victim provocation, it can be readily hypothesized that voluntary sex play would antecede the aggressive experience. Earlier studies provide us with substantial data for expecting aggressive behavior to be grounded upon a superstructure of consensual sexual activity (Kanin, 1957, 1969). However, these coeds report a surprisingly large percentage of episodes beyond the kissing level which were spontaneous male sexual gestures not preceded by any consensual erotic activity. Approximately 44% of the sexual aggressions beyond kissing did not follow any consented-to sex play![2] Quite unexpected is the finding that the more sexually advanced the level of offense, the greater the probability that the episode was not preceded by prior sexual interaction. While it can be imagined—albeit with a little difficulty—how 36% of the breast fondling aggressions were not preceded by consensual kissing, it is somewhat perplexing to ponder the fact that 54% of the intercourse efforts were abruptly initiated without benefit of previous sex play.

### Female's Sexual History

A rather conspicuous hypothesis that must be negotiated in pursuing the problem regarding why some females become persistent victims of aggression focuses on the female's sexual history. One can speculate that the sexually initiated female—one with coital experience—could more readily find herself a target of sexual aggression. Feasibly, a variety of cues favorable to the encouragement of male advances can be readily associated with the sexually experienced female. First, the possibility exists that the male believes that his companion has been sexually active, through either direct or indirect information supplied by his male associates, or even by the female herself. Double-standard males particularly would find rejection of their sexual solicitations by these females as intolerable and without rational basis, leading to aggressive sexual efforts (Kanin, 1969). Second, the sexually experienced female may in some fashion convey the impression, through either seductive or verbally provocative behavior, that she is sexually experienced and therefore accessible.

Inspection of these data reveals that the offended female cannot be distinguished from her nonoffended peers with respect to their coital histories. Approximately 50% of each group were nonvirgin. But perhaps this hypothesis suffers from being too general. Prior sexual experience may have little influence, if any, in precipitating the more innocuous forms of offensive aggression. Her wantonness or nonvirginity, however individual male definitions may run, is not necessarily a prerequisite for the attempt to kiss or sexually fondle a female companion. A variety of other cues can satisfy the encouragement for such interaction. However, it can be hypothesized that coital experience is associated with coitally directed aggressions. Taking into account the relationship between the maximum experienced level of aggression and prior coital history reveals a very interesting pattern. The females reporting the more serious aggressions also tend to be the more sexually experienced (Table 2). Considering now only the offended female, it is found that nonvirginity is increasingly reported as we progress from those females who were offended at the kissing and breast-fondling stage (45%), to the genital fondling stage (55%), to the intercourse levels

**Table 2.** *Coital History of Offended Females by Levels of Offensive Experience*[a]

|          | KISSING AND BREAST FONDLING (%) | GENITAL FONDLING (%) | INTERCOURSE AND INTERCOURSE WITH VIOLENCE (%) |
|----------|------|------|------|
| Virgin   | 55.2 | 45.5 | 33.3 |
| Nonvirgin | 44.8 | 54.5 | 66.7 |
| Total    | 100.0 | 100.0 | 100.0 |
| number   | 58 | 44 | 36 |

[a]Total $N = 138$ since five respondents failed to provide information on coital history. $\gamma = 0.29$.

(67%). Although the nonvirginal victim is the recipient of more advanced aggressions, we should not ignore the possibility that she may be the one who more readily acquiesces to the more casual sexual invitations and therefore unwittingly invites the coitally directed aggressions.

Sexually Aggressive Females

Continuing in the context of female provocation prompts us to consider another facet of conduct wherein the offended female can be seen as having presented a different sexual self from the nonoffended. The respondents were offered the opportunity to report whether they were ever sexually aggressive and offended a male companion by their "forward or provocative behavior." This question was asked in our quest for information that might show the offended female to be more "suggestive" or seductive and hence "inviting" male advances. The findings demonstrate that indeed it is the offended rather than the nonoffended female who reports having been aware of sexually offending a male companion, 34.3% and 16.5%, respectively ($\gamma = 0.45$). Viewing this finding from the perspective that offending a male is the independent variable shows that 68% of the sample who offended males were themselves also offended, in contrast to 44% of the nonoffended. Again, there is additional evidence that there may be something in the demeanor of the offended female that contributes to her "victimization."

## PAIR RELATIONSHIPS

In previous studies, it was found that the nature of the pair relationship was associated with the level of aggression, *viz.*, the more advanced aggressions tended to be reported by those involved in the more durable pairings, i.e., steady and regular dates, pinned, and engaged. It was also previously observed that about half (49%) of the offensive episodes occurred within the casual date; exclusion of the necking level revealed only 30% of the episodes to be reported for casual pairings (Kirkpatrick and Kanin, 1957).

These current data offer a radically different pattern in that the majority of episodes are reported for casual pairings. In fact, *each* level of erotic intimacy is concentrated among the casuals. Table 3 rather dramatically reflects the 1957–1974 figures and tells us, in effect, that now the offensive acts are largely concentrated among the less involved and less durable pairings. Although time contrasts based on accidental samples offer shaky grounds for comparative analysis, the dramatic and exaggerated reversal observed here deserves consideration. Speculation prompts us to consider that advanced pairings today are more apt to involve rather extensive sexual activity and that aggression at these advanced pair levels is uncalled for. Furthermore, it may be that male sexual aspirations are significantly higher today, especially in the early stages of pair interaction, and that males manifest a diminished tolerance for the uncooperative female, i.e., for erotic intimacy short of coitus. The prolonged bouts of stabilized noncoital sex play would not only seem to fail to conform with current sexual aspirations but also may appear juvenile.

The frequency and nature of dating behavior can be viewed as the basic opportunity structure which could account for aggressive encounters. Considering dating as an exposure variable, then, we could hypothesize that aggression would be associated with increased frequency of dating and with spontaneous dating, i.e., "pick-ups" and chance meetings, rather than planned encounters. This hypothesis receives no support from these data in that offended women report that during the month previous to the administration of the schedule they had fewer planned dates than the nonoffended, 6.8 and 9.4, respectively, and the same number of spontaneous dates, 4.6. However, this does indicate the offended female to have a greater proportion of her dates of the spontaneous variety than the nonoffended, 41% and 33%, respectively.

Now if we look at the different number of men dated in the same context of exposure to aggressive situations, we can see that the offended females are "dating around" considerably more than the nonoffended, 3.3 dates per man dated vs. 7.5 dates per man dated. Breaking down this finding into an analysis by spontaneous and planned dates shows that it is the nonoffended female who can command relationships without incurring aggressive episodes. For example, for planned dates,

Table 3. *Relationship Involvement and Erotic Intimacy Level at Which Offensiveness Occurs, by Episodes, 1957 and 1974*

| Relationship involvement | BREAST FONDLING (%) | | GENITAL FONDLING (%) | | ALL EFFORTS AT INTERCOURSE (%) | |
|---|---|---|---|---|---|---|
| | 1957 | 1974 | 1957 | 1974 | 1957 | 1974 |
| Casual pairings | 43.8 | 82.9 | 31.4 | 71.9 | 30.1 | 75.4 |
| Involved pairings | 56.2 | 17.1 | 68.6 | 28.1 | 69.9 | 24.6 |
| Total | 100.0 | 100.0 | 100.0 | 100.0 | 100.0 | 100.0 |
| number | 381 | 187 | 191 | 107 | 83 | 69 |

the mean number of dates per man per month for the offended is only 3.7 in contrast to 7.5 for the nonoffended. For spontaneous dates, the findings are comparable. The nonoffended female who gets involved in an unplanned encounter has 7.5 dates with that person while the offended female who makes an unplanned date has but 2.8 dates with that male. Again, we have to speculate on the meaning of these findings. Does the offended female have less bargaining power? Does she simply have a philosophy of "dating around," thereby exposing herself to a greater number of males and increasing the probability of being offended? Going out with a "dating-around" female may be viewed by males as an indication of relationship futility, that one should be pre-pared to capitalize on "short-term investments." On the other hand, if a female gives the impression that the relationship will be brief, either reputationally or directly, the imputation of sexual promiscuity is not unusual and could well accelerate the sexual efforts of many males.

## SUMMARY AND CONCLUSIONS

From the foregoing analysis, certain summary statements and conclu-sions are in order.

1. Sexual aggression in dating-courtship pairings continues to be a common experience for college females. Approximately 50% of these coed respondents reported being offended at some level of erotic inti-macy during the academic year studied.

In spite of the dramatic social changes that have come to bear on premarital male-female relationships during the past decade or so, the incidence and frequency of sexually offensive male conduct in dating-courtship relations, according to our data, appear to have remained rela-tively unchanged. The normative pattern of sexual aggression for males, and its frequent escalation into offending force, has apparently not been disturbed by the various social movements that stress sex-role egalitari-anism, intrasex communication, and a more permissive sexuality. In fact, from high school through college, sexual offending aggression is shown to be an experience of the majority of females. We must acknowl-edge, however, that these social changes could very well have polaristic functions. "Liberated" females may be viewed as sexually rebellious since they advocate the abolition of traditional constraints on the female. The sexual revolution could very well persuade some males that females possess malelike sex drives. And the youth movement could also have consequences of a comparable nature, e.g., the imputation that liberation from traditional youth roles and the open communication regarding sexual matters indicate more sexually engageable females.

2. The currently offended female demonstrates an overall history of being sexually victimized. She is victimized more frequently and more seriously, in both her high school and college years. And although we can offer evidence that the genitally and coitally aggressed females are more apt to be nonvirgin, and that females who are sexually aggressive are more apt to be victims, no significant evidence can be mustered to show that this habitual victimization is associated with any social and personal characteristics that would help account for this condition. We have to acknowledge, however, that personality traits that could be instrumental in precipitating the offended females' difficulties were not accounted for in this study.

The inability of our data to demonstrate the significance of personal and social variables such as age, social class, and intelligence, as either individual or comparative variables, comes as a surprise, particularly in view of past research findings. The patterning of these variables which formerly led to interpretations of male exploitation of females possessing "inferior" or heterogamous characteristics is patently absent. We are tempted to speculate on the foregoing negative findings. It was originally anticipated, although without much conviction, that certain conspicuous social changes would be responsible for altering the incidence of sexual aggression. Our data could not demonstrate this. However, there is something in our findings that could be related to these social changes. The male role of sexual pursuit may not have changed but perhaps a modification of the mechanics of the pursuit has taken place. It would appear feasible that although these changes did not modify male sexual exertions, they did alter the nature of the sexual target. Additional supportive evidence for this position comes from the finding that male sexual aggression currently shows greater disregard for the nature of the pair relationship. All females appear to have become suitable sexual targets regardless of the stage of premarital intimacy, including the most casual and impersonal. This finding was the most dramatic change from the 1957 evidence. It may well be that impersonality in the sexual encounter is one of the most dominant of the new sexual folkways, regardless of the much-publicized quest for "meaningful relationships."

## NOTES

1. The 1957 study (Kirkpatrick and Kanin) found 55.7% of the respondents reporting themselves offended at some level of erotic intimacy during the academic year. The mean number of episodes per offended female tallied out at 6.3. The distribution of episodes by level of intimacy reveals the 1972 data strikingly comparable to the 1957 findings.

2. A study of high school senior girls in 1956 (Kanin, 1957) found only 25% of the aggressive episodes beyond kissing to be "abrupt," and this by males whom we can more readily characterize as younger and inexperienced.

---

# REFERENCES

Kanin, E.J. (1957). Male aggression in dating-courtship relations. *Am. J. Sociol.* 63: 197–204.

———— (1969). Selected dyadic aspects of male sex aggression. *J. Sex Res.* 5: 12–28.

Kirkpatrick, C., and Kanin, K. (1957). Male sex aggression on a university campus. *Am. Sociol. Rev.* 22: 52–58.

# WIFE BEATING

## 1. WIFE BEATING AND OTHER FORMS OF FAMILY VIOLENCE IN HISTORICAL PERSPECTIVE

Not only has wife beating generally been legal throughout history; it has often been considered a man's duty to beat his wife occasionally in order to keep her from giving in to temptation. Countries such as Iran, Italy, and Scotland did not make wife beating illegal until after 1970. And women were not the only family members who were dependent upon the whims of their husbands for their physical well-being. Children were also subject to beatings from their fathers that, in many societies, could be fatal without criminal penalty. We live in a society today that has its roots in practices favoring a high level of family violence, all of it proceeding from the father/husband to the other members of the household.

## 2. ESTIMATES OF THE PREVALENCE OF WIFE BEATING

Studies of wife beating historically have suffered from the same methodological problems as studies of rape. Samples used have been selected from legal records or from treatment populations, which distorted results and made it impossible to make any reliable estimate of the prevalence of wife beating in America. The first national study focusing on family violence was recently published by Straus (1978), and Gaquin (1978) has performed an analysis of previously unpublished data from the National Crime Survey program. Gaquin's analysis suggests that there were more than a million incidents of spouse abuse in the United States between 1973 and 1975. Assaults by spouses constituted 25 percent of all assaults on women who had ever been married at some time in their lives or who were currently married. For women who were currently divorced, assaults by the husbands accounted for 28 percent of all the assaults they suffered from all sources, and spouse assaults were responsible for an incredible 55 percent of all assaults experienced by separated women. Violence is not less serious because it occurs in the family. Gaquin found that spouse abuse was more likely to involve physical injury and to require hospital treatment or other medical care than assaults against women occurring outside of the family.

234

Straus administered a nationwide study of a representative sample of more than 2,000 couples. Based on these interviews, he estimated that approximately 1.8 million wives are beaten by their husbands in America each year. A third of the beaten wives in his sample experienced at least five beatings during the year, another third were beaten only once during the year prior to the study, and the remaining third were beaten between two and four times during the year. Straus himself regards these figures as a drastic understatement of the true incidence of wife beating in America, suggesting that the true rates may be more than twice as high as the estimates derived from his study.

These estimates of the prevalence of wife beating in the United States show us that whereas rape is a low-incidence crime that impacts many women only through its symbolic effects, wife beating directly affects a much larger proportion of American women. If alcoholism can be said to affect every family in America through one or another of its members, then what can we say about wife beating, which is even more common?

## 3. THE CAUSES OF WIFE BEATING

The same general emphasis on violence in American society that encourages rape also encourages wife beating as a solution to marital conflict. This is similarly true of many of the cultural factors that have been discussed by Pagelow (1978a) in an article that is reprinted in this reader. However, there are also factors that are specific to marital violence, such as the historic legitimacy of marital violence in Western civilization. Marital violence that previously had the sanction of law has now become at least partially illegal, but the practices of husbands have been slow to conform to these changes in legal and moral standards. One reason for the hesitancy of any husbands to view wife beating as inappropriate and immoral is that the law still does not give wives the same degree of protection from assaults by their husbands that it gives to citizens in general. This legal situation, as interpreted to the public by police officers who are called upon to aid beaten wives, tends to encourage husbands to continue to beat their wives "so long as they keep the situation from getting out of control."

In addition to these general sociocultural factors, there are specific situational and psychological factors that tend to promote wife beating in specific instances. For example, men who have observed wife beating when they were children or who have otherwise been exposed to a great deal of violent behavior are more likely than other men to beat their wives. If a wife is better at arguing than her husband, he may be tempted to resort to physical violence in order to maintain his marital dominance in the face of his lack of verbal skill. Another situation which is particularly conducive to marital violence occurs when a man loses his job or suffers some other kind of status-diminishing loss, so that he may feel the need to reestablish marital dominance through violence to make up for power that he no longer possesses as the main breadwinner of the family. Finally, general stress factors such as those described by Farrington (1975) tend to increase the probability that marital violence will occur.

## 4. WHY DON'T MOST BEATEN WIVES LEAVE?

Many beaten wives try to influence their husbands to behave decently, and after the beatings continue beyond all hope of reformation, they leave their husbands temporarily, or perhaps forever. And yet there are other beaten wives who stay on. Why is this? In the case of beatings that are infrequent and not very physically damaging, it is understandable that wives may continue to hope that their husbands will reform after each scattered incident and that this pattern can continue indefinitely. What is harder for many people to understand is why a number of wives who are severely beaten or who are beaten frequently also choose to stay with their husbands and attempt to cope with the situation rather than leave it.

Understanding why these women continue to stay with their husbands requires that we look at both the effects of wife beating on victims and at the general effect of the status of women as second-class citizens upon their ability to leave an undesirable marriage. Women do not have access to the same societal resources that men do. There are few institutional resources that are available for battered women, and these women also have very limited personal resources. For them, leaving home may mean that they will immediately become destitute and, if they take their children with them, they may have no idea how they are going to support them. A second article by Pagelow (1978b) analyzes the reasons why women remain with abusive spouses in terms of (1) lack of personal and material resources, (2) the negative institutional response that they receive when they seek help in the larger society, and (3) their personal commitment to a traditional ideology. Some women have been literally beaten into submission, while others believe that it is their place to be beaten just as they saw their mothers beaten when they were young. The sum of all these diverse factors makes it extremely difficult for battered women to leave their husbands. Indeed, in some ways, leaving becomes increasingly difficult the more one is battered.

## 5. WIFE BEATING AND MARITAL POWER

Except for wives who are so severly beaten that they sustain serious physical injuries, the most negative effects of wife beating are probably social and psychological rather than physical. Beaten wives spend a great deal of time trying to figure out how to avoid angering their husbands in the future so that beatings will not recur. At the same time, they become much more timid about meeting their own needs through their marriage. Their self-images become more negative, and they become increasingly fearful of exercising any initiative. On the social level, their shame may tend to isolate them from social contacts in the same way that rape victims sometimes become progressively isolated. Another social consequence of wife beating is that it decreases the power of wives relative to that of their husbands in marital decision making. This subject is treated by Adler (1977) in a paper included in this section.

Adler studied 50 married couples who were graduate students, white, and predominantly from the middle class. Although this is not a group that one would expect to be high in marital violence based on the stereotypes that are common in the literature, she found that 34 percent of the husbands and 32 percent of the wives had used violence against their spouses during their marriage. These acts included hitting, pushing, kicking, and punching. The idea that husband beating is approximately as common as wife beating is supported by the findings of Straus (1978) and has been given wide circulation in the work of Steinmetz (1978). Does this mean that husband beating is as important a social problem as wife beating? Not at all, and Adler's article tells us why. A number of the "battered husbands" whom she interviewed defined their battering as ineffective, nonthreatening, amusing, or annoying. In contrast, not one of the wives who had been assaulted took this position. Adler found the husbands to be larger than their wives in 48 of 50 couples, which is probably about what one would find in a national sample of American families. All but one of the husbands and two of the wives agreed that in their marriage the husband was much stronger than the wife. In short, violence directed toward husbands by wives in Adler's sample was much less often perceived as threatening than violence against wives by husbands.

The crucial test of the impact of marital violence is the way in which it impacts marital power. Adler shows us that the use of violence by wives was essentially unrelated to the balance of power in the families she studied, but the use of violence by husbands was strongly associated with dominance over their wives. Her findings are therefore supportive of feminist theory on wife beating in that they suggest that the power implications of wife beating are significant in family decision making. Although we do not yet have as much evidence as we would like on this matter, it appears fair to say that wife beating has the effect of making wives second-class citizens in their families just as discriminatory laws and customs have traditionally made them second-class citizens in the larger society.

## 6. STRATEGIES FOR DEALING WITH WIFE BEATING

Pagelow (1978b) gives us a classification of alternatives that can be used by beaten wives to improve their situation. Obviously, these women can either stay or leave; if they leave, they can either stay away forever, or they can return home at a later date to try again. If they stay away permanently, they can choose to file for divorce, or they can be satisfied with either a formal or informal separation. Women who stay within the family and try to solve the problem there can attempt to deal with their husbands entirely on their own, or they can seek the help of friends or neighbors, counselors, medical personnel, criminal justice personnel, or specialized services such as battered-women shelters. If they are able to utilize their internal resources plus some combination of external resources to bring about a successful termination of wife beating, then this may mean an improved relationship with their husband in the future, or it may mean that they have succeeded in having him evicted from the family. Should all of these strategies fail, they may become resigned to their fate and continue to suffer periodic beatings throughout their lives. There are many cases on record in which women who chose the road of resignation were rewarded by being beaten to death by their husbands or became so depressed that they committed suicide, or who killed their husband in moral if not legal self-defense. The anonymous interview that concludes this section of the text illustrates the homicide solution to the problem and shows how wife beating and female criminality can be intertwined.

Scientists do not know what techniques work best with which kinds of wife beaters under what conditions. Bowker (1979) is undertaking a series of research studies in an attempt to provide an answer to the question of what women can do about wife abuse. The first step in this research will be to construct a typology of wife beating that takes into account the frequency of the beatings, the severity of the beatings, the circumstances of the family, and the characteristics of the spouses. Then, women who have successfully checked wife beating in their lives will be asked to explain what techniques they tried unsuccessfully and what techniques were ultimately successful for them. The possibilities are many and complex, encompassing all of those mentioned by Pagelow and ranging from psychological strategies through the use of informal helping networks and legal action. When enough cases of the successful termination of wife beating have been examined, then it will be possible to say something about which techniques or combinations of techniques work best in which wife beating situations. Beaten wives, unlike rape victims, have a great deal of time in which to analyze their situation. Thus, information based on scientific research should be able to be successfully applied by many of them.

# REFERENCES

Adler, Emily. Perceived marital power, influence techniques and marital violence. Revision of a paper presented at the annual meeting of the American Sociological Association, Chicago, 1977.

Bowker, Lee H. *Beating wife-beating: An exploratory study.* A Research proposal funded by the National Institute of Mental Health, 1979.

Farrington, Keith. Toward a general stress theory of intra-family violence. Paper presented at the annual meeting of the National Council on Family Relations, Salt Lake City, 1975.

Gaquin, Deirdre A. Spouse abuse: Data from the national crime survey. *Victimology,* 1978, *2,* 632–643.

Pagelow, Mildred D. *Sex roles, power, and woman battering.* Paper presented at the 9th World Congress of Sociology, Upsala, Sweden, 1978a.

————. Secondary battering and alternatives of female victims to spouse abuse. Revision of a paper presented at the annual meeting of the American Sociological Association, San Francisco, 1978b.

Steinmetz, Suzanne K. The battered husband syndrome. *Victimology,* 1978, *2,* 499–509.

Straus, Murray A. Wife beating: How common and why? *Victimology,* 1978, *2,* 443–458.

## FOURTEEN

# Sex Roles, Power, and Woman Battering*

MILDRED DALEY PAGELOW

Woman battering is one of many violent crimes perpetrated by men against women down through the ages and in many cultures. Attempting to discover root causes for male violence against females in the context of power, domination, and control of one sex by the other raises the idea that primordial fear and envy of men may have generated an anti-woman phobia that underlies male-female relationships. Basic biological and physiological differences of the female could have generated subliminal hostility sometimes expressed in violence. Structural conflict theory provides a framework to examine ways that realistic conflict may be diverted into nonrealistic conflict against women. Since men are power holders vis-a-vis other men, it is postulated that intrasex conflict is realistic but largely unresolvable, and intersex nonrealistic conflict is a functional alternative. Men's conflict with women is nonrealistic in the sense that while women do not have power relative to men, they can provide a sense of power by being dominated and subordinated. The concepts of scapegoating, safety valves, and ambilvalence seem to give support to these ideas. An anti-woman phobia may have been transmitted through the generations and cultures by a variety of modes, some of which are examined here.

*© Mildred Daley Pagelow, January 1981.

## INTRODUCTION

After centuries of recorded atrocities documenting "man's inhumanity to man," the modern world reacted in shock and disbelief at revelations in the last few years of man's inhumanity to women. Specifically, this refers to *his* woman: *his* wife, lover, girlfriend. Although *man*kind has periodically set out to annihilate whole segments of the population in wars, massacres, pillage, looting, rape, and wholesale genocide in gas chambers, it seemed inconceivable to many that more than an insignificant number of men could possibly beat the women who are closest and dearest to them: women who share sexual intimacy with them and are, frequently, the mothers of their children. People in positions of power demanded evidence.

Evidence came from Great Britain (Dobash and Dobash, 1976; Middleton, 1977, 1978; Pizzey, 1977) and Europe (Andersen, 1977). The International Tribunal on Crimes Against Women held in Brussels, Belgium, in March 1976, attended by 2,000 women from 33 countries declared woman battering a serious international crime (Russell and Van de Ven, 1976), and the American National Organization for Women established a Task Force on Battered Women/Domestic Violence. Later, the U.S. Commission on Civil Rights and subcommittees of the U.S. Congress held hearings where witnesses came to describe the enormity of the problem, trying to convince persons in positions of power that there is, indeed, a national problem of such magnitude and seriousness that it requires federal intervention (Pagelow, 1978a, 1978b). In the meantime, each community group that emerges across the country has had to follow the same procedure, gathering local statistics to prove to the satisfaction of potential money-grantors that woman battering is a serious problem in their community (Hampton, 1978). Next, they have had to educate powerholders to show that existing community services either cannot or do not adequately serve the needs of victims so that grantors will approve the establishment of crisis shelters and related services for victims. Apparently the same pattern of providing proof and justification of need is followed in other countries also (Joutsen, 1978; Middleton, 1977). Rather than seeming strange that men physically abuse their spouses, it is far stranger, in view of historical evidence, that men in positions of power should doubt that they do so.

## OVERVIEW OF RESEARCH

One United States study recently completed by Straus et al. attempted to measure interpersonal violence within the family by means of a large-scale survey. Among other types of violence, including sibling violence and intergenerational violence, they found that there was a high incidence of spousal violence (Straus, 1977). Data were gathered from 2,143 intact couples by structured interviews which asked for a count of violent acts and which indexed severity of violence along a continuum by use of the Conflict Resolution Techniques (CRT) scale. When Straus confined attention to responses to the item "beat up," he reports that: "This gives a figure of 1.1% during the year, with an average of 5.5 beatings per year among the couples who reported a beating" (Straus, 1977:6). However, this reference is to couples who were reporting on incidents recalled in the year prior to the poll only. When the focus of inquiry was expanded to include violent acts *before* the previous year "irrespective of who initiated the act," Straus states:

> Thus our data for item P, beating up, indicate that such a beating had occurred at some time in 5.3% of the marriages. Of these, I estimate that about two out of three were instances of husbands beating wives, or about 3.5% of American couples. Or in numbers of couples, over a million and a half. However . . . this is almost surely a considerable underestimate. . . . These considerations . . . suggest that the true incidence rates are probably double those I have just mentioned. (1977:7–8)

Straus also weighed implications of violent acts by wives against their husbands but for a variety of reasons concludes that, "In short, wives are victimized by violence in the family to a much greater extent than are husbands and should therefore be the focus of the most immediate remedial steps." (1977:10)

A preliminary report and theoretical framework of another study have been discussed in detail in earlier papers (Pagelow, 1976, 1977a, 1977b). This 2-year research project that is currently nearing completion investigates female victims of domestic assaults and professionals in both helping and law enforcement agencies. Data from a sample of 200 battered women were primarily obtained at shelters in the United States, a small proportion from shelters in London and Dublin, and about one-fourth from volunteers who heard about the study. A variety of methodologies were employed, including survey questionnaire, unstructured depth interviews, observation, participant observation in group discussions, and records analysis.

The underlying theoretical perspective is a tripartite model that was developed because of unsuitability of alternative theories that are either individual psychopathological or violent culture models that are too general, hence untestable. Based on social learning theory, it suggests why some couples become involved in physical violence and why some do not, and why some continue physically violent relationships. A set of independent variables are postulated to explain why many women remain in violent relationships after primary battering; these are: resources, institutional response, and traditional ideology. Resources are defined as the set of personal and material life circumstances in the social environment of victims.[1] Institutional response is the real or perceived reactions by social agents to spouse abuse, the victims, and the aggressors. Traditional ideology is a construct that encompasses the belief systems that influence behavior; it includes such ideas as rigid sex-role division of labor, the patriarchal family, inequality of the sexes, and so forth. Assumptions are that traditional sex-role socialization in the hierarchal structure of the patriarchal family leads men to expect positions of power, domination, and control over subordinates—women and children—without clearly defined limits to the way they maintain subordination. On the other hand, women are socially conditioned not only to accept subordination but also to be dependent and powerless in intrafamily relationships. The major proposition is:

> *The fewer the resources, the more negative the institutional response; and the more intense the traditional ideology of women who have been battered, the more likely they are to remain in relationships with the batterers and the less likely they are to perform acts that will significantly alter the situation in a positive direction.* (Pagelow, 1978c:2)

Although data analysis is still incomplete, indications are that this study will provide support for the underlying theoretical assumptions.

Another study initiated several years ago, which examined police and court records in two cities in Scotland, has recently been completed (Dobash and Dobash, 1976, 1978). This investigation also included in-depth interviews with 109 women who had been battered by their spouses, with results highly compatible with inferences drawn thus far from the Pagelow study. Cross culturally, victims tend to reveal striking similarities in experiences and perceptions regarding the violence itself and interactions with spouses and social agencies. These researchers show that in spousal assaults, wives are far more frequently the victims than are husbands. Out of 1,044 cases of assaults occurring between family members, 791 wives were victims compared to 12 husband; of the total assaults, 75.8 percent were directed against wives, while only 1.1 percent were directed against husbands (Dobash and Dobash, 1978: 436–437). It is obvious that official records only reveal the "tip of the iceberg" (Martin, 1976), because the Dobashes found through their interview sample that only 2 out of every 98 assaults were reported to the police.

The research team from Scotland draws conclusions that the hierarchal structure of the patriarchal family has historically legitimized wife beating for the subordination, domination, and control of women and that women are victims of men's brutality to a far greater extent within marriage than outside of marriage. They conclude:

> Females, whether they be sisters, mothers, wives or daughters, are more likely to be subject to control through the use of physical force than are their male counterparts—and it is in their capacity as wives that the risk is the highest and the danger the greatest. . . . Women were very rarely assaulted by strangers on the streets, only 15 percent of the cases involving female victims occurred outside the family setting. (Dobash and Dobash, 1978:437)

The Dobashes' conceptualization and analysis make a valuable contribution to our knowledge of spouse abuse. They have made great strides over the popular narrow focus on problems within the victims themselves (see Pagelow, 1978c, for a discussion on "Blaming the Victim") and by itemizing all types of family violence have produced statistics to show that the most common type is wife beating. Although the Dobashes confine their focus on woman battering within the marital relationship, they provide data pertinent to generalized male-female violence which is the focus of this paper. They write:

> Almost all of the violent offenders reported to the police were males (91.4 percent) while a mere 8.6 percent of the offenders were females. . . . Though men and women are almost equally likely to be victims they are not equally likely to be aggressors. Men are disproportionately represented as offenders. . . . violence occurring between family members almost always involved male offenders and female victims, a pattern which prevailed in almost 94 percent of the cases. In every type of relationship, marital, parental, or sibling, the assaults followed the same pattern; males attacking females. In only 2.6 percent of the cases was the female the offender, but she was the victim in nearly 95 percent of the cases. (Dobash and Dobash, 1978:436)

Using the Dobash stance as a point of departure, we can take one more step beyond the realm of contemporary husband-wife relationships in the patriarchal family and examine the broader question of male-female relationships in general over recorded history. Although the patriarchal family has generated, accepted, and fostered physical abuse of women, violence against women occurred long before, and outside of, monogamous marriage. [For commentary on this, see Russell's Introduction to Martin's Book *Battered Wives* (1976:ix).] If we want to understand why contemporary men batter their wives, this crime should be placed in the context of other crimes of violence against women such as rape, incest, femicide, castration, torture, and execution—atrocities that occurred in the past and continue to the present time (Russell and Van de Ven, 1976). To say that some men are jealous, possessive, and want to control and dominate women who are often nearest and dearest to them is to attend to symptoms, not the underlying genetic causes.

## THE BROADER QUESTION OF MALE POWER, DOMINATION, AND CONTROL

It is impossible to fully develop a thesis on male power and domination of suitable depth and magnitude in a paper of this length. The most that can be attempted here is to raise questions and to explore possible explanations based on evidence gathered from a multiplicity of sources. Straus briefly mentions phrases that are relevant to this topic when he discusses "compulsive masculinity"; he notes the "mutual antagonism between the sexes" (1976:553). Earlier in the same article he mentions "the more general phenomenon of male hostility to women" (1976:550); another reference is to the "battle of the sexes" (Straus et al., 1976:19). These clues served as a catalyst toward consideration of the possibility of deep subliminal hostility or even hatred between men and women. But if this hostility is "mutual," why is it that male violence is disproportionately greater against women than the reverse, as the Dobashes point out? In fact, for all the violent crimes under their consideration, females were even more frequently violent against other women: 5.1 percent were females assaulting females, as compared to 3.5 percent females assaulting males (Dobash and Dobash, 1978:436). On the other hand, males attacked females at almost the same rate that they attacked males. While the antagonism itself may be mutual, something we can neither prove nor disprove, it does not manifest itself equally in the form of violence on the part of men and women.[2]

   Empirical evidence of hostility, contempt, or violence largely reveals a one-directional arrow, from male to female. In homicide, "Husbands killed their wives violently in *significantly* greater proportion than did wives who killed their husbands" (Wolfgang, 1958:214). In battering, Straus addresses the "striking imbalance in the extent to which wives are victims of violence by husbands" (1976:545) and looks for factors to account for it. Except in sex-segregated confinement institutions, rape is almost always committed by males with female victims (Bart, 1975; Brownmiller, 1976). As for incest and molestation of children, almost all victims are female, and almost all perpetrators are male. The Burgess and

Holmstrom sample of sexual trauma victims included only 3 pre-adult males (2.8 percent), and all 20 offenders were male (1975). A state of Washington assault center for sexually abused children found that 97 percent of the victims were female, and 99 percent of the offenders were male (Klingbeil and Berliner, 1977).

Infanticide has been largely a crime of destroying female babies because of economic considerations, and it appears to some writers that, universally, girl babies are considered of lesser value than boy babies (Belotti, 1975, 22–31). The Papuans practiced female infanticide, but the Zulu are kinder, according to Hays. When a boy is born, the Zulu slaughter an ox, but not for the birth of a girl, saying, "Why should we kill an ox for a girl? She is merely a weed" (Hays, 1964:12). In an extraordinary book that searches primitive behavior, history, myth, and literature for understanding of male anti-woman behavior, Hays produces a Bulgarian folk rhyme that he aptly suggests is the "ultimate in savagery" which supposedly expresses sentiments of a man who has nine daughters:

If the tenth, too, is a girlchild,
I will cut both of your feet off,
To the knees I'll cut your feet off,
Both your arms up to the shoulders,
Both your eyes, too, I will put out,
Blind and crippled you will be then,
Pretty little wife, young woman. (quoted in Hays, 1964:12)

Hays is one of several writers in recent years who has addressed the topic of hatred, fear, and envy of women by men (Delaney et al., 1976; Dworkin, 1974; Haskell, 1974; Montagu, 1968). Power that men hold over women's lives was addressed long ago by Mill (1971), and historical documents written by others concerned with male power have been gathered by Kraditor (1968) and Rossi (1974). These volumes give a wealth of evidence that throughout the years few people were concerned about the imbalance of power between the sexes. A few writers focus on particular institutions in society that have contributed to anti-woman ideology and the powerlessness of women: medicine (Ehrenreich and English, 1973a; Frankfort, 1972); psychoanalysis (Chesler, 1973; Miller, 1974); and religion (Daly, 1974, 1975; Hageman, 1974; O'Faolain and Martines, 1973). Masters and Lea compiled almost 500 pages of ancient and contemporary articles steeped in misogyny aptly titled *The Anti-Sex* (1964). In the introductory article, Masters raises the topic of woman battering among other abuses of women and describes the sixteenth-century Russian domestic code that demanded absolute obedience for women saying:

> Disobedient wives were to be soundly thrashed, but "not straight on
> the face or on the ear," since the husband would be sorely dis-
> advantaged should his spouse thus become blind or deaf or other-
> wise incapacitated. "Keep to the whip," enjoined the Code, "and
> choose carefully where to strike." (1964:19)

Masters later states:

> Husbands have, in many times and places, been able to beat, muti-
> late, and even murder their wives with impunity. Fathers have been
> accorded the right to determine whether a female child should be
> killed or permitted to live. Widows have been compelled to destroy
> themselves upon the death of the husband. . . . Men have for centur-
> ies, in the literatures of many lands, poured out their grievances
> against and contempt for women. Misogyny, or a close approxima-
> tion thereto, has been cultural and ideological, not just individual
> and deriving from other personal experiential sources. The Battle of
> the Sexes—for the female has found ways of striking back—is a
> product of both conscious and unconscious, rational and irrational
> causes, and has long since become a maiming way of life. (1964:44)

## IS THERE A PRIMORDIAL ANTI-WOMAN PHOBIA UNDERLYING MEN-WOMEN RELATIONSHIPS?

Even though history books, almost exclusively written by men, do not
emphasize the many crimes against women, individually and as a caste,[3]
that have been committed by men, the evidence is there. The gynocide of
seven million witches in Europe (Dworkin says this may be a conservative estimate, 1974:130), the crippling of millions of women over ten
centuries in China, the enforced slavery of untold millions of women to
their husband-owners, the current practice of female circumcision that
has mutilated an estimated 25 to 30 million girls and women in Africa
(Hosken, 1978:491), the wholesale rape and slaughter of women and
children as the aftermath of men's wars as recently as Bangladesh (Goldman, 1972)—all these are evidence that misogyny is not confined to a
few warped individuals in each century or in particular cultures. At
about the same time that women from around the world gathered in
Belgium to denounce crimes against women, movie producers were making a film called "Snuff" that portrayed female torture, rape, murder,
and mutilation so convincingly explicit that viewers could not be sure if
it was actual or simulated (rumors hold that the movie showed actual,
brutal murder).

Based on the surplus of evidence that anti-woman feelings are strong, pervasive, have existed over recorded history up to and including the present, and are cross cultural in scope, the question arises: Why? Why does one-half of the population evidence massive contempt for the other half? Perhaps the question should be rephrased to read: Why do most of the population have contempt for women? It seems apparent that many women themselves show contempt for women as a caste. As Laws points out, the "Token" identifies herself with the "Sponsor," but the "Sponsor" remains aware of her "ineradicable primary-deviant class membership" and, thus, she can never fully participate in the dominant group (1975:62). In other words, she sees herself as "one of the boys," as an exception to the rule, not like "them" but a rare individual. (Feminists dub such women "Queen Bees.")

The point is, if there is a subliminal anti-woman phobia underlying men-women relationships transmitted over generations, what could possibly be the genetic cause? We begin by examining basic differences between the sexes, avoiding cultural and social trappings, trying to see what women, by possession of a female body and female genitalia, are capable of doing, having, being, and producing (that males are incapable of).[4] If the anti-woman phobia has elements of envy, as some claim, then we must search for perceived or real advantages women may have over men. What is there about the female body, the *being* female, that could arouse fear and envy strong enough to culminate in hatred, or at least contempt, for the female sex? Stripped of all else except immutable biological and physiological differences, there are two differences that are generically female that may arouse fear and envy in males. First, the female body is parturient (concomitant with the reproductive processes of menstruation and lactation): a woman knows *without question* that the child her body produces is her own. Second, the female body is unrestricted by physiological limitations in sexual performance as is the male body. It is not necessary for women to have erections for intercourse; therefore, compared to men, their sexual capacity is seen as relatively limitless. The physical processes of coitus are different.

## Reproductive Capabilities

The first of the two basic sex differences, the reproductive processes and lactation, have had tremendous impact on male thinking, reflected in taboos and rituals from ancient and primitive societies to present-day industrialized societies. Long before primitive man learned that he had any share in the creating of new life, it was obvious to him that woman produces new life. Terror of the unknown may have led to some of the magic, rituals, and taboos associated with childbirth, menstruation, and lactation. Not only does the contemporary male Orthodox Jew daily offer thanks to God for not having created him woman (Hays, 1964:12), but the ancient taboos that kept husband and wife apart during her menses are still observed (Richardson, 1974). As recently as 1972, the chief rabbi of Israel issued a warning against violation of the taboo in "Family Purity," a statement that "goes to every couple in Israel who apply for a wedding license" (Delaney et al., 1976:16). Hays documents in detail many cultural fears and anxieties associated with female biological processes, particularly in his chapter "The Perils of Love" (1964: 49–63).

The need for men to know with certainty the identity of their own progeny (information that is clearly available to all mothers) was probably one of the strongest motivating factors in the establishment of the patriarchal family. Doubts about paternity, according to Montagu, gave rise to strict rules of conduct for women, fear and suspicion, and a "catalogue of horrors" inflicted upon women either to prevent or punish adultery while "adultery of the male has usually gone unpunished" (Montagu, 1968:52). Economics had much to do with it, because men wanted assurance that the male child to whom a man bequeathed his fortune was unquestionably his rightful heir. As Dobash and Dobash remark: "The husband's authority had to remain inviolate in order that there would be no question about the pedigree of the male children who were to inherit the family name and possessions" (1978:428). Gilder, who worries about surviving the "rising tide of feminism" and agonizes over being "doomed to a life without family and marriage," apparently agrees, for he says: "The desire of men to claim their children may be the crucial impulse of civilized life" (1975:93).

Anthropologists have documented a wide variety of rites, rituals, and punishments administered to women that are associated with menstruation and childbirth and that reveal both fear and envy (Delaney et al., 1976; Frazer, 1927; Hogbin, 1970). In some cultures, one or both female processes are imitated by men: men seeking to cause their own purification by blood or fathers "giving birth" to the young (Hoebel, 1972; Hogbin, 1970). Another anthropologist, Montagu, introduces the idea of envy, mentioning "feminine" phraseology in creative instances which is counter to men's linguistic penchant to use masculine phrases and to "avoid anything of the feminine" (1968:42). Montagu says, "Man's drive to achievement can, at least in part, be interpreted as an unconsciously motivated attempt to compensate for the lack of biological creativity" (1968:42).

Sexual Capabilities

The second of these basic differences between the sexes is unlimited performance in the sex act itself on the part of women and the actual physical processes of coitus. Commenting on the fragility of male sexuality,
Hays explains:

> Women can fulfill their sexual role in society without effort, by
> mere acceptance; their need for orgasmic experience has varied with
> the culture's expectations. Men, however, must be capable of erec-
> tion and discharge or they are not performing their duty in carrying
> on the race. At the same time loss of semen and erection in the sex
> act seems also to have troubled them. Thus men have worried about
> their potency from the beginning of history. (1964:283)

There abounds ample evidence that men identified women as carnal
creatures with *insatiable lust;* the "myth of feminine evil" so frequently
quoted by these authors may well have stemmed from envy (Daly, 1974;
Hays, 1964; Masters and Lea, 1964). Mark Twain satirically commented
on the "competent candlestick" and the "decrepit candle" (1975:474–478).
In his posthumously published manuscript "Letters from the Earth,"
Twain states:

> [Woman] is ready for action, and *competent.* As competent as the
> candlestick is to receive the candle. Competent every day, competent
> every night. Also, she *wants* that candle—yearns for it, longs for it,
> hankers after it. . . . But man is only briefly competent. . . . After
> fifty his performance is of poor quality, the intervals between are
> wide, and its satisfactions of no great value to either party; whereas
> his great-grandmother is as good as new. . . . Her candlestick is as
> firm as ever, whereas his candle is increasingly softened and weak-
> ened by the weather of age, as the years go by, until at last it can no
> longer stand, and is mournfully laid to rest in the hope of a blessed
> resurrection which is never to come. . . . His procreative compet-
> ency is limited to an average of a hundred exercises per year for fifty
> years, hers is good for three thousand a year for that whole time—
> and as many years longer as she may live. Thus his life interest in
> the matter is five thousand refreshments, while hers is a hundred
> and fifty thousand. . . . Now if you or any other really intelligent
> person were arranging the fairnesses and justices between man and
> woman, you would give the man a one-fiftieth interest in one
> woman, and the woman a harem. Now wouldn't you? (1975:
> 476–477)

Twain humorously berated the injustices toward females and chided the unfairness of males who came to the conclusion that "the Creator intended the woman to be restricted to one man" instead of the reverse. Anthropologist Hoebel shows that while 16 percent of all societies have adopted a monogamous marriage form, 83 percent accept either polygynous or a mixture of monogamous and polygynous, and a mere 1 percent accept polyandry (1972:430). Hoebel states: "The actual marriage of several men to one woman is as rare (occuring in 4 of the 854 cultures in the *Ethnographic Atlas*) as the marriage of several women to one man is common" (1972:431). Two of these cultures, the Tibetan and Eskimo, practice female infanticide, which contributes to the idea that multiple husbands are not an adjustment of the scales of justice for the "competent candlestick" as much as for the economic and sexual benefit of men who otherwise would not have legal access to one.

But there is another element of the basic differences between the sexes that may promote male primordial fear of females. Many writers suggest this idea (cf. Hays, 1964:283), but Dworkin seems to express it most cogently when she states:

> Here the definition of woman . . . is her carnality; the essence of her character . . . is her malice and avarice. . . . we are dealing with an existential terror of women, of the "mouth of the womb," stemming from a primal anxiety about male potency, tied to a desire for self (phallic) control; men have deep-rooted castration fears which are expressed as a horror of the womb. These terrors form a substrata of a myth of feminine evil which in turn justified several centuries of gynocide. (1974:134)

Dworkin stresses not only the fear of loss of potency or virility but also

> a dread of the loss of cock and balls. The reason for this fear can perhaps be located in the nature of the sex act per se: men enter the vagina hard, erect; men emerge drained of vitality, the cock flaccid. The loss of semen, and the feeling of weakness which is its biological conjunct, has extraordinary significance to men. Hindu tradition, for instance, postulates that men must either expel the semen and then vacuum it back up into the cock, or not ejaculate at all. For those Western men for whom orgasm is simultaneous with ejaculation, sex must be a most literal death, with the mysterious, muscled, pulling vagina the death-dealer. (1974:136)

Although expressed in the vernacular, Dworkin may have identified the root cause of castration fears: They are found, she theorizes, in the natural, physiological process of vaginal intercourse. Another author agrees with the concept of "womb envy"; Chesler states: "To create without killing, to make something out of 'nothing' the way women seem to make new life out of nothing, naturally, effortlessly . . . or so it seems to men: male science, male alchemy, is partially rooted in male uterus-envy, in the desire to create something miraculous." (1978:79)

But then Chesler looks at the relationship of men to other men, particularly fathers, and the willingness of Biblical fathers to sacrifice their sons, which she claims contributes to men's passionate longing for paternal benevolence. She writes:

> The difficult truce between sons and fathers proceeds from *both* recognizing the importance of what they have in common: a penis. This simple anatomical fact is what makes all men "alike" and all men different from women. Based on this fact, men come to share a belief that women are "other"—not really human beings. But when the penis becomes the root sign of humanity and . . . divinity, then men may wince at the pain or humiliation inflicted upon other men—but not at the pain and humiliation inflicted upon women. (Chesler, 1978:50,79)[5]

Perhaps this helps explain why male-only clubs are found in almost every culture around the world. Hays devotes a chapter to the subject, "Men Without Women" (1964:63–78), and Richardson has an interesting discussion on all-male groups (1971:12–14). Even today in the United States, "brotherhoods," fraternal organizations, clubs, and service and community organizations (some of which grudgingly capitulated to the demands for membership by racial and ethnic minorities) are digging in their heels and refusing to admit females to their ranks as full-fledged members.

Yet men do want to socialize with women publicly and, especially, privately.


## CONFLICT THEORY REVISITED

It seems possible that both of these very basic female differences, apparently producing male mass envy and fear, are the root cause of the misogyny or anti-woman phobia that has triggered atrocities against women as individuals and as a caste. Yet there is also ambivalence of most men toward women—the fine line between love and hate, rage and benevolence, fear and envy—that has been transmitted through the generations in the literature and symbolically through mythology and religion (Hays, 1964; Mirande and Enriquez, 1976). How is this inconsistency to be explained or understood?

Building largely upon the earlier works of Simmel and also of Marx,
Coser provides a framework that seems tailored to the dimensions of the
problem (1964). If we can recognize that the sexes have sources of hostility and tension, both within the same sex category and between sexes,
then we can establish two simultaneously conflictual relationships on the
part of men and also on the part of women. Coser states:

> Each social system contains sources of realistic conflict insofar as
> people raise conflicting claims to scarce status, power and resources,
> and adhere to conflicting values. . . . Realistic conflicts arise when
> men clash in the pursuit of claims based on frustration of demands
> and expectancies of gains. Nonrealistic conflicts arise from depriva-
> tions and frustrations stemming from the socialization process and
> from later adult role obligations, or they result . . . from a conver-
> sion of originally realistic antagonism which was disallowed expres-
> sion. (1964:54)

The following typology of conflict is derived from Coser (1964:48-60).

Realistic:
- Against frustrating agents themselves for specific results
- Pursuit of legitimate claims
- A means toward realistic goals—abandoned if another way is found
- If there are no, or insufficient, safety-valves, tend to explode
- Stable—will cease if functional alternative ways to achieve ends are found (e.g., compromise, treaty, etc.)

Nonrealistic:
- Release of tension in aggressive action against shifting objects
- Conversion or originally realistic antagonism which was dis-allowed expression
- Satisfaction derived from the aggressive act itself
- Plays a reinforcing role for realistic conflict
- Unstable—there exist only functional alternatives as to object (could also be called scapegoating)

It should be noted that the two types are not as conceptually distinct as
suggested here, for in the tradition of Weber, Coser says:

> The distinction between realistic and nonrealistic conflict involves a
> conceptual abstraction from concrete reality in which the two types
> actually may be merged. . . . Realistic conflict situations may be
> accompanied, especially where there are no adequate provisions for
> the carrying out of the struggle, by unrealistic sentiments which are

deflected from their source. In concrete social reality an admixture of both "pure" types will be found. (1964:53)

At this point, it seems appropriate to reveal assumptions derived from the structural conflict perspective regarding the phenomenon of cross-cultural and long-term abuse of women by men. Based on Simmel's and Coser's distinctions between realistic and nonrealistic conflict, the key proposition is that: *men engage in realistic conflict with other men and unrealistic conflict with women, whereas with women the opposite is true. Women engage is realistic conflict with men and nonrealistic conflict with other women.* The sets of suggested interrelationships are shown below:

|         | MALES     | FEMALES     |
|---------|-----------|-------------|
| MALES   | Realistic | Nonrealistic |
| FEMALES | Realistic | Nonrealistic |

Before continuing the examination of the hypothesis, it should be mentioned that women's conflict types will be largely excluded from this discussion, partly for the purposes of clarity and brevity. Since men are universally the category with the most power, consideration here will be generally limited to two of the four cells, i.e., men's realistic and nonrealistic conflict. As we have seen, when hostility and conflict erupt into violent aggressive acts, the actors are usually male, whether their targets are males or females. It may be noted that male violence against other males is greater than violence against females, especially when wars and other mass phenomena are considered (Haavio-Mannila, 1978). But the issue of overall male violence, although it is important and deserves consideration, cannot be fully addressed here because it is largely outside the focus of this paper. Male-to-male violence is realistic because it largely conforms to the criteria outlined by Coser, although it seems obvious that men also engage in nonrealistic conflict with other men when they use each other as scapegoats. Women's realistic conflict undoubtedly is directed toward men, since men are the agents with the "scarce status, power, and resources," just as men are more likely to be in conflict with other men over these same advantages. If women are frustrated from deprivation of status, power, and resources, they are most likely to displace "antagonism which was disallowed expression" onto other women (and children, too, in true scapegoating fashion), as men are most likely to displace hostility and aggression toward women.

This conceptualization allows us to see how displacements onto substitute objects may in fact reinforce realistic conflict by emphasizing the major group relationship. While a man may displace blame and hostility on the "little woman" at home, he may reinforce his "brotherhood" with other men at the club or tavern in a spirit of "us" camaraderie, even though his competition and conflict with other men is the major conflict that must be repressed. In the same way, a woman can engage in hostile and destructive behavior toward other women and then find solace and belongingness in her marital relationship within which she is in an unequal power struggle that has no appropriate way of being conducted overtly and that therefore must be repressed. Coser suggests three possible ways of expressing hostile feelings:

> (1) direct expression of hostility against the person or group which is the source of frustration, (2) displacement of such hostile behavior onto substitute objects, and (3) tension-release activity which provides satisfaction in itself without need for object or object substitutes. (1964:41)

When Coser gives credit to Simmel for a "safety-valve theory" of conflict, he gives examples of both duels and witchcraft as socially approved expressions of hostility against the adversary and also says: "The voluminous literature on witchcraft abounds with cases in which those accused of witchcraft had not in any way harmed their accusers or aroused hostility, but were singled out as a means for the release of hostility which could not be expressed safely against the original object" (1964:42). Nevertheless, Coser's main references are to socially approved witchcraft, apparently within the context of preliterate tribes. He fails to mention that the wholesale persecution of people (mostly women) for witchcraft was both socially sanctioned by power holders and probably served as a "safety-valve" for the male to male conflict group, reinforcing in-group solidarity (Erikson, 1969).

Writing about the four centuries of European witch hunting, Ehrenreich and English say: "The witch-craze was neither a lynching party nor a mass suicide by hysterical women. Rather, it followed well-ordered, legalistic procedures. The witch-hunts were well-organized campaigns, initiated, financed and executed by Church and State" (1973b:9).

Scapegoating does receive some attention from Coser, who says:

> The well-known "scapegoating" mechanism operative in group conflict is relevant in this context. . . . Racial and religious prejudice (and I would add: sexism), by channeling hostilities onto powerless targets, may contribute as much to the stability of existing social structures as the safety-valve institutions discussed above. . . . The availability of safety-valve institutions leads to a displacement of goal in the actor: he need no longer aim at reaching a solution of the

unsatisfactory situation, but merely at releasing the tension which arose from it. In this way, the unsatisfactory situation will remain unaltered or become intensified. (1964:45–46)

It seems clear that nonrealistic conflict is the vehicle whereby safety valves and scapegoating come into great importance for the continuance of the social system without major change.

Both Simmel and Coser were to address hostility in close social relationships, although Coser limited his discussion of conflictual intimate relationships to the realistic conflict category. Nevertheless, it seems reasonable to suggest that men's conflict with women, at least in comparison with their conflict with other men, largely fits the nonrealistic dimension better. These two writers seem to offer some logical explanation for the seemingly illogical love-hate, rage-benevolence, fear-envy phenomena mentioned earlier. Simmel speaks of two tendencies, monistic and antagonistic, explaining: "Erotic relations offer the most frequent illustrations. How often do they not strike us as woven together of love and respect, or disrespect . . . of love and an urge to dominate or the need for dependence" (1955:22–23). Coser continues along the same lines:

> Simmel asserts that social relationships are likely to involve both converging and diverging motivations, both "love and hatred," which generally are intricately linked. One frequently hates the person one loves; hence it is often invalid to separate the two elements in concrete reality. (1964:60–61)

Coser links Simmel's proposition—the greater the involvement of total personality, the greater the probability of love-hate/attraction-hostility —to Freud's concept of ambivalence and the greater the likelihood of repression of hostility. Coser says: "In such cases feelings of hostility tend to accumulate and hence to intensify" (1964:62).

## AMBIVALENCE: NEED-DEPENDENCY IS ANTITHETICAL TO MALE SEX-ROLE EXPECTATIONS

Based upon these ideas, it is suggested that a need-dependency state is largely the root basis for the ambivalence of men toward women that has sustained the anti-woman phobia over the ages. In contradiction to the male sex role of dominance, superordination, control, and independence, men *need* women; there is a strong need-dependency element in men-women relationships. Women also have a need-dependency for men, but it is compatible with sex-role expectations, thus does not exert the same pressures toward conflict for women. In one of his recent articles, Goffman comments on mutual need-dependency (1977:313), and Hays makes this contribution to the topic:

> The feelings that surround contact . . . and the alien and unusual are the same as the earliest ambivalences of the small child. . . . all nonrational human behavior is organized in this scheme of duality, of attraction and repulsion, of love and hatred. (1964:37)

Even the umbilical cord may represent a tie that binds man to woman—his mother. For example, Masters discusses the misogyny of famous religious leaders (as do many other writers), and while telling about the power of the Jesuits in the sixteenth century states: "One prominent Jesuit declared himself much aggrieved and ashamed that a woman should have brought him into the world" (1964:19). It must have been a terrible irony for so many "Holy Men of God" who reviled women as something less than human and argued over their even possessing souls, that despite all their rage and hatred, the immutable fact was that all of them were born of the despised creatures: women. In fact, for Christians there was another conundrum: Jesus, the Son of God, was also formed in a woman's body, emerging from the despicable womb, an organ that "consorted with devils" (Sprenger and Kramer, 1964:215). To resolve this dilemma, at least, the Holy Men declared the miracle of the Immaculate Conception, elevating the Virgin Mary to heights beyond the reach of all mortal women.

The institution of the family was created by male power holders and upheld ever since by church and state as a most basic and sacred institution. Monogamous marriage has largely been shown to be beneficial for men and detrimental for women (Bernard, 1973; Durkheim, 1966). If society is to survive, people must procreate, and at least until now, procreation has usually required man-woman sexual intercourse. If we add into our consideration the normal human sex drive and that the majority of men prefer coitus with females, then we can distinguish a sexual need-dependency relationship. There are many other types of need-dependency, a very important one of which is economic (Bernard, 1972; Chapman and Gates, 1977; Chesler and Goodman, 1977; Deckard, 1975).

The ambivalence stemming from hate-love, rage-benevolence, fear-envy plus domination-dependency may have resulted in a dichotomy—not only in the extremes in division of labor and sex-role differentiation between the sexes, but also in the mutually exclusive sex-role expectations among women as a caste. In literature, plays, mythology, religious dogma, and even in law, women have been dichotomized into saint and sinner, virgin and whore. (For a discussion of the sharp dualism of *La Malinche and La Virgen de Guadalupe* in Mexican culture, see Mirande and Enriques, 1976.) One writer introduces a contemporary third category when he discusses nun, witch, and playmate (Richardson, 1974). Cultural stereotypes have largely either projected women onto an impossible pedestal or thrown them into the gutter; the polar extremes of love-hate have created love-hate objects—virgin-whore. Many writers have produced evidence that supports these ideas; a few examples follow. Delaney et al., have this to say:

> We have already mentioned that the male treats the menstruating woman with ambivalence; he both envies her ability to create and fears her power to destroy. The love-fear relationship is nowhere so potent as when it involves the act of love itself. A man is as likely to be sexually aroused by a women when she is menstruating as he is at any other time. But the blood of the menstruating woman is somehow dangerous, magical, and apparently not something he wants to get on his penis. It is thus necessary to protect the penis from the menses. . . . But official explanations for the intercourse taboo range from the holy to the hygienic, and they do not acknowledge that the male is afraid of *anything.* (1976:14–15)

Virginia Woolf, in her famous "A Room of One's Own," noted that women did not exist in literature except in the printed words of men (1974). Woolf saw clearly the dichotomized image—the two extreme portraits of "woman":

> It was certainly an odd monster that one made up by reading the historians first and the poets afterwards—a worm winged like an eagle; the spirit of life and beauty in a kitchen chopping up suet. But these monsters . . . have no existence in fact. What one must do to bring her to life was to think poetically and prosaically at one and the same moment, thus keeping in touch with fact. (1974:637)

In fiction, Woolf found woman:

> a person of the utmost importance; very various; heroic and mean; splendid and sordid; infinitely beautiful and hideous in the extreme; as great as a man. . . . But this is woman in fiction. . . . A very queer, composite being thus emerges. (1974:637)

Woolf's double image of poetry and history revealed:

> Imaginatively she is of the highest importance; practically she is completely insignificant. She pervades poetry from cover to cover;

she is all but absent from history. She dominates the lives of kings and conquerors in fiction; in fact she was the slave of any boy whose parents forced a ring upon her finger. Some of the most inspired words, some of the most profound thoughts in literature fall from her lips; in real life she could hardly read, could scarcely spell, and was the property of her husband. (1974:637)

Interestingly, Woolf looked up "Woman" in *The History of England* and found "Woman: possession of" and there read that:

"Wife-beating was a recognised right of man, and was practiced without shame by high as well as low. . . . Similarly, the daughter who refused to marry the gentleman of her parents' choice was liable to be locked up, beaten and flung about the room, without any shock being inflicted on public opinion. Marriage was not an affair of personal affection, but of family avarice, particularly in the 'chivalrous' upper classes." (1974:636)

The next reference Woolf found regarding the position of women in the history of England was 200 years later.

During her discussion of the thousand years of mutilation of women's bodies in China, the "beautification" process of footbinding, Dworkin tersely states:

It demonstrates that man's love for woman, his sexual adoration of her, his human definition of her, his delight and pleasure in her, require her negation: physical crippling and psychological lobotomy. That is the very nature of romantic love, which is the love based on polar role definitions, manifest in herstory as well as in fiction—he glories in her agony, he adores her deformity, he annihilates her freedom, he will have her as sex object, even if he must destroy the bones in her feet to do it. Brutality, sadism, and oppression emerge as the substantive core of the romantic ethos. (1974:112)

As an anthropologist friend mentioned when we were discussing the theme of this paper, "Men literally love us to death!" (Baizer, 1978), which is an interesting variation on the old saw, "Kill them with kindness."

## PERPETUATION AND TRANSMISSION OF ANTI-WOMAN PHOBIA

If an irrational and illogical phobia underlies (and undermines) man-woman relationships, how is it that modern society has developed to great technological and scientific heights and still carries along baggage

of ancient fears, envy, and hatred? One answer is that it has been transmitted through generations by a multitude of "carriers" of this ancient
"wisdom." New generations are socialized by adults, and each of us is
"carefully taught" our sex role expectations beginning very early in life.


Nursery Rhymes, Fairy Tales, Mythology, Taboos, and Law

Collectors Baring-Gould and Baring-Gould provide a nursery rhyme
that was supposed to teach little children the day of the week. They
write, "Charles Lamb liked it [this rhyme] so much he would send copies
of it—in Latin—in letters to his friends" (1962:105). It reads:

> I married a wife on Sunday,
> She began to scold on Monday,
> Bad was she on Tuesday,
> Middling was she on Wednesday,
> Worse was she on Thursday,
> Dead was she on Friday,
> Glad was I on Saturday night,
> To bury my wife on Sunday.

Another version had three lines changed to read: Bought a stick on
Tuesday, Beat her well on Wednesday, Sick was she on Thursday (Baring-
Gould and Baring-Gould, 1962:105). While this "teaching aid" was
malevolent, it was a long time ago when children chanted either version
of this nursery rhyme. However, consider Mother Goose rhymes which
not very long ago our own children learned:

> Peter, Peter, pumpkin eater
> Had a wife and couldn't keep her
> He put her in a pumpkin shell
> And there he kept her very well.

The message: Peter must be a man because he has a wife; men *keep* their
wives—locked up? In a fairy tale, Hanzel and Gretel's mother abandoned them in the forest and then an old lady prepared to cannibalize
them. Fairy tales are full of the violence and wickedness of women,
whether they are mothers, stepmothers, or wicked witches: They are
malicious, envious, greedy, cunning, and evil. The heroine is either passive and downtrodden (Cinderella) or asleep/dead (Sleeping Beauty,
Rapunzel, Snow White). Prince Charming is rich, powerful, strong, and
brave. Dworkin reviews the symbolism and implications for sex-role
socialization of the young through fairy tales:

> The lessons are simple, and we learn them well. Men and women are different, absolute opposites. . . . The good father can never be confused with the bad mother. Their qualities are different, polar . . . . There are two definitions of woman. There is the good woman. She is a victim. There is the bad woman. She must be destroyed. The good woman must be possessed. (Dworkin, 1974:47–48)

These common nursery rhymes and fairy tales are cross cultural in origin and have been handed down through antiquity with slight cultural variations along the way.

Almost any anthropological study of preliterate cultures contains a series of myths interlocked with taboos associated with mating and marriage, menstruation and childbearing. Most of these myths and taboos served to widen the social distance between males and females, to reinforce superiority of males and inferiority of females, and to set women apart as unclean and evil, creatures to be feared and avoided (Delaney et al., 1976; Hogbin, 1970). Hays points out that while there are myths and taboos applying to men as well as to women, it is men who set the norm. He says:

> We must remember . . . that the male is dominant, he sets the pattern of the human being and the alien. . . . he can see that other males are the same and therefore can be accepted into the category of the self versus the alien. But women are different. Despite a man's need for his mother's breast and his sexual attraction to her, she is not of his kind. Even though he entertains unconscious hostilities toward his father he can identify with him. Woman . . . is alien, peculiarly filled with mana . . . [he feels] that her bad mana is more important than her beneficial potentialities. (Hays, 1964:38)

Hays' comprehensive review of myths provides evidence of irrational fear associated with female sexuality. From vastly different and geographically distant cultures, he produces myths that associate women's vaginas with snakes, live dogs' heads, sharp teeth, and thorns, all of which symbolize the fear of castration (Hays, 1964). According to myths about creation, including Eve and Pandora and all the variations in between, women were held responsible for all accumulated sorrows and evils in the world.

Myths and taboos moved into law tend to remain there long beyond the time when hoary superstitions and fears should have faded into antiquity. As ancient (male) Israel's fears of the sexual power of females gave rise to taboos against women based on biological processes of childbirth and menstruation, they became institutionalized and expressed in ritual law (Richardson, 1974:11). These laws are still in effect today, as are many in other cultures. Changes are particularly slow to occur in family law, which perhaps affects the lives and welfare of women more than any others. One excellent account reviews myths, religious mis- ogyny, Bonaparte's Civil Code, British Common Law, and their impact upon American law (Davidson, 1977:2–23). The transition from mythol- ogy to law seems to take a very short step, as Davidson (1977) and Dobash and Dobash (1978) clearly show. On the other hand, recalci- trance of the law to change to give more equitable justice to women may be found in Schulder's review (1970:153–175; also De Crow, 1975), or a cursory reading of a recent review of California law on the status of homemakers (Bersch, 1977). Perhaps the most convincing testimony to the unwillingness of the law to change to recognize women as full and equal human beings is the 55-year struggle (as yet still unsuccessful) to enact into law the Equal Rights Amendment to the United States Consti- tution which merely states: "Equality of rights under the law shall not be denied or abridged by the United States or by any State on account of sex."

## History, Textbooks, and Literature

As men's laws have been written by men for men, history has been recorded and traced almost exclusively by men; history books have les- sons to teach, not only by what they include, but what they exclude. As noted earlier, women were almost a second thought in the history books Woolf examined; among the few exceptions were female monarchs—an inherited state. When women were mentioned, it was usually in their "proper" role: "Behind every great man there's a good woman." In one history book, Madame Curie was illustrated "peering mildly from behind her husband's shoulder while he and another distinguished gen- tleman loom in the foreground, engaged in serious dialogue" (U'Ren, 1972:323). Being famous in her own right apparently was not enough to justify taking even this woman out of her "natural place."

In the dominant culture, textbooks prepare young girls and boys to know their proper places. Young adults later turn to fiction, and some to the classics in literature. Regardless of the level, books available today strongly tend to reinforce sex-role stereotypes. What they learn overall is that boys progress from competitiveness and aggressiveness in sports and nature to competitiveness and aggressiveness in sex and occu- pation (Martin, 1971; Millet, 1970; Woolf, 1974). The role of girls scarcely changes. As women they are still "girls," passive, supportive, nurturent, and dependent on males—only now the men they depend on are not brothers and fathers but lovers or husbands. In addition, these female characters are either willing to do anything and everything for their men or men soon show them the expediency of doing anything and everything, whether they are willing or not (e.g., Shakespeare's Kate).

Today, feminists are searching the archives and libraries, trying to reconstruct the pages of history in which women rightfully belong, as are blacks, Chicanos, and other minorities. Mackenzie complied a magnificent collection of words, photographs, and illustrations for a documentary of the suffragette movement in England (1975). This volume helps to fill the gap. As Mackenzie says, "I discovered this feat had been almost successfully erased from the history books. The women who fought for the vote had vanished from out history" (1975:ix). Another outstanding contribution is a documentary history on *Black Women in White America* by Lerner (1973): over 600 pages of articles, communications, and other documents which had largely been lost to, or ignored by, white historians. These efforts will undoubtedly help fulfill the need for oppressed categories such as women and minorities to find new ways to define themselves and to develop a sense of pride and self-worth (Brown and Seitz, 1970; Kraditor, 1968, Rossi, 1974). Feminist groups now analyze current and new textbooks to guard against sex-role stereotyping and negative female images.

But the work has just begun, and present and past generations have been educated through texts and history books selectively recorded, written, and interpreted by members of the dominant sexual, racial, and ethnic category.


Religion and Psychotherapy

Religion has been a true carrier of The Word through the ages, and that Word constituted a powerful force supporting the hierarchal relationship of humans to each other and to their god, reading from top to bottom, God, men, women, children. Where mythology and the shaman left off, the clergy took over; and by dogma, theology, and sermons to the faithful, an anti-woman phobia has been nurtured and transmitted through the generations to the present. One writer observes: "All religions preach subordination of women not just to God, but to men, as an article of faith. . . . Moreover, judeo/christian theological writings are explicitly misogynous" (Gardner, 1977). Burning women at the stake as witches was a massive hate campaign engendered by the clergy that publicly destroyed millions of women (Dworkin, 1974; Ehrenreich and English, 1973b; Hays, 1964), but to this day millions of individual women are privately sacrificed to a masculine diety whose spokespersons deny them control over their own bodies or lives (Daly, 1973, 1975; de Beauvoir, 1974; Hardin, 1974; Richards, 1974).

As Daly points out, "theology and ethics which are overtly and explicitly oppressive to women are by no means confined to the past" (1973:4), whether they are manifested in ritual law of Judaism (Richardson, 1974), the theology of Christianity (Daly, 1973), or the Eastern religions such as the Moslem (Goldman, 1972). We have read in the present decade of 200,000 Bengali women who were double victims of men and religion: raped by West Pakistani soldiers and made social outcasts by their husbands because "no Moslem will live with a wife who has been touched by another man" (Goldman, 1972:84). We have heard little about the forced motherhood of women in Roman Catholic countries where the church and state combine to prohibit contraceptives, abortion, and divorce (Russell and Van de Ven, 1976). No headlines tell of the millions of women who die as the result of crude and unsanitary attempts at abortion or of the unwanted infants who are directly or indirectly killed by these unwilling "breeders." Daly calls Catholic pressures against birth control "the reduction of the woman to the condition of biological beast . . . " (1975:55). Even in countries where constitutional law declares the separation of church and state, as in the United States, one religion has thrown its money and power behind and organized opposition to the Equal Rights Amendment, and a California Bishop excommunicated members of his diocese who belonged to the National Organization for Women because of NOW's pro right-to-choose stance on abortion. We are aware that women are refused entry into the ministry of most religions around the world, and that they still cannot participate in the most sacred rites of the religions that circumscribe their lives.

In some contemporary cultures, religion has lost power and efficacy, but where the church leaves off, the new religion of psychotherapy, psychiatry, and psychology has taken over in the relay race of anti-woman phobia. The psychiatrist now assumes the role of the high priest and the shaman before him (Szasz, 1970). Daly states:

> To a large extent in recent times the role of religion in supporting the sexual caste system has been transferred to the professions of psychiatry and psychology. . . . Psychiatry and psychology have their own creeds, priesthood, spiritual counseling, rules, anathemas, and jargon. Their power of psychological intimidation is is enormous. . . . Together these professions function as "Mother" Church of contemporary secular patriarchal religion, and they send missionaries everywhere. (1973:4)

Other writers have detailed the anti-woman and oppressive nature of psychotherapy and its damaging effects on women in relation to men and society, (Chesler, 1973; Weisstein, 1972). The big difference is that now not only do women have an insatiable lust, but they have a whole host of other inherent sex-specific problems. Shainess writes, "Freud's thinking not only had its roots in Jewish theology, but was a direct extension of the New Testament and the thinking of St. Thomas Acquinas" (1970:259).

Thus women moved from Eve-Pandora, Cleopatra–Virgin Mary, to "permanently sick" because they suffer from penis envy, masochism, and so forth. The numbers of writers are growing who are showing that psychotherapy has established itself as the new religion that changes heresy and sin into sickness, neurosis, and psychosis and attaches labels to dichotomized gender roles of masculine and feminine (Broverman et al., 1970; Miller, 1974; Shainess, 1970; Szasz, 1970).

The Media: Television, Movies, Advertising, and Pornography

In the United States, one of the earliest socializing agents is television (Bandura, 1973), which has been denounced by citizen groups across the country for lack of program quality and, in particular, for the heavy emphasis on violence and sex, separately or together. Very young children begin by watching juvenile-fare cartoon characters who engage in a wide variety of violent activities, as well as watching adult fare that clearly shows stereotyped, mutually exclusive, masculine-feminine gender roles. Many viewing hours are filled with movies, and when we analyze their content, we find that they are sending messages in the form of entertainment that closely reflect cultural values. Haskell has written a comprehensive analysis of American movies that extends from silent movies to the present (1974). Haskell notes the popularization of the double standard, the evil woman, the standards of virginity, motherhood, and family responsibility for women, and the attacks by the press and clergy when some actresses refused to project the intended image, either in their personal lives or on the screen. Haskell found in American movies, their producers and directors, the sense of anti-woman phobia being described in this paper, for she summarizes:

> Because woman did not fight back, man quickly took the advantage and made her the scapegoat for all his vices and fears. He was abashed that his penis moved, unbidden, when he looked at Eve, and so he invented penis envy. He was terrified by the prospect of his own demise, and so he invented God and His Son to resurrect

and redeem him. He was resentful that another man had preceded him and made love to his mother, so he invented the Virgin Birth and vasectomized his father. He was intimidated by woman's sexual desire, and so he invented the mutually exclusive virgin and the whore. He was worried lest woman, resenting his freedom, should want to live and work as he did, and so he invented and ordained the mother in honored vassalage to him. He was ashamed of growing old and ugly . . . and so he invented female vanity to exorcise and account for these fears. (1974:227–278)

Later Haskell writes, "This fear and awe of woman-as-mother, or wife-as-mother, is the prime source of female grotesques in American movies" (1974:341–342). Television viewers in the United States are still receivers of such films within their homes, often with the youngsters gathered around. The whole family will also be treated to commercials every few minutes, whether the program is the daily news, old movies, or new television productions of violence and sex. Some writers have turned to media images of women in magazines, television, and advertisement and have found there more of the same sex-role stereotyping of women and men (Embree, 1970; Florika, 1970; Komisar, 1972).

Perhaps one of the important side effects of the media is to reach out to women who do not have the money to pay therapists. Soap opera gives millions of daytime viewers a vicarious "other life" to escape the pain and boredom of their own. One local radio station offers a talk show conducted by a psychologist who receives telephone calls from listeners and who in turn dispenses wisdom, advice, and methods for coping with the callers' most vexing problems. Similarly, there are two sisters who each write nationally syndicated columns that are to be found in newspapers in almost every city and hamlet in the United States. Spiced with wit now and then, their advice clearly reflects traditional beliefs of rank-and-file Americans. If a problem presented in serious, the reader is invariably urged to consult a psychiatrist, psychologist, medical doctor, or pastor. Magazines, too, regularly provide problem-solving feature articles. Surely the media function as the modern-day safety valve mentioned by Coser (1964). Incidentally, Embree mentions that "William Paley, now Chairman of the Board of Columbia Broadcasting System, was deputy chief of the Psychological Warfare Division" (1970:197), an interesting background for chief executive of one of the three most powerful broadcasting corporations in the country.

The media reinforce mutually exclusive sex roles: Women learn that they find their greatest satisfaction in "Kinde, Kuche, Kirche" (Weisstein, 1970; Hays, 1964), and men learn that they are aggressive animals.

Yet another side of media socialization is the insidious emphasis on women and beauty, with clear instructions that women *need* cosmetics to protect against their own body odors as well as to create the image of beauty so very desirable to all men. The damage done by creating objects out of women is costly to women primarily and men secondarily (Dworkin, 1974; Montagu, 1968:50). Hays remarks, "It has remained for Americans to make of her [woman] an abstract commodity" (1964:284). Montagu mentions that men complain about women's artificial beautification, yet he writes: *"The behavior of women in our culture has largely been conditioned by and in response to the behavior of males toward them.* Men have placed a high premium upon sexual attractiveness; the promised dividends are high, and women, therefore, concentrate on making themselves sexually attractive" (1968:50). In the United States today one can spend whole evenings devoted to watching feminine objects of beauty parade their bodies, adornments, and "talents" in institutionalized beauty contests. This practice of inspecting and appraising sexual objects like so many pieces of meat has extended competition ages downward to teenaged, and finally to pre-teenaged, girls. A national commentary program recently devoted television time to the beauty competitions of little girls from about ages 8 to 13, shown preening and marketing themselves under the proud eyes of mothers introducing them to the ecstasy and heartbreak of being a packaged commodity. Hays makes the following comments on this sad spectacle:

> No more dehumanized victim could be found than a Marilyn Monroe . . . the bitter conflict between herself as an industry and a frustrated, undeveloped, and wholly unrealized female destroyed her. Hers was a feminine American Tragedy. In a merchandising civilization everything is marketable. By marketing legs, breasts, and haunches, a male-dominated society . . . [panders to fantasy] but it goes further by patenting and mass-producing a pseudo image upon which a nationwide audience may vent its hostile and degrading eroticism. (1964:283)

If the little girls who walk onto a judging platform are "lucky," they will be the next generation of "sex symbols," movie stars, happy housewives in TV ads, objectified on billboards and record covers or even the centerfolds of *Playboy*. If not quite so lucky, they may turn to modeling for porno movies or one of the many pornographic magazines that have such staggering circulations *(Newspage,* 1978).

There is perhaps no better support to be found for the idea of an anti-woman phobia than materials on American magazine and newspaper racks, liberally sprinkled around every city on sidewalks, in supermarkets, and "mom and pop" grocery stores, and so forth. A hometown newspaper and three magazines were recently purchased: one a detective story, the second an erotic "love" story, the third a copy of *Hustler*.[6] The first four pages of the newspaper produced nine articles reporting violent acts that totaled 11 killings: one husband murdered his six children to "spite" his wife; another husband killed his wife, son, and himself; another man ran his wife down with his automobile after an argument; and finally there was a 13-year-old boy who shot his teacher. The other violent acts included assault, mugging, and destruction of a church interior. *All* of these crimes were committed by males. The major headline on the front page told of the kidnap and rape of a 13-year-old girl brutally beaten and left for dead—starkly similar to a rape-murder of a 14-year-old girl the week before. In the lower left corner of the same page was a short item telling of the release without bail of a convicted multiple rapist-kidnapper *(Daily Pilot,* 1978:1–4).

The detective and erotic magazines were overflowing with lurid sex. Several color photographs on the covers showed scenes depicting women being tortured by men, with bold captions of story topics to urge potential readers to turn inside by learn about torture, mutilation, male castration, rape, incest, and murder. But most graphic of all was the cover illustration of the June 1978 issue of *Hustler*. It showed a meat grinder. Before it was a dish filled with pink "meat" and from the top of the grinder protruded the bottom half of a female body upside down: the inverted buttocks and legs of a woman. To the left of the meat grinder scene was a quotation ascribed to the publisher: "We will no longer hang women up like pieces of meat" and to the lower right corner was a pseudo meat stamp indicating prime meat quality.[7]

In the United States, pornography has become more and more explicit as the country has become more liberal and sexually frank. There are limitations to how many ways copulation and the female body can be depicted, and gradually the accent has focused on torture and degradation of women for the titilation of the almost exclusively male readership and for increased sales. Recent trends are moving toward child pornography in magazines and movies, but the theme remains the same: Sex is linked with violence, power, domination, and control of women and children by men. Lederer and Russell point out that many people who have acted against pornography in the past "have usually ignored the misogyny . . . expressed in it" (1977:2). These writers see the upsurge in violence and child pornography "as part of the backlash to the women's liberation movement. Enough woman have been rejecting the traditional role of subordination to men to cause a crisis in the collective male ego" (1977:3). Lederer and Russell reviewed pornographic movies, books, advertisements, and magazines and found violence rampant; all previously mentioned forms of sexual violence were included in the constant theme of degradation of women as sex objects being subjected to "masculine" domination and control for male pleasure. Even when violence and sadism are missing, Lederer and Russell say that all pornography objectifies women, which "means that women are not seen as human beings, but as things. . . . Men are reared to view females in this way, pornography thrives off this, and feeds it, and rape is one of the consequences" (1977:1). Other writers have taken a similar stance (Brownmiller, 1976; Dworkin, 1974; Hays, 1964; London, 1978: Women Against Violence in Pornography and Media, 1977).

An unusual component of a scientific journal recently was eight pages of photographs accompanying an article by London, "Images of Violence Against Women," in *Victimology* (1978:511–518). These black-and-white photographs showed record covers, advertisements, cartoons, and a birthday card which vividly portrayed, overtly or symbolically, all the forms of violence and sadism referred to above. One of these most clearly illustrates the imprint of ancient misogynist mythology. It is a cover for the record "Hydra." *Victimology's* staff provided this commentary:

> [It shows] Woman as monster that must be eliminated. The Hydra is a many-headed serpent or monster of Greek mythology slain by Hercules each head of which when cut off was replaced by two others. Thus it represents a multifarious, long lasting, deep seated and difficult evil to eradicate. The snakes portrayed here are poisonous. The misogynic implications of this picture are obvious. Women are often associated with sin and snakes and are seen as the cause of evil. (1978:516)

To deny that ancient fears and envy of women gave birth to an anti-woman phobia that is rampant today, resulting in crimes of violence against women, may well be taking a "head in the sand" approach (Martin, 1976:15). Hatred is a word that few of us like or want to hear, but we cannot deny that it exists—even if it is irrational—any more than we can deny that racism, homophobia, and sexism do exist.


## CONCLUSIONS

The private crime of woman battering was taken out of a localized dyadic interaction within the home and marriage and placed in a cross-cultural and cross-temporal context of crimes of violence against women. This led to a shift in emphasis away from individuals at a specific time period into a group phenomenon of long endurance. From prehistoric times to the present, men apparently have both feared and envied women because of biological and physiological differences which generated an anti-woman phobia. Based on structural conflict theory, the hypothesis was presented that suggests that the dominant category, men, are in realistic conflict with other men and nonrealistic conflict—largely based on need-dependency—with women. Using women as scapegoats, men have projected onto women greatly undesirable features that have set them apart as alien beings: the "Other." The anti-woman phobia has been transmitted through cultures and ages via nursery rhymes, fairy tales, mythology, taboos, and law; history, textbooks, and literature; religion and psychotherapy, and the media. There seems to be abundant evidence to support the idea of an undercurrent of conscious and subconscious anti-woman phobia that has set women up in a we-them dicotomy as appropriate victims—scapegoats—in male-to-male conflict. That the phobia is pervasive seems clear; that it is an integral heritage in the psyche of *all* men is not clear. Evidence to the contrary can be found everywhere if one looks, and particularly in the person-hood of many of the male authors cited here who recognize and abhor anti-woman sentiments (cf. Hays, 1964; Masters and Lea, 1964; Mill, 1971; Montagu, 1968; Richardson, 1974; Szasz, 1970). Goffman has also pointed out that differences between the sexes are no longer important because of technological and scientific advancement, but they have been artificially maintained and perpetuated in what he terms "institutional reflexivity" for the affirmation of mutually exclusive gender identity and social distance (1977). Hays writes of the injustices done to women *qua* woman by men saying, "he has either imprisoned her, made her an out-cast, or treated her as a scapegoat," and concludes:

> If we are to go forward, therefore, it is time the male abandoned his magical approach to the second sex. It is time he learned to accept his existential anguish; it is time he realized the menace of the female lies within himself. And when he is ready to accept her as a partner in work and love, he may even begin to find out what she is like. (1964:295)

Montagu also discussed crimes men have committed against women over the ages:

> These have been for the most part unconscious crimes, and men have no more been aware of what they were doing to women than women have, on their part, been aware of the unjustness of what was being done to them. On the whole, the motivations of men have been unconscious and where they have not been unconscious men's

behavior toward women has been conditioned by the social heredity represented by their tradition. Men as well as women have been the victims of this tradition, and as long as it continues injustice will continue to be as frequent as it is. (1968:51)

Faced with ageless conflict between men and between men and women, any of us could be led to despair of ever having a kind and just world. To read the many pages required for the construction of this paper has led to feelings of hopelessness and depression; this has not been an easy paper to write. Atrocities and violently destructive behavior are found on page after page of the literature under review until it begins to appear that the whole world is a cesspool of conflict and hatred. Yet the fact of doing research on one form of men's violence against women, whether it is woman battering, rape, incest, or any other form of violence, inevitably raises the question: Why? What are the causes? Some investigators have pointed to personality traits—jealousy and possessiveness, emotional insecurity, alcoholism, and so on—but these are merely symptoms, not the cause, of male violence directed at women. In this search for root causes, years of civilization's cosmetics and cultural decorations had to be peeled away, layer by layer; and if the ugly festering sore of an irrational, primordial anti-woman phobia is at the source, then we must look at it well before it can be eradicated. Only by exposing it can we begin to deal with it directly. While an anti-woman phobia may have been generated from prehistoric ignorance, fear, and envy based on biological and physiological differences between men and women, this does not mean that it will always survive to contaminate man-woman relationships. The *differences* are generic, while *attitudes* creating phobias (such as fear and envy) are not immutable to change. Ideas and attitudes are learned and may be unlearned or reformulated. Thus, it is hoped that raising these questions here will lead to even more questions, and finally to some answers.

One writer offers comfort; Hunt reminds us that there is the other side of human interactions which gives some hope that the Lorenzes and Ardreys of the world are wrong, for he says:

The record of man's inhumanity to man is horrifying, when one compiles it—enslavement, castration, torture, rape, mass slaughter in war after war. But who has compiled the record of man's kindness to man—the trillions of acts of gentleness and goodness, the helping hands, smiles, shared meals, kisses, gifts, healings, rescues? . . . [man] is a beast and perhaps at times the cruelest beast of all— but sometimes he is also the kindest beast of all. He is not all good

and not perfectible, but he is not all bad and not wholly unchange-
able or unimprovable. That is the basis on which one can have hope
for him; but it is enough. (1973:37–38)

Ironically, these comforting words by Hunt were first printed in the July
1970 issue of *Playboy* magazine.

## NOTES

1. A few examples of personal resources are health of self and/or dependent children, age, appearance, education, employability, and number of children
and their ages. Material resources include money, property ownership, etc.
Resources may be positively or negatively weighted.

2. It should be noted that even if the antagonism may be "mutual," the
advantage lies proportionately on the side of the group with power. Even if
women were to be equally antagonistic toward men, their capacity for revenge
and violent acts is both socially and physically less. Evidence of women's retaliation or "punishment" of men may be found in covert vengeful acts, subterfuge or
deviousness, or coy "feminine" manipulation of men to achieve goals they could
not obtain by direct confrontation. Montagu says, "The female's inability to
cope with the physically stronger male obliges her, from an early age, to develop
traits that will enable her to secure her ends by other means. . . . When one has
a stubborn mule in the house, one has to learn to get around him. Women early
developed a strategy of devices or 'artful dodges' for dealing with the problem"
(1968:43–44). Sometimes ridicule is used, such as among the Wogebo of New
Guinea, where the women to go a mountain top and loudly mock the men's
sacred rites from which they are absolutely excluded (Hogbin, 1978:87).

3. The term caste is used herein to denote an ascribed category in rigid
social stratification: women by nature of their sex automatically are members of
the subordinate caste, regardless of class membership. Daly explains:
There exists a worldwide phenomenon of sexual caste, basically the same
whether one lives in Saudi Arabia or in Sweden. This planetary sexual caste
system involves birth-ascribed hierarchially ordered groups whose members
have unequal access to goods, services, and prestige and to physical and
mental well-being. (1973:2)

4. There are, of course, differences inherent in the male body and male
genitalia that enable him to do, have, be, produce, etcetera, what the female is
either incapable of or restricted from. For purposes of this discussion these differences will not be addressed here. These differences might well be considered
advantages to the male by men (as well as women), but therefore would be
unlikely to produce fear and envy leading to an anti-woman phobia.

5. One example of how men are likely to intercede when a man is attacked
by another man, or a woman attacked by another woman, but not when a

woman is attacked by a man is found in the social-psychological experiment by Shotland and Straw (1976). Straus says their study reflects male hostility to women, and along with the study cites his own unpublished experiment with Churchill regarding punishment to an assaulter (1976:550–551). Straus also mentions that some bystanders who did not intervene in the Kitty Genovese murder explained that they thought the victim was the man's wife.

    6. *Hustler* magazine reportedly "boasts a readership of 7 million men per month in the United States. *Playboy* magazine sells 6 million copies per month" *(Newspage,* 1978:1).

    7. These items were purchased at a "mom and pop" neighborhood store. the clerk who handled my purchase was the 14-year-old son of the owners who helped locate the gruesome detective magazine, saying he had been looking it over just that morning.

---

# REFERENCES

Andersen, Ingerlise, *Wife battering in the Netherlands: Needs and incidence.* Paper presented at the International Sociological Association Seminar on Sex Roles, Deviance, and Agents of Social Control in Dublin, Ireland, 1977.

Baizer, Carol. Excerpt from a personal conversation on May 23, 1978.

Bandura, Albert. *Aggression: A social learning analysis.* Englewood Cliffs, NJ: Prentice-Hall, 1973.

Baring-Gould, William S., and Baring-Gould, Ceil. *The annotated mother goose.* New York: Bramhall House, 1962.

Bart, Pauline B. *Rape and the criminal justice system.* Paper presented at the annual meeting of the Society for the Study of Social Problems, San Francisco, California, 1975.

Bernard, Jessie. *Women and the public interest: An essay on policy and protest.* Chicago: Aldine, 1972.

———. *The future of marriage.* New York: Bantam, 1973.

Bersch, Blanche C. The legal status of homemakers in California. Committee on Homemakers, National Commission on the Observance of International Women's Year. (Washington, D.C.: U.S.) Government Printing Office, 1977.

Broverman, Inge, Broverman, D. M., Clarkson, F. E., Rosenkrantz, P. S. and Vogel, S. R. Sex-role stereotypes and clinical judgments of mental health. *Journal of Consulting and Clinical Psychology,* 1970, *34*(1), 1–7.

Brown, Connie, and Seitz, Jane. 'You've come a long way, baby': Historical perspectives. In Robin Morgan (Ed.), *Sisterhood is powerful.* New York: Vintage, 1970, 3–28.

Brownmiller, Susan. *Against our will: Men, women and rape.* New York: Bantam Books, 1976.

Burgess, Ann Wolbert, and Holmstrom, Lynda Lytle. Sexual trauma of children and adolescents. *Nursing Clinics of North America,* 1975, *10*(3), 551–563.

Chapman, Jane Roberts, and Gates, Margaret. *Women into wives: The legal and economic impact of marriage.* Beverly Hills: Sage, 1977.

Chesler, Phyllis. *Woman and madness.* New York: Avon, 1973.

———. A psychologist takes on male mythology. *Ms. Magazine,* 1978, *6*(1), 50, 79.

———, and Goodman, Emily Jane. *Women, money and power.* New York: Bantam, 1977.

Coser, Lewis A. *The functions of social conflict* (Second printing). Glencoe, Illinois: Free Press, 1964.

Daily Pilot. Orange County, California: May 19, 1978, pp.1-4.

Daly, Mary. *Beyond god the father: Toward a philosophy of women's liberation.* Boston: Beacon Press, 1974.

———. *The church and the second sex.* New York: Harper and Row, 1975.

Davidson, Terry. Wifebeating: A recurring phenomenon throughout history. In Maria Roy (Ed.), *Battered women: A psychosociological study of domestic violence.* New York: Van Nostrand Reinhold, 1977, 2–23.

de Beauvoir, Simone. *The second sex.* New York: Vintage Books, 1974.

Deckard, Barbara. *The women's movement: Political, socioeconomic, and psychological issues.* New York: Harper and Row, 1975.

De Crow, Karen. *Sexist justice.* New York: Vintage Books, 1975.

Delaney, Janice, Lupton, Mary Jane and Toth, Emily. *The curse: A cultural history of menstruation.* New York: E. P. Dutton, 1976.

Dobash, R. Emerson, and Dobash, Russell P. *Love honour and obey: Institutional ideologies and the struggle for battered women.* Paper presented at the annual meeting of the Society for the Study of Social Problems, New York, 1976.

———. Wives: The 'appropriate' victims of marital violence. *Victimology,* 1978, *2* (3-4), 426–442.

Durkheim, Emile. *Suicide.* New York: Free Press, 1966.

Dworkin, Andrea. *Woman Hating.* New York: E. P. Dutton, 1974.

Ehrenreich, Barbara, and English, Deirdre. *Complaints and disorders: The sexual politics of sickness.* Old Westbury: The Feminist Press, 1973. (a)

———. *Witches, midwives, and nurses: A history of women healers.* Old Westbury: The Feminist Press, 1973. (b)

Embree, Alice. Media images 1: Madison avenue. In Robin Morgan (Ed.), *Sisterhood is powerful.* New York: Vintage Books, 1970, 194–212.

Erikson, Kai R. *Wayward puritans: A study of the sociology of deviance.* New York: John Wiley and Sons, 1969.

Florika. Media images 2: Body odor and social order. In Robin Morgan (Ed.), *Sisterhood is powerful.* New York: Vintage Books, 1970, 212–219.

Frankfort, Ellen. *Vaginal Politics.* New York: Bantam Books, 1973.

Gardner, Jo Ann Evans. *Varieties of discontent: Female response to religious misogyny.* Paper presented at the annual meeting of the American Psychological Association, San Francisco, California, 1977.

Gilder, George E. *Sexual suicide.* New York: Bantam Books, 1975.

Goffman, Erving. The arrangement between the sexes. *Theory and Society,* Fall 1977, *4*(3), 301–331.

Goldman, Joyce. Women of Bangladesh. *Ms. Magazine,* August, 1972, 84–86.

Haavio-Mannila, Elina. Suggestions in a letter, dated July 11, 1978.

Hageman, Alice L. *Sexist religion and women in the church: No more silence!* New York: Association Press, 1974.

Hampton, Marilynne Brandon. Testimony on domestic violence before the senate subcommittee on child and human development, March 4, 1978.

Hardin, Garrett. *Mandatory Motherhood: The true meaning of "Right to Life."* Boston: Beacon Press, 1974.

Haskell, Molly. *From reverence to rape: The treatment of women in the movies.* New York: Holt, Rinehart and Winston, 1974.

Hays, H. R. *The dangerous sex: The myth of feminine evil.* New York: G. P. Putnam's Sons, 1964.

Hoebel, E. Adamson, Antropology: The study of man. New York: McGraw-Hill Book Company, 1972.

Hogbin, Ian. *The island of menstruating men: Religion in Wogebo, New Guinea.* Scranton: Chandler Publishing, 1970.

Hosken, Fran P. Female circumcision in Africa. *Victimology,* 1978, *2*(3–4), 487–498.

Hunt, Morton. Man and beast. In Ashley Montagu (Ed.), *Man and Aggression* (Second Edition). New York: Oxford University Press, 1973.

Joutsen, Matti. Letter dated June 4, 1978 describing events in Helsinki, Finland.

Klingbeil, Laril, and Berliner, Lucy. Report of Operations by LEAA Grantees, Washington, D.C., December 12. Sexual Assault Center, Harborview, Hospital, Seattle. Washington, D.C.: LEAA.

Komisar, Lucy. The image of woman in advertising. In Vivian Gornick and Barbara K. Moran (Eds.), *Woman in sexist society.* New York: Mentor, 1972, 304–317.

Kraditor, Aileen S. *Up from the pedestal: Selected writings in the history of American feminism.* Chicago: Quadrangle Books, 1968.

Laws, Judith Long. The psychology of tokenism: An analysis. *Sex roles,* 1975, *1*(1), 51–67.

Lederer, Laura, and Russell, Diana. Questions we get asked most often. *Women Against Violence in Pornography and Media Newspage,* November 1977, *1*(6), 1–4.

Lerner, Gerda. *Black women in white America: A documentary history.* New York: Vintage Books, 1973.

London, Julia. Images of violence against women. *Victimology,* 1978, *2*(3–4), 510–424.

Mackenzie, Midge. *Shoulder to shoulder: A documentary.* Middlesex: Penguin Books, 1975.

Martin, Del. *Battered wives.* San Francisco, Glide Publications, 1976.

Martin, Wendy. Seduced and abandoned in the new world: The image of woman in American fiction. In Vivian Gornick and Barbara K. Moran (Eds.), *Woman in Sexist Society.* New York: Basic Books, 1971, 329–346.

Masters, R. E. L., and Lea, Eduard. *The anti-sex.* New York: The Julian Press, 1964.

Middleton, Audrey. *A refuge in Belfast.* Paper presented at the International Sociological Association Seminar on Sex Roles, Deviance, and Agents of Social Control, Dublin, Ireland, 1977.

————. Incest or rape? *Fortnight,* January-February 1978, *160,* 8, 18.

Mill, John Stuart. *On the subjection of women.* Greenwich: Fawcett Premier Book, 1971.

Miller, Jean Baker. *Psychoanalysis and women.* Baltimore: Penguin Books, 1974.

Millett, Kate. *Sexual politics.* New York: Doubleday, 1970.

Mirande, Alfredo, and Enriquez, Evangelina. Chicanas: Their triple oppression as colonized women. *Sociological Symposium,* Fall 1976, *17,* 91–102.

Montagu, Ashley. *The natural superiority of women.* New York: Macmillan, 1968.

O'Faolain, Julia, and Martines, Lauro. *Not in god's image: Women in history from the Greeks to the victorians.* New York: Harper and Row, 1973.

Pagelow, Mildred Daley. *Preliminary report on battered women.* Paper presented at the Second International Symposium on Victimology, Boston, 1976.

————. *Battered women: A new perspective.* Paper presented at the International Sociological Association Seminar on Sex Roles, Deviance, and Agents of Social Control, Dublin, Ireland, 1977.(a)

————. *Secondary battering: Breaking the cycle of domestic violence.* Paper presented at the annual meeting of Sociologists for Women in Society section of the American Sociological Association, Chicago, 1977.(b)

————. *Needs assessment of victims of domestic violence.* Testimony for the U.S. Commission on Civil Rights Consultation on Battered Women and the House Committee on Science and Technology Hearings on Domestic Violence, 1978.(a)

————. *Research on domestic violence: What we have and what we need.* Testimony Hearings on Domestic Violence, 1978.(b)

————. *Secondary battering: Alternatives of female victims to domestic violence.* Paper prepared for the annual meeting of the American Sociological Association, San Francisco, California, 1978.(c)

Pizzey, Erin. *Scream quietly or the neighbors will hear.* Short Hills, NJ: Ridley Enslow, 1977.

Pornography: Some facts and figures you should know. *Women Against Violence in Pornography and Media. Newspage,* 1978, *2*(5), 1–4.

Richardson, Herbert W. Nun, witch, playmate: The Americanization of sex. New York: Harper and Row, 1974.

Rossi, Alice S. *The feminist papers.* New York: Bantam, 1974.

Russell, Diana E. H., and Van de Ven, Nicole. *Crimes against women: Proceedings of the international tribunal.* Millbrae, CA: Les Femmes, 1976.

Schulder, Diane B. Does the law oppress women? In Robin Morgan (Ed.), *Sisterhood is powerful.* New York: Vintage Books, 1970.

Shainess, Natalie. A psychiatrist's view: Images of women—Past and present, overt and obscured. In Robin Morgan (ed.), *Sisterhood is powerful.* New York: Vintage Books, 1970.

Shotland, R. Lance, and Straw, Margaret K. Bystander response to an assault: When a man attacks a woman. *Journal of Personality and Social Psychology,* 1976, *34*(5), 990–999.

Simmel, Georg. *Conflict.* Glencoe, Illinois: Free Press, 1955.

Snell, John E., Rosenwald, Richard J., and Roby, Ames. The wifebeaters wife. *Archives of General Psychiatry,* August 1964, *11,* 107–112.

Sprenger, James, and Kramer, Heinrich. Malleus Maleficarum. In R. E. L. Masters and Eduard Lea (Eds.), *The anti-sex: The belief in the natural inferiority of women.* New York: Julian Press, 1964, 201–218.

Steinmetz, Suzanne K., and Straus, Murray A. *Violence in the family.* New York: Harper and Row, 1974.

Straus, Murray A. Sexual inequality, cultural norms, and wife-beating. In Emilio Viano (Ed.), *Victims and society.* Washington: Visage Press, 1976, 543–559.

———. *Wife-beating: How common, and why?* Paper presented at the Conference on Battered Wives: Defining the Issues, Stanford University, May 20, 1977.

———, Gelles, Richard, and Steinmetz, Suzanne K. *Violence in the family: An assessment of knowledge and research needs.* Paper presented at the meeting of the American Association for the Advancement of Science, Boston, 1976.

Szasz, Thomas S. *The manufacture of madness.* New York: Harper and Row, 1970.

Twain, Mark. Letters from the earth. In N. Tavuchis and William J. Goode (Eds.), *The family through literature.* New York: McGraw-Hill Book Company, 1975, 474–478.

U'Ren, Marjorie B. The image of woman in textbooks. In Vivian Gornick and Barbara K. Moran (Eds.), *Woman in sexist society.* New York: Mentor, 1972, 318–328.

Weisstein, Naomi. 'Kinde, kuche, kirche' as scientific law: Psychology constructs the female. In Robin Morgan (Ed.), *Sisterhood is powerful.* New York: Vintage Books, 1970.

——— Psychology constructs the female. In Vivian Gornick and Barbara K. Moran (Eds.), *Woman in sexist society.* New York: Mentor Books, 1972.

Wolfgang, Marvin E. *Patterns in criminal homicide.* Philadelphia: University of Pennsylvania Press, 1958.

Women against violence in pornography and media. Berkeley: Berkeley Women's Center, 1977.

Woolf, Virginia. A room of one's own. In Alice S. Rossi (Ed.), *The feminist papers: From Adams to de Beauvoir*. New York: Bantam Books, 1974.

---

FIFTEEN

# Secondary Battering and Alternatives of Female Victims to Spouse Abuse*†

## MILDRED DALEY PAGELOW

## INTRODUCTION

Until the last few years, the phenomenon of domestic violence was almost totally ignored by social scientists; Americans generally regarded the home as *the* safe haven away from the troubles and violence of the outside world. Then, after centuries of lone voices "crying in the wilderness," Kempe coined the term "the battered-child syndrome," and a select few scientists gave recognition to this form of domestic violence (see Helfer and Kempe, 1968; Gill, 1971; Gelles, 1974, 1977). A few others turned attention to sibling violence, here and there one heard about aged parents abused by their adult children (Kelly, 1975), and Straus and his colleagues wrote about interspousal violence (Straus, 1974, 1977a; Steinmetz and Straus, 1974; Gelles, 1972; Straus, Gelles and Steinmetz, 1976). As a by-product of their studies on domestic violence, both Straus (1976, 1977b, 1977c) and Gelles (1975, 1976) have addressed the specific issue of wife beating.

The purpose of this paper is to examine the question of the alternatives of female victims to repeated batterings by spouses. The term "secondary battering" was coined earlier to theoretically distinguish between the initial occurrence of physical assault, "primary battering,"

---

*© Mildred Daley Pagelow, January 1981.

†Sincere thanks are offered to William Ryan, who introduced the author to the concept of victim blaming through his book and whose comments on an earlier draft of this paper were most helpful. The dependable support, insightful criticisms, and scholarly guidance received from Maurice Jackson are very gratefully acknowledged.

with its attendant social-psychological factors (Pagelow, 1977a, 1977b), and the progression into the second stage of repeated batterings that most researchers have found escalate in frequency and intensity over time (Gayford, 1975a;196; Nichols, 1976:31; Pagelow, 1977a:24; Scott, 1974:436). Many puzzled persons in the "helping professions" appear to shrug off responsibility of caring for victims by the often repeated question-statement: *"If they really don't want to be beaten—if it's really as bad as they say—why don't they leave? They must like it, or they wouldn't stay!"*

The dissonance associated with conflicting feelings toward victims— of sympathy on the one hand and anger or disgust on the other—seems to be resolved somewhat by blaming the victim (Ryan, 1971; Pagelow, 1977c). One sociologist has addressed the question directly, asking, "Why do they stay? (Gelles, 1976); Martin devoted a chapter and much of her book to providing answers (1976); and this paper will attempt to outline some of the alternatives—and obstructions to alternatives—of female victims of secondary battering, based on research findings (Dobash and Dobash, 1976, 1978; Pagelow, 1976, 1977b, 1978a).


## THE STUDY

The investigation of woman battering within the context of domestic and/or intimate relationships was initiated early in 1976. The focus of the study is in keeping with that of the March 1976 International Tribunal on Crimes Against Women held in Brussels that largely addressed violent crimes committed by males against female victims such as rape, femicide, political torture, castration, and so forth, as well as battering (Russell and Van de Ven, 1976). Scope conditions are broader than wife abuse and narrower than generalized violence between family members. Violence in this study is defined as intentional acts of physical aggression and the use of force or threat of force to cause another to do, or prevent them from doing, something against his or her will.[1] Spouse abuse under consideration here is to be distinguished from reciprocal acts of violence engaged in between some couples, dubbed "mutual combat" in an earlier paper (Pagelow, 1976:46). A distinction must also be made between woman battering and sadomasochistic practices engaged in by couples for sexual arousal or enjoyment (Pagelow, 1977a:8–9). The type of violence discussed here is congruent with "one-sided aggressive acts" (Steinmetz and Straus, 1974:11), sometimes occurring without warning and seldom defended or retaliated.

Methodology

This exploratory investigation takes two approaches. One includes field interviews of varying depth with social agents most likely to be contacted by victims of spouse abuse, for example, persons in the fields of law, law enforcement, the judiciary, medicine, psychology, the ministery, and social welfare. The other component includes a sample of adult female victims of domestic violence: Women who were battered by the men with whom they had maintained intimate relationships that generally included cohabitation at some point.[2] There was no effort made to restrict the sample to women, but much of the study was conducted either at shelters or through shelters for victims of spouse abuse and their children, and none of these victims were men. While there is little reason to doubt that at least some men are victims of spouse abuse, the probabilities of the intense fear and desperate need for safety and the lack of alternatives and resources experienced by most women victims are extremely slim (Pagelow, 1978a). Many shelters have never received a call for assistance from male victims (Pagelow, 1978b:7), and the relatively few that have report that they channel these victims into existing community services that can adequately meet their needs, which are generally counseling or legal services.[3]

There were several methodological techniques employed in the component of the study regarding victims. They included in-depth interviews, participant observation in discussion groups, records analysis, and observation during more than one hundred hours spent as a volunteer worker at shelters. A self-administered questionnaire, distributed at shelters located mainly in California, was designed to elicit demographic data about victims and abusers, the nature of the violence and extent of injuries, and victims' help-seeking efforts and response. Over one hundred questionnaires have been completed and returned; the majority came from shelter residents and about 25 percent came from women who had heard about the study and had volunteered to provide information.

Underlying theoretical assumptions of this investigation, stimulated by observational impressions, and preliminary analysis of the data obtained from the pilot study, are detailed in earlier papers (Pagelow, 1977a, 1977b). The third part of this tripartite theoretical perspective focuses on secondary battering. The major proposition is: *The fewer the resources, the more negative the institutional response; and the more intense the traditional ideology[4] of women who have been battered, the more likely they are to remain in relationships with the batterers and the less likely they are to perform acts that will significantly alter the situation in a positive direction.*

There are advantages and disadvantages inherent in the design of this study. Nonrandom sample selection and use of self-report limits its generalizability, but there are at least four major advantages. First, the study was not restricted to one geographic area; thus, it avoids parochialism. Second, the sample base was not restricted to one source, and it thus avoids socioeconomic class bias. Third, the employment of a variety of methodologies, quantitative and qualitative data collection, provides analysis of underlying dynamics, verification, and development of case histories. Fourth, the unavailability of contrasting evidence from the point of view of batterers[5] is somewhat compensated for by the field interviews with social agents in the criminal justice system, medical fields, and others. Data derived from two sources—social agents and victims—provide a base for analysis and comparison, serve as checkpoints against each other, and provide a better understanding of the interaction between battered women and the agents/agencies they turned to for assistance. If they did not seek help, a better understanding can then be reached as to why they did not.[6]

## OVERVIEW

During the course of this exploration, the impression developed that in the case of woman battering, the female victim is perceived as the "deviant," not the batterer. It suggests the following hypothesis: If a woman has been subjected to secondary battering, then others will respond to the victim as one who deviates from socially acceptable norms by "breaking the rules" (Becker, 1966). This leads to a second hypothesis: If the victim is designated (symbolically labeled) a deviant, social pressure will be differentially applied to enforce conformity with the rules, which will tend to obstruct alternatives.

The "rules" that the victim has broken are in relation to the sacred norms of "belonging" to a man, and in exchange for this privilege, women are expected to provide a happy home or at least to maintain that impression: "The myth of the happy housewife." The "Sanctity of the Home" (Kremen, 1976) is an institutionalized ideal, and contemporary women almost without exception were carefully socialized to play particular roles in the home. An exchange was expected: the burden of financial support was placed squarely on the man, and the burden of making his home life enjoyable and comfortable was placed squarely on the woman (Bernard, 1973). Traditional sex roles were clear and unambiguous, and until recently there has been little doubt that if the home is not a place of love and harmony, it is up to the woman to correct the wrongs. If she fails to do so, it is clearly her "fault" (Martin, 1976: 80–82). Then, if she makes private disharmony a subject of public knowledge, she has exposed the family "skeletons in the closet" (Martin, 1976) and proved her "disloyalty" to her spouse. It is thus through the combination of her *failure* to make her spouse happy in addition to public *exposure* of private beatings that a woman becomes a "deviant." Even with changing mores that lessen sanction against cohabitation without legal marriage, produce less stigmatization of women employed outside the home, and allow some relaxation of rigid sex roles, women are still generally expected to take major responsibility for expressive "home-making," to be sensitive to the needs and desires of their spouses, and to make the union "successful" (Andelin, 1976; Morgan, 1975). As Steinmetz and Straus state about the family:

> The idealized picture of family life is a useful and perhaps even a necessary social myth. The utility of the myth results from the fact that the family is a tremendously important social institution. Therefore, elaborate precautions are taken to strengthen and support the family . . . one of these supportive devices is the myth or ideology of familial love and gentleness. This ideology helps encourage people to marry and to stay married. . . . Thus, from the viewpoint of preserving the integrity of a critical social institution, such a mythology is highly useful. (1974:6–7)

Any woman who publicly declares to the police, a doctor, emergency room personnel, or a judge that her spouse physically assaulted her is not only challenging the myth but is also admitting "failure" in her assigned role expectations vis-à-vis her spouse. Martin quotes one battered women, who said, "I knew I had to keep the family together," reflecting the viewpoints of many people in this culture (1976:80). When a woman who was privately battered by her spouse goes "public," she moves from the category "discreditable" to "discredited," to borrow Goffman's terms (1963). Following Goffman's typology, a battered woman can be considered stigmatized by "blemishes of individual character" (1963:4). As long as her beatings and suffering stay hidden behind closed doors, the public can choose to ignore them, turn up the "tele" to drown out disturbing noises (Pizzey, 1977), and contribute to their neighbor's impression management to maintain self-presentation consistent with role expectations (Snyder, 1977:115–146). When "deviance" becomes known, the actor becomes labeled as outsider according to Becker, who says that deviance is the "product of a transaction that takes place between some social group and one who is viewed by that group as a rule-breaker" (1966:10).

The point is, rules are broken when a woman accuses her spouse of battering, and those "rules" according to Becker were created by social groups who apply them to particular people and label them "deviant" (1966:9). These rules that demand women stay at the side of their spouses, even if staying may be to the disadvantage of women, have been well documented by many writers (see especially Bernard, 1973, 1975). Long ago, Durkheim advocated marriage and large numbers of children for the good of "society." Yet, at the same time that he showed that permanent unions were beneficial for men, he showed they were detrimental for women. Durkheim states: "Conjugal society, so disadvantageous for women, must, even in the absence of children, be admitted to be advantageous for men" (1966:193). As Bernard and others were to show years later with more sophisticated research techniques, Durkheim said:

> Indeed, marriage may very possibly act in an opposite way on husband and wife. . . . As partners their interests are different and often hostile (1966:269). . . . By fixing the conjugal state permanently, it prevents all retreat, regardless of consequences. . . . There is no compensation or relief for the woman. Monogamy is strictly obligatory for her. . . . it prevents her from changing it if it becomes intolerable. The regulation therefore is a restraint to her without any great advantages. (1966:272)

Of course Durkheim was addressing formal marriage, but on the other hand, not all women who are battered are married to their batterers—many are cohabitees and some are even divorced wives or former lovers.[7] These women by definition are already "deviants" by rejecting the rule of institutional marriage and are further stigmatized when the issue of battering arises. In other words, depending on the particular social environment in which the cohabitation or divorce takes place, they may be severely stigmatized or merely "discreditable" as long as they keep a low profile and behave in other matters in a socially approved manner. Becker discusses degrees of response; they vary, and they depend on who the rule breaker and the offended group may be (1966:12). He also states, "Some rules are enforced only when they result in certain consequences" (Becker, 1966:13). In the case of divorcees or cohabitees, the stigmatization may occur or become greater only when they reveal that the men they lived with have beaten them.[8]

Why, we might ask, if it is the institution of marriage and family that is threatened by public revelation of violence, is not the batterer equally stigmatized? Examination of our social structure suggests two possible answers: first, the sexist foundations of our society promote "masculine" aggression and male violence directed against women (Straus, 1976), and second, the strong tendency to "blame the victim" (Ryan, 1971). The question is complex, and these are only two out of many possibilities and combinations of answers that may shed some light on the imbalance. There are some sanctions against a man who beats his spouse, but they are differentially enforced, and usually only when he has gone "too far" (Dobash and Dobash, 1978:430).

The first explanation is elaborated on in detail by Straus when he insightfully describes the "cultural norms legitimizing intrafamily violence" (1976:545–551). Straus introduces this section of the article with a few words on "norms glorifying aggression and violence" regarding intrafamily violence and then concentrates on spousal relations, noting, "similar norms are present and powerful, but largely implicit, unrecognized or covert" (1976:546). In its entirely, this section addresses male violence against females with only one slight reference to the reverse.[9] By this, one may conclude that the norms Straus is referring to that legitimate husband-wife violence in actuality permit or approve violence by husbands against wives, that is, *husband-administered* violence. This is not a daring presumption because the fact that neither aggression nor violence is considered gender-appropriate behavior for females within this culture is well documented in the many sex-role and gender-role texts available (Bernard, 1972; Chafetz, 1974; Forisha, 1978; Oakley, 1972; Pleck and Sawyer, 1974; Roszak and Roszak, 1969).[10] It should not be too surprising that this disparity exists, when one considers the differential response from adults when a boy or a girl behaves aggressively or violently—for the boy it is most likely to be considered a manifestation of "masculinity," whereas it is considered "abnormal" for the girl. Men—*but not women*—receive cultural approval for violence. That there are culturally approved norms of violence for men in this country is most powerfully expressed by Straus when he states: "But the most explicit contemporary legal expression of the right of husbands to use physical force is found in the immunity of husbands from prosecution for rape of a wife" (1976:550).

The second suggested reason why battered women are more stigmatized than the batterers—the tendency to blame the victim—seems almost too obvious. Victims who are blamed are generally the occupants of the lowest rung of the cultural ladder, and within every group, category, or socioeconomic class, women are assigned lower status realtive to men—they are the "Other" (Bernard, 1975b; de Beauvoir, 1974; Rosaldo and Lamphere, 1975). Consider Ryan's words: "The generic process of Blaming the Victim is applied to almost every American problem" (1971:5). Cultural deprivation, the culture of poverty, and stress and frustration theories all have one thing in common—they find the problem is within the victims. When "experts" looked at the ghetto, they targeted on the black family, and the ultimate victim for blaming was the black woman—labeled the "matriarch."

In his report, Parnas gives a quotation from an "extremely articulate and well-read Negro [police] sergeant" that reveals the pervasive effect such targeting can have (1967:952). Parnas relates the officer's viewpoint:

> The Negro family in America, he pointed out, has long been matriarchal (referring to the recent "Moynihan Report"). The man's main function in the low class Negro family, he said, is to satisfy the woman's sex needs. The woman is in control and will therefore complain if the man takes advantage of her. (1967:952)

In this particular case, the person who accepts these ideas is a police officer who is frequently called to protect the lives and safety of women—including Black women. Wolfgang wrote of "different" cultural values and norms that made stabbings common and accepted in situations where "assaultive behavior is necessary, expected, or desirable" (By whom? The victim or the aggressor?) and where there exist "unconscious destructive impulses" (1958:329). These powerful ideas are still widely accepted today and are influential in blaming the victims of spouse abuse. Parnas writes: "Subculture differences, whether real or imagined, affect patrol practices" (1967:953). They also affect the attitudes and behavior of lawyers, district attorneys, judges, and legislators—people in positions of power and influence who are predominantly male, as are most individuals in the fields of power and influence that affect public policy and initiate cultural change.

## ALTERNATIVES

The foregoing discussion was necessary to unmask some of the hidden assumptions that are within the social and cultural environment adjacent to female victims. To rephrase the quotation, "'No man is an island'— neither is any woman." People who find themselves in a violent domestic situation cannot, totally and by themselves, either create or alter the situation in a vacuum. If we address alternatives, we should also examine forces that would tend to prevent, block, or obscure alternatives. If it is true that female victims of domestic violence, far more than the aggressors, are culturally defined as rule breakers ("deviants") and as such will be the objects of social pressure to enforce conformity, then we can expect that female victims will meet resistance when they seek alternatives. Empirical evidence shows that victims do find resistance or obstructions to alternatives (Gelles, 1976; Hilberman and Munson, 1977; Kremen, 1976; Martin, 1976; Pagelow, 1976; Pizzey, 1977; Straus, 1976).

Alternatives have been systematically obstructed, obscured, or blocked. Traditional social agencies have remained deaf and unresponsive to the needs of battered women while taxpayers have poured billions of dollars into these agencies to address community needs. Psychiatrists have treated patients' symptoms for years without discovering that some patients were victims of spouse abuse (Hilberman and Munson, 1977). Medical doctors have prescribed tranquilizers, and emergency room personnel have healed wounds and sent victims home without giving the kind of help that was needed. Police have insisted crime in the home was a "private matter," clergymen have advised prayer, counselors have advised communication, and parents have advised, "You made your bed, now you lie in it." Victims have been "locked up" (in shelters), while the perpetrators of this crime remain free; "victims' rights are constantly abrogated and defendant's rights are constantly applauded and approved" (Fields, 1978). Only a tiny segment of the world's population has come to recognize that for centuries women and their children have been coerced, beaten, tortured, and killed by their male "protectors."

It took the feminist movement, composed of a relatively small proportion of the population dedicated to equality and freedom of choice, to see the problem, reveal it to others, and attempt both to aid victims and generate social change. It seems obvious that systematic avoidance, neglect, and determination for such a long time span not to see, hear, feel, or respond to a serious social problem of such great magnitude (for which evidence is growing daily), when it existed right in our midst, required massive disdain for the victims. This evidence seems to provide some support for the hypotheses proposed earlier.

Although at first it may seem to be an oversimplification, ultimately there are two major alternatives for battered women: one is to stay and attempt changes while remaining in the relationship, and the second is to leave the relationship.[11] The diagram shown here illustrates some of the complexities of decision making for victims of secondary battering.[12] This diagram does not take into account the constellation of negative and positive resources of victims both personal and material or the interlocking considerations of victims after leaving, such as economic, social, and religious penalties. If there are dependent children, these considerations are even more serious.

FIG. 1. Alternatives of female victims to domestic violence.

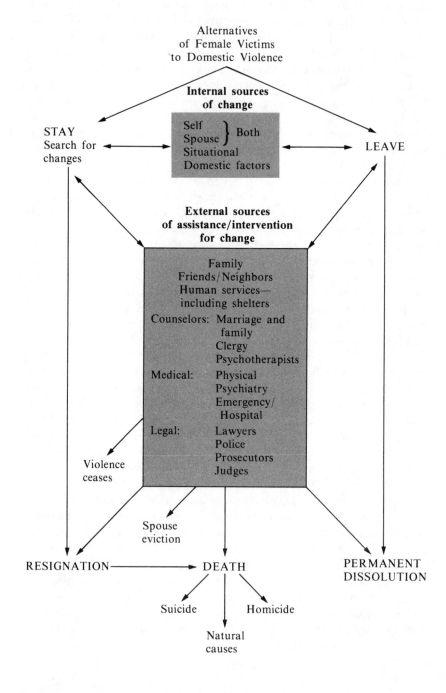

Almost all victims initially try the first alternative, sometimes attempting for years to change themselves, their spouses, or both, or whatever situational factors their spouses may claim "cause" their outbursts of violence, for example, meals, finances, housekeeping, childrearing, and so on. When those efforts fail, they can either resign themselves to their "fate" or attempt to get help external to the home. Depending on the type of institutional reaction they receive, they may leave, effect change, or resign themselves to the violent situations and wait for release by death—their own or their spouse's. Some try to escape through suicide; a few succeed. Almost half the survey respondents indicated they contemplated suicide at some point, and 21.7 percent attempted suicide at least once. Escape is also sought by attempting to kill their spouses; a few of these succeed. Others leave the relationships when they are murdered by their spouses. Until very recently, untold millions of women were limited to the alternative of staying and attempting change from within, largely because they received negative institutional response when they tried to get external help and lacked the necessary resources for leaving. In addition, they had no safe place to go.

Here are some brief examples of 138 survey respondents' contacts with community agencies. According to this sample, 47.8 percent had been medically treated for injuries (in hospitals, clinics, doctors' offices). Two-thirds of those who did not receive professional treatment said they believed their injuries serious enough for medical care but were unable to obtain it (no money, no transportation, or restraint by spouse). Police were called at least once for 58.5 percent, and in almost half of these cases, police were called more than once. Two-thirds of these women state they asked that their spouse be arrested; half of the arrest requests were dropped and charges were pressed for the other half. Of the total number of respondents reporting police intervention, 11.6 percent of the abusing spouses were convicted. Twenty-one percent said they received assistance from a legal agency, half of which were private attorney offices the other half of which were public agencies. Social agencies were contacted at least once by 39 percent of the total sample. A psychiatrist, psychologist, or an analyst was consulted by 37.7 percent of the total sample: 10.5 percent said clearly that this form of assistance was helpful, while 26 percent as clearly stated that it was not helpful.

Two-thirds of these women described their family of origin as moderately or deeply religious, while only 28 percent classified themselves as not at all religious today. Even though 72 percent of the sample expressed a range of religious conviction from moderate to deep, only 28 percent sought help from a member of the clergy. Of these, 80 percent recorded their experiences as: (1) go home, wife's duty, forgive repentant husband; (2) go to a marriage counselor/didn't want to get involved; or (3) no helpful advice/only religious advice. The balance received either sympathy or were told to leave their husbands. Marriage counselors were consulted by 21 percent; one respondent said abuse stopped.

Regarding potential child support, 41 percent believed their spouses earned enough to pay, but only one-third of these women expressed belief that their spouses would pay child support. They were more optimistic about their ability to support themselves and their children: 58 percent felt they could earn enough to support themselves and their children, while the others were unsure or felt they could not.

As for help from other family members, 42 percent said they had relatives *able* and only 39 percent had relatives *willing* to give them and their children, if they had any, a place to stay. The distance to the residence of their nearest relatives was 20 miles and over for 60 percent of the sample, and for half of these the distance was over 500 miles.

In recent years, with modification of divorce laws, increasing female employment, awakening social consciousness, and the opening up of new options—particularly the establishment of shelters—an ever increasing number of women are taking the second alternative and leaving the relationship. Over 70 percent of the shelterees in my sample reported at least one previous attempt to leave, and of these, 81 percent had attempted to leave the relationship two or more times. Leaving is no guarantee that they will not return; the majority who leave usually return several times before some of them make the final break. The decision itself may not be enough; a woman frequently returns involuntarily: Either the assaulter follows her and brings her back, or he applies coercion— threats and fear for the safety of herself, her children, family, friends, or the people who gave her assistance. Eighty-four percent of those who had left at least once earlier said they returned because their spouses found them, convinced them they were repentant/would change, or threatened them. Children may be used as pawns in a hostile game, "kidnapped" by their fathers/step-fathers. Leaving was not sufficient to terminate violence for 18 percent of my sample because the spouses of these women reportedly were unwilling to accept rejection and appeared to become obsessed with the notion of "punishing" them. Disruption, harassment, threats, property damage, and even more physical abuse were all part of their lives, lasting as long as 10 years for some. These women changed names, residences, used post office box addresses, unlisted telephones, and so forth, only to find their car tires slashed or to awaken in the middle of the night to a threatening voice on the telephone, and so on. Welfare regulations and having school age children made it particularly difficult for some of these fugitives to keep their identity and location secret.

Shelters are a relatively recent addition to sources of external assistance for battered women, but as they are severely restricted financially, many shelters have rules preventing reentry of a victim on grounds that space is needed for desperate others on waiting lists. Some shelters limit residence to 6 days, a week, or a month; few in the United States allow longer. There is not enough space to explain what these shelters do and cannot do for female victims and their children; this topic has been addressed previously in some detail (Pagelow, 1978a, 1978b). However, it should be remembered that whether the victim gains entry to a shelter or not, the heavy social pressures when she leaves home or shelter make it extremely difficult for her to maintain autonomy and independence, especially if she lacks personal and material resources (Pagelow, 1977b).

There was a small minority of women in my sample who reported that the violence stopped in the "primary stage"—in other words, about 8 percent said they were beaten once or no more than two times. Most stopped the violence by use of the second alternative—leaving; a very few stopped the violence while maintaining the relationship. Interestingly, the ones who continued the relationships were those who met violence with violence with only two exceptions: a woman who began divorce proceedings that could be reinitiated by a telephone call to her attorney, and the survey respondent who said violence ceased after counseling. The following are some examples of the violent responses: one woman struck her husband unconscious with an iron skillet; another kicked her 200-pound husband in the groin (she weighed 125 pounds); and another woman waited until her drunken husband fell asleep, later awakening him with a knife held at his throat. She reminded him that if he beat her in the future, he had better kill her then, because he could not stay awake forever. For all those who retaliated with violence, there was one, and only one, counterattack, and batterings ceased.

The women who left the situation after primary battering were above average in personal and/or material resources. They had more education, better employment or employment potential, nearby relatives willing and able to assist, few or no children, and so on. They also expressed less commitment to traditional ideas; close to 50 percent had remarried, and they described these new marriages as good relationships. A few of the others were cohabitating, saying this was preferable to marriage for them.

Most of this subsample was composed of volunteers who heard about the study and called, wrote, or stepped forward after an oral presentation to offer help. All of these women were healthy; none of the

relationships, regardless of the ages of the women, existed more than 5
years (shorter investment period); and only one of them had a dependent
child. Although generalizations cannot be made on the basis of such a
small comparison group, these women do appear to have some advantages in resources over others in the sample. They seemed to have one or
a combination of relatively better resources, a more favorable institutional response, or less commitment to traditional ideology[13] than the
victims of secondary battering—which offers tentative support to the
theoretical assumptions underlying the investigation.

## IMPLICATIONS FOR SOCIAL POLICY

As victims of poverty and racial bigotry are blamed for being the *cause*
of their victimization (Ryan, 1971), so are victims of spouse abuse
blamed for being the cause of *their* victimization (Pagelow, 1977c), or,
even more basically, women categorically are blamed for men's aggressive behavior (Pogrebin, 1974; Straus, 1977:550). The common denomi-
nator is that women in all of these categories are barred from social
power, control over their own life opportunities, and access to wealth
relative to power holders and policy makers.[14] The blaming is not necessarily vicious, although there is some social-psychological evidence from
experimental research that individuals can be more hostile toward victims than aggressors. Wrightsman comments, "Possibly the subjects
. . . felt that, as a victim, he must have deserved the beating he was so
obviously getting. Therefore, subjects shocked him all the more, merely
because he 'deserved it'" (1977:224). In the case of victims of spouse
abuse, the reaction is not usually as overt and hostile. For example,
when observers see a woman being publicly assaulted by a man, other
men do not jump in to help him beat her—they merely do not help her
(Pogrebin, 1974:55; Straus, 1976:550).

    Victim blaming applied to battered women is much more subtle. It
is remarkably like the process described by Ryan:

> Victim-blaming is cloaked in kindness and concern, and bears all
> the trappings and statistical furbelows of scientism; it is obscured by
> a perfumed haze of humanitarianism. In observing the process of
> Blaming the Victim, one tends to be confused and disoriented
> because those who practice this art display a deep concern for the
> victims that is quite genuine. . . . Its adherents include sympathetic
> social scientists with social consciences in good working order, and
> liberal politicians with a genuine commitment to reform. (1971:6–7)

Victim blaming takes several forms within the context of violent crimes against women, such as the studies of personality factors of the victims—not the aggressors—which "discover" personality defects in victims. Probably the best known of these is the report by Snell et al. (1964). A lesser known study is one by Gayford, a British psychiatrist who studied victims at Chiswick Women's Aid. After several comparatively scholarly articles, Gayford wrote a popularized account of female victims in which he "divided battered women into nine 'types' and [gave] them names such as 'Tortured Tina,' 'Violent Violet,' and 'Fanny the Flirt,'" as well as 'Go-Go Gloria' (Wilson, 1976:8). The mask of scientism slipped off. One study which has received substantial media attention, "Comparing Battered and Nonbattered Women," is based on a sample obtained at a shelter where *all* the women were refugees from abuse—physical and nonphysical. The sample consisted of 57 women, 46 of the former type of abuse and 11 of the latter. The author concludes, "The battered women in this study repressed anger, were timid, emotionally reserved and had lower coping abilities" (Star, 1977:16). While the report says they showed no signs of being "submissive," personality inventories and attitude scales led to a diagnosis of "passivity."

Ryan warns of "The Art of Savage Discovery" surrounding social problems (1971), and Weis and Borges show that even the relatively new discipline of victimology has taken a turn from earlier interests in helping the victim toward "the art of how to blame the victim" (1976:231). While these writers try to draw out attention to social and cultural causes, many social scientists persist in locating the problem *within* the victim. Evidence of this propensity is common in the literature: Amir speaks of "victimization as a universal condition of every woman" (1971:253); Schafer began by working for victim assistance which turned later to "functional responsibility" of the victim (*Victimology,* 1976:224); another writer, addressing criminal homicide (all examples are of women killed by spouses), says victims can be "partially or wholly to blame," followed by the phrases: "invites," "asking for trouble," "direct invitation," and "directly encourage" (Mushanga, 1978:483). Mushanga writes of East and Central African victims, but he seems not too distant from American Schafer who mentions victim negligence, precipitating action, or provocation (Holmstrom and Burgess, 1976:1–2).

Provocation is another favorite way to blame victims. Probably the most commonly accepted notion is that women wage an unfair "war of words," because they are more verbally facile (Goode, 1975:197). Gelles concluded that the combination of comparatively "superior verbal skills" as well as knowledge of sensitivity points "can lead to" physical abuse of the woman (Straus et al., 1976:23). While it is true that "can lead to" is not the same as either "invite" or "encourage," many other persons do not make such distinctions. Straus makes the point quite clear that regardless of whether or not complaints of "nagging wife" are true, it is no justification for physical violence (1977b:221). The message is not nearly as clear when it comes from Gayford, who suggests that victims not only provoke attacks, but also seek out violent men (1975:197). There are many who openly agree with these ideas of victim provocation, *particularly violent men, whether batterers or rapists* (Copeland et al., 1976:82; Landau, 1976:12; Pagelow, 1977c).

The implications of victim blaming have a direct relationship to what will happen in the near future regarding social policy. In a comparatively short time, feminists and others exposed the previously hidden problem of woman battering, and the media took up this newly "discovered" social problem. Community groups began emerging in response across the country and struggled to establish shelters and otherwise provide direct services for victims and their children. They spent millions of unpaid hours trying to educate their fellow citizens at every level in their communities to the needs of victims, endeavoring to establish a network of existing community services so they would respond with appropriate victim services. They studied complex and sometimes unintelligible guidelines in order to write proposals for funding without "grantsmanship" expertise. They tried to educate police departments, they held fund raisers, and they appealed to politicians for help. Some succeeded in raising enough money to serve a few of the many victims who came to them for help. Most shelters have to turn away more women and children than they can serve. The Emergency Services Program in Hayward, California, admitted to residence 913 women and children, and they had to refuse an additional 1,776 in one year (*Congressional Record*, 1978:S3906).

Gradually, some legislators proposed bills calling for changes in police recording of incidences of spousal assault, for the strengthening of existing laws, and the introduction of new laws, and even for the provision of money for shelters and direct services. Finally, legislators at the federal level began writing bills to "prevent domestic violence and to assist victims." Along with increasing political interest there was an imperceptible, growing "concern" within the tax-funded establishment agencies to "help" victims, assaulters, and their children. "Grant junkies," as Representative Mikulski dubbed them, are everywhere, ready and eager to move in as soon as funds are appropriated (1978). Suddenly, many established agencies and some nonprofit service organizations that for many years were unhearing and unresponsive to the cries for help from victims are springing to life with their humanitarian services and programs. Some social scientists, meanwhile, are sharpening pencils preparatory to tailoring proposals to obtain research funds.

It is interesting to note what has been happening within those hard-working community groups that established shelters and provided services when the rest of society ignored the problem. Some maintain original ideals, ever struggling for funding. For others, their ranks have been infiltrated by humanitarians who spread the gospel of "curing" the victim, her assaulter, and her children, too. The original philosophy of some shelters has shifted from the feminist ideals of providing nontherapeutic support services for victims to the new philosophy of "treatment" for victims. Administrators of these shelters allow researchers to subject victims to psychological attitude and personality scales; they have mandatory psychological counseling; and at least one had until recently a male psychiatrist on the staff with the power to determine whether or not a woman could stay (psychiatric screening was one of the mandatory conditions of residence). Other small, nonprofessional groups have lost out in the "battle for the bucks" to emerging groups possessing necessary proposal writing skills: One of these "treats" the family as a unit, with the expressed purpose of restoring family stability and permanence. Couples counseling is a growing "fad," particularly among the middle class, where the victim is faced with severe economic penalties for herself and her children in the event of the dissolution of the marriage relationship (Lynn, 1977).

It appears that we have not progressed very far from the time when the female victim went alone to the marriage and family counselor to the present when she now goes accompanied by her spouse—the desired outcome in both cases is to restore harmony and keep the family "together." Have we come full circle? Ryan's words have a contemporary ring when he says:

But the stigma, the defect, the fatal difference—though derived in the past from environmental forces—is still located *within* the victim inside his skin. With such an elegant formulation, the humanitarian can have it both ways. He can, all at the same time, concentrate his charitable interest on the defects of the victim, condemn the vague social and environmental stresses that produced the defect (some time ago), and ignore the continuing effect of victimizing social forces (right now). It is a brilliant ideology for justifying a perverse form of social action designed to change, not society, as one might expect, but rather society's victim. . . . there is a terrifying sameness in the programs that arise from this kind of analysis. . . . The formula for action becomes extraordinarily simple: change the victim (1971:7–8)

Thus, millions of dollars will be appropriated, a massive bureaucracy will take most of it, the "grant junkies" will move in, and the nonprofit grassroots service providers will get whatever small amount remains. The end result will be that American citizens, formerly disturbed by unpleasant evidence of brutality within the family, will congratulate themselves that "something is being done" about the problem and, thus, placated, put it out of mind (Wilson, 1976). If they should hear screams coming from the home next door, they can turn the televised ball game up louder, confident that the victim can now get all the help she needs.

## NOTES

1. This definition deliberately excludes psychological violence and is limited to physical acts or threats of physical force, not because it is an unimportant feature of violence between spouses but rather because of a need to arbitrarily restrict limits to physical, rather than psychological, evidence. There is little doubt that the two types of violence are closely related. My own study clearly shows that almost all physical acts of violence are preceded by psychological abuse and later accompanied by psychological abuse. On the other hand, there may be—and often is—psychological abuse without physical abuse.

2. Since the sample includes both marital and quasi-marital relationships, the term "spouse" is used in this paper for consistency and convenience as an alternative designation for wife, husband, lover, and so on.

3. Training Coordinator Nancy Lynn of the Victims Information Bureau in Suffolk County related that her agency had received over 6,000 calls in 15 months on their hot line, 600 persons used their counseling center, and 96 percent of their clients contacted them about spouse abuse (1977). During that time span, Lynn said there were three men who said they were victims of spouse abuse, one who was himself a former batterer whose wife began beating him after taking self-defense lessons.

4. Major variables—resources, institutional response and traditional ideology—have been discussed at length in earlier papers (Pagelow, 1977a, 1977b). Summary definitions are: resources: personal (health of self/dependent children, age, appearance, education, employability, etc.) and material (money, property, etc.). Institutional response: real or perceived reactions by social agents to spouse abuse, victims, and aggressors. Traditional ideology: belief systems that include ideas such as rigid sex-role division of labor, patriarchal family, inequality of the sexes, and so forth.

5. Although names and addresses of batterers were available through shelters for most respondents, contacting these men for interviews could have promoted more danger for victims, other shelter residents, and possibly even the researcher. It was uncomfortable enough to be on one end of a shelter's "hot line" telephone when an enraged spouse blasted orders from his home to "get this crazy woman out of here—now—before I kill her!" The 3-hour negotiation that followed trying to convince the man not to further abuse his spouse was convincing evidence that a sociological researcher is not necessarily qualified to be a war correspondent. In addition, the batterer refuses in most cases to admit that there is any "problem," and if he does admit to one, maintains that the problem is hers, not his, and withdraws from discussion (Pagelow, 1976; Snell et al., 1964).

6. For example, during interviews with law enforcement officers, the complaint is lodged against battered women that "they don't want the guy arrested, they just want us to stop him from beating her." By comparison, these explanations are repeatedly offered by the victims: (1) the police would not even record the call; (2) the officers refused to take their complaint; (3) they recorded the complaint but it was later dropped without their knowledge or wishes; and (4) they were pressured against such action by the police, who reinforced their fear and reminded them of their vulnerability. One woman in England described the sequence of events very similar to the experiences of many American victims. She said, "I was lying in a pool of blood on the floor with broken ribs when this man stood over me and asked me if I wanted my husband arrested. I asked, 'Can you keep him?' and he said, 'No. Do you want him arrested?' He [her spouse] was standing right there. Naturally, I answered 'No.' What else could I do? I couldn't even walk, much less run!"

7. This point brings to mind the case (although the source has been forgotten) of a woman divorced from a man who continually came after her and beat her. When the woman called the police after a beating to have him arrested and complained about the behavior, the officer remarked that, after all, it was *her* fault because she married him in the first place.

8. A parallel may be drawn with the rule breakers who defy society's laws regarding heterosexual marriage and those who defy society's laws regarding sexual preference, e.g., homosexuals. Both are seen by many as threatening the institution of marriage and, following that line of reasoning, a threat to society itself. In an article soon to be published, Warren develops the case that many of the Dade County, Florida, "homophobics" were determined to push gays back "in the closets" because they were terrified that overt gays might provide positive role models and reference groups, educate to dispel old fears, and thereby lighten the stigma attached to homosexuality (Warren, 1978). She quotes a newspaper journalist who tells that a major objection is not in the *being* gay but in the *flaunting* of it.

9. The lone reference Straus gives to wife-administered violence in this section is to a 1974 newspaper article and a 1967 article by Parnas in which Parnas gave 25 illustrations of spousal violence from the Chicago police department

files. Only three of those chosen (12 percent) indicated that a female was the
abusing spouse: two used weapons, one threw hot water. On the other hand, in
illustration 18, the husband killed his wife by striking her in the head with an
axe after the police departed (1967:941). An example from these police files gives
some support to the contention of an "old boys club" spirit of camaraderie
between policemen and accused assaulters frequently complained about by battered women. Illustration 14 describes the intervention techniques employed by
officers toward "white immigrants from Mississippi living as common law husband and wife." The statement ends: "Before they left, one of them whispered to
the man, 'Why don't you go out and buy her a can of snuff—maybe you'll get a
little more tonight.' This policeman then gave the man a good-natured slap on
the back and he laughed uproariously" (1967:935).

10. In recent years, aggressive and violent behavior has been viewed as less
appropriate for men, but, unfortunately, this is still a minority view, subscribed
to primarily by feminists and young men.

11. Included in the alternative to stay is to have the man leave, but the
prospects for this to happen are slim, unless he decides to leave voluntarily. In
most cases, if the couple has shared a residence, the only way a woman can evict
a man is through court processes, and the requirements are so overwhelming for
the average woman that it is easier for her to leave, even if there are children. In
the event she has the man evicted, the woman may be in even greater danger of
attack, regardless of restraining orders or orders of protection—merely a piece
of paper to some dispossessed men. In nonmarital relationships it may be easier,
but not necessarily. A neighbor once tried to evict her lover from the home she
owned for a beating, but when the man told police he was her "tenant," the
police said she would have to readmit him into her home until she had given him
the required landlord-tenant 30-days notice to vacate.

12. The possibility of "violence ceases" must be included as one potential
outcome, although in relationships involving secondary battering discussed here,
the probabilities appear to be decidedly slim. As mentioned earlier, almost all
studies, including my own, have shown that violent behavior tends to increase
rather than decrease over time. Couples counseling seems to repress violent
behavior—at least for the duration of the counseling. Observations lead to expectations that the shorter the time span in which there has been violent behavior and the more intense the interventional pressures to change, the more likely
violence will cease and vice versa.

13. Less commitment to traditional ideology may be an *effect* of their battering experiences rather than a predisposing factor that was present at the time
of termination of violence. Most, but not all, of this subsample had not been
beaten for at least 2 years, although the time span ranged from 6 months to 20
years. Traditional ideology (as well as the other two variables, resources and
institutional response) is likely to change over time. It is possible that with
increasing resources, for example, and demonstration of independence and
adaptability, a person may become less committed to belief systems subscribed
to earlier in different circumstances.

14. Many readers of this statement will pull themselves up indignantly and
say *Not so!* Some women are poor and some are rich, and rich women who are

victims of domestic violence are not powerless. The response to that claim has been discussed in detail in an earlier paper that attempts to show that, regardless of socioeconomic class, women are relatively powerless economically (Pagelow, 1978a). Terry claims that this holds true, even for the wealthiest women, for they, like minorities, do not belong to "the club" (1974). Terry maintains that power lies in the hands of white men; the club excludes women and minorities from membership. He defines "the club" as the group whose members receive material and psychological benefits and which "distributes influence and power among its members and then uses that power to dominate groups unlike itself (consciously or unconsciously)" (Terry, 1974:66).

# REFERENCES

Amir, Menachem. *Patterns in forcible rape.* Chicago: University of Chicago, Press, 1971.

Andelin, Helen B. *Fascinating womanhood.* Santa Barbara: Pacific Press, 1976.

Becker, Howard S. *Outsiders.* New York: Free Press, 1976.

Bernard, Jessie. *The sex game.* New York: Atheneum, 1972.(a)

————. *Women and the public interest: An essay on policy and protest.* Chicago: Aldine, 1972.(b)

————. *The future of marriage.* New York: Bantam, 1973.

————. *The future of motherhood.* Penguin Books: New York, 1975.(a)

————. *Women, wives, mothers: Values and options.* Chicago: Aldine, 1975.(b)

Chafetz, Janet Saltzman. *Masculine/feminine or human? An overview of the sociology of sex roles.* Itasca: F. E. Peacock, 1974.

Congressional Record. Proceedings and debates of the 95th Congress, Second Session, March 16, 1978, *124*(38), S3906–3915.

Copeland, Lorraine, Marks, C. J., Mahabir, C., Jacobs, R. S., Valensuela, A. M., and Brody, J. G. *Rape: Prevention and resistance.* San Francisco: Queen's Bench Foundation, 1976.

de Beauvoir, Simone. *The second sex.* New York: Vintage Books, 1974.

Dobash, R. Emerson, and Dobash, Russell P. *Love, honour and obey: Institutional ideologies and the struggle for battered women.* Paper presented at the annual meeting of the Society for the Study of Social Problems, New York, 1976.

————, Wives: The 'appropriate' victims of marital violence. *Victimology,* 1978, *2*(3/4), 426–442.

Durkheim, Emile. *Suicide.* New York: Free Press, 1966.

Fields, Marjorie D. Excerpts from her testimony before the House of Representatives Subcommittee on Select Education of the Committee on Education and Labor, March 16, 1978.

Forisha, Barbara Lusk. *Sex roles and personal awareness.* Morristown: General Learning Press, 1978.

Gayford, J. J. Wife battering: A preliminary survey of 100 cases. *British Medical Journal,* January 1975, *1,* 194–197.

Gelles, Richard J. The violent home: A study of physical aggression between husbands and wives. Beverly Hills: Sage Publications, 1972.

———. "Child abuse as psychopathology: A sociological critique and reformulation." In Suzanne Steinmetz and Murray Straus (Eds.), *Violence in the family.* New York: Harper and Row, 1974, 190–204.

———. Violence and pregnancy: A note on the extent of the problem and needed services. *The Family Coordinator,* January 1975, 81–86.

———. Abused wives: Why do they stay? *Journal of Marriage and the Family,* 1976, *38*(4), 659–668.

———. *Violence towards children in the United States.* Paper presented at the annual meeting of the American Association for the Advancement of Science, Denver, 1977.

Gil, David G. Violence against children. *Journal of Marriage and the Family,* November 1971, *33,* 624–635.

Helfer, Ray E., and Kempe, C. Henry. *The battered child.* Chicago: University of Chicago Press, 1968.

Hilberman, Elaine, and Munson, Kit. *Sixty battered women: A preliminary report.* Paper presented at the annual meeting of the American Psychiatric Association, Toronto, Canada, 1977.

Holmstrom, Lynda Lytle, and Burgess, Ann Wolbert. *Rape victimology: Past, present, and future research.* Paper presented at the annual meeting of the American Association for the Advancement of Science, Boston, 1976.

Kelly, John. The battered parent. *Practical Psychology for Physicians,* 1975, *2*(9), 65–67.

Kremen, Eleanor. *The 'discovery' of battered wives: Considerations for the development of social service network.* Paper presented at the annual meeting of the American Sociological Association, New York, 1976.

Lynn, Nancy. *Middle class violence: Spouse abuse in the suburbs.* Paper presented at the annual meeting of the American Sociological Association/ Sociologists for Women in Society, Chicago, 1977.

Martin, Del. *Battered wives.* San Francisco: Glide Publications, 1976.

Mikulski, Representative Barbara A. From her statement to the Subcommittee on Select Education of the Committee on Education and Labor, March 16, 1978.

Morgan, Marabel. *Total woman.* Old Tappan, New Jersey: Revell, 1975.

Mushanga, Tibamanya mwene. Wife victimization in East and Central Africa. *Victimology,* 1978, *2*(3/4), 479–485.

Oakley, Ann. *Sex, gender and society.* New York: Harper and Row, 1972.

Pagelow, Mildred Daley. *Preliminary report on battered women.* Paper presented at the Second International Symposium on Victimology, 1976.

———. *Battered women: A new perspective.* Paper presented at the International Sociological Association Seminar on Sex Roles, Deviance, and Agents of Social Control in Dublin, Ireland, 1977.(a)

————. *Secondary battering: Breaking the cycle of domestic violence.* Paper presented at the annual meeting of the Sociologists for Women in Society Section of the American Sociological Association, Chicago, 1977.(b)

————. *Blaming the victim: Parallels in crimes against women—rape and battering.* Paper presented at the annual meeting of the Society for the Study of Social Problems, Chicago, 1977.(c)

————. *Needs assessment of victims of domestic violence.* Testimony for the U.S. Commission on Civil Rights Consultation on Battered Women and the House Committee on Science and Technology Hearings on Research into Domestic Violence, 1978.(a)

————. *Research on domestic violence: What we have and what we need.* Testimony for the U.S. Senate Child and Human Development Subcommittee of the Human Resources Committee, 1978.(b)

Parnas, Raymond. Police response to domestic disturbances. *Wisconsin Law Review,* Fall 1967, 914–960.

Pizzey, Erin. *Scream quietly or the neighbors will hear.* Short Hills, NJ: Ridley Enslow Publishers, 1977.

Pleck, Joseph H., and Sawyer, Jack. *Men and masculinity.* Englewood Cliffs, NJ: Prentice-Hall, 1974.

Pogrebin, Letty Cottin. Do women make men violent? *Ms. Magazine,* November, 1974, 49–50,80.

Rosaldo, Michelle Zimbalist, and Lamphere, Louise. *Woman, Culture and Society.* Stanford: Stanford University Press, 1975.

Roszak, Betty, and Roszak, Theodore. *Masculine/feminine.* New York: Harper and Row, 1969.

Russell, Diana E. H., and Van de Ven, Nicole. *Crimes against women: Proceedings of the international tribunal.* Millbrae, CA: Les Femmes, 1976.

Ryan, William. *Blaming the victim.* New York: Random House, 1971.

Scott, P. D. Battered wives. *British Journal of Psychiatry,* November 1974, 433–441.

Snell, John E., Rosenwald, Richard J., and Robey, Ames. The wifebeaters wife. *Archives of General Psychiatry,* August 1964, *11,* 107–112.

Snyder, Mark. Impression management. In Lawrence S. Wrightsman, *Social Psychology* (Second Edition). Monterey: Brooks/Cole, 1977, 115–146.

Star, Barbara. *Comparing battered and nonbattered women.* Unpublished paper, 1977.

Steinmetz, Suzanne K., and Straus, Murray A. *Violence in the family.* New York: Harper and Row, 1974.

Straus, Murray A. Leveling, civility, and violence in the family. *Journal of Marriage and the family,* February 1974, *36,* 13–29.

————. Sexual inequality, cultural norms, and wife-beating. In Emilio Viano (Ed.), *Victims and society.* Washington: Visage, 1976.

————. Normative and behavioral aspects of violence between spouses: Preliminary data on a nationally representative USA sample, 1977.(a)

————. A sociological perspective on the prevention and treatment of wifebeating. In Maria Roy (Ed.), *Battered women.* New York: Van Nostrand Reinhold, 1977.(b)

————. *Wife-beating: How common, and why?* Paper presented at the conference on Battered Wives: Defining the Issues, Stanford University Center for Research on Women, May 20, 1977.(c)

————, Gelles, Richard, and Steinmetz, Suzanne K. *Violence in the family: An assessment of knowledge and research needs.* Paper presented at the annual meeting of the American Association for the Advancement of Science, Boston, 1976.

Terry, Robert. The white male club: Biology and power. *Civil Rights Digest,* Spring 1974, *6*(3), 66–77.

Warren, Carol A. B. *Homosexuality and stigma: Behavior, identity and community.* Unpublished manuscript. Los Angeles: University of California.

Weis, Kurt, and Borges, Sandra S. Rape as a crime without victims and offenders. In Emilio Viano (Ed.), *Victims and society.* Washington: Visage, 1976, 230–254.

Wilson, Elizabeth. *The existing research into battered women.* Camden Women's Aid: National Women's Aid Federation, Camden, NJ, 1976.

Wolfgang, Marvin E. *Patterns in criminal homicide.* Philadelphia: University of; Pennsylvania, 1958.

Wrightsman, Lawrence S. *Social psychology.* Monterey: Brooks/Cole, 1977.

SIXTEEN

# The Underside of Married Life: Power, Influence, and Violence*

EMILY STIER ADLER

## INTRODUCTION

Robert Blood has suggested that much of the research in the sociology of the family "tends to run in ruts" and one of those "ruts" is the study of marital power (1976:8). Since the publication of the original study by

*This is a revised version of a paper presented at the annual meetings of the American Sociological Association, Chicago, September 1977. The research was supported in part by a Rhode Island College faculty research grant.

Blood and Wolfe (1960), the topic of marital power has received wide-spread attention (for example, Bahr, 1972; Cromwell and Olson, 1975; Heer, 1962; Hoffman, 1960; Safilios-Rothschild, 1970; Scanzoni, 1972; Turk and Bell, 1972). However, in spite of the work done during the past two decades, the field is still far from coherent. To date, studies of marital power have employed different definitions of the concept, used different methodologies and operationalizations, presented divergent interpretations of the findings, found the data supportive of multiple theoretical models, questioned the explanatory utility of the concept itself, and even postulated as to sociologists' underlying motivations for expending so much time and energy on the topic.

Given these complexities, one might wonder about the wisdom of yet another paper on marital power. The answer is simple: The issue simply is not going to go away. In its methodology, the analysis of marital power must face the relationship between "subjective" and "objective" realities; in its theoretical underpinnings, it must face the relationship between structural and normative characteristics; and empirically, it must face the complex interrelationship of many variables that beg to be classified.

The goals of this article are modest. First, an alternative operationalization of the concept of marital power will be presented. In addition, two aspects of married life that are theoretically important to an understanding of, and are empirically correlated with, marital power are considered.

## SAMPLE

The data for this study were obtained from in-depth interviews with 50 couples. The population selected was that of married part-time graduate students at a New England state college. This population ($N=1579$) was chosen because it was assumed that part-time students (who had already completed a B.A. degree) and their spouses would be more likely to have other roles in addition to that of student (e.g., worker, parent).

In order to obtain the sample, contact was made with 79 members of the population, selected by systematic random sampling. The initial contact was a letter sent to the homes of members of the population. The second contact was a phone call to answer any questions about the study and, if the respondents were willing, to schedule an interview. In four cases the second contact did not take place (no listed telephone or answer), in two cases the couple was no longer part of the sample (divorce or separation), and in two cases time conflicts did not permit the interview to take place. Of those who received the second contact and were in intact marriages, 21, or 25 percent, refused to participate.

It is recognized that the findings of this study can only be generalized to a small, relatively homogeneous, and highly educated population. Like the population, the sample was white, middle class, and predominantly Catholic. There was, however, a wide range in the characteristics of age (from 21 to 63 years of age), length of marriage (1 to 29 years), number of children (0 to 5), and wife's work status (employed part-time, full-time, and not employed in a wage-earning job).

Pretesting of the interview schedule and questionnaire was conducted during the fall of 1974. The interviews with the sample took place between January and July 1975.

## PERCEIVED MARITAL POWER

Power is most often defined as the ability of an individual to change the behavior of other members of a social system (Olson and Cromwell, 1975a:5). Family power is a multidimensional concept that is measured through behavioral acts in which the degree of one's power is put to the test (Safilios-Rothschild, 1970:540). In this study, *perceived* marital power is defined as the spouses' perceptions of the extent to which each controls the other's behavior.

Defining perceived marital power in terms of the way that family members themselves see the power structure means that the researcher is interested in a "subjective" rather than "objective" view of the family. Interest in the "intersubjective world" of the spouses directs the researcher to focus on the "texture of meaning" of the respondents' everyday lives (Schutz, 1963:309). Therefore, a self-report method was used in this study instead of an evaluation of observed family members' behavior in, for example, a discussion or game situation (as, for example, in Kenkel, 1957, and Straus, 1967). "Self-report methods tap the subjective reality by measuring power from the perspective of those individuals involved in the relationship" (Olson and Cromwell, 1957b:137).

Previous research in the field contained some methodological pitfalls which were avoided in this study. Other studies, for example, had obtained data from only one spouse, usually the wife, based on the dubious assumption that the other spouse's responses would be similar (Safilios-Rothschild, 1969:290). In addition, even when researchers have obtained data from both spouses, they have continued to look for a measure of power that would act as a reflection of the one "valid reality" rather than viewing the discrepancies between husbands' and wives' reports as valid. Rather than assuming that both spouses' reports would be similar, this study interviewed both the husband and the wife in each couple at the same time in different rooms. In this way the possibility that the husband's and wife's realities might not coincide could be examined.

This study relied primarily on broad, open-ended questions concerning each spouse's perception of the power structure. In this way the study avoided the concerns about the validity of measuring power by asking respondents which spouse makes the decision in a given set of areas. This method of measuring power, which has been used in the bulk of previous research, has been questioned on numerous grounds: that the specific decisions which are used have a direct impact on the study's findings (Centers, Raven, and Rodrigues, 1971:265–267); that calculating an overall decision-making score makes the untenable assumption that all decisions are equally important (Safilios-Rothschild, 1970:543); and that response alternatives like "both make decisions" in a culture that supports an equalitarian ideal may tend to distort findings by an artificial over-selection of this type of choice (Safilios-Rothschild, 1970: 544). Finally, since a whole field of decision making may be relegated to a weaker partner (Safilios-Rothschild, 1970), and each area of decision making may not be equally salient to the spouses (Komarovsky, 1967), it was important to use a methodology that emphasized general questions to allow these issues to be explored.

Operationalization of Perceived Marital Power

To classify the couples according to their perceived marital power structures, both spouses were interviewed separately and were asked a series of questions that explored their perceptions of their ability to influence and control each other. These included questions concerning (1) the respondent's feelings about who usually gets his or her way when the couple disagrees, (2) the outcome(s) of the example(s) of decision making that the respondent cites when asked about recent decisions, (3) the respondent's feeling about his or her ability to force the spouse into something the spouse was initially opposed to, and (4) the respondent's feeling of satisfaction about the amount of power that the spouse sees him or herself as having. The last question was considered especially important because it was asked after quite a bit of discussion about power and influence. It usually involved a restatement of the respondent's perception of the balance of power; sometimes it included a clarification of, and occasionally a reevaluation of, the situation.

Based on the answers, each spouse was classified as to his or her individual perception of the balance of power into one of three categories: equalitarian, husband dominated or wife dominated. As a check on the initial classification, the responses to questions that asked about the respondent's view of the spouse's view of the situation, about the extent to which he or she delegated responsibility to the spouse, and about decision making in 22 specific areas were considered as "backup information." In general, the answers to these questions were in agreement with and tended to support the initial classification of each spouse's view of the perceived marital power structure.

After the husband and wife were each classified as to his or her perception of the marriage, these perceptions were compared. In 46 of the 50 couples, the spouses' perceptions of the distribution of marital power were substantially the same. In the other four couples, "his" marriage was clearly different from "her" marriage. There were four types of perceived marital power type identified: equalitarian (22 couples), husband dominated (19 couples), wife dominated (5 couples), and differently perceived (4 couples).

### The Equalitarian Marriage: "It Balances Out"

The most important characteristic of the equalitarian marriage is that both the wife and the husband feel that neither one of them is dominant in terms of making decisions or exerting influence. In all of these families the spouses perceived themselves as exerting joint and equal influence over at least a sizeable proportion of family matters. In all of these families, each spouse also was seen as having more influence in some areas than he or she did in other areas—either because he or she knows more about a particular area, is more affected by what happens, and/or feels more strongly about the particular area.

The proportion of matters defined as "personal" issues as opposed to "family" issues varied from family to family. At one end of the continuum are those couples who defined quite a few issues as "personal." Among these couples the husband and wife each had almost complete autonomy in areas defined as "his" and "hers"—perceived by both as being of equal importance. On the other end of the continuum are the couples in which most matters were defined as concerning both of them. Among these couples almost all things were seen as being decided after a lot of "give and take" in which both spouses were seen as equally likely to do the "giving."[1]

All 22 of the husbands and 21 of the wives were satisfied with the amount of influence they have. They felt that they had "enough" but not "too much." As Mrs. 19 said, "I like it the way it is. When I feel pushy he gives me room." Similarly, her husband commented that he would not make any changes. Mr. 19 explained, "I have control over me. I decide what time to get up in the morning and what time to go to bed at night. My children, I have the power to tell them they must go to school. I don't have power over my wife. I don't rule her and she doesn't rule me."

## The Husband-Dominated Marriage: "But He Respects My Opinion"

The predominant characteristic of the husband-dominated marriage is that both the husband and the wife perceive the husband as having more power than the wife does. In all 19 of these couples, although the wife was seen as having control in at least some areas, the husband was perceived as having final or overall control on family matters. In addition, in seven of the couples, the wives' areas were defined as less important than the husbands' areas.

However, even if the husband was seen as the dominant spouse, in most cases this was seen as being tempered by his "reasonableness." In the majority of cases (13 couples) the husband was perceived as consulting the wife on at least some of the things he decided. These wives were pleased to be consulted and believed that their husbands respected their opinions and considered them carefully before deciding. Similarly, in 12 cases the wife felt that if she *really* wanted something, she could get her own way. Furthermore, seven husbands said they gave in to their wives on minor issues in order to "keep the peace" in the family. These attributes made the great majority of the wives (14 cases) satisfied with the balance of power. Mrs. 33, for example, told us that

> if it's financial, I think he makes the final decision. We wanted to get an apartment before we got this place and I found one that I liked but it was more than he wanted to spend, and he said "No, we can't do it," and I didn't really fight with him. [Are there things that would be more your decision than his?] Like we need a new bedspread and I want to spend $20 or $30, he goes along. He doesn't deny me things. . . . I guess I see him as more of the head of the house. I think for all the practical purposes you need someone. When there are two people you can be more 50-50, but with a family it's different.

And Mr. 33 noted that, "I have no desire to be any more authoritarian than I am."

The Wife-Dominated Marriage: "If It Makes Her Happy"

The essential characteristic of the wife-dominated marriage is that the husbands and wives share the perception that the wife is the more influential spouse. Although one husband felt the situation had occurred because his wife was the more logical person, the other four said it was basically because giving in made their wives easier to live with. Three of these husbands implied that *if* they were willing to take the consequences of their actions, they could become more powerful than they were at the present time.

In contrast to the husband-dominated marriage, three of these wives saw at least a portion of their power as covert and manipulative rather than as power that could openly control. And, in similar contrast, three of the husbands were dissatisfied with the balance of power and preferred to have more. In every case the husband was seen as having at least some areas under his control and as being consulted by his wife on the other decisions as well—even if he would ultimately give in to her.

Mr. 9 illustrated this type of relationship when he said he gives in because he doesn't want to live with "a miserable wife," but that he is not always happy with the way things are. He told us, "If I say, 'Let's go eat here,' and she doesn't want to, she won't. If I say, 'Let's go skiing this weekend,' she won't go if she doesn't want to. I can't get her to do it or go. I could say, 'Well, I'm leaving. I'm not coming back.' She'd say, 'Goodbye.'" In her view, Mrs. 9 feels that she usually wins because, "If I think it's best, I tell him he doesn't know what's best."


Marriages with Differently Perceived Power Structures:
"His" Marriage versus "Her" Marriage

In some marriages, husband and wife had different perceptions of the power structure. In two of these families, each spouse felt that he or she was the more powerful and believed the other spouse to share that perception. In both couples the spouses felt able to force the other into accepting something. Each believed that if the other spouse knew how much something meant to him or her, then he or she would "give in to please me." During the interviews with both couples, the spouses related different decisions, each remembering the ones where he or she felt dominant. The spouses all felt satisfied with the power structure.

The other two couples had wives who perceived themselves as dominant and husbands who felt they were equal. All four spouses felt they could force the spouse into something. Among these two couples, the wife appeared to believe she had control because of the "power vacuum" the husband left. In each case the husband's career is a top-priority item—the couple had either moved because of it or planned much of the family life around it. The husband did not feel at all "infringed upon" in this important area and therefore defined the situation as equal. The wife, on the other hand, felt that because of her husband's interests, she has charge of the other areas of family life and therefore is dominant. It may be that only when the husband is interested in exerting control in these other areas that the differences in perception need to be reconciled. While one husband felt satisfied with the situation as he saw it, the other reported that, although previously he was satisfied, he now wanted more control. Both wives felt that they have too much power. They see power and involvement in family life as related: in order to get more power their husbands will have to get more involved.

## ON POWER AND MARRIED LIFE

The most important reason for pursuing the concept of marital power is its utility for understanding other aspects of marriage. In this paper I will briefly describe the spouses' influence techniques, patterns of marital violence, and the relationship they have to the perceived power structure.

Influence Techniques

"The investigation of the influence dynamics between spouses is extremely important, if not indispensible, for the assessment of familial power structure" (Safilios-Rothschild, 1969a:7). Analyzing the way in which spouses attempt to influence each other can clarify the concept of marital power as well as provide an understanding of one aspect of family sex roles. Specifically, we can examine the validity of the widely held stereotype that women often get their way in families through manipulative and covert means, while men get their way by using open and forthright tactics.

Respondents were asked how they would try to make their spouses go along with them in the event that their spouses opposed something that they felt to be very important. In describing the most frequently used technique(s), many respondents indicated that they saw the question as asking about techniques specifically designed to influence the spouse (for example, "Oh, you mean what's my *strategy* for getting my own way. . ."). Others were careful to present the techniques as not consciously manipulative ("Well, I don't do it on purpose, you know, to get my own way, but I cry when I'm upset and I guess he knows. . . "). Of all the respondents, only one husband said he did not do anything to influence his wife.

Wives listed more influence techniques than did the husbands. The mean number of techniques for wives was 2.2; for husbands it was 1.4. In addition, the lists of primary techniques and total techniques used were somewhat different for husbands and wives (Table 1).[2] More wives said they would keep bringing the topic up for discussion (Mrs. 20: "Just bringing it up repeatedly. If he sees it coming up all the time and it's important enough he usually gives in."); argue or get angry about it (Mrs. 7: "I would slam things around the house and throw a fit."); become withdrawn and silent (Mrs. 18: "A very feminine technique, I guess. The only one I resort to is not speaking. He explodes. I don't; I keep it in."); and become emotionally upset or cry (Mrs. 11: "I get depressed and may cry or be moody. I'll go off by myself but I'll never yell."). More husbands say they discuss the topic logically (Mr. 41: "Point out the merits, stay away from the points you don't want brought up. Give a good sales pitch."); and act stubborn (Mrs. 13: "If I'm strongly for it, it would be perseverance, stubbornness. If I was strongly for it, I would keep after her. I would not drop it. Persistence—for a long time.").

When the techniques used are grouped into three types, "emotional techniques" (becoming withdrawn, pouting, using the "silent treatment," crying, becoming emotionally upset and witholding sex), "argumentative techniques" (being angry, arguing, yelling, telling spouse that he or she would do it anyway, and being stubborn), and "discussion techniques" (bringing topic up for discussion again, discussing it logically and telling the spouse how he or she feels about the issue), sex is found to be moderately associated with influence techniques (Table 2, gamma = -.49).[3] The major difference between husbands' and wives' influence techniques is that while only 1 husband said he used an "emotional technique," 24 of the wives said they did; that is, the wives used as many of the more "open" influence techniques, such as discussion and argument, as the husbands did, but used more "manipulative" techniques, such as crying or the silent treatment, as well. Perhaps wives have more success with and/or feel more comfortable with the traditional, and more acceptably "feminine," techniques.

In addition to the sex of the spouse, it was hypothesized that those who see themselves as relatively powerful would use different influence techniques than those who perceive themselves as less powerful. Feeling

**Table 1.** *Influence Techniques Used by Husbands and Wives*

| Influence Techniques Cited by Spouse: | PRIMARY INFLUENCE TECHNIQUES | | TOTAL INFLUENCE TECHNIQUES | |
|---|---|---|---|---|
| | Husbands | Wives | Husbands | Wives |
| I would keep bringing the topic up for discussion | 4 | 11 | 9 | 27 |
| I would discuss the topic logically, and tell him/her how I felt about it | 34 | 27 | 34 | 32 |
| I would be very stubborn | 8 | 5 | 13 | 5 |
| I would get angry, I'd argue, I'd yell about it | 0 | 3 | 4 | 11 |
| I would tell him/her that I'd do it anyway | 3 | 0 | 6 | 5 |
| I'd become withdrawn, I'd pout, I'd use the "silent treatment" | 0 | 2 | 1 | 12 |
| I'd cry; I'd become emotionally upset | 0 | 2 | 0 | 16 |
| I'd withhold sex | 0 | 0 | 0 | 2 |
| Total | 49 | 50 | 67 | 110 |

**Table 2.** *Relationship between Sex of Respondent and Influence Techniques Used[a]*

| Sex of the Respondent | INFLUENCE TECHNIQUES | | | |
|---|---|---|---|---|
| | One or more "argumentative" techniques used | One or more "discussion" techniques used | One or more "emotional" techniques used | Total |
| Husbands | 17 | 35 | 1 | 53 |
| Wives | 17 | 39 | 24 | 80 |
| Total | 34 | 74 | 25 | 133[b] |

[a]gamma = -.49

[b]The total number of influence techniques is greater than 100 because some spouses listed more than 1 technique.

less need to negotiate or be "reasonable," spouses who perceive themselves as powerful may be more likely to demand their own way, be
stubborn, or tell the spouse that they will do something anyway. On the
other hand, spouses who feel that they have less power may feel the need
to convince or coax the spouse.

The data support this hypothesis. Influence techniques used by
wives and husbands are substantially correlated with marital power type.
Only about one-third of the wives who used "argumentative" and "discussion" techniques were in husband-dominated marriages versus two-
thirds of those who used "emotional" techniques (Table 3). On the other
hand, 58 percent of the husbands who used "argumentative" techniques
were perceived to be dominant, and 70 percent of the husbands who
used "discussion techniques" were in marriages perceived differently by
the spouses or perceived as being equalitarian or wife dominated (Table 4).

The data presented may explain more fully some sex-role stereotypes. Perhaps, in addition to the spouse's sex, it is the perceived
amount of power that he or she has that determines the influence techniques that he or she will use. It may be that because women are more
likely to perceive themselves as less powerful than men, they use emotional manipulation more often. However, when wives feel they are not
dominated by their husbands they can rely more on presenting their
desires logically and, if that does not work, can go on to argue forcefully
for their goals. On the other hand, men who are not perceived as dominant may not be as able to be as demanding and argumentative in
approaching their wives as other men. Instead, lacking the power that
dominant men have to "bully" their wives, they may need to rely more
on discussion.

Marital Violence

There have been relatively few studies of marital violence to date. Of
those studies, most selected at least part of their sample in a way that
had potential bias (i.e., divorcing couples, police "blotter" families).
While the sample used in this study does not contain those biases, there
are, in addition to the sampling considerations previously discussed, two
factors which might have resulted in an underrepresentation of violence-
prone couples. Studies have found violence greater among poor families
(Gelles, 1974) and among families where husbands are unemployed
(Gelles, 1974) or underachieving (O'Brien, 1971). In contrast, the families in this study were very middle class (mean years of education was
16), and all the husbands were employed.[4]

**Table 3.** *Influence Techniques Wife Says She Uses by Marital Power Type[a]*

| | INFLUENCE TECHNIQUES | | | |
|---|---|---|---|---|
| Perceived Marital Power Type | One or more "argumentative" techniques used | One or more "discussion" techniques used | One or more "emotional" techniques used | Total |
| Husband dominated (n = 19) | 6 | 15 | 16 | 37 |
| Non-husband dominated (n = 31) | 13 | 27 | 8 | 48 |
| Total | 19 | 42 | 24 | 85[b] |

[a]gamma = -.57
[b]The total number of influence techniques is greater than the number of wives because some wives listed more than one technique.

**Table 4.** *Relationship Between Influence Techniques Husband Says He Uses by Marital Power Type[a]*

| | INFLUENCE TECHNIQUES | | |
|---|---|---|---|
| Perceived Marital Power Type | One or more "argumentative" technique used | One or more "discussion" technique used | Total |
| Husband dominated (n = 19) | 10 | 12 | 22 |
| Non-husband dominated (n = 31) | 7 | 27 | 34 |
| Total | 17 | 39 | 56[b] |

[a]Yule's Q = -.53
[b]The total number of influence techniques is greater than the number of husbands because some husbands listed more than one technique.

Given these considerations, we can turn to an examination of the frequency with which marital violence occurred in this sample of 50 families. Physical violence is defined as the intentional use of physical force on another person (Steinmetz and Straus, 1974:3). Data on violence were obtained by asking each spouse if he or she had ever hit or tried to physically hurt his or her spouse, and if he or she had ever been hit by the spouse.[5] Although the husbands' and wives' reports of the use of physical violence against the spouses were very highly correlated, there were some discrepancies in reporting. Because of the social undesirability of using physical force on family members, it was assumed that if only one spouse reported violence, that spouse was giving the more accurate version.

In 20 of the couples (40 percent), spouses reported hitting, slapping, punching, scratching, kicking, pushing, or throwing things at the other at least once during the marriage. In eight of the couples (16 percent), violence had occurred several times. Among the couples in which violence had occurred, husbands and wives were about equally likely to initiate the violence and to respond violently once the other had begun.

Although husbands' and wives' uses of physical force against each other were highly correlated, there were three couples in which the wife used violence against the husband at least once, but he had never used violence against her, and four couples in which the husband had used violence against the wife, but she had not reciprocated. We therefore need to analyze separately the violence used by husbands and the violence used by wives.

There were approximately the same number of violent spouses of each sex. Seventeen of the husbands (34 percent) used violence against their wives at least once during their marriage, and 6 husbands (12 percent) used it at least several times. Of 33 husbands who had never used violence, 3 did use what can be considered "threatening" gestures. That is, the husband's actions, while not directed at the wife, may have served as a warning that they *could* be. Two spouses described these episodes as follows:

> Mrs. 25: "He slams things around. Not at me, but in general."
>
> Mr. 11: "Once I got so mad I threw a sandwich at her. Back about four years ago, I was giving the kids a haircut, and she was giving me a hard time about something and I picked up the shears and walked around the kitchen with them for awhile."

Most couples reported more than one kind of violence used against the wife. The most frequent kind of violence that husbands used was hitting, slapping, kicking, or punching their wives. Throwing things and pushing or shoving were also fairly common. Only one husband used a weapon. In this case the husband threatened the wife with a knife by throwing it near, but not at, her.

Sixteen of the wives (32 percent) used violence against their husbands at least once during the marriages. Of these, six (12 percent) used violence at least several times. None of the wives used "threatening" gestures. Slapping, hitting, scratching, punching, and kicking were clearly the most common kinds of violence in which the wives engaged. One wife used a weapon. In this case she held a razor against the husband's throat but did not cut him.

It is important to note that in 6 of the 16 cases in which the wife used violence, her behavior was defined as ineffective and/or not threatening. The following comments illustrate how her actions were perceived.

> Mr. 9: "Oh yes! [My wife hits me] but she can beat me all over my head and it won't hurt me."
>
> Mrs. 19: "Yes, I hit him. One night he got me really aggravated and I hit him a couple of times in the arm. And as he stood there laughing at me I belted him a couple of times; I belted him again. I felt better after. He laughed. He thought it was hilarious." (Mr. 19 commented that while the episode didn't bother him, his wife hurt her hand and was so upset that she cried).

As these spouses' comments illustrate, in over one-third of the cases where a wife used violence against her husband, she was not taken seriously. Her behavior was defined as amusing or, at most, annoying. In the 17 cases where husbands were violent, however, not one wife felt this way about his use of violence. In all 17 cases his use of violence was defined as far from trivial.

## Violence and Perceived Marital Power

Because families, like all other social units or social systems, are power systems, it can be argued that their foundations rest to some degree on force or its threat (Goode, 1971). Even though marital violence is not defined as normative in our society or among the respondents,[6] as Steinmetz and Straus (1974) have pointed out, family members can use physical violence to compensate for the lack of other resources in order to maintain their positions.

When the relationships between violence and power are examined, the correlation between violence against the wife and power type is found to be quite a bit higher than that of violence against the husband and power type (Tables 5 and 6). The proportion of husbands who have had violence used against them is fairly similar in both husband-dominated and non-husband-dominated marriages (37 percent versus 29 percent).

Table 5. *Relationship Between Physical Violence by the Husband Against the Wife and Perceived Marital Power Type*[a]

| Physical violence used against the wife | PERCEIVED MARITAL POWER TYPE | | |
| --- | --- | --- | --- |
| | Husband-dominated | Non-husband dominated | Total |
| Physical violence was used against the wife | 9 | 8 | 17 |
| No physical violence was used against the wife | 10 | 25 | 35 |
| Total | 19 | 33 | 50 |

[a]Yule's Q = .48

Table 6. *Relationship Between Physical Violence by the Wife Against the Husband and Perceived Marital Power Type*[a]

| Physical violence used against husband | PERCEIVED MARITAL POWER TYPE | | |
| --- | --- | --- | --- |
| | Husband-dominated | Non-husband dominated | Total |
| Physical violence was used against the husband | 7 | 9 | 16 |
| No physical violence was used against the husband | 12 | 22 | 34 |
| Total | 19 | 31 | 50 |

[a]Yule's Q = .18

One explanation for the low correlation between use of violence and power for wives may be found in the wives' abilities, rather than in their willingness to use violence:

> Women may be as motivated to violence as men are, but since their physical equipment for violence is less effective in actual use, they are at a great disadvantage in a physical encounter. It is true that here, as elsewhere, technology modifies "natural relationships." Guns, bombs, and poisons are great equalizers between men and women as well as between men. (Bernard, 1971:251)

Evidence of Bernard's point can be found in this study. Among the 50 couples, there was only 1 in which the husband was judged to be physically smaller than the wife, and one 1 in which the spouses were judged to be the same size. In addition, 49 of the husbands and 48 of the wives felt that the husband was physically stronger than the wife. (The other respondents reported that the husband *had* been the stronger, prior to an illness.) Therefore, without the use of weapons,[7] it was possible for almost all of the husbands to have used physical force as a means of controlling their wives.

Therefore, the lack of correlation between power and violence for the wives can be attributed to their size, strength, and, as previously discussed, the fact that their husbands often did not take seriously their use of violence.

As one wife in a husband-dominated marriage declared:

I stand on the toilet bowl because he's so much taller than me. I'll stand there and punch him in the arm because he gets me so mad. I want to be supreme. He won't give into me because I don't have the height or strength and he laughs at me.

In contrast to the wives' situations, the husbands—bigger, stronger, and posing a more serious threat—clearly have the ability to use what Allen and Straus (1975) call the "ultimate resource"—physical violence—in order to obtain control over the marriage.

We found that the wives in husband-dominated marriages were the recipients of violence twice as frequently as wives in non–husband-dominated marriages (47 percent versus 24 percent; Table 5). Wives in equalitarian marriages had the lowest rate of violence used against them (22 percent) and were more likely than those in husband-dominated marriages to retaliate if it was the husband who initiated the violence.

Before we conclude, however, that violence is simply a way of obtaining power, we must consider the possibility of feedback from power to violence. Specifically, it is equally possible to hypothesize that in addition to obtaining power through the threat or actual use of violence, *those with more power* may be more willing to use violence. As O'Brien (1971:693) argues:

Conflict in a social group is thought to be most likely to occur during the decision making process. Such a process is conducted according to some established authority pattern that is vested in a status hierarchy . . . Hence from an external perspective, violence is most often seen to be constituted of actions through which the incumbents of different status positions are maneuvering for control of some decision outcome. In the process of that struggle, if the members of the subordinate status position fail to concede the decision, then the superior group will typically exert coercive power in order to influence the outcome of the decision.

We can conclude that men who have used violence even once may have an additional power resource. Violence need not be used frequently to be a resource. One significant episode of violence to which the wife has responded passively or ineffectually must make her aware of the continued possibility of violence directed at her. The *threat* of violence in these cases may be sufficient to make it a power resource.

Examples from wife-dominated and equalitarian marriages help to illustrate the interconnection between the two variables. Spouses in two of the five wife-dominated marriages did report violence used against the wife. However, in one of the cases it was not an especially significant event. The wife said he husband had never hit her; the husband just said, "No," thought a minute, and then reported that during their 8-year marriage, "I think I hit her once, one month after we were married—nothing serious." In the other case, the results of the violence were significant, but the wife took decisive action. She felt so strongly that her husband had violated the norms of acceptable marital behavior that she imposed negative sanctions.

> Mrs. 9: I took him to court. It was at the point it was at and it was retaliation on my part. I wear glasses and he hit me. It wasn't intentional, but I had slippers on and he hit me in such a way that I banged and broke my glasses and cut myself on my cheek. We had such a terrible argument. As soon as he saw me bleeding, he ran. And I immediately called my family, and I didn't know what to do. And we called the police and I brought him to court. I went to the accident room, and the first thing they asked me was "Were the police notified?" and all this, and it seemed like, it *was* an accident. We knew it, and I know it. It seemed as though I had to prove something to him. You don't do these things, and this is what can happen.

Furthermore, she reported that while the episode happened early in their 11-year marriage, "he's never lived it down." Her husband said nothing like it ever happened again.

As the following comments illustrate, some of the wives in marriages perceived to be equalitarian were aware of the possibility of marital violence and had an explicit position concerning its use.

> Mrs. 35: I've never hit him and I never will. And if he ever touched me, I'd leave him.

Mrs. 37: He kids about the fact that he once spanked the boys' mother and I made it clear that this had better never happen here.

These women may be in a better bargaining position because the men have never used violence against them, *or* their relatively equal power position may protect them in part from an attempt to do so.

## SUMMARY AND CONCLUSIONS

This research has suggested an alternative methodology for the study of marital power that avoids some of the problems of the previous research. The classification scheme used does more than tabulate simple "win scores." It deals with the way in which spouses view their marriages, how they feel the other spouse sees the marriage, and how satisfying they find the perceived reality to be. It allows an outsider to get two "inside" views and to compare them. In this way the couple can be classified and the quality of the marriage examined. For example, it is interesting to note that the power structures that conform to patterns that are about equally acceptable in American society are satisfying to the great majority of the spouses in them. Equalitarian couples fulfill the American ideals of equality and marriage for companionship. Husband-dominated marriages are in keeping with the norm of the male as the "head of the household" that traditional sex roles support. On one level or the other, both of these marital power types are living an American dream. It is the spouses in wife-dominated families who are more likely to feel dissatisfied. Although objectively the structure of these families is much like that of the husband-dominated families, the husbands in these families feel keenly the societal stigma. Given societal norms, the "henpecked" husband and the "rooster-pecked" wife are likely to perceive very different realities.

This research has also examined the relationships between sex, power type, and the kind of influence techniques spouses use. Finally, it has analyzed the interconnections between the use of violence and the perceived ability to control the spouse.

Marital power, influence, and violence are important areas for social research. The view of the family, "romanticized and idealized *ad nauseam* by sociologists as the cornerstone of society and the bedrock of social stability" (van de Berghe, 1973:99), must be balanced by an examination of the "underside" of family life. Families may be nurturant and supportive groups; they also may be conflict-ridden and potentially harmful autocracies.

## NOTES

1. In this way, the equalitarian couple classification is similar to Komarov-sky's "balance of power" type which included "equalitarian" couples who make decisions jointly, "stalemate" couples in which each spouse was only strong enough to frustrate the other's wishes and those couples in which spouses had supremacy in different but equal areas (1967:223).

2. Given that some techniques are more socially acceptable for one sex than the other to use, there are possible challenges to the validity of self-report data for measuring the concept.

3. Davis's guidelines for Goodman and Kruskal's gamma and Yule's Q are followed (1971:49).

4. And, it is also very possible that the families with the most violence were most likely to refuse to participate in this study.

5. Behavior that spouses described as "playful," "fooling around," or mock fighting was not classified as violence since the object was not to hurt the other spouse.

6. 74 percent of the respondents said that under no condition would it be acceptable for one spouse to hit the other.

7. In this study, only one husband and one wife were reported to have threatened their spouses with weapons. As Goode (1971) suggests, although fam-ilies may *ultimately* be based on force, the fact that other "resources" are likely to be used first probably acts to limit the use of weapons in families. A family member using a weapon has not only admitted he or she has no other social resources but has seriously violated the ideology of the family as a system based on affection.

---

## REFERENCES

Allen, Craig M., and Straus, Murray A. Resources, power and husband-wife violence. In Murray A. Straus and Gerald T. Hotaling (Eds.), *The Social Causes of Husband-Wife Violence*. Minneapolis: University of Minnesota Press, in press.

Bahr, Stephen J. Comment on 'The study of family power structure: A review 1960–1969.' *Journal of Marriage and the Family*, May 1972, *34*, 239–243.

Blood, Robert O., and Wolfe, Donald M. *Husbands and wives*. Glencoe, Illi-nois: Free Press, 1960.

———. Research needs of a family life educator and marriage counselor. *Journal of Marriage and the Family*, February 1976, *38*, 7–12.

Centers, Richard, Raven, Bertram, and Rodrigues, Aroldo. Conjugal power structure: A re-examination. *American Sociological Review*, April 1971, *36*, 264–278.

Cromwell, Ronald E., and Olson, David H. *Power in families.* New York: John Wiley and Sons, 1975.

Davis, James A. *Elementary survey analysis.* Englewood Cliffs, NJ: Prentice-Hall, 1971.

Gelles, Richard. *The violent home: A study of physical aggression between husbands and wives.* Beverly Hills: Sage Publications, 1974.

———. Abused wives: Why do they stay? *Journal of Marriage and the Family,* November 1976, *38,* 659–668.

Heer, David. Husband and wife perceptions of family power structure. *Marriage and Family Living,* February 1962, *24,* 27–35.

Hoffman, Lois Wladis. Effects of the employment of mothers in parental power relations and the division of household tasks. *Marriage and Family Living,* February 1969, *22,* 27–35.

Kenkel, William F. Influence differentiation in family decision making. *Sociology and Social Research,* September 1957, *42,* 18–25.

Komarovsky, Mirra. *Blue collar marriage.* New York: Random House, 1967.

Levinger, George. Physical abuse among applicants for divorce. In Suzanne Steinmetz and Murray Straus (Eds.), *Violence in the family.* New York: Dodd, Mead and Company, 1974.

O'Brien, John E. Violence in divorce-prone families. *Journal of Marriage and the Family,* November 1971, *33,* 692–698.

Olson, David H., and Cromwell, Ronald E. Power in families. In Ronald E. Cromwell and David H. Olson (Eds.), *Power in families.* New York: John Wiley and Sons, 1975.(a)

———. Methodological issues in family power. In Ronald E. Cromwell and David H. Olson (Eds.), *Power in families.* New York: John Wiley and Sons, 1975.(b)

Safilios-Rothschild, Constantina. Patterns of familial power and influence. *Sociological Focus,* Spring 1969, *2,* 7–19.(a)

———. Family sociology or wives' family sociology? A cross-cultural examination of decision-making. *Journal of Marriage and the Family,* May 1969, *31,* 290–301.(b)

———. The study of family power structure: A review 1960–1969. *Journal of Marriage and the Family,* November 1970, *32,* 534–553.

Scanzoni, John. *Sexual bargaining: Power politics in the American marriage.* Englewood Cliffs, NJ: Prentice-Hall, 1972.

Schutz, Alfred. Common sense and scientific interpretation of human action. In Maurice Natanson (Ed.), *Philosophy of the social sciences.* New York: Random House, 1963.

Sprey, Jetse. Family power structure: A critical comment. *Journal of Marriage and the Family,* May 1972, *34,* 235–238.

Steinmetz, Suzanne, and Straus, Murray A. *Violence in the family.* New York: Dodd, Mead and Company, 1974.

Straus, Murray A. The influence of sex of child and social class on instrumental and expressive family roles in a laboratory setting. *Sociology and Social Research,* October 1967, *52,* 7–21.

Turk, James, and Bell, Norman. Measuring power in families. *Journal of Marriage and the Family,* May 1972, *34.*

van den Berghe, Pierre. *Age and sex in human societies: A biosocial perspective.* Belmont, CA: Wadsworth Publishing, 1963.

---

SEVENTEEN

# An Interview with Sara Smith— One Woman's Experience with the Cycle of Violence*

## ANONYMOUS

Sara Smith was a law-abiding citizen, a Sunday school teacher, and a mother of two well-behaved schoolgirls when she killed her husband, who had recently left her for another woman, and burned their house down in 1978. Initially sentenced to a state correctional institution, she was subsequently transferred to a state mental health institution. Discovering that other women in these institutions had, like herself, experienced child abuse and neglect during childhood, Sara wrote to the Center for Women Policy Studies to ask about the relationship between child abuse and neglect and adult violence. Learning of this, the author talked with Sara on February 17, 1979, in her locked ward about Sara's own background and feelings concerning the cycle of violence.

Interviewer:   Apparently you agree with the TV ad showing an adult prisoner as the victim of child abuse and suggesting that violence is transmitted from generation to generation.

Sara Smith:    I know I committed a violent crime and lived with a violent husband for many years partly because I grew up feeling that being kicked around meant I wasn't any good. I was also surprised to hear other women prisoners describing much the same kind of physical, sexual, and psychological abuse as kids as I had known.

---

*Sara Smith is a fictitious name; however, no other facts in this interview have been changed from what actually was reported.

Interviewer: It is difficult for the general public and even some professionals to recognize the importance of preventing and treating child abuse and neglect as a way of reducing adult crime.

Sara Smith: I suppose so, but I feel so strongly that violence breeds violence.

Interviewer: Some of the textbooks on violence make that point, but hearing your story in your own words should convince any doubters that crime prevention begins with reducing child abuse and neglect.

Sara Smith: Okay, where shall I begin?

Interviewer: What do you remember most about your childhood?

Sara Smith: What I remember most is that there was always some kind of violence going on in the house, and neither my father nor my mother seemed to be around much to stop it. For example, I remember seeing the farmer who owned the place where we lived beating up one of my brothers. He had my brother Joe across the bed and was pounding away at him while I was standing behind the door watching. My older brothers would often get mad and kick the table over or throw things around, and the smaller kids like myself would be herded outside to get out of the way of whatever would be flying.

Interviewer: Did you come from a large family?

Sara Smith: Yes, there were 10 children. My mother was only 14 when she was married, so she was almost a child herself when she started having babies, and she didn't know much about taking care of children. One of my sisters died when she was a baby because my grandmother had told my mother to put the baby in front of an open window in the wintertime as a way of recovering from a bad cold. Needless to say, she developed pneumonia and later died.

Interviewer: Did your parents attempt to discipline the children at all?

Sara Smith: No, nothing was ever said about controlling behavior or explaining that "you are not supposed to do this" or "you should do that." It was like we would have to decide on our own, somehow, how we should function. We set up our own value system without any parental guidance.

Interviewer: What happened if you asked questions for guidance?

| Sara Smith: | I never learned how to ask, I guess, and in fact I never developed enough confidence to ask questions. |
| --- | --- |
| Interviewer: | Children are so instinctively curious and questioning, I am wondering if you hadn't been abused very early and punished for asking questions. |
| Sara Smith: | That could be. I know that I don't recall any curiosity, and in fact I don't recall ever having any enthusiasm for life. At one point, all the kids were taken away from mom and dad. From what I gather, dad had lost his job so we were living in a culvert under the road like a bunch of gypsies. The welfare department took all the kids away, and we were placed in the county home for children for several months. |
| Interviewer: | Was your family together then again for the rest of your childhood? |
| Sara Smith: | Oh, no. Some time later my dad took four or five of us younger kids to Kentucky and left us there for 4 or 5 months with a woman who later became my step-mother. There was no explanation; we were just carted down there and deposited with her. Without warning, they appeared again and off we went. It was a gypsy type of existence, always moving, never finishing a whole grade in school, and never getting to know kids. We didn't have anything to say about it, and we were just dragged along sort of like furniture or baggage. |
| Interviewer: | Did your family have any other contacts with the welfare department or legal authorities during your childhood? |
| Sara Smith: | Yes. When I was 8 I remember some guys came to our house and dragged my mother away. No one said she was going to be gone for awhile, but in fact she was in prison for about a year. Neither my mother nor my father was ever willing to discuss this subsequently, so I don't know for sure why she was sentenced. |
| Interviewer: | What do you remember about your older brothers besides their throwing things and fighting? |
| Sara Smith: | Well, some of them sexually abused some of my sisters and me. |
| Interviewer: | Did your dad ever do this too? |
| Sara Smith: | No. He just wasn't around that much. My mother wasn't either, so there wasn't anyone to stop the boys. As I said before, we kids sort of took care of each other. |

Interviewer:  Do you have any recollection of being physically abused as a child?

Sara Smith:  Yes. My sister wouldn't just spank me, she would use a whip or a butcher knife, and I remember once she hit me so hard the knife broke. Now with my husband, spanking was a daily part of his childhood. His father used to beat him unmercifully and try to get him to cry, but my husband was determined to act like it didn't hurt, and his dad would just sort of throw up his hands and say, "There's nothing more I can do." My husband felt that his parents were ogres, that they stood in the way of things he wanted to do, and he transferred that feeling to teachers and everybody else. All his life he was determined to do what he wanted to do, even if it was unreasonable.

Interviewer:  Tell me more about him.

Sara Smith:  I always felt that he abused me because that is what he wanted to do, but couldn't, to some of the other people in his life, especially his mother. He had a big thing about his mother. He hated her. It seemed she was the one who always stopped him from having what he wanted. He felt like she was responsible for everything that happened to him in his life, and he transferred those frustrations to me.

Interviewer:  Was he in trouble with the law?

Sara Smith:  Yes, to some extent, both as a kid and as an adult for things like traffic tickets, stealing hub caps, drinking. He told me that he was in the brig more than he was out of it while he was in the service because he would get into fights with his superior officers. He hated authority and could not take orders from anybody, and he could always excuse himself from any responsibility.

Interviewer:  You mentioned drinking, and I'm wondering if it was a major problem.

Sara Smith:  Oh, yes. Drinking was part of his life. When he got drunk, he could forget his problems, and it was a sort of macho thing with him. I think he started drinking when he was about 11.

Interviewer:  Did your husband only abuse you when he had been drinking?

Sara Smith:  Oh, no. When he was sober, too, and it started even before we were married. That was the only time I ever had to go to a doctor or a hospital because of his abuse.

He knocked me down one time while we were dating, and it turned out that I had to have a rib removed. At the time I looked at it as an accident and chalked it off as just a little too much roughhousing.

Interviewer: If he continued to abuse you after you were married, why did you stay with him?

Sara Smith: I stayed with him because I was afraid to go out on my own. I didn't have any job training or experience and anyway this was the pattern of my life. This is what I had been led to expect. My parents didn't think I was good enough to be treated decently, so why should anyone else?

Interviewer: You had no goals for yourself?

Sara Smith: No. I made my husband's goals my own. During the time I was married to my husband I really didn't exist as an individual. I was just sort of a part of him. When I killed him, it was really like killing myself. It took me a long time to get over that idea and to realize that there was something left for me in this world. Only my two girls gave my life any purpose or meaning.

Interviewer: You came into the marriage ready to blame yourself for anything that went wrong, and he came into the marriage ready to blame you also. Does that sound about right?

Sara Smith: Yes, and really I felt so sorry for him much of the time. It would seem that everything he touched, everything he came in contact with would turn out wrong. He had finished high school via a correspondence course and was a good auto mechanic when he was sober.

Interviewer: Did you talk to anyone about your husband's abusing you or about marital or other problems in general— friends, neighbors, relatives, etcetera?

Sara Smith: No. My husband was adamant that nobody should know what was going on with us. It was like a big secret. At one point I suggested we should have some marriage counseling, and my husband told me to keep my mouth shut. He alienated me from the one brother I was close to, so I couldn't talk to my brother either.

Interviewer: How did you hide your black and blue marks?

Sara Smith: Oh, I made excuses that I fell down or hit myself or something like that. I really didn't have any friends because my husband didn't let me. He didn't let me see my relatives either. It wasn't until after my husband's death that I realized that it was my husband who had created friction that kept me apart from my brothers and sisters.

Interviewer: Would you care to comment on your husband's attitude toward sex?

Sara Smith: He thought women were good for two things—keeping house and sex. He lumped all women together in a group and identified them as stupid. His attitude was that they should stay home and mind their own business but be available to go to bed with or provide meals, clean clothes, etcetera. He always had his own way as far as sex was concerned. He would either force me physically to go along with him or just keep nagging until I gave in. I usually would let him have his own way so he wouldn't hurt me.

Interviewer: I suppose he knew you weren't getting much enjoyment from it?

Sara Smith: Oh, yes, but he said that didn't matter as long as his needs were met.

Interviewer: When he left you and started living with another woman, did your feelings change?

Sara Smith: At first, no. I still blamed myself, but gradually, particularly during and after my trial when I got help from both professionals and the National Organization for Women, I started realizing that there were some good things about me. I am gradually building up a sense of self-worth and self-esteem.

Interviewer: Where did you go for help and what seemed to be effective?

Sara Smith: After my husband left me, I first went to a public mental health service, but the social worker wasn't much help, partly perhaps because I didn't know what I wanted at the time. I guess I was still blaming myself. When a *guardian at litem* was appointed for the two girls—my husband was trying to get custody—I heard my oldest daughter tell him that my husband was molesting her. I had told the social worker this too. When the *guardian ad litem* decided that my husband and I were equally fit as parents, I was very distressed. By then I also had an attorney, but he too said not to make a big issue out of the sexual abuse. To me, however, it

was an important issue and not one of these professionals agreed. How could I know that he wouldn't go
ahead and rape one of the girls? I think this is when my
trust in him really cracked.

Interviewer: You are highly motivated to be a good mother, aren't
you?

Sara Smith: Yes, I always tried to show my girls that at least one
parent was involved with them and really cared. My
husband thought that we were there for his convenience, and the kids weren't allowed to make any noise
or play in the same room where he was. If the kids
vanished when he appeared, he would be infuriated and
force them to sit down and watch TV with him or whatever. I felt very uncomfortable about this because if I
didn't speak up to defend the children, I felt guilty, like
I wasn't doing my job as a mother, but if I did speak
up, he would explode and perhaps hit me.

Interviewer: In view of the lack of positive parenting in your own
childhood, I am wondering how you developed a supportive and caring relationship with your own girls.

Sara Smith: I definitely had to learn this. Mostly I watched other
people. I did some reading too, and talked with other
parents. Religion has helped me too.

Interviewer: Were you always religious?

Sara Smith: Oh, no. My husband had gone to a Lutheran school,
but I had never gone to Sunday school or church until
after we were married. My husband didn't want me to
go to church at first, but then he changed his mind and
decided I should go. He quit going altogether. After my
husband left me, I talked to the minister, but I was still
blaming myself so it didn't do much good. I know now,
though, that faith has really saved me and I think that
it is part of a parent's responsibility to help children
develop some religious values.

Interviewer: You seem to feel that you are able to stay in touch with
your girls even though you are confined here.

Sara Smith: I am still their mother, and I want them to know that I
care about them. They visit me nearly every weekend
and I write to them often.

Interviewer: Do you find that the other mothers confined here feel
the same way?

Sara Smith: I regret to say that I am afraid many of them have a
hopeless attitude about nearly everything. Many have

known little but violence throughout their lives. I discovered this when I was in group therapy and so many women talked about being abused, both in childhood and as wives.

Interviewer: Could you give me some examples?

Sara Smith: Mary, who was beaten by her husband all the time, had been in an incestuous relationship with her father since the time she was 14. Instead of protecting her, Mary's mother just told her she was no good and it didn't matter what her father did to her. Ann said that her father set her hair on fire and beat her up—he is a confirmed alcoholic—and her uncle tried to get her involved in a sexual relationship. Janet was 4 years old when her father died, and she had total care of a number of younger siblings while her mother went off to work. Marie has talked about her father verbally abusing her all the time, and now she has an abusive husband.

Interviewer: How abusive?

Sara Smith: Oh, he ran over her with a car one time, but she is going to go back and live with him when she gets out of prison. She said one reason they were always having a problem was because they were both on drugs much of the time and she thinks now things will be different.

Interviewer: Since all of the women you have mentioned are mothers, do you think it would be helpful to have classes on parenting in locked wards of mental health institutions such as this or in prisons?

Sara Smith: Yes, I think it would be a very good idea because it does seem that so many of these women have very little understanding of how to deal with children. Many do not know what is involved in parenting and therefore can hardly be blamed for neglect. I have met a woman here who didn't know that it was wrong for her son and daughter to be involved sexually with each other.

Interviewer: Do you think these women would be motivated to be involved in a parent group?

Sara Smith: That's a good question. I know that a job training program was started at the prison and since all of the women seemed to want jobs, I thought they would flock to it. However, it went over like a lead balloon and was a real flop. As I said before, so many have a "What's the use" attitude about everything. It seems to me that some of them would rather withdraw and say,

"Poor me, I've never had a chance in my life," rather than taking the risk of doing something about themselves.

Interviewer:    You have certainly raised an important point for social workers and other helping professionals. How can we break this cycle? I want to thank you for your willingness to talk to me and share your story so that others can understand the cycle of family violence somewhat better.

# PROCESSING FEMALE OFFENDERS IN THE CRIMINAL JUSTICE SYSTEM

---

# PART THREE

# WOMEN, THE POLICE, AND THE COURTS

## 1. WOMEN AND THE LAW

As Armstrong (1977) has pointed out, females under the law are "protected" but unequal. So-called protective statutes protect women primarily from themselves rather than from the predatory activities of others, and do so by giving them longer periods of time in correctional confinement than are meted out to men who have committed similar acts. As an example of this, the Muncy Act, which was adopted in Pennsylvania in 1913, resulted in women serving 50 percent more time in prison than men sentenced for similar offenses. Women were often sent to Muncy, the state institution for women, as punishment for crimes for which men served shorter terms in local jails where they were more accessible for visits from relatives and friends. Throughout American history, criminal and civil law has not only discriminated against females, but it has also consistently embodied traditional stereotypes of women's character and morals. A woman's legal status locates her somewhere between a child and an adult male (Cavanagh, 1971).

There are many parallels between the legal status of blacks and of women in America (Kanowitz, 1969). For example, both have historically been denied the privilege of voting in elections and, therefore, their rights as citizens. Neither has been taken as seriously as white males when testifying in the courts of law. Students who argue that these forms of discrimination against blacks and women have long passed into history should be reminded that the Equal Rights Amendment has received very strong opposition in the United States and still has not been ratified in enough states to come the law of the land as of the writing of this book. Even if it is eventually passed, the strength of the opposition to the amendment, the delays in its ratification, and the defeats that it suffered in many states will remain as an historical monument to the unwillingness of men to grant legal equality to women.

## 2. VICTIMS AND CRIMINALS: TWO KINDS OF CLIENTS FOR THE CRIMINAL JUSTICE SYSTEM

Aside from the relatively small proportion of criminal justice system employees who are female, there are two ways in which women and girls come into contact with criminal justice personnel. These are as victims and as offenders. In one case, women who have criminal offenses committed against them voluntarily become clients of the criminal justice system when they ask for protection and/or that justice be carried out. In contrast, female offenders are the unwilling clients of the criminal justice system and ask only that they be left alone. As they are coerced clients, female offenders are unlikely to be satisfied with the services rendered to them by the criminal justice system. This has little effect upon the criminal justice system because the number of female offenders is small and because the opinions of felons and misdemeanants are not highly valued in American society. The situation with regard to female victims is very different in that they are much larger in number than female offenders and they also have higher status. Despite these factors, there is considerable evidence that female victims are substantially dissatisfied with the treatment they receive from the criminal justice system, often reporting that they are treated more like offenders than the victims (Bowker, 1978).

We know very little about the criminal justice system treatment of the female victims of economic crimes. The studies that are represented in the literature are largely limited to the victims of sex crimes and domestic assaults. Le Grand (1977) tells us that many police departments have typically followed a policy of no arrests in domestic violence incidents. This situation was so severe that it led to class action suits against police departments in California and New York. One reason why police officers prefer to avoid domestic violence incidents is that they are dangerous to themselves as well as to the victims, and they seem to be becoming more dangerous all the time. In the period from 1968 to 1972, responding to disturbance calls was the second most common situation in which law enforcement officers were killed. By the 1973–1977 period, disturbance calls produced 121 officer deaths as compared with 104 deaths from robberies, 72 deaths from traffic pursuits and stops, and lesser numbers of deaths associated with other law enforcement situations (Federal Bureau of Investigation, 1978). A second reason why police departments often try to minimize their response to domestic disturbance calls is that these calls rarely result in a case that stands up in court. In light of their limited resources, police departments tend to try to put most of their efforts into cases that they feel will be successfully terminated by prosecution and a guilty verdict. Finally, and perhaps more important than either of these two reasons, is the general sexist ideological position that wife beating is not "real violence" and is therefore not a "real crime."

These policies are not merely the product of the prejudices of individual police officers. They are often a matter of public policy. Langley and Levy (1978), writing in the *FBI Law Enforcement Bulletin,* give a number of examples of police or sheriff's department regulations or policies that specifically discourage making arrests on domestic disturbance calls. They state that these are typical of the official police tactics currently used in the United States. They find that the battered wife is generally put on the defensive instead of being comforted when the police arrive on the scene of a wife beating incident. The shame of these policies is revealed by several recent studies that suggest that in 85 to 90 percent of the spouse murders, the police had already been at the residence of the victim on a previous call for a domestic disturbance. In half of the cases studied in one investigation, the police had been summoned five or more times previous to the date of the marital homicide (Fleming, 1979).

Until recent years, women could not expect much better treatment as rape victims than as beaten wives. Rape victims were almost always interviewed by male police officers who felt bound to "suggest that she was not *really* raped, and that she enjoyed the experience, that she is not a 'good' woman or that she encouraged the encounter" (Weis and Borges, 1973:103). Officers have been quoted asking irrelevant and obscene questions such as "How big was he?"; "How many orgasms did you have?" and "What were you thinking about while he was doing it?" (Wood, 1973:348). One still hears these horror stories today, but many police departments in the more progressive jurisdictions have instituted special rape units with female police officers that are giving greatly improved service, just as the same progressive departments are giving selected officers specific training in dealing with domestic disputes or pairing them with treatment personnel in special domestic dispute team units.

Police officer attitudes toward rape victims result in more than an unpleasant and inappropriate social situation for rape victims. The offense incident report that they write up and submit to the district attorney's office reflects these attitudes and impacts the decision to prosecute the case. An unusually thorough and perceptive analysis of this process by Randall and Rose (1979) is one of the original articles that has been written for this reader. When the case comes up in court, the forced reliving of the crime and the brutal cross examination may be as bad as the original rape event. In one recent incident ("Voice from Grave Helps to Jail Slayer," 1979), a woman who had bravely fought to survive after suffering multiple rapes and eight gunshot wounds committed suicide rather tha face the trial. The rapist was sentenced to life plus 20 years after her taped account of the attack was played in court.

## 3. THE JUVENILE JUSTICE SYSTEM

The juvenile justice system has often been harder on girls than on boys. Boys were defined as needing to be institutionalized only if they had committed serious criminal acts, while girls who did no more than engage in sexual activity with their boyfriends were sometimes incarcerated for long periods of time.

> Juvenile court sessions were often like scenes from a Kafka novel. One could never be sure that the disposition of a case would be on the basis of the accusations or on the quality of evidence. Despite these uncertainties it was almost guaranteed that a girl would be sent to a reformatory if either she or her parents, especially her mother, were not blushingly contrite about the girl's sexual adventures. (Schlossman and Wallach, 1978:75).

Juvenile justice theory included the idea that serious illegal acts committed by boys were indicators of an underlying developmental problem so that what they required was treatment rather than punishment. Consistent with this, juvenile court practices offered neither the rigors nor the constitutional protections of the adult courts. This logic was twisted around when applied to females so that acts of no criminal consequence committed by young girls could also be taken as indicators of an underlying developmental problem which required that they receive treatment. In practice, the "treatment" to which they were subjected involved longer periods of incarceration than those suffered by boys who had committed serious delinquent acts such as assault and robbery.

Examples of the discriminatory handling of girls in the juvenile justice system abound in the literature. For example, a study of the children appearing before the New York family court between 1964 and 1974 found that a higher percentage of girls than boys was committed in every year even though the boys had committed more serious delinquencies (Conway and Bogdan, 1977). The same discriminatory pattern was found in a middle-sized Eastern city (Datesman and Scarpitti, 1976), in Honolulu (Chesney-Lind, 1973), and in many other jurisdictions. The situation of judicial paternalism is fully discussed in a recent article by Chesney-Lind (1977) that is reprinted in this volume. Although the blame for the overrepresentation of female status offenders in the juvenile justice system has been almost uniformly placed upon criminal justice practitioners, a recent report by Teilman and Landry (1978) provides us with an alternative interpretation. They found inconsistent gender biases in juvenile justice system statistics collected from a number of different sites and concluded that female status offenders are disportionately represented in the juvenile justice system more as a result of parental actions than the actions of justice system personnel.

## 4. FEMALE CRIMINALS AND THE POLICE

What should a woman do if she is caught by a police officer while engaging in a criminal activity? There is some evidence that she can increase her chances of avoiding arrest if she behaves in stereotypically female ways, but if she is aggressive or hostile, she may be even more likely to be arrested than a man apprehended under similar circumstances (DeFleur, 1975). In an article that is included in this volume, Moyer and White (1979) report on an experimental study in which they administered questionnaires containing episodes involving offenders with differing sets of characteristics to a sample of police officers in a large Southeastern city. Although they also found that the direct influence of the offender's demeanor was somewhat stronger for women than for men, most of the variation in the police officers' statements about how they would respond to female offenders was determined by the type of crime involved rather than by demeanor.

These two studies are exceptional in that very little research has been carried out on the subject of police attitudes toward female offenders. We know quite a bit more about the interaction between police officers and prostitutes. Laws against prostitution, like all laws against crimes without victims or against private behavior between consenting adults, are almost impossible to enforce fairly. When citizens complain loudly about the presence of prostitutes in their neighborhoods, the police often respond by harrassing the prostitutes so they will simply move to another area. Harrassment techniques consist of picking up the prostitutes, holding them overnight in a local jail, and then releasing them the next morning because of the lack of a legitimate charge on which they could be prosecuted. The net effect of this technique is that prostitutes lose a night's wages each time they are pulled in, and once it becomes known "the heat is on" in any given neighborhood, prostitutes will move elsewhere. In the drive to gain information about prostitution, the vice officers are often forced to engage in quasi-ethical and even illegal activities (Atkinson and Boles, 1977). In addition to these invasions of the constitutional rights of prostitutes themselves, police tactics also infringe upon the rights of nonprostitutes who happen to be in an area that is known for heavy prostitution, as LaFave (1965) has described in Detroit.

## 5. CRIMINAL JUSTICE PROCESSING FROM THE POLICE TO CORRECTIONS

Drawing on criminal cases from 194 counties in all 50 states, Nagel and Weitzman (1972) found that the criminal justice processing of women in the United States was consistent with the paternalistic model. Under this model, women who fit the traditional stereotype of how females should behave and live their lives are likely to receive less severe treatment by the criminal justice system than men arrested for the same offense. Since that time, there have been a number of other studies of the criminal justice system processing of females, ranging from pre-trial diversion to sentencing. In general, these studies fail to support consistently the thesis of paternalism. The problem with most of these studies is that they deal only with case-processing statistics, which means that they ignore both the demeanor of the offender and a consideration of how criminal justice system decision makers come to their conclusions about defendants.

Investigations such as Stanko's (1979) study of early case screening in prosecutors' offices are more likely to detect gender-related irregularities in criminal justice system processing than studies that consider only data having to do with the externalities of case processing. She found that robbery complaints by prostitutes were labelled as "phony" because these women were considered to have "asked" to be victimized by placing themselves in situations where victimization was likely to occur. Similarly, there were no cases in which the complainant and defendant knew each other prior to the robbery (such as when the offender was a boyfriend or separated husband of the victim) that were given felony treatment during the period studied by Stanko (1977). Since women are more likely than men to be victimized by people they know, this kind of unwritten policy discriminates against them. Stanko (1979) also found similar difficulties in the way prosecutors deal with domestic assault and rape complaints.

# REFERENCES

Armstrong, Gail. Females under the law—'Protected' but unequal. *Crime and Delinquency,* April 1977, *23,* 109–120.

Atkinson, Maxine, and Boles, Jacqueline. Prostitution as an ecology of confidence games: The scripted behavior of prostitutes and vice officers. In Clifton Bryant (Ed.), *Sexual deviancy in a social context.* New York: Franklin Watts, 1977, 219–231.

Bowker, Lee H. *Women, crime, and the criminal justice system.* Lexington, MA: D. C. Heath, 1978.

Cavanagh, Barbara K. 'A little dearer than his horse': Legal stereotypes and the feminine personality. *Harvard Civil Rights—Civil Liberties Law Review,* 1971, *6,* 260–287.

Chesney-Lind, Meda. Judicial enforcement of the female sex role: The family court and the female delinquent. *Issues in Criminology,* Fall 1973, *8,* 51–69.

———. Judicial paternalism and the female status offender—Training women to know their place. *Crime and Delinquency,* April 1977, *23,* 121–130.

Conway, Allan, and Bogdan, Carol. Sexual delinquency—The persistence of a double standard. *Crime and Delinquency,* April 1977, *23,* 131–135.

Datesman, Susan K., and Scarpitti, Frank R. *Unequal protection for males and females in the juvenile court.* Paper given at the annual meeting of the American Society of Criminology, Tucson, Arizona, 1976.

DeFleur, Lois B. Biasing influences on drug arrest records: Implications for deviance research. *American Sociological Review,* February 1975, *40,* 88–103.

Federal Bureau of Investigation. *Crime in the United States 1977.* Washington, D.C.: U.S. Government Printing Office, 1978.

Fleming, Jenifer B. *Stopping wife abuse.* Garden City, NJ: Doubleday, 1979.

Kanowitz, Leo. *Women and the law.* Albuquerque, NM: University of New Mexico Press, 1969.

La Fave, Wayne R. *Arrest, The decision to take a suspect into custody.* Boston: Little, Brown, 1965.

Langley, Roger, and Levy, Richard C. Wife abuse and the police response. *FBI Law Enforcement Bulletin,* May 1978, *47,* 4–9.

LeGrand, Camille. Rape and other crimes against women. In George Nicholson, Thomas W. Condit, and Stuart Greenbaum (Eds.), *Forgotten victims: An advocate's anthology.* Sacramento, CA: California District Attorneys Association, 1977.

Moyer, Imogene L., and White, Garland F. *Police processing of female offenders.* Paper given at the annual meeting of the Academy of Criminal Justice Sciences, Cincinnati, 1979.

Nagel, Stuart, and Weitzman, Lenore J. Double standard of american justice. *Society,* March 1972, *9,* 18–25, 63, 63.

Randall, Susan C., and Rose, Vicki M. The effect of police perceptions on the processing of rape/sexual assault cases. A preliminary draft of this paper was given at the annual meeting of the Society for the Study of Social Problems, Boston, 1979.

Schlossman, Steven, and Wallach, Stephanie. The crime of precocious sexuality: Female juvenile delinquency in the progressive era. *Harvard Educational Review,* February 1978, *48,* 65–94.

Stanko, Elizabeth A. *These are the cases that try themselves.* Unpublished doctoral dissertation, City University of New York, 1977.

———. Would you believe this woman? Crime and its victims: The interactive effects of myths and stereotypes during the routine operations of the criminal justice system. Paper given at the annual meeting of the Academy of Criminal Justice Sciences, Cincinnati, 1979.

Teilman, Katherine S., and Landry, Pierre H. *Gender bias in juvenile justice.* Unpublished paper, University of Southern California, 1978.

Voice from grave helps to jail slayer. *Milwaukee Journal,* October 9, 1979.

Weis, Kurt, and Borges, Sandra S. Victimology and rape: The case of the legitimate victim. *Issues in Criminology,* Fall 1973, *8,* 98–107.

Wood, Pamela L. The victim in a forcible rape case: A feminist view. *American Criminal Law Review,* Winter 1973, *11,* 335–354.

EIGHTEEN

# Barriers to Becoming a "Successful" Rape Victim[*]

## SUSAN CAROL RANDALL AND VICKI McNICKLE ROSE

### INTRODUCTION

Although the act of rape has long been regarded as serious, not until the late 1960s did a widespread definition of rape *as a social problem* begin to emerge (Rose, 1977a; 1977b). During the past decade, feminists and other interest groups, constituting an anti-rape movement, have assumed an active role in advocating changes in rape legislation and attitudes about sexual victimization, as well as in the way rape victims are treated by criminal justice officials.

---

*The research reported herein is being conducted under the auspices of grant number 5 RO1 MH31711–02, National Center for the Prevention and Control of Rape, National Institute of Mental Health.

Reforms in several areas—in the legislative arena, in the judicial sphere, and at the community level—have been noted. Nevertheless, the actual execution of current modifications in policies and laws cannot be automatically assumed at the present time. That is, whether genuine long-term changes in traditional attitudes and application of the law will be effected by these reforms is as yet uncertain.

Substantial legislative revision has been accomplished, largely as a consequence of anti-rape efforts. If not the major achievement of the movement, it is nevertheless the one which has received the most publicity. In the past, rape laws in every state were based on the assumption that the victim's accusation should be regarded with suspicion. For example, some states required that juries in rape cases be instructed that rape is "an accusation easy to be made, hard to be proved, but harder to be defended by the party accused, though innocent" (The Laws Respecting Women, 1974:312). Since 1972, when the trend toward legal reform began (Rose, 1977a; 1977b), more than 40 states have revised their rape laws (Dedmon, 1978). These laws still vary from state to state, but the various types of changes include:

1. Repeal of the above-mentioned "Lord Hale instructions" to juries.
2. Elimination of corroboration requirements which formerly necessitated evidence—*in addition to* the victim's testimony—that the alleged offense did, in fact, occur.
3. Limiting the defense attorney's ability to inquire into the victim's past sexual conduct during the trial.
4. Broadening the legal definition of "rape" so that the conception of a sexual offense is not limited to a single act (i.e., forced sexual intercourse perpetrated on a woman by a man). Generally, reform statutes define various coerced sexual acts as crimes.
5. Making rape a "sex-neutral" offense, thereby providing for prosecution of cases in which the victims are males.
6. Elimination of "spousal immunity." (In a few states, rape laws now apply to married couples; previously, in all states a man could not be charged with raping his wife.)
7. Repeal of laws requiring evidence of resistance on the part of the victim.

Although the tenor of media coverage of such changes tends to be optimistic ("Major revisions in rape laws protect victim, aid prosecution," Dedmon, 1978), the extent to which such legislation is actually having an effect is presently debatable. For example, a recent *Time* article noted that:

The Michigan law has helped dramatically increase the number of rape convictions. In that state, there were 90% more successful prosecutions in 1977 than in 1972, while rapes that have been reported climbed by 30% and arrests by 62%. ("A revolution in rape," 1979:50)

On the other hand, several researchers had previously concluded that there appeared to be no significant difference between conviction rates for rape in states with "traditional" rape legislation, as compared with states in which substantial revisions had been on the books for a sufficient length of time for effects to be evaluated (cf. Reich and Chappell, 1976; Ben-Horing, 1975:113; Chappel and Singer, 1977:266).[1]

To complicate the issue, there is a difference between the law in action and the law on the books. That is, although legislatures may enact statutes that make certain provisions, it does not necessarily follow that those specifications will be precisely followed by law enforcement agencies, the prosecutor's staff, or judges. For example, a prosecutor's criteria for deciding whether to prosecute a rape case may include *de facto* corroboration requirements. That is, even though the written law does not require evidence that supports the victim's charge, the prosecutor may assume (based upon past experience) that a conviction without such evidence is unlikely. Therefore, corroboration requirements are imposed, although they are not legally sanctioned. Similarly, a prosecutor may "require" evidence of resistance before taking a case to court.

Nor do judicial attitudes always reflect the "spirit" of the law. For example, the Texas Court of Criminal Appeals ruled in 1979 that a threat of serious bodily injury is required for conviction on the charge of aggravated rape; "[a] man who beats a woman with his bare fists does not sufficiently threaten her to make a rape an aggravated offense . . . " ("Beating ruled insufficient for aggravated rape charge," 1979). Therefore, the Court struck down the life sentence of a convicted rapist, stating that the evidence in the case was not sufficient to convict the defendant of aggravated rape or to warrant a sentence of more than 20 years. The majority opinion further noted that:

The complainant's bodily injuries consisted of black and swollen eyes, a swollen face, cuts inside her lip, bruised chest and breasts, scratched and abraded buttocks and legs, a rash from poison ivy, and pain . . . . She suffered no concussion, no broken bones, no internal injury, no scars, no serious permanent disfigurement and no protracted loss or impairment of any part of her body. ("Beating ruled insufficient for aggravated rape charge," 1979)

This ruling overturned the conviction, although the alleged offender might be retried on a lesser charge.

At the community level, the organization of rape crisis centers designed to aid victims is another major achievement of the anti-rape movement. Services rendered by such centers include counseling; staffing emergency phone lines; providing victims with information on medical, police, and court procedures; organizing community education programs on rape prevention; and the like. However, funding problems are a constant for such centers.

Another major accomplishment within the community is the provision of special services for rape victims by several institutions (in many instances at least in part due to the advocacy of rape crisis staffers)—by law-enforcement agencies, mental health centers, medical organizations, etcetera. For example, some police departments have created special units for the investigation of rapes. Nonetheless, the Law Enforcement Assistance Administration (LEAA) concluded that, "even when reforms are introduced, institutional traditions are often resistant to change; there is still a tendency for responses to rape cases and rape victims by police, hospitals and prosecutors to be 'poor,' 'inadequate,' and 'haphazard'" (Brodyaga, et al., 1975). Activists in the anti-rape movement stress redoubling anti-rape efforts in terms of attacking the societal roots of rape, and they continue to criticize the ineffectiveness of the criminal justice system (cf. D. C. Area Feminist Task Force on Violence Against Women, 1979; McDonald, 1977; "Conferences we have known . . . ," 1977).

## OFFICIAL PROCESSING OF RAPE COMPLAINTS: BARRIERS TO BECOMING A "SUCCESSFUL VICTIM"

The "common sense" view of what happens in criminal cases is one of an almost automatic progression of events: A citizen is victimized; the citizen reports the crime to the police, who apprehend the suspect; the suspect is prosecuted and punished. In reality, however, there is nothing "automatic" in the handling of criminal cases, particularly those that involve rape.

First, only a fraction of females who are raped ever report the offense to the police. Estimates of the number of unreported rapes range from approximately 4 times as many offenses as reported (President's Commission, 1967:21) to 10 times as many (Griffin, 1971; Horos, 1974; Offir, 1975) to even as high as 20 times the reported number (Kitty

Genovese Women's Project, 1977:16). There are a number of reasons why women choose not to report rape, including: concealment of the offense from parents, husband, and/or friends; fear of retaliation by the offender; shame; fear of stigma; desire to protect one's reputation; and the feeling that it would be futile to report the offense (Wood, 1972; Weis and Borges, 1973; Congressional Record, 1973). Failure to report may also be related to fear of the treatment one anticipates receiving from criminal justice officials. Dukes and Mattley (1977:73) report that three of the four most important variables for discriminating statistically between women who reported being raped and nonreporters were related to the victim's impressions of police handling of rape cases. And Schram reports that over half of the nonreporters interviewed in an LEAA survey said they feared the type of treatment they might receive from police or prosecutors ("Rape study finds irony in cases," 1978:1).

Of the more than 56,000 rapes that *were* reported in the 1975 Uniform Crime Report statistics, only 51 percent of these offenses were "cleared by arrest"; 12.4 percent resulted in conviction on the original charge, with another 3.5 percent resulting in conviction for a lesser offense (FBI, 1975:22–24). The statistics from a recent LEAA survey on rape cases in five cities are even more dismal. The arrest rate for reported rapes ranged from a low of 20 percent in Detroit to a high of 36 percent in New Orleans; in Seattle and Kansas City the prosecution rate for reported rapes was approximately 5 percent and the conviction rate around 2 percent ("Rape study finds irony in cases," 1978:1).

Of course, one reason that conviction rates in rape cases are so low is that a very large percentage of the suspects are never apprehended. Other reasons, though, have to do with the difficulty a rape victim has in becoming a "successful victim" (cf. Gagnon, 1974:245; Reynolds, 1974:64–65; Kitsuse and Cicourel, 1963:133–139). Although in most types of criminal cases both the police and the prosecutor attempt to verify a victim's allegations, the charge of rape and the victim of rape are subjected to far closer scrutiny than is the case with any other type of criminal complaint. In the remainder of this article, research conducted by the authors and others on the problem of becoming a "successful rape victim" will be examined.

Legality vs. Legitimacy

Another "commonsense" view regarding the handling of criminal cases is that if the details of an offense meet the legal requirements for definition of a "crime," the occurrence will be dealt with as a "real crime" by the officials to whom it is reported. For example, in many state penal codes the legal elements necessary to prove forcible rape include: (a) that the victim be female, the offender male[2]; (b) that the victim and offender not be married[3] or cohabiting; and (c) that the victim testify that sexual intercourse occurred, without her consent, and that she relay this information to a third party within a specified period of time. The legal criterion for lack of consent is met if the victim submitted due to force *or* the threat of force. Legal criteria, however, tell us little about the practical definition of rape used by officials. In the authors' research, for example, it was found that, although the state merely requires the victim to tell a third party about the rape within 6 months, even a day's delay in reporting to the police may raise serious suspicions concerning the victim's allegations. And, in their survey of police reporting practices, the National Institute (1977a) found that many police departments ignored the "threat of force" legal requirement for nonconsent to intercourse and instead required that *actual* physical force be used before they would define an offense as forcible rape. Approximately 28 percent of the agencies required, in addition, the use of a weapon and/or evidence that the victim had resisted (1977a:15–16). Clearly, the legal elements of the offense constitute a necessary, but not a sufficient, condition for the official handling of rape complaints.

Because criminal justice officials are deluged with many more complaints than they have resources to handle, they develop classification schemes that aid them in sifting through the myriad of offenses reported to them and in deciding which complaints merit further attention. Officials make these decisions not only on the basis of personal bias or idiosyncratic whim; they scan whatever information they have available on a case for clues as to what type of case this is based on their working knowledge of events and people, subsequently categorizing the case to typifications developed over years of experience in dealing with such complaints [cf. Skolnick's (1966) description of the "symbolic assailant" and Sudnow's (1965) discussion of "normal crimes"]. The classification schemes and discretionary decisions of particular officials are also affected by the pressures exerted from other sectors of the criminal justice system. For example, police investigators must take into account pressure from supervisors not to ignore certain cases, especially those which might result in outraging influential members of the community, as well as pressure from the prosecutor's office not to file cases which have little chance of resulting in a conviction.

Based on our own and others' research, it appears that the major classificatory scheme for rape cases that is brought to bear at the patrol stage and the early part of the police investigative stage has to do with "victim legitimacy." Legitimacy has to do with whether a victim can successfully persuade the police that she is "deserving" of the status of rape victim. The unsuccessful victim is one who is unable to convince the police or other officials that her definition of the situation is correct. The status of victim is not granted immediately; instead, a negotiation process with officials is required (Gagnon, 1974:247–248). The negotiation of the status of legitimate victim is more difficult to accomplish than other types of victimization when the allegations involve rape due to the pervasive suspicion among officials regarding such complaints. For example, Grimstad and Rennie (1973:149) note that the Chicago police training manual, as recently as 1972, instructed officers that "the first thing to do is determine if a woman [who reports a rape] is lying." And it was recently disclosed that police in Yakima County, Washington, routinely require rape *victims* to submit to polygraph tests. One of the victims, who thought that "she knew the identity of her attacker requested that the suspect be tested as well. Authorities refused, explaining that requiring a suspect to take a polygraph would violate his constitutional rights" (Faller, 1979:10). The following discussion of research on police processing of rape cases should serve to clarify the concept of legitimacy by showing what factors need be present in order to become a successful victim.


Police Discretion and Victim Legitimacy

Police patrol officers have an enormous amount of discretionary power in this country because many of the decisions they make are low-visibility, unrecorded ones that are never reflected in official records. For example, police may use their discretionary power in deciding whether or not to make an arrest when they see an offense being committed or when they learn of an offense from a victim or other citizen. Police may decide whether to accept a citizen- or victim-initiated complaint as "valid" and investigate the allegation further or simply ignore the complaint without filing an official offense report. If they do file a report on behalf of the complainant, they can decide, within certain limits, what offense to record, which may or may not be the same as the offense alleged by the victim.

In contrast with many other types of offenses, police mobilization in rape cases is usually citizen initiated rather than police initiated. Research (cf. Skolnick, 1966; Black and Reiss, 1967, 1970) has shown that in cases where there is a complainant, it is not as easy for police simply to ignore an offense as it is when they are the only ones who

observe the behavior. Nevertheless, patrol officers have considerable lee-
way in deciding how to handle rape complaints. If patrol officers decide
that a rape victim's complaint is unsubstantiated, they may refuse to
investigate further. Rather than filing an official report, they may engage
in what is called "unofficial unfounding" of a complaint. This is done by
recording the rape complaint not as a rape but in a catchall category
such as "investigations of persons" (Comment, 1968:279n), "suspicious
circumstances" (Skolnick, 1966:170–172), or, in the author's research, a
category called "meet complainant." In other words, many rape complaints may never be recorded as officially reported crimes.

There has been little systematic research conducted so far on the
characteristics of victims who are able to lodge their complaints successfully as compared with those whose allegations of rape wind up as unof-
ficially unfounded. However, Peters (1975:186) found, in a study of rape
victims in Philadelphia, that what may be termed a victim's "legitimacy"
is influenced by such factors as (a) the amount of physical harm (in
addition to the rape) suffered by the victim, (b) the victim's relationship
with the offender, and (c) the amount of resistance offered by the victim.
In addition, the National Institute's (1977a:27) findings from its survey
of police department practices in the handling of rape complaints may
be useful in distinguishing the characteristics of victims who are likely to
be seen as legitimate. The Institute asked respondents to select the factors they viewed as most important in deciding whether to proceed with
the investigation of an alleged rape. The most frequently chosen factors
were proof of penetration; use of physical force; promptness of reporting; extent of injury to victim; relationship between victim and suspect;
and circumstances of initial contact. It should be noted that most of the
factors mentioned in Peters' and the National Institute's studies are
related to external verification that the offense did indeed occur (e.g.,
physical injury) and to evidence of the nonconsensual nature of the
offense (e.g., victim-offender relationship).

Even when police officers decide to file an official report concerning
a victim's rape allegation, they may not report the offense as rape. For
example, in the National Institute's survey of police handling of rape
cases, they found *over one hundred* different charging options used by
police as an alternative to a rape charge, including such charges as public indecency, lewd and lascivious acts, sexual misconduct, and indecent
exposure, as well as some property crimes such as burglary and trespass-
ing (National Institute, 1977a:16). In multiple-offense cases (i.e., where
the offender engages in a nonsexual offense along with rape), the sexual
offense may never be recorded. As Skolnick found, in a combined rape-
robbery offense, "the robbery may appear easier to prove than the

rape—for example, if corroborating evidence has been found on the person of the defendant—[so] the patrolman reports a robbery and includes the surrounding circumstances" (1966:171).

If the police officer who initially talks to the victim defines her and her complaint as sufficiently legitimate to warrant the filing of an official rape offense report, the case then generally moves into the jurisdiction of a police investigator or detective.[4] Investigators, like patrol officers, are overburdened with cases, and they too must mentally classify the reports they receive in terms of their priorities. Their first concern is usually to check the report made by the patrol officer and make their own determination of legitimacy of the case and the victim, in order to decide which cases merit immediate attention.

Investigators do not have quite as extensive discretionary power as patrol officers as they cannot totally ignore a complaint referred to them; they must file a report stating their decision as to how to dispose of a case. They do, however, have wide discretion as to how actively to pursue a case. Their response to the offense report submitted by a patrol officer can range from the extreme of officially unfounding the complaint—without ever even contacting the victim, witnesses, or suspect—to launching a full-scale investigation of the complaint. Again, official action or inaction on rape complaints is related to how legitimate the victim and her case are perceived as being. Generally, the patrol officer's offense report is the first tool an investigator has on which to base a determination of the merits of a complaint. This can present serious problems for the successful processing of a rape complaint, as patrol reports frequently omit important information (e.g., whether there were witnesses; whether the victim received a medical examination for rape; whether a weapon was used, etc.) and sometimes even contain inaccurate data (e.g., the wrong phone number and/or address for the victim; misleading information about the victim's interaction with the suspect, etc.). Later, if the investigator views the initial report as worthy of being pursued, the information in the offense report will be supplemented or modified by interviews with the victim, with witnesses (if any), and with available physical evidence such as the medical report on the victim, fingerprints of the suspect, and so on.

Rape complaints that are viewed by investigators as illegitimate are frequently disposed of by being classified as unfounded.[5] The FBI's Uniform Crime Report guidelines state that an offense can be unfounded *only* if "investigation shows that no offense occurred or was attempted" (FBI, 1974:43). However, police agency practices rarely conform to this regulation. For example, in 18 percent of police departments surveyed by the National Institute, it was their practice to unfound an offense if too much time elapsed between its occurrence and the report to the police (1977a:17). In addition:

> The vast majority said that lack of victim cooperation or withdrawal of the complaint by the victim could lead to the unfounding of a report *despite the fact that UCR guidelines specifically state that lack of victim cooperation is not a legitimate reason to unfound a report of a crime* [emphasis added]. (1977a:17)

Not only did the National Institute's survey reveal wide variation in unfounding practices between jurisdictions but also such extensive variation in procedures for unfounding crimes *within* agencies that "the delineation of a department-wide policy has little meaning" (1977a:17).

In short, the term *unfounded* need not imply that a rape did not in fact occur. LeGrand (1973:228–29) lists some of the reasons given for unfounding rape complaints that bear no necessary relation to the question of whether or not the offense took place: (1) evidence that the victim was intoxicated; (2) delay in reporting by the victim; (3) lack of physical condition supporting the allegation; (4) refusal to submit to a medical examination; (5) the previous relationship of victim and offender; and (6) the use of a weapon without accompanying assault and battery. LeGrand notes that police also unfound complaints because victims fail to preserve necessary physical evidence (for instance, they may douche or shower before reporting the crime), or because victims are too emotionally upset, too young, too afraid, or too embarrassed to cooperate with the ordeal of an official investigation.

A comprehensive study of official unfounding practices was conducted in Philadelphia in 1966 and 1967 (Comment, 1968). The researchers reviewed a sample of investigative reports detailing rape and attempted-rape allegations and interviewed investigators to determine what factors affect the likelihood of a complaint being deemed unfounded. Following is a brief summary of some of the major findings:

1. *Physical condition of the victim and promptness of report:* "During the interviews with investigators, . . . the physical condition of the complainant was one of the factors most frequently mentioned as being determinative of the investigator's initial reaction to the complaint and of the 'tone' or nature of the investigation. The other factor was promptness of complaint" (1968:287n).

2. *Medical evidence:* "negative violence reports caused 47 percent of the offenses to be unfounded, while positive violence reports resulted in only 8 percent being unfounded. . . . [T]he police

place much greater reliance upon the violence aspect of the medical report than upon the intercourse aspect" (1968:288). This appears to be due to the recognition of the inaccuracy and inconclusiveness of medical reports on penetration. "However, the complainant's refusal to submit to medical attention resulted in an unfounded offense 56 percent of the time" (1968:289).

3. *Victim-offender relationship:* The largest percentage of unfoundings came from cases in which the alleged offender was a date (43 percent) or an acquaintance (28 percent) as compared with a friend (19 percent) or a stranger (18 percent) (1968:291).

4. *Alcohol involvement:* Where the investigative report mentioned intoxication of the victim, 82 percent of the complaints were unfounded as compared with 15 percent where there was no mention of it (1968:292).

5. *Presence of a weapon and evidence of victim resistance:* When a weapon was present, only 16 percent of the cases involving no victim resistance were unfounded by the police in comparison with 32 percent where there was neither a weapon nor resistance (1968: 299).

### The Issues of Victim Credibility and Consent

In the previous section the findings of several researchers were presented concerning factors associated with patrol officer and investigator decisions about whether and how to proceed with rape complaints. But why are variables such as "promptness of reporting, use of a weapon in the perpetration of an offense, victim-suspect relationship," and so on, important in police determinations of the legitimacy of a victim and hence their willingness to process a rape complaint? Part of the answer to this question was alluded to earlier: Criminal justice officials are presented with many more cases than they can possibly investigate and process fully, including many cases about which they have little doubt as to whether the offense did, in a strict legal sense, occur. The presence of necessary legal elements, then, becomes only one criterion of a rape case that is "worthy of further attention." The other factors that research as found to effect police processing are largely related to what may be called the issues of victim "credibility" and "consent." That is, a legitimate victim is one who was not only victimized in a legal sense but who shows herself to be a credible complainant and who can convince the police that her assault was nonconsensual.

A rape victim establishes her credibility as someone who "deserves to be believed" by behaving in a manner and showing emotions that police deem appropriate to someone who has "really" been raped. The most important actions a woman who has been raped must engage in if she is to become a successful victim are prompt (which generally means immediate) reporting of the offense to the police (or at least to a third party, such as a parent) and prompt submission to a medical (pelvic) examination. Delays in reporting raise questions in the minds of officials as to whether the victim was really assaulted or whether she merely fabricated a story to cover illicit sexual behavior on her part which she wishes to hide from her parents, friends, or spouse. The first response of someone who has "really" been raped, according to most police, is to notify the authorities. That this view is not limited to police is well illustrated by the reaction of a prosecutor in a recent case. In 1978 several football players at a university in Florida were accused by a coed of gang raping her in a dormitory. The prosecutor in charge of presenting cases to the grand jury "said there was a good possibility the players might not be charged because the incident wasn't reported until 12 hours after it allegedly happened" ("Charges may not be filed . . .," 1978:A-3). Similarly, if a victim delays having a pelvic examination performed (in order for physicians to obtain samples of semen or other evidence of recent intercourse), this raises serious doubts concerning her credibility. Great emphasis is placed on the medical examination despite the fact that the evidence obtained is often inconclusive. Still, the assumption is that a "truly legitimate" victim will do everything possible to provide officials with evidence concerning her attack. A major problem with this assumption is that many women are not aware of the importance of having such an examination and/or of not bathing or douching prior to it. Although in most jurisdictions patrol officers are supposed to instruct rape victims concerning the importance of preserving this evidence and to provide transportation of the victim to a hospital or clinic where she can obtain this examination, this is by no means a universal practice.

In addition to prompt reporting and submission to medical examination, a "legitimate" victim must display visible emotional trauma appropriate to the ordeal she has suffered as well as an attitude of active cooperation with the authorities. Research on the "rape trauma syndrome" experienced by many victims indicates, however, that women are likely to display behavior greatly at odds with official perceptions of what is "appropriate" to such a victim (cf. Burgess and Holmstrom, 1974). For example, denial of the offense to oneself is not uncommon, resulting in reporting delays; emotional shock frequently results in a calm outward appearance that may be misinterpreted as lack of caring;

and a frequently early impulse is to rid oneself of all remnants of the attack (e.g., by throwing out underclothing and by bathing), thus inadvertently destroying essential evidence. In general, the less a victim's attitude and behavior correspond to the official conception of what is appropriate, the more important *external* verification of her story becomes, in the way of witnesses and physical evidence of the attack. If such corroboration of her story is absent, it is indeed difficult for her to successfully press her complaint.

In addition to establishing her credibility, the "legitimate" victim must also convince authorities that she was in no way responsible for her victimization. This is often not an easy task as the view that rape is quite frequently victim precipitated (and hence not really a crime) is prevalent throughout the criminal justice system, from the police to judges. For example, the Philadelphia judges interviewed by Bohmer (1976:227-228) divided rape victims into three basic categories: (1) "genuine victims," (2) "women who are 'victims' but who were 'asking for it,'" and (3) "vindictive females." A Wisconsin judge, Archie Simonson, gained nationwide attention in 1977 when he gave two youths extremely light sentences for rape, claiming that most rape victims bring the crime on themselves by wearing provocative clothing (i.e., they fit in the "asking for it" category above) ("Judge claims support . . . ", 1977: A-5). That Simonson was later recalled by voters does not mean that his opinion concerning victim precipitation is unique. Shortly after his infamous statements on rape, the California Court of Appeals voted unanimously to free a convicted rapist because the victim had been hitchhiking (Shearer, 1977:9).

When patrol officers review a victim's story or investigators a patrol officer's report, they look for clues that might give them reason to suspect the nature of the victim's involvement in the offense. For example, if the relationship between the victim and the offender is anything other than "total strangers," this gives rise to suspicions concerning the role the victim may have played in precipitating the offense. The doubts are generally the greatest if the victim and her assailant have ever the consensual sex or have even dated; if the victim was picked up voluntarily by the offender (e.g., at a bar, a party, etc.); or if the victim and offender partook of alcohol or other drugs prior to the offense. In order to counteract suspicions regarding the consent issue, evidence that the victim actively resisted and that she was overcome by overwhelming physical force or a weapon is important. As with the credibility issue, external confirmation (e.g., eye-witnesses, physical injuries, torn clothing) of her claim of nonconsensual assault becomes increasingly crucial the more her victimization departs from the "total stranger with a gun" motif.

## Concluding Remarks

Being able to persuade the police that one is a legitimate rape victim is not enough, however, to ensure that one's complaint will be actively pursued by the police and/or prosecutor. A successful victim is one who is *both* legitimate *and* whose case is prosecutable. Although the first condition for a rape to be seen by officials as prosecutable is that the victim be legitimate, many such victims to not have prosecutable cases. For example, the legitimacy of elderly victims who are raped in their homes in the middle of the night is rarely questioned by police. However sympathetic the police may be, they can rarely proceed with the complaint because such victims frequently have poor eyesight and poor hearing and thus are unable to provide the police with leads as to the offender. The second of prosecutability, then, is that the police be able to apprehend a suspect and be provided with evidence (e.g., conclusive identification of the perpetrator by the victim) that links the suspect with the offense. Unless there are no doubts at all as to a victim's legitimacy, corroborating evidence (i.e., evidence *other than* the victim's identification of the suspect and her testimony) is usually required for a prosecutable case. And such external evidence that corroborates the victim's story is of special import if the *suspect* is not easily seen as legitimate (i.e., as the type of man who would do such a thing).

The issues of victim legitimacy and case prosecutability raise important questions regarding the rights of rape victims to have their cases fully processed. In recent years there has been some attention given to the idea of victim rights (cf. Drapkin and Viano, 1975), and some states have established victim compensation programs although these are generally poorly funded and often require the victim to wait months before any compensation is forthcoming ("Victims of crime ask . . .," 1977:16). However, victims do not legally have a right to force the state to prosecute a case. Criminal violations are offenses against the state, not, strictly speaking, against the individual; hence, the state's representative, the district attorney, has complete discretionary power[6] to decide what cases to accept for prosecution. And, of course, in order for the district attorney to accept a case for prosecution, the police must have been able to apprehend a suspect and there must be sufficient evidence (i.e., satisfying the probable cause requirement) to charge the suspect with the offense. The only legal remedy available to a rape victim who is dissatisfied with the processing of her case or with the sentence imposed on the defendant is to file a civil suit against the defendant (cf. "Angry rape victim sues. . .,"1976:7; "Victims of crime ask . . .," 1977:16). Again, though, there must be an identified suspect and sufficient evidence linking the suspect to the crime for a civil suit to be successful.

That only a relatively small number of rape cases are ever successful can, to a large extent, be accounted for by three factors:

1. Inadequate resources in the criminal justice system to handle all criminal complaints,
2. General lack of knowledge on the part of women as to how they should react when they have been raped (e.g., prompt reporting, preservation of evidence, etc.).
3. Societal attitudes concerning the crime of rape and the victim of rape (which are reflected in the attitudes of criminal justice officials).

The anti-rape movement can, and already has to some extent, affected the second and third problems listed here. Whether or not the movement can provide the impetus for taxpayers to provide additional resources for the official handling of rape and other crimes is less certain.[7] It is very unlikely, at any rate, that the high level of movement activity evidenced in the mid-1970s can be maintained for an extended period of time (cf. Mauss, 1975:57–71; Rose, 1977a, 1977b).

While it will be some years before we can make an overall assessment of the movement's legacy (Rose, 1977a, 1977b), educational and consciousness-raising efforts of anti-rape organizations *have* had some impact, although apparent changes may be largely superficial: "Encountering people who know the 'correct' phrases about rape without a corresponding change in consciousness is becoming quite common" (Klein, 1977:9). Further, some feminists allege that the anti-rape movement is being co-opted and warn that activists must not lose sight of the ultimate goal: *eliimination* of rape—as well as all other forms of violence against women—via attacking its social causes and the sexist attitudes that support it ("Conferences we have known . . . ,' 1977: Klein, 1977).

## NOTES

1. It may be several years before this issue is resolved, as some time must elapse between the passage of legislation and the evaluation of its implementation. For example, the effect of Michigan's 1975 sexual conduct law, which has served as a model for legislative changes in other states, is currently being studied ("New rape law evaluated," 1979:5).

2. More than two dozen states have now made their rape laws sex neutral thus recognizing that women may be perpetrators and men may be victims

("Major revisions in rape laws . . . ," 1978:B-8). However, rape complaints lodged by males against females are exceedingly rare and convictions almost nonexistent.

3. Approximately one-quarter of the states have recently repealed "spousal immunity" clauses which prevent husbands from being charged with rape of wives. In all but New Jersey, Oregon, and South Dakota, however, the husband and wife must be living apart in order for the rape law to apply ("Major Revisions in Rape Laws . . . ," 1978:B-8). Despite the changes in these laws, it is still extremely rare for a husband to be charged, much less convicted, of raping his wife although a Massachusetts jury recently (September 1979) did so. At the time of the offense for which the man was convicted, the couple had been granted a divorce but the divorce decree was not yet final ("Man convicted of raping wife," 1979).

4. Some of the large metropolitan police departments now have special sexual assault investigative units, but in most departments rapes are handled by general assault investigators with little or no specialized training in dealing with rape cases.

5. Other methods of disposing of such cases include (a) classifying them as "suspended, pending further developments" (and then not actively pursuing them), or (b) filing a prosecution report with a "special designation" (e.g., "grand jury referral") indicating to the prosecutor that the investigator has serious doubts about the case.

6. In many of the jurisdictions that have a grand jury system, grand juries have investigative powers of their own and may bring indictments directly. Generally, though, the grand jury reviews only those rape cases presented to it by the prosecutor.

7. The movement may have effected a switch in priorities in some jurisdictions so that rape cases receive more attention than they did in the past; however, as this entails diverting important resources from other areas of criminal investigation and processing, such a move may be met with resistance by advocates of other interests. For example, homicide investigators and/or prosecutors may protest that the offense with which they deal is the most heinous and deserves the greatest resource allocation.

# REFERENCES

Angry rape victim sues, jury shares her anger. *The National Observer,* February 14, 1976, 7.
A revolution in rape. *Time Magazine,* April 2, 1979, 50.
Beating ruled insufficient for aggravated rape charge. *Dallas Morning News,* June 14, 1979.
Ben Horin, Daniel. Is rape a sex crime? *The Nation,* August 1975, *221,* 112–115.

Black, D. J., and Reiss, A. J. Patterns of behavior in police and citizen inter-
actions. Section 1 of Studies of Crime and Law Enforcement in Major
Metropolitan Areas, Volume II. Washington, D.C.: U.S. Government
Printing Office.
————. Police control of juveniles. *American Sociological Review*, 1970, *35*,
63–77.
Bohmer, Carol. Judicial attitudes toward rape victims. In William B. Sanders
and Howard C. Daudistel (Eds.), *The criminal justice process*. New York:
Praeger Publishers, 1976, 225–232.
Brodyaga, Lisa, Gates, Margaret, Singer, Susan, Tucker, Marna, and White,
Richardson. Rape and its victims: A report for citizens, health facilities, and
criminal justice agencies. National Institute of Law Enforcement and Crimi-
nal Justice, Law Enforcement Assistance Administration, U.S. Depart-
ment of Justice, 1975.
Burgess, Ann W., and Holmstrom, Linda L. Rape trauma syndrome. *American
Journal of Psychiatry*, 1974, 131, 981–986.
Chappell, Duncan, and Singer, Susan. Rape in New York City: A study of
material in the police files and its meaning. In Duncan Chappell, Robley
Geis and Gilbert Geis (Eds.), *Forcible rape*. New York: Columbia Uni-
versity, 1977, Chapter 12.
Charges may not be filed in alleged campus rape case. *Dallas Times Herald*,
February 4, 1978, A-3.
Comment: Police discretion and the judgment that a crime has been committed:
Rape in Philadelphia. *University of Pennsylvania Law Review*, 1968, *117*,
277-322.
Conferences we have known . . . and money we haven't seen. *Feminist Alliance
Against Rape Newsletter*, May/June, 1977,10.
Congressional Record. 93rd Congress, 1st session, Vol. 119, No. 134, Septem-
ber 17, 1973.
D. C. Area Feminist Alliance Task Force on Violence Against Women. March
to stop violence against women: Underlying principles. *Aegis*, May/June,
1979, 37–41.
Dedmon, Jonathan. Major revisions in rape laws protect victim, aid prosecu-
tion. *Pittsburgh Press*, November 26, 1978, B-8.
Drapkin, Israel, and Viano, Emilio. *Victimology: A new focus* (Volume III).
Lexington, Massachusetts: Lexington Books, 1975.
Dukes, Richard L., and Mattley, Christine L. Predicing rape victim reportage.
*Sociology and Social Research*, October 1977, *62*, 63–84.
Faller, Nancy. Lie test for rape victims. *Mother Jones*, July, 1979.
Federal Bureau of Investigation. *Uniform crime reporting handbook*. Washing-
ton, D.C.: U.S. Government Printing Office, 1974.
————. *Uniform crime reports*. Washington, D.C.: U.S. Government Print-
ing Office, 1975.
Gagnon, John H. Sexual conduct and crime. In Daniel Glaser (Ed.), *Handbook
of criminology*. Chicago: Rand McNally College Publishing Company,
1974.

Griffin, Susan. Rape: The all-American crime. *Ramparts,* September 1971, 26–35.

Grimstad, Kirsten, and Rennie, Susan. *The new woman's survival catalog.* New York: Coward, McCann and Geoghegan Berkley Publishing Corporation, 1973.

Horos, Carol V. *Rape.* New Canaan, Connecticut: Tobey Publishing Co., Inc., 1974.

Judge claims support for his views on rape. *Dallas Times Herald,* May 28, 1977, A-5.

Kitsuse, John I., and Cicourel, Aaron. A note on the use of official statistics. *Social Problems,* Fall 1963, *11,* 131–139.

Kitty Genovese Womens' Project. Kitty Genovese Womens' Project Report on Rape Offenders in Dallas County. New York: 316 5th Avenue, Suite 301, 1977.

The laws respecting women (reprinted from the J. Johnson edition, London, 1977). Dobbs Ferry, NY: Oceana Publications, Inc., 1974.

Klein, Freada. Developing new models: Rape crisis centers. *Feminist Alliance Against Rape News,* July/August 1977, 9–10.

LeGrand, Camille E. Rape and rape laws: Sexism in society and law. *California Law Review,* May 1973, *63,* 919–941.

Man convicted of raping wife. *Dallas Times Herald,* September 22, 1979.

Major revisions in rape laws protect victim, aid prosecution. *Pittsburgh Press,* November 26, 1978, B-8.

National Institute of Law Enforcement and Criminal Justice. Forcible rape: A national survey of the response by police (Volume I). Washington, D.C.: U.S. Government Printing Office, 1977.

Offir, Carole Wade. Don't take it lying down. *Psychology Today,* January 1975,73.

Mauss, Armand L. *Social problems as social movements.* Philadelphia: J. B. Lippincott Company, 1975.

McDonald, Nancy. 'All in the family' Reviewed. *Feminist Alliance Against Rape Newsletter,* September/October 1977, 11–12.

Peters, Joseph. The Philadelphia rape victim study. In Israel Drapkin and Emilio Viano (Eds.), *Victimology: A new focus* (Volume III). Lexington, Massachusetts: D. C. Heath, 1975.

President's Commission on Law Enforcement and Administration of Justice. *The challenge of crime in a free society.* Washington, D.C.: U.S. Government Printing Office, 1967.

Rape study finds irony in cases. *Dallas Times Herald,* August 7, 1978, 1.

Reich, Jay, and Chappell, Duncan. *The prosecutorial response to Michigan's criminal sexual conduct law: Business as usual.* Unpublished manuscript, 1976.

Reynolds, Janice M. Rape as social control. *Catalyst,* Winter 1974, 62–67.

Rose, Vicki McNickle. Rape as a social problem: A byproduct of the feminist movement. *Social Problems,* October 1977, *25,* 75–89. (a)

————. The rise of the rape problem. In Armand L. Mauss and Julie C. Wolfe (Eds.), *This land of promises: The rise and fall of social problems in America.* Philadelphia: J. B. Lippincott Company, 1977, 167–195. (b)

Shearer, Lloyd. Rape and judges. *Parade Magazine,* October 21, 1977,9.

Skolnick, Jerome. *Justice Without Trial.* New York: John Wiley and Sons, 1966.

Sudnow, David. Normal crimes: Sociological features of the penal code in a public defender office. *Social Problems,* Winter 1965, *12,* 255–276.

Victims of crime ask: 'What about our rights?' *Chicago Tribune,* January 30, 1977, 16.

Weiss, Kurt, and Borges, Sandra S. Victimology and rape: The case of the legitimate victim. *Issues in Criminology,* Fall 1973, *8,* 71–115.

Wood, Pamela Lakes. The victim in a forcible rape case: A feminist view. *American Criminal Law Review,* Fall 1972, *11,* 335–354.

NINETEEN

# Judicial Paternalism and the Female Status Offender: Training Women to Know Their Place*

MEDA CHESNEY-LIND

The controversy surrounding the juvenile court system's jurisdiction over youth charged with noncriminal or status offenses has taken on the character of a national debate, and yet one important aspect of this issue seems consistently neglected. Although females constitute only about a quarter of the juvenile court populations across the country, they may be a majority of those charged with noncriminal offenses.[1] Young women, it seems, are far more likely than their male counterparts to be arrested and referred to court for offenses which apply only to youth: "running away from home," "incorrigibility," "waywardness," "curfew violation," or being a "person in need of supervision." One recent national study found, for example, that 75 per cent of the females in the juvenile justice system were there for status offenses rather than criminal

*Reprinted from *Crime and Delinquency,* Volume 23, Number 2, April 1977.

behavior.[2] Simply stated, girls account for an inordinate proportion of persons brought into the juvenile justice system for status offenses.

Why are women, who generally constitute a very small proportion of those in the criminal justice system, so frequently charged with status offenses? The answer to this question supplies both a major explanation of the court's relatively harsh response to youth labeled as status offenders and an important argument for the removal of these cases from court jurisdiction.

## ENFORCEMENT OF PATRIARCHAL AUTHORITY

A brief look at the history of the juvenile court provides a partial explanation for the preponderance of women charged with status offenses in the court populations across the country. Contrary to the popular myth that juvenile courts were established to prevent juveniles from being tried and sentenced as adults, the actual history of the institution reveals quite different motives. In 1899, the first juvenile court was established in Chicago, culminating a long campaign to create a separate judicial system for youthful offenders. While using rhetoric about protecting children from the horrors of the adult system, the court's founders were actually interested in a system which would shore up "traditional" American institutions like the family. Imagining these to be threatened by foreign immigration and urbanization, the largely middle-class, Anglo-Saxon conservatives set up a court to reinforce their definition of appropriate adolescent deportment.[3]

Consequently, they were not interested in children accused of the classic crimes against property, nor were they opposed to the imprisonment of youth. Instead, says sociologist Anthony Platt, they were concerned with insuring the normative behavior of youth by instilling proper attitudes toward authority, family relationships, and personal morality. Assuming the natural dependence of children, they created a special court to prevent "premature" independence and to monitor and enforce traditional family authority.

This mission, which originally supplied the logic for the arrest, detention, and incarceration of youth for "incorrigibility," "ungovernability," or "running away from home," is not simply of historical interest. The court's continuing commitment to the enforcement of family authority is clearly reflected in recent statistics that show a steady increase in the proportion of these cases in the court populations.[4] But more to the point, the institution's undiminished willingness to involve itself in the enforcement of traditional family values is particularly ominous for young women.

The traditional family has always exerted greater control over the behavior of its daughters in order to protect their virginity or virginal reputation. A "good girl" is obedient to parental demands and, while sexy, is never sexual. Sons, on the other hand, are encouraged by their parents to "sow wild oats," and their independent behavior is, if not encouraged, then at least tolerated.

Like good parents, police and court personnel respond differently to the indiscretions of young men and women. Routine procedures encourage officials to ignore all but the most extreme misbehavior of boys while looking very closely at all girls' delinquency. The juvenile justice system is concerned that girls allowed to run wild might be tempted to experiment sexually and thus endanger their marriageability.

The court involves itself in the enforcement of adolescent morality and parental authority through the vehicle of status offenses. The use of these offense categories, it will be shown, creates a *de facto* double standard of juvenile justice in America, one for men and another for women, and results in the preponderance of young women facing such charges before the court.


## POLICE DISCRETION

Much attention has been given recently to the startling increases in the "female crime rate," and there seems to be some basis for this concern. The number of female arrests is increasing, and this is especially true for adolescent women. Between 1960 and 1974, arrests of adult women were up 76.5 per cent; during the same period, arrests of women under eighteen were up 235.1 per cent.[5] The meaning of this dramatic increase is less clear, however; and facile characterizations of adolescent women enthusiastically breaking into formerly male bastions of criminal activity obscure more than they explain.

Self-report studies measuring the actual volume and character of juvenile misconduct have shown that official statistics consistently underestimate girls' criminal activity and overestimate status offenses.[6] One of these studies, for example, showed that status offenses comprised "only 8 per cent of girls' delinquent acts and not much less of boys', 6 per cent."[7] The overemphasis of girls charged with status offenses has been explained, in part, by the routine police practice of ignoring (or releasing without arrest) girls accused of criminal activity and arresting those suspected of juvenile offenses.[8]

Recent arrest statistics published by the Federal Bureau of Investigation indicate a possible change in police behavior and an increase in the number of juvenile women arrested for criminal behavior (particularly larceny and drug offenses). These changes in enforcement patterns, while producing dramatic percentage increases in certain offense categories, do not signal a basic change in female delinquency or the official response to it. Nearly one-third (28.6 per cent) of the young women arrested in 1974 were taken into custody for either running away from home or curfew violations, and these women, along with others arrested for uniquely juvenile offenses, are far more likely to remain in the juvenile justice system than are their counterparts charged with crimes.

Decisions after arrest, which determine whether a youth will be "counseled and released" or "referred to court," reveal a consistent pattern of police paternalism that penalizes women. In 1965, the last year for which national data are available, girls charged with juvenile offenses made up about a third of those arrested but about half of those referred to juvenile courts. Only about 20 per cent of the boys were referred to court for these offenses. Boys were more likely to find their way to court for criminal offenses: burglary, larceny, and car theft. [9]

More recent statistics from Honolulu indicate that the situation has not changed. [10] In 1972, girls charged with noncriminal offenses were far more likely than girls charged with crimes to be referred to juvenile court. Only 6.1 per cent of the girls arrested for the most serious adult offenses and 12.7 per cent of the girls arrested for less serious adult offenses were referred to court, compared with 33.7 per cent of those arrested for juvenile offenses. The police were also a good deal more likely to refer a girl than a boy arrested for a juvenile offense to court (33.6 per cent and 22.7 per cent, respectively).

This harsh police response to the noncriminal activity of young girls is, in some respects, the result of parental attitudes. Boys and girls who are brought to the attention of the police for criminal offenses have natural advocates in their parents; but three out of every four youths charged with status offenses are, according to one study, brought to the attention of the police by their parents. [11]

The parental role in the initiation of police action also explains why girls make up so preponderant a part of persons charged with these noncriminal offenses. Parents have different standards of behavior for their sons and daughters; and they tend to demand greater obedience and chastity from their daughters. For example, they would seldom ask police to arrest a son who fails to come home from a date at the expected time, but this is a common reason for seeking a daughter's arrest. Since the statutes simply require adolescents to obey their parents, the police often find themselves unwittingly involved in the unequal application of the law.

## DISCRIMINATION IN DETENTION

After arrest, this double standard victimizes females who enter the juvenile justice system in yet another fashion. Not only are girls charged with violations of their sexual role more likely than boys to be referred to court, but they are more likely than boys to be held in jails or juvenile detention facilities across the nation.

In 1971, girls constituted only 22.3 per cent of all juvenile arrests but 33 per cent of those held in juvenile detention centers. Further, 75 per cent of the detained girls but only between 20 and 30 per cent of the detained boys are charged with noncriminal offenses. Girls may also stay longer in detention since youths detained for juvenile offenses stayed longer in these facilities than did youths charged with crimes.[12] Data collected by Paul Lerman in New York indicated that adolescents charged with juvenile offenses were twice as likely as youths charged with crimes to be detained for more than thirty days. Since girls are overwhelmingly charged with these offenses, it seems likely that they spend more time in detention than their male counterparts.

These statistics are startling and indicate that girls who have not violated the law are punished more severely after arrest than either boys or girls charged with crimes. Like good parents, the family court officials feel the need to "protect" their "daughters"—usually from sexual experimentation.

Further evidence of this paternalistic interest in girls' sexuality is found in the widespread use of pelvic examinations in detention centers across the nation. Elizabeth Gold reports that all girls brought before the family the court in New York are given vaginal smears, even girls brought before the court for nonsexual offenses.[13] Similarly, in Philadelphia, each girl who enters the Youth Study Center, regardless of age, must submit to an internal examination. Some may argue that, given the problem of venereal disease among teen-agers, such examination is medically justified. However, it must be remembered that the exam takes place in an institutional setting and in concert with other entry rituals and, thus, is both degrading and depersonalizing.

For example, one detention center surveyed by the National Council of Jewish Women required all girls to undergo a pelvic exam "to determine if they are pregnant" and at the same time subjected them "in a group" to the Cuprex Delouse test, in which their bodies are sprayed with a "burning substance."[14] The director of the Philadelphia Youth Study Center was a little more specific about the administration of the pelvic exam required of all women who entered his institution:

"We do put a girl on the table in the stirrups and we have a smear
. . . . We do have a swab. You go in and get a smear." When asked
whether a girl who refused to undergo this pelvic exam would be
placed in "medical lock-up"—a polite term for solitary confinement—he responded, "Yes, we may have to."[15]

Aside from being a degrading experience for a young girl and probably a violation of her right to privacy, the routine administration of
pelvic exams demonstrates the court's assumption that girls who come
to the attention of the police and the courts are quite probably engaging
in "promiscuous" sexual activity; in short, the court tends to equate
female delinquency with sexuality. Like adult women, girls are more
likely to be labeled as "carriers" of venereal disease and at fault if they
are pregnant and unwed. Such labels as "runaway" and "incorrigible"
are buffer charges for suspected sexuality, providing legal categories to
cover the court's real interest in the girl's obedience to sexual norms. It
is for this reason that girls charged with these offenses are so often incarcerated and subjected to pelvic exams.

This perspective also explains why the court sees no problem with
the lengthy incarceration of girls who are not charged with crimes.
Court personnel argue that the girls "have no place to go." In fact, court
officials demand that the girl choose between continued incarceration
and some form of court-arranged and court-approved living situation.
Like the girl's parents, they feel that the girl must be controlled and
"protected" from the temptations of the street. Only rarely does the
court manifest the same concern for the protection of boys in its jurisdiction.

## JUDICIAL PATERNALISM

It is within the court system proper that the paternalistic nature of juvenile justice becomes explicit. While girls are about one-quarter of the
total juvenile court population, they are apparently the majority of those
charged with juvenile offenses.

What happens to girls charged with these juvenile offenses once they
enter the system? Since they have committed no crime, they would be
expected to disappear from the system rapidly. Yet, while some girls do
indeed receive lenient treatment, all evidence seems to suggest that they
are the ones referred for law violations.

At intake, probation officers determine which of the cases are the
most serious, and those are generally referred to a formal hearing before
a juvenile court judge. One would assume that the serious categories of

offenses would have higher rates of referral. But such is not the case. Astonishingly, many "PINS" or noncriminal cases are referred by the intake officer to a hearing rather than to informal procedure.

The New York researchers found that, to intake officers, parental objection to a daughter's boy friend (64 per cent of the referred cases) was more serious than a charge of larceny (57 per cent of the cases referred). Referral rates are higher for verbal abuse than for assault; a refusal to obey and coming home late will get you before a judge more quickly than arson or illegal entry.[16] Data from Honolulu during 1967–72 are less specific but show that girls were six times more likely than boys to appear before a juvenile court judge on their first offense.

This treatment is often the result of pressure from parents. In the New York study, for example, Andrews and Cohn reported that parents come to probation interviews armed with a long list of offenses that the child has allegedly committed. These charges may range from running away from home or being truant to having a boy friend the parents do not approve of, staying out late at night, "having an abortion against parental wishes, sleeping all day,, . . . banging a door in reaction to a parental command, wanting to get married, . . . and being an "invertebrate [sic] liar.'"[17]

Juvenile court judges also seem to participate enthusiastically, though perhaps unconsciously, in the judicial enforcement of the female role. Part of their behavior, while discriminatory, is understandable. Their legal background provides them with clear guidelines when confronting youths charged with crimes. Standards of evidence are clear, elements of the crime are laid down by statute, and the youth's civil rights are, at least to some extent, protected by law.

But in the case of a boy or a girl charged with incorrigibility or ungovernability, the court is without legal guidelines. Many of these judges find themselves in a legal never-never land; and, in this void, fall back on the role of benevolent but harsh parent which is built into the juvenile justice system.

Andrews and Cohn's review of the handling of cases of ungovernability in New York concluded with the comment that judges were acting "upon personal feelings and predilections in making decisions" and gave as evidence for this statement several courtroom lectures they recorded during the course of their study. For example: "She thinks she's a pretty hot number; I'd be worried about leaving my kid with her in a room alone. She needs to get her mind off boys."[18]

Similar attitudes expressing concern about premature female sexuality and the proper parental response are evident throughout the comments. One judge remarked that at age fourteen some girls "get some crazy ideas. They want to fool around with *men,* and that's sure as hell trouble." Another judge admonished a girl:

> "I want you to promise me to obey your mother, to have perfect school attendance and not miss a day of school, to give up these people who are trying to lead you to do wrong, not to hang out in candy stores or tobacco shops or street corners where these people are, and to be in when your mother says . . . . I don't want to see you on the streets of this city except with your parents or with your clergyman or to get a doctor. Do you understand?"[19]

The judges are not apologetic about the consequences of their double standard of justice. Comments made in June 1975 by Hunter Hurst, director of the Juvenile Justice Division of the National Council of Juvenile Court Judges, are very revealing in this regard:

> The issue is that status offenses are offenses against our values. Girls are seemingly over-represented as status offenders because we have a strong heritage of being protective toward females in this country. It offends our sensibility and our values to have a fourteen year old girl engage in sexually promiscuous activity. It's not the way we like to think about females in this country. As long as it offends our values, be sure that police, or the church or vigilante groups, or somebody is going to do something about it. For me, I would rather that something occur in the court where the rights of the parties can be protected.[20]

Hurst's enthusiasm about the quality of the court's commitment to the rights of women should be tempered by the legal controversy presently surrounding the issue of the rights of minors charged with juvenile status offenses. He should also be somewhat troubled by an argument that lumps the juvenile justice system with vigilante groups in the enforcement of community prejudices against women. The fact that these sexist community norms exist is no justification for involving agencies of the law in their enforcement.

## TRAINING WOMEN

"For her own protection. . . . " These words take on a very special meaning in the juvenile justice system. The logical extension of judicial paternalism, they mask the fact that the young woman is being sentenced to a juvenile prison.

The most recent census of these institutions indicated that, at any one time, over eight thousand young women are held in training schools across America.[21] Young women account for over 20 per cent of those held in training schools—in marked contrast to adult women, who are only 3.2 per cent of those held in state and federal prisons in 1971. Looking at these figures in another way, we see that girls, while only 40 per cent of all arrests of all females, constituted 60 per cent of all females in prisons, because after arrest a girl is almost seven times more likely than her adult counterpart to end up in prison.[22]

Girls tend to be placed in training schools "for their own protection," which actually means protection from "temptation" and their own sexuality. Thus, 70 per cent of the girls committed to training schools across the nation are there for juvenile offenses.[23]

A detailed review of one training school in Connecticut reveals the true meaning of the court's protection. In her study of Long Lane, Kristine Rogers reports that the staff express a great deal of interest in the girl's sexual history and habits:

> A girl is subjected to several interrogations upon entrance to Long Lane about her past sexual relations, her menses, any vaginal discharges, etc. Pregnancy is seen as "getting what she deserves," and the staff hope that if girls are made to live through one in such a punitive surrounding perhaps it won't happen again.[24]

The evidence seems to indicate that the girls at Long Lane get the message about the evils of sexuality. Rogers reported that the girls referred to their own pregnancies as "unmentionable situations," a variation on the school's "UM" designation for their "unmarried" status.

The school's twin remedies for sexual precosity are clear: training in the womanly arts and lengthy incarceration. Emphasis in this institution is on "religious" training coupled with sewing, cooking, and "beauty culture" to prepare the girls for their eventual role as "homemakers." No other vocational training occurs at the school and, while boys in Connecticut were paid for their work in the institution, girls were not.

This archaic regime was complemented in Connecticut by incarcerating the girls for longer periods of time; girls spent an average of seven months in the institution, compared with five months for boys. This pattern is not unique to Long Lane. In 1965, the nation-wide median stay for girls was two months longer than for boys; and more recently, girls in New York averaged twelve-month stays while boys averaged nine months.[25]

As to the reasons for this policy, the court officials in Connecticut are quite candid:

"Why most of the girls I commit are for status offenses. I figure if a girl is about to get pregnant, we'll keep her until she's sixteen and then ADC [Aid to Dependent Children] will pick her up!"[26]

The pervasive concern about potential sexual misconduct at this school in Connecticut is not atypical. An ambitious survey of fifty training schools across the nation concluded with this comment: "The fact is that many girls wind up in institutions for sexual offenses."[27] In essence, these "training schools" are the logical culmination of a pattern of paternalistic justice that characterizes all stages in the juvenile system. At a time when sex roles are clearly changing, the wisdom of involving official agencies of the government in the enforcement of a nineteenth-century view of womanhood is, to say the least, questionable.

## CONCLUSION

This paper has reviewed evidence that the juvenile court's historic commitment to traditional morality and obedience to parental authority results in a *de facto* double standard of juvenile justice. Routine police and court procedures seem to select out girls whose offenses threaten parental authority and boys whose offenses cannot be explained away as "boys will be boys." The court does this because both its history and its structure encourage extra-legal paternalism as well as law enforcement.

The evidence is clear that girls charged with status offenses receive harsher treatment than girls suspected of crimes at the level of referral to court, pretrial detention, and incarceration. It is also apparent that girls are far more likely than boys to be brought into the court system as status offenders despite evidence that boys commit as much of this type of behavior as girls.

Putting this another way, status offenses have allowed the construction of a double standard of juvenile justice. These vague offense categories coupled with the court's commitment to operate *in loco parentis* encourage the court to involve itself in the maintenance of traditional sex roles which require women to be obedient and chaste while encouraging young men to "sow wild oats."

The court is clearly applying the law in an unequal manner. But more importantly, the court is punishing the noncriminal behavior of girls as harsly as the criminal behavior of boys. Incarceration, white-washed by such phrases as "for her own protection," is incarceration nonetheless. Most of the girls incarcerated in American training schools and detention centers have not violated any law or committed any crime. They are there because they cannot get along with their parents and the court will not allow them to be free. These abuses of judicial discretion make it imperative that the court's authority over the status offender be limited and other sorts of responses to youth in trouble be sought. Fortunately, encouraging movement in this direction is under way.

While efforts to extend due process rights to the status offender have been disappointing,[28] challenges that status offenses are unconstitutionally vague have been more successful. Two recent federal court decisions have held that statutes which permitted officials to take children into custody because they were "in danger of leading an idle, dissolute, lewd or immoral life" *(Gonzalez* v. *Maillard)*[29] or because they were "in danger of becoming morally depraved" *(Gesicki* v. *Oswald)*[30] were impermissibly vague. In may 1972 the United States Supreme Court affirmed the *Gesicki* decision without opinion.[31]

Pressure for legislative reform of the court's broad authority over status offenders is also building. The Juvenile Justice and Delinquency Prevention Act of 1974, which provides resources for states and communities to set up new programs for juvenile offenders, requires that states receiving funds must develop and implement plans to treat the status offender without recourse to juvenile detention or correctional facilities.[32]

While neither of these reforms removes the status offender from court jurisdiction, they do begin to place limits on the court's power to intervene in the lives of adolescents who have not committed crimes. Clearly, these efforts must be supported and other community resources must be created to deal with family problems. Runaway shelters and halfway houses for young people in conflict with their parents already exist in many communities, and their success should encourage others to explore these options.

While these reforms can be, and have been, supported for a wide variety of humanitarian reasons, this paper has not suggested that one of the most compelling is that status offenses have encouraged the uncritical enforcement of a restrictive female role. This in turn may mean that the juvenile justice system has engaged in the violation of the civil rights of most of the females who have come into its jurisdiction.

## NOTES

1. National data on this are unavailable. However, recent statistics cited for the New York area in R. Hale Andrews and Andrew H. Cohn, "Ungovernability: the Unjustifiable Jurisdiction," *Yale Law Journal,* June 1974, pp. 1383-1409,

indicate that 62 per cent of those charged with "ungovernability" are girls. My research in Hawaii indicates that girls are roughly 60 per cent of all status offenders.

2. Rosemary C. Sarri and Robert D. Vinter, "Juvenile Justice and Injustice," *Resolution,* Winter 1975, p. 47.

3. Anthony M. Platt, *The Childsavers: The Invention of Delinquency* (Chicago: University of Chicago Press, 1969).

4. Nora Klapmuts, "Children's Rights," *Crime and Delinquency Literature,* September 1972.

5. Federal Bureau of Investigation, *Uniform Crime Reports* (U.S. Department of Justice: Washington, D.C., 1975), p. 184.

6. For a more complete summary of these self-report studies see Meda Chesney-Lind, "Judicial Enforcement of the Female Sex-Role: The Family Court and the Female Delinquent," *Issues in Criminology,* Fall 1973, p.55.

7. Martin Gold, *Delinquent Behavior in an American City* (Belmont, Calif.: Brooks/Cole, 1970), pp. 63–64.

8. Thomas P. Monahan, "Police Dispositions of Juvenile Offenders," *Phylon,* Summer 1970.

9. Children's Bureau, Department of Health, Education and Welfare, "Statistics on Public Institutions for Delinquent Children, 1965," Washington, D.C., 1967.

10. Meda Chesney-Lind, "Juvenile Delinquency: The Sexualization of Female Crime," *Psychology Today,* July 1974, pp. 43–46.

11. Kathryn W. Burkhart, "The Child and the Law: Helping the Status Offender," Public Affairs Pamphlet No. 530, 1975, p. 4.

12. Rosemary Sarri, *Under Lock and Key: Juveniles in Jail and Detention* (Ann Arbor: University of Michigan, 1974).

13. Jean Strouse, "To Be Minor and Female: The Legal Rights of Women under 21," *Ms.,* August 1972, p. 74.

14. Edward Wakin, *Children without Justice: A Report by the National Council of Jewish Women* (New York: National Council of Jewish Women, 1975), p. 45.

15. Loretta Schwartz, "The Kids Nobody Wants." Paper distributed by the Philadelphia Program for Women and Girl Offenders.

16. Andrews and Cohn, *supra* note 1, p. 1388.

17. *Id.,* note 33, p. 1388.

18. *Id.,* note 124, p. 1403.

19. *Id.,* notes 126, 129, p. 1404.

20. Hunter Hurst, "Juvenile Status Offenders," a speech given to the New Mexico Council on Crime and Delinquency, June 20, 1975.

21. U.S. Department of Justice, "Children in Custody: A Report on Juvenile Detention Facility Census" (Washington, D.C.: U.S. Govt. Printing Office, 1973), p. 7.

22. These figures were complied by comparing statistics on juvenile and adult female offenders contained in the U.S.Department of Justice's *Sourcebook on Criminal Justice Statistics,* 1973.

23. U.S. Justice Dept., *supra* note 21, p. 9.

24. Kristine Rogers, "'For Her Own Protection . . . ': Conditions of Incarceration for Female Juvenile Offenders in the State of Connecticut," *Law and Society Review,* Winter 1972, p. 235.

25. Linda Singer, "Women and the Correction Process," *American Criminal Law Review,* Winter 1973, p. 299.

26. Rogers, *supra* note 24, p. 227.

27. Wakin, *op. cit. supra* note 14, p. 79.

28. See Linda Riback, "Juvenile Delinquency Laws: Juvenile Women and the Double Standard of Morality," *UCLA Law Review,* 1971, p. 313; and "The Dilemma of the 'Uniquely Juvenile Offender,'" *William and Mary Law Review,* Winter 1972.

29. Civil No. 50424 (N.D. Cal. 1972).

30. 336 F. Supp. 371 (S.D.N.Y. 1971).

31. 523 F. Supp. 781 (1971).

32. Public Law 93-415, 93rd Congress, S. 821, Sept. 7, 1974.

## TWENTY
# Police Processing of Female Offenders
IMOGENE L. MOYER AND GARLAND F. WHITE

## STATEMENT OF THE PROBLEM

Traditionally, official measurements of the frequency and seriousness of criminal activities have shown that men exhibit much more involvement in crime than women. Social scientists and officials in the criminal justice system have therefore overlooked the systematic study of the female offender, and scientific inquiry has been concentrated on the male criminal offender.

There have been basically two general ideas constructed to account for the low involvement of women in criminal activities. The first centers on the premise that female criminality is relatively infrequent because of the constraints of the traditional female social role. The second explanation that has provided a focus for the study of women offenders centers around the working of the criminal justice system. Its premise is that women indeed frequently engage in criminal activities but are not detected, apprehended, or convicted in proportion to the frequency that men engaged in criminal activities are.

Pollak was one of the first sociologists to advance the sex-role argument to account for women's apparently low involvement in crime. He advanced the theory of "hidden" female crime to account for what he considered unreasonably low official arrest rates for women. He stated that our cultural norms of relative inactivity for women and chivalrous behavior for men protect against the detectability of female crime (Pollak, 1950:2). Although Freud had stated that women turn to crime as a perversion of or rebellion against inferior biological sex organs (Freud, 1964:124–127), Pollak suggested that women learn concealment and deceit through their passive role in the sex act. A major reason for hidden crime, according to Pollak, lies in the nature of women themselves. They are instigators of crime rather than perpetrators of criminal activity (Pollak, 1950:10). Early writers thus explained female criminal behavior in terms of the biological inferiority of women, as well as speculation concerning the passive, deceptive role of women during the sex act.

Recent years have witnessed a growth in arrests for women. The Uniform Crime Reports, for example, indicate that arrests for women have increased from 10.6 percent of all arrests in 1958 to 15 percent of all arrests in 1977. This trend has stimulated increased interest in the causes as well as the extent of female crime. A major interest centers around the increase of female arrests for crimes such as robbery and burglary that are typically committed by males. Adler, using an updated version of the sex-role argument, provides a series of anecdotes to support her contention that women are committing more burglaries and robberies as a result of their increasing liberation from traditional roles. Utilizing the UCR, Bales and Steffensmeier argue that the dramatic increase in burglaries and robberies by women (400 percent from 1960 to 1972) is only an artifact of small numbers. Further analyzing the UCR, both Simon and Steffensmier agree that the increase in women's crime is found in white-collar crimes such as fraud, embezzlement, forgery and counterfeiting, and larceny/theft. Minimizing the increases in women's participation in property crimes in general, Steffensmeier states:

> Comparison of male and female levels of property crime revealed that, with the exception of stolen property, the relative gap between the sexes has been narrowing since 1960. This closing of the gap, however, does not necessarily mean that females are catching up with males in propensities to commit property crimes. While females have made relative gains, absolute differences are still large and have generally increased so that female property crime levels continue to lag far behind those of males. Catching up appears to be the case only for the offenses of larceny and fraud/embezzlement. (Steffensmeier, 1978:576)

Rita Simon states, however, "that if this trend continues approximately equal numbers of men and women will be arrested for fraud and embezzlement by the 1990s and for forgery and counterfeiting the proportions should be equal by the 2020s (Simon, 1975:41). Simon further suggests that the increases in white-collar crimes may be explained by the trend of women moving from positions as housewives into employee positions. This movement of women into the labor force has provided women with differential socialization and differential opportunities for committing these crimes.

While Simon has utilized differentiation in the sex roles to explain the lower arrest rates of women, other authors, such as Anderson, Price, Adler, and Haskell and Yablonsky, have used the second premise that differential methods of control may explain the low arrest rates for women. Analyzing official crime statistics, Price states:

> A further look at the new rapidly accumulating data and observations relating to women offenders tends to buttress the view that women offenders may have existed for some time in proportions larger than we cared to acknowledge. These statistics support the contention that the criminal justice system has related to women differently from the way it does to men at every stage of its process. (Price, 1977:105)

In 1950 Pollak proclaimed, "Men hate to accuse women and thus indirectly to send them to their punishment, police officers dislike to arrest them, district attorneys to prosecute them, judges and juries to find them guilty and so on" (Pollak, 1950:151). Similar remarks are made by Haskell and Yablonsky, who state that "police are less likely to arrest women than they are men under identical circumstances" (Haskell and Yablonsky, 1973:61).

These studies illustrate the ideas sociologists have about the participation of women in the criminal enterprise. While there does seem to be increased interest in the female criminal offender, the positions taken by most of the writers are based on speculations and theoretical assumptions about the meaning of data acquired from secondary sources; for example, the Uniform Crime Reports. As argued by Anderson, these assumptions about the nature and etiology of female criminality and the preferential treatment of women within the criminal justice system have not been supported by research utilizing data collected independently of police records.

The need for original empirical research is greatest in the area of the treatment of female offenders by police officers—the first step into the criminal justice system. The necessity of police discretion in processing offenders through the criminal justice system is suggested by Goldstein. The difficulties of "total law enforcement" are presented by Goldstein to support his argument that "selective law enforcement" is the only way the criminal justice system can function (Goldstein, 1972:110–112). Furthermore, numerous studies of police decisions have presented evidence that the decision to arrest an offender varies according to the attributes of the offender, such as race and demeanor.

The study reported in this paper was conducted in order to provide additional information for the understanding of female crime. As pointed out, many researchers argue that agents of the criminal justice system respond differently to female offenders than they do to male offenders. In an attempt to further illuminate this issue the authors analyzed police officers' reactions to male and female offenders described in several different hypothetical episodes of criminal acts. The following hypotheses were explored

*Hypothesis One:* Police officers are inclined to react less harshly to women than to men for most offenses. This is designed to test the assumptions of authors such as Anderson, Haskell and Yablonsky, and Price that police officers are reluctant to arrest females since officers tend to be protective of females. In addition, police officers have generally been socialized to see women as delicate and unlikely to commit most crimes. In discussing the police officer's "working personality," Skolnick suggests:

> The policeman, because his work requires him to be occupied continually with potential violence, develops a perceptual shorthand to identify certain kinds of people as symbolic assailants, that is, as persons who use gesture, language, and attire that the policeman has come to recognize as a prelude to violence. This does not mean that violence by the symbolic assailant is necessarily predictable. On the contrary the policeman responds to the vague indication of danger suggested by appearance. (Skolnick, 1966:45)

Thus, since it is assumed that police officers are unlikely to define women as dangerous, they will be inclined to react less severely to women for most offenses.

*Hypothesis Two:* The variation in police dispositions across type of offense will be greater for women than for men. Along with attitudes of chivalry toward women, police officers also hold stereotyped views of feminine behavior. Women who violate these stereotypes by committing offenses traditionally considered nonfeminine will be more likely to receive severe dispositions by police than women committing offenses

traditionally considered female offenses (Anderson, Haskell and Yablonsky, and Price).

*Hypothesis Three:* Women whose demeanor involves traditionally
masculine behavior (loud, boisterous, aggressive, vulgar, and disrespect-
ful) are more likely to provoke a severe reaction from police than men
with similar demeanor, regardless of the offense. Previous studies of
police discretionary power indicate that the police officer's decision to
arrest is related to the degree of respect the offender shows the officer as
well as the general demeanor of the alleged offender. Studies further
show that officers develop stereotyped cues concerning the offender's
moral character based on the offender's demeanor during encounters
with the police. (Lundman, Skolnick, and Piliavin and Briar).

*Hypothesis Four:* Black women are more likely to receive severe
reactions from police than white women. The studies noted above suggest differential use of discretionary power by police officers according
to the demeanor and social circumstances that fit the police officers'
stereotypes of guilty persons and/or persons in need of social control.
Skolnick has stated that in the process of doing police work the officer
develops a "perceptual shorthand to identify certain kinds of people"
(Skolnick, 1966:45). In examining the issue of the influence of racial bias
on the officer's discretionary judgment, Skolnick suggests that it is the
tendency of the officer to stereotype that gives the black and white liberal the impression of racial discrimination. Skolnick utilizes the discretionary judgment of warrant police officers to illustrate how stereotyping can give the impression of racial discrimination:

> In the simple case in which the defendant has one warrant for fifteen
> dollars outstanding, the policeman's primary consideration is the
> apparent stability of the defendant's residence, because the police-
> man does not want to lose control over his physical presence. If the
> defendant owns his own home, or if he owns furniture, he cannot
> afford to move in order to escape the payment of fifteen dollars.
> Since Negroes tend to be less stable residentially, the police are less
> likely to give Negroes time to raise bail. (Skolnick, 1966:85)

Skolnick concludes that although police officers deny racial bias, the
practice of stereotyping results in the more frequent arrest of blacks.
This hypothesis in intended to test whether the practice of stereotyping
demeanor and appearances results in black women receiving severe
responses from police officers more frequently than do white women.

## RESEARCH METHODS AND PROCEDURES

The study reported in this paper is part of a larger research project to examine police decisions in a large, metropolitan area in a Southeastern state. From September to November 1978, 282 questionnaires were completed by police officers and detectives to determine how police react to a variety of persons and behaviors in hypothetical situations. To measure the effects of the independent variables (type of offense, race of the offender, sex of the offender, and demeanor of the offender) on the decisions made by patrol officers and detectives (the dependent variable), 40 brief hypothetical cases were constructed. The episodes were written to conform to a 5 X 2 X 2 X 2 design with five types of offenses (public drunkenness, traffic offense, assault, shoplifting, and possession of marijuana), and with male and female offenders, both black and white, displaying either a cooperative (positive) demeanor or a hostile (negative) demeanor. The following episode, for example, was used to indicate hostile demeanor of black women involved in a drunkenness offense:

> During routine patrol duty, an officer observed two black women arguing loudly in the Northern Shopping Center parking lot. As the officer approached, he realized the two women were drunk and arguing over a bottle of whiskey. When the officer attempted to question the two women, they became hostile and told the officer to mind his own business. Then the women began to curse the officer for not being out catching the real criminals.

A second example illustrates how the cooperative demeanor of a white man involved in a shoplifting offense was conveyed to the respondents:

> An off-duty police officer was shopping at a local discount store. At the shoe department he noticed a white man had tried on a pair of shoes and started walking into another section of the store wearing the new shoes. He next observed him dropping two transistor radios and an instamatic camera into his shopping bag. As he walked toward the front of the store he put two candy bars in his pocket. Then, he looked at his watch and walked out the door. When the officer stopped him and identified himself, he became very embarrassed, apologized, and started to cry.

The hypothetical episodes were presented to police officers in a questionnaire format during precinct roll call sessions. Eight different questionnaires were used, each containing a set of five episodes. Table 1 illustrates the distribution of the 40 hypothetical episodes on the eight different questionnaires (A through H). Sets of episodes were constructed so that each questionnaire contained each of the five types of crime, and the other independent variables were balanced across the questionnaires so as not to duplicate any particular combination of the independent variables. Along with demographic questions, each set of five episodes constituted a separate questionnaire. The eight different questionnaires (A through H) were randomly ordered before distribution to the officers. Thus, the particular questionnaire an officer received was determined by random assignment.

After reading each episode officers were instructed to indicate the course of action which should be taken. They responded by selecting one of the following alternatives:

1. Do nothing
2. Question the offender(s) and release
3. Take the offender(s) to the police department for interrogation
4. Issue a misdemeanor/traffic summons
5. Arrest and book

Officers' responses to these alternatives constitute the dependent variable.

**Table 1.** *Distribution of Hypothetical Offense Episodes Across Questionnaires A — H*

| | TYPE OF CRIME | | | | | | | |
|---|---|---|---|---|---|---|---|---|
| | Men ◄——————— Sex ———————►Women | | | | | | | |
| | Black | | White ◄——— Race ———► Black | | | | White | |
| | Posi-tive | Nega-tive | Posi-tive | Nega-tive | ◄Demeanor► | Posi-tive | Nega-tive | Posi-tive | Nega-tive |
| Public Drunkenness | H | C | A | B | | E | G | D | F |
| Traffic Offense | F | E | C | H | | B | D | G | A |
| Assault | C | D | H | G | | A | E | F | B |
| Shoplifting | G | A | F | H | | D | C | B | E |
| Marijuana | A | B | E | D | | H | F | G | C |

## ANALYSIS OF DATA

An analysis of variance procedure was used to determine the amount of variance explained in the officers' dispositions of the episodes by each of the independent variables. A multiple regression approach to the analysis of variance allowed the calculation of the amount of variance explained by each of the independent variables while simultaneously adjusting for the effects of all other independent variables and interaction effects.

Since each police officer in the sample responded to five different hypothetical cases, the total number of responses analyzed was five times as great as the number of responding officers. Thus, judgments are not independent; and, for this reason, F values which are customarily used along with the analysis of variance technique will be excluded. At this stage in the research, the omission of significance tests is not a particularly critical loss since the respondents include the total number of police officers in the participating departments who were both available and willing to participate in the study. Additionally, the primary focus of this study is to explore the relative influences of the independent variables on the police officers' dispositions; not to determine if they have a statistically significant impact on these dispositions.

## FINDINGS

The analysis of the effects of the four experimental factors—sex, race, and demeanor of the offender, and the type of crime—indicates that these factors account for about one-fourth of the total influence on the severity of the officers' reactions. The other factors that influence the officers' decisions are unknown. Among the experimental factors which we tested, the type of crime had the most influence.

Among the types of crimes, shoplifting received the most severe reaction from the police. Shoplifting was followed in descending order of severity by possession of marijuana, public drunkenness, traffic offense, and assault. Thus, the police indicated they they would take the most serious action in the hypothetical shoplifting cases and the least serious action in the assault cases.

The demeanor of the offender, whether the offender was described as exhibiting a cooperative or hostile attitude, had only a small influence on the officers' dispositions. A negative or hostile demeanor produced a slightly harsher reaction from the police than did a positive attitude.

Another part of the study concerned the analysis of the combined or joint effects of the four experimental factors. It was important to see if combinations of factors such as race and sex, for example, might produce strong effects on the officers' decisions. Hypotheses two, three, and four all involved the combination of variables. Only the joint effect of type of offense with the demeanor of the offender exhibited a strong effect on the officers' decisions. This interaction accounted for 13 percent of the total variance in police officer dispositions. This finding suggests that the kinds of demeanor displayed by the offenders exerted more influence on the officers' decisions for some types of crimes than for others. The remaining two-way and three-way combinations seemed to have little influence on the dependent variable. All together the separate and combined effects explained about a third of the total variation in the officers' dispositions.

A closer examination of the only influential combined effect, demeanor and type of crime, revealed that the demeanor which was displayed by the offender exerted a much more pronounced effect on officers' decisions for some crimes than for others. The proportion of the total variation in the officers' dispositions explained by variation in demeanor ranged from 1 percent for possession of marijuana to 40 percent for public drunkenness. Thus, whether the public drunk was cooperative or hostile to the confronting police officer determined, to a large extent, how that officer processed the offender. On the other hand, if the offender was found in possession of marijuana, his or her demeanor apparently did not influence the arresting officer's response.

## DISCUSSION AND CONCLUSIONS

The findings indicate quite clearly that none of the hypotheses were supported. The first hypothesis speculated that police officers would react to men more harshly than women, for most types of crimes. Thus, sex should have explained a large proportion of the variation in officers' dispositions. As pointed out earlier, it did not.

The second hypothesis predicted that the variation across types of crimes would be greater for women than for men; that is, the interaction effects for sex with the type of offense should have accounted for a large share of variation in the police officers' decisions.

The third hypothesis predicted that a negative demeanor displayed by females would produce a more severe reaction than a similar demeanor exhibited by male offenders. If so, the interaction between sex of

offender and demeanor would have accounted for a much larger proportion of variance than it, in fact, did.

The final hypothesis predicted that black women would receive
more severe reactions from the police officers than white women. This
hypothesis, of course, failed to be supported by the data as well. When
sex was held constant, race should have accounted for a sizable proportion of the variation, but it did not.

The analysis of the responses of the police officers to the hypothetical crime episodes, therefore, indicated that decisions of police officers
were not contingent on the sex or race of the offenders. Whether what
police officers say they should do in response to a hypothetical crime
episode corresponds to how they actually behave in the course of their
daily occupational duties will have to remain on a speculative level until
additional research is conducted. However, on the basis of this research,
we think there is some justification for believing that neither sex alone
nor race alone directly determined the police officers' responses. The
questionnaire was constructed to minimize attempts to adjust responses
artificially on the basis of race and sex. While officers certainly perceived variation by race and sex across the episodes, demeanor and type
of crime were also varied. Thus, it would be difficult to deliberately
equalize the severity of responses based on race and sex.

The major variables in determining how police officers responded
were the nature of the offense and the manner in which the offender
behaved when confronted by the officer. The effect of demeanor was,
however, contingent upon the type of crime committed. As stated previously, how the offender behaved had very little to do with the officers'
response to some offenses and a great deal to do with the responses to
other kinds of crimes.

The examination of differences in specific responses to black versus
white offenders revealed no differences. This suggests that race did not
have a direct influence on the officers' responses. It further suggests that
officers did not respond differently to cues from blacks than to those
from whites. Thus, at least considering the variables included in this
study, police officers respond quite uniformly to black and white
offenders.

A detailed examination of differences in police responses to men
and women offenders found that most of the variance in the officers'
responses to women offenders was due to main or direct effects of type
of crime and demeanor. That is, the types of offenses women commit
seemed to have a much greater *direct* influence on police officers' decisions than the kinds of crimes in which male offenders engage. Demeanor, as well, affects officers' decisions in a more direct fashion for
women offenders.

In comparison, decisions about male offenders were made in a more complicated fashion. The type of offense in interaction with the demeanor displayed by the male offender exerts the heaviest influences on police officer dispositions. What this suggests is that more subtle cues were used in the decisions about male offenders than female offenders. Thus, while the dispositional outcomes were the same, the process of arriving at the disposition was more complex.

In summary, this research has found thus far that officers use basically two out of four pieces of information considered in the experimental design in making dispositions about criminal offenders. First, the offense committed by the offender was considered. Second, the demeanor the offender displayed was considered. The effect of demeanor, however, was significantly more important for some crimes than for others.

These pieces of information were used with approximately equal impact for male and female offenders. The differences were that for female offenders, the type of crime committed was the first and most important piece of information, followed by the interaction of the demeanor contingent upon types of crime and demeanor. Neither of these attributes was straightforward for men.

The hypotheses for this research, therefore, have not been supported by this study thus far. It is possible that the speculations of writers such as Pollak and Haskell and Yablonsky concerning the differential treatment of women by police are simply a myth. On the other hand, it is also possible that more data are needed to test the hypotheses. This is the first research study to utilize primary data to examine police disposition of female offenders. Further, as stated earlier in this paper, this study is part of a larger research project that will include field observations as well as the administration of additional questionnaires to police officers. It is, therefore, anticipated that future research will further clarify how police officers determine the dispositions of female offenders.

## REFERENCES

Adler, Freda. *Sisters in crime.* New York: McGraw-Hill Book Company, 1975.

Anderson, Etta A. The "chivalrous" treatment of the female offenders in the arms of the criminal justice system: A review of the literature. *Social Problems,* February 1976, 350–357.

Boles, Jacqueline. *Women in crime: Changing patterns.* Paper presented at the meeting of the Southern Sociological Society, Washington, D.C., April 1975.

Freud, Sigmund. *New introductory lectures on psycho-analysis and other works.* London: The Hogarth Press, 1964.

Goldstein, Joseph. Police discretion not to invoke the criminal process: Low-visibility decisions in the administration of justice. In G. F. Cole, (Ed.), *Criminal justice: Law and politics.* Belmont, California: Wadsworth Publishing Company, 1972, 108–129.

Haskell, Martin R., and Yablonsky, Lewis. *Crime and delinquency.* Chicago: Rand McNally, 1973.

Hoffman-Bustamante, Dale. The nature of female criminality. *Issues in Criminology,* Fall 1973, 117–135.

Klein, Doris. The etiology of female crime: A review of the literature. *Issues in Criminology,* Fall 1973, 3–30.

Lundman, Richard J. Routine police arrest practices: A commonwealth perspective. *Social Problems,* October 1974, 127–144.

Piliavin, Irwin, and Briar, Scott. Police encounters with juveniles. *The American Journal of Sociology,* September 1964, 206–214.

Pollak, Otto. The criminality of women. New York: A. S. Barnes & Company, Inc., 1950.

Price, Ray R. The forgotten female offender. *Crime and Delinquency,* April 1977, 101–108.

Simon, Rita. *The contemporary woman and crime.* Rockville, Maryland: National Institute of Mental Health, 1975.

Skolnick, Jerome. *Justice without trial: Law enforcement in a democratic society.* New York: John Wiley and Sons, Inc., 1966.

Steffensmeier, Darrell J. Crime and the comtemporary women: An analysis of changing levels of female property crime, 1960–1975. *Social Forces,* December 1978, 565–584.

# WOMEN IN CORRECTIONS

## 1. THE HISTORICAL DEVELOPMENT OF FEMALE CORRECTIONAL INSTITUTIONS

Correctional institutions for women were established in Indiana and Massachusetts in the 1870s. Before that time, female prisoners were incarcerated in male prisons, sometimes in separate rooms and sometimes mixed indiscriminately with the male prisoners. The mixing of male and female prisoners provided numerous opportunities for sexual victimization, as did the fact that all of the correctional officers charged with supervising the prisoners were also male. Freedman (1974) tells us much about how female reformers worked for an amelioration of these terrible conditions and finally succeeded in gaining acceptance for the ideology of separate treatment for women in institutions run by women. This was not an easy task, for in Freedman's words,

> To convince the correctional profession to accept plans for separate women's prisons, reformers had to overcome resistance based on three fears: that women were incapable of controlling, let alone reforming, female criminals; that female-controlled institutions would lack a "natural" familial structure and, less explicitly expressed, that women's institutions threatened to reduce male dominance in society and would destroy femininity. (1974:86)

In their triumph over male prejudices, female reformers were satisfied with the establishment of matriarchal reformatory institutions for women that inculcated the ideals of domesticity rather than of freedom and equality between the sexes. Some social changes come in a continuous surge, while others occur only sporadically, with long periods of stability or decay in between. The reform movement in women's prisons is an example of the latter rather than the former pattern. Feinman's article (1979), which appears later in this section, explains this in detail. The domestic programs instituted in the late 1800s and early 1900s are still in evidence in American correctional institutions. There has been no period in the twentieth century during which public attention was focused on the problems of females in corrections the way it was at the end of the nineteenth century. Only with the rise of the women's movement has any serious attention been given to programs and conditions in women's prisons. Even now, the orientation of the women's movement is much more toward problems that impact the middle class, such as employment, than problems that are largely limited to lower classes, of which correctional processing is a prime example. It appears that a thoroughgoing reformation of female correctional institutions in the style of the late nineteenth century reforms will not occur until the composition of the women's movement changes to include many more women from the lower classes who will demand that their incarcerated sisters be given the same privileges and benefits as prisoners in male institutions.

## 2. POPULATION TRENDS IN FEMALE CORRECTIONS

The proportion of prisoners who are women has never been more than 4 percent in the United States. The number of women in federal and state correctional facilities was 5,808 in 1950, rising to 7,700 in 1960 and then declining to 6,269 in 1972. At that point, female prisoner populations began to increase rapidly, reaching 8,580 in 1975. The number of women in prison increased nearly 20 percent between 1974 and 1975. In addition to the females who are incarcerated in state and federal prison systems, there are also many females in institutions for girls or in female wings or cells in county and city jails, as well as many females who participate in probation, parole, and other community corrections programs. The number of females in nonprison corrections is much larger than the number of women incarcerated in prisons. For example, a national census of delinquents in detention found 10,139 girls in 1974. This constituted almost 23 percent of all delinquents in detention, a much higher proportion than the proportion of adults in women's prisons (Bowker, 1978). As an example of the relative numbers of females placed on probation and in correctional institutions, the state of Wisconsin placed 1,255 females on probation in 1977 and institutionalized only 167 (Wisconsin, 1978a; 1978b, 1978c, 1978d). Although no exactly comparable statistics on females in state and county jails are available for Wisconsin, a survey of women in 40 Wisconsin jails in 1975 found that 400 different women had been confined in the last full month previous to the date of the survey (The Women Offender in Wisconsin Jails, 1975).

## 3. CHARACTERISTICS OF FEMALE PRISONERS

What kinds of women serve time in correctional institutions? The national survey by Glick and Neto (1977) contains a considerable amount of information about the characteristics of female prisoners. They found that two-thirds of the incarcerated women were under 30 years of age, and their median age was 27 years. Half of the women were black, 20 percent were currently married (although 60 percent had been married at some time), 73 percent had borne children (with more than three-quarters of them having children living at home when they were arrested), and more than half of them had been on welfare at one time or another. They tended to be less educated than women as a whole, half of them came from broken homes, and 40 percent had worked at a legitimate job outside their homes in the two months before they were arrested. Incarcerated felons in the Glick-Neto study had been convicted of violent crimes in 43 percent of the cases, property crimes in 29 percent of the cases, and drug offenses in 22 percent of the cases. Drug or alcohol use was a major problem in the lives of more than 22 percent of these women, for a number of the property and violent crimes were also drug related.

## 4. COMMUNITY CORRECTIONS FOR WOMEN

In the broader sense of the term, community corrections includes pre-trial programs, probation, work and training release from correctional institutions, parole, and the use of certain small scale residential programs that depend on community resources rather than internal resources to provide a range of services to the client. McArthur (1974) mentions that a number of the 30 pretrial intervention projects with which he is familiar accept female applicants. Some pretrial programs have the capability of diverting female offenders completely out of the criminal justice system in return for their participation in certain treatment or work programs. Other programs help them with problems of bail, legal needs, or special problems such as those related to the care of dependent children of the offenders.

Probation and parole allow women to be free in the community under the supervision of a probation or parole officer. The general difference between these two programs is that probation occurs instead of imprisonment while parole follows imprisonment. Although true, this difference can be misleading, for many women who are placed on probation have served time in jail before the trial, and this jail time is sometimes longer than the jail sentences meted out to convicted misdemeanants. Being released to the community does not guarantee that women will be accepted in the community; as Feinman (1979) points out, the prison reform movement which righted many of the wrongs that were occurring in female corrections during the previous century was not successful in changing the willingness of the community to accept female felons.

In their national study of women's correctional programs, Glick and Neto (1977) identified six categories of residential programs operating at the community level. These were halfway houses, work-release/prerelease centers, academic prerelease centers, therapeutic communities for drug abusers, mixed modality programs, and residential centers for alcoholics. Although these programs seemed more traditional and criminal justice oriented than they needed to be, they had four clear advantages over prison programs. The racial/ethnic distribution of their staff members was closer to that of their residents; they were much more likely to employ ex-offenders; they had a higher level of family and community involvement with their clients; and they made heavier use of community resources as opposed to in-house resources. Because of these advantages, particularly the opportunities for increased contact with family and other community members, it would be beneficial to greatly expand the use of these alternatives to incarceration while at the same time diminishing the number of women who are imprisoned in the coming decade.

## 5. PRISONS, JAILS, AND PROGRAMS

The LEAA 1970 National Jail Census identified only nine jails that were used exclusively for women (American Bar Association, 1974). In other American jails, women continued to be housed in separate wings or cells in the main male institution. In some institutions, certain cells are swing cells in that they are used for both male and female prisoners according to the needs of the institution. In no case, however, are males and females simultaneously housed in the same cells the way they were a century ago. Because many jails are quite small, convicted misdemeanants and legally innocent arrestees who are awaiting trial are mixed together as are relatively young and inexperienced offenders and hardened criminals with long records of serious offenses. Therapeutic, educational, and work-related programs are rare in jails, for they are limited both by a high degree of prisoner turnover and by anemic funding policies. In some cases, jail visiting regulations are more stringent than prison visiting regulations, so that family members who live nearly are prevented from taking advantage of their easy access to their incarcerated relatives.

When Chandler (1973) surveyed programs in women's prisons, she found severe deficiencies in both educational and vocational programs. It was impossible for women to take any college classes (except by correspondence) in most of the prisons, although typing classes were available in all but one of them. Vocational training programs concentrated on traditional domestic tasks such as sewing, baking, cleaning, laundry, domestic service, and nursing. As Stellpflug (1978) has pointed out, these traditional educational programs simply fall sort of meeting the needs of women in correctional institutions.

When Arditi and Goldberg (1973) surveyed male and female prisons in the United States, they found a number of differences which they attributed to the two primary factors of stereotyping and scale. Stereotyping refers to the persistence of traditional programs and attitudes that do not adequately prepare female prisoners for reentry into the modern world. These problems could be easily solved if correctional administrators could be persuaded that it was in their best interest to do so. In contrast, problems of scale cannot be dealt with quite so easily. Scale refers to the fact that there are not enough women offenders in most states to make it efficient to offer them the same variety and quality of programs that may exist in male institutions. As a matter of fact, some states have so few incarcerated female offenders that they farm them out to adjacent states and pay a fee for them to be boarded there. Having a small number of female offenders not only affects the programs that they are offered, it also makes it difficult to classify them into different institutions or segregated settings by custody grading as is done with men. This means that female prisoners have to deal with a much wider range of criminality in their fellow prisoners than do male prisoners.

A major problem in American corrections that is partially a product of scale and stereotyping is how to meet the needs of women associated with reproductive functioning. There are medical needs related to being pregnant upon intake into an institution and there are social needs concerning the welfare of children who are born to women while incarcerated as well as of the children that they were forced to leave behind in the community when they entered the institution. The years in which people are most likely to commit crimes coincide exactly with the years of greatest biological productivity, so that a higher proportion of women are pregnant at entrance into an institution than one might expect. The proportion of women in prison who have children on the outside is larger still, amounting to perhaps two-thirds of all incarcerated women. The lack of adequate provision for continuing relations between these mothers and children is a national scandal. Part of McGowan and Blumenthal's (1978) brilliant analysis of this problem is reprinted as an article in this reader.

## 6. PRISONER BEHAVIOR IN CORRECTIONAL INSTITUTIONS

Human beings fight to establish a semblance of normal social relations even under the most stressful conditions. The more difficult the conditions, the harder it is to approximate normal social relations, and so social arrangements tend to take on unusual forms. The forms that grow up between inmates in correctional institutions are called prisoner subcultures (Bowker, 1977). Academic investigators of prisoner subcultures first concentrated on male correctional institutions so that it is only recently that female prisoner subcultures have been adequately understood. Norms, roles, and statuses in female subcultures are structured in response to two main classes of restricting conditions: the sexual stereotypes in larger society that women bring into the prison with them, and the pressures and deprivations that exist within the prison walls. Two articles on the subject of female prisoner subcultures have been included in this section. In the first, Bowker (1979) discusses the differences between male and female prisoner subcultures, and in the second, Carter (1973) provides us with some ethnographic detail on courtship and pseudofamily relations in a reform school for delinquent girls.

## REFERENCES

American Bar Association. Commission on Correctional Facilities and Services. *Women in detention and statewide jail standards.* Washington, D.C., 1974.
Arditi, R. R., and Goldberg, F. The sexual segregation of American prisons. *Yale Law Journal,* May 1973, *82,* 1229–1273.
Bowker, Lee H. *Prisoner subcultures.* Lexington, MA: D. C. Heath, 1977.
———. *Gender differences in prisoner subcultures.* Paper presented at the annual meeting of the American Psychiatric Association, Chicago, 1979.
Carter, Barbara. Race, sex and gangs: Reform school families. *Society,* November/December 1973, *11,* 38–43.
Chandler, Edna W. *Women in prison.* Indianapolis, ID: Bobbs-Merrill, 1973.

Feinman, Clarice. Sex role stereotypes and justice for women. *Crime and Delin-quency,* January 1979, *28,* 87–94.

Freedman, Estelle B. Their sisters' keepers: An historical perspective on female correctional institutions in the United States: 1870–1900. *Feminist Studies,* 1974, *2,* 77–95.

Glick, Ruth M., and Neto, Virginia V. *National study of women's correctional programs.* Washington, D.C.: Government Printing Office, 1977.

McArthur, Virginia A. *From convict to citizen: Programs for the woman offender.* Paper produced for the District of Columbia Commission on the Status of Women, Washington, D.C., 1974.

McGowan, Brenda G., and Blumenthal, Karen L. *Why punish the children? A study of children of women prisoners.* Hackensack, NJ: National Council on Crime and Delinquency, 1978.

Stellpflug, Kay. Traditional education falls short of women's needs in institutions. *American Journal of Correction,* November/December 1978, *40,* 26–27.

Wisconsin. Department of Health and Social Services. *Admissions to juvenile institutions, calendar 1977.* Madison, WI 1978a.

———. *Adult probation admissions, 1977.* Madison, WI, 1978b.

———. *Juvenile probation admissions, 1977.* Madison, WI, 1978c.

———. *Offenders admitted to adult correctional institutions, calendar 1977.* Madison, WI, 1978d.

The woman offender in Wisconsin jails, a survey. Milwaukee, WI: Wisconsin Program for Women and Girl Offenders and the Benedict Center for Criminal Justice, 1975.

TWENTY-ONE

# Sex-Role Stereotypes and Justice for Women[*]

CLARICE FEINMAN

Since the development of the modern prison system 200 years ago, obvious physical improvements in the housing and supervision of incarcerated women have been made. We no longer herd convicted women

---

[*]Reprinted from *Crime and Delinquency,* Volume 25, Number 1, January 1979.

into attics or sections of male institutions or subject them to virtually
unrestrained abuse by male guards.[1] Today, both the federal government
and most states have separate penal institutions for women, supervised
by other women. However, separate does not necessarily imply equal or
just.

Regardless of the changes in the physical treatment of female
offenders, three main facts stand out throughout the history of women
in jail and prison. First, the treatment of incarcerated women reflects the
sex role stereotypes which society has relegated to women. Second,
although women have played a major role in improving the conditions
of incarceration, they have perpetuated those role stereotypes. Third, sex
stereotypes have significantly affected the exoffenders' opportunity to
succeed in the community after release.

These three factors have intruded—and they continue to intrude—
on the treatment of women in prison and their reception in the community following release. That the problem is as much contemporary as it is
historical is a conclusion that will be illustrated by a discussion of programming and problems affecting inmates in the New York City Correctional Institution for Women.

## SEXUAL STEREOTYPING:
## THE CONSEQUENCES OF DEVIATION

Coinciding with the advent of the modern American prison system in
1790 was the development of the "cult of true womanhood,"[2] wherein
the ideal woman was defined as the wife and mother in the home.
Women were expected to be pious, pure, submissive, and oriented
toward the family. Historians Barbara Welter and David B. Davis have
both cited this American obsession with women's role in society, which
reached its first peak in the period between 1820 and 1860,[3] a time when
the United States experienced significant political, economic, social, and
territorial changes. In addition, the first women's rights movement was
organized during this period. Fearful for the strength and security of the
nation, religious, political, and literary spokesmen pointed to true womanhood as the only constant in a rapidly changing society. Since that
time, these sex roles, steeped in religious and moral values, have had a
decisive impact on the manner in which nonconforming women have
been defined and treated. The deification of the spiritually pure wife/
mother brought demands for laws to punish the nonconforming woman
as unnatural, as the symbol of sin.[4] Thus, in the first half of the nineteenth century, those female offenders who had "fallen" from their natu-

rally pure state were viewed as more depraved than their male counter-parts; as such, they were dealt with more harshly while incarcerated. Moreover, they continued to carry the stigma imposed upon them by an unforgiving society when they left prison.[5]

The special threat presented by delinquent women stemmed from the popular conviction that women were generally passive and domestic—unlike men, who were naturally aggressive. Women who went against their natural tendencies were considered to be "monster[s],"[6] the "embodiment of the evil principle,"[7] and unable to distinguish right from wrong. An experiment such as the penitentiary movement could have no effect on these creatures, for redemption was clearly out of the question. The result was that female criminals were simply removed from public view. Women were crowded together into small, unsanitary, poorly ventilated quarters in male institutions such as Auburn and Sing Sing. There they were subjected to the demands of male guards.[8] Under this "policy of calculated neglect,"[9] women were flogged, sometimes impregnated, and they often died from the abuse. The horrible condi-tions in Auburn and Sing Sing impelled B. C. Smith, chaplain at Auburn Prison during the 1820s, to state that to be a woman in prison was "worse than death."[10]

In 1828, De Witt Clinton, governor of New York, recommended to the state legislature that a separate penitentiary be built for women. In rejecting the proposal, members of the legislature expressed fear that, when released, the women would corrupt the morals and contaminate the young men in the vicinity of the institution.[11] Even the exposure of the unbearable conditions at Auburn and Sing Sing failed to temper the views of these opponents to reform.[12]

## FEMALE REFORMERS: PERPETUATION OF THE STEREOTYPE

In 1830, despite public hostility toward the project, a group of middle- and upper-class women, motivated by religious impulses and aiming to reform their fallen sisters, established a home for delinquent women. The Magdalen Society of New York City opened the Magdalen Home to serve female offenders who manifested a desire to repent and assume their proper role. The home provided vocational training in the domestic arts for those women who gave "evidence that true womanhood [was] really returning"[13] and secured employment for them as domestics in good Christian families.[14] In 1845, the Women's Prison Association of New York City opened the Issac T. Hopper Home, which operated according to the principle that delinquent females could be redeemed if separated from men and guided by virtuous women. Pregnant women, alcoholics, and narcotics addicts could not live or receive help at the home. Those who did qualify received medical care and vocational training in traditional skills. If redeemed, they too were placed as domestic workers in respectable Christian homes.[15]

Throughout the nineteenth century, women continued to lead the efforts to reform delinquent women and to improve the conditions of their incarceration. While these reformers were unusual in assuming an aggressive role,[16] their fundamental approval of their own social positions and their deeply embedded religious and moral values resulted in a perpetuation of those very stereotypical sex roles that imposed restrictions on them.

During the years between 1870 and 1930, prevailing attitudes toward the female offender began to change, partly because of these women involved in penal reform. Errant women were no longer castigated as generically depraved but were seen as the victims of male lust and imposed sex roles which afforded women few opportunities to work and earn an adequate wage. Many reformers at the end of the nineteenth century considered themselves morally superior to men and therefore singularly capable of uplifting their fallen sisters, and they crusaded for separate, wholly female penal institutions as the only means of uplifting the poor unfortunate fallen women. With separate institutions came careers and employment for a number of these reformers, who became professionals in female correction and penology—a field in which they did not compete with men or threaten the stereotypical sex role structure.[17]

One would have hoped that these reformers would develop an iconoclastic approach to correction and provide alternatives to stereotypical sex roles. But education and career orientation notwithstanding, the time had not yet come for a break with traditional values. Female administrators established an atmosphere that simulated a homelike environment, with a mother-child relationship between matron and inmate. Inmates were taught to be good homemakers and were prepared for their proper role in society.[18]

The assumption that women were naturally passive, and thus less dangerous than their male counterparts in prison, did give female administrators one advantage—that of being free to experiment with programs and innovations. Some of these innovations later became part of the institutional programming in men's prisons. Elizabeth Farnham, head matron of the women's division at Sing Sing in 1844, introduced educational classes, a library, and art and music programs. She attempted to simulate a homelike atmosphere by decorating the women's quarters with flowers, pictures, and lamps.[19] Dr. Katherine B. Davis, the first superintendent at the New York State Reformatory for Women at Bedford Hills, introduced in 1901 a formal school program, vocational training, and recreation. She also developed a research project to study career patterns of female prisoners.[20]

As effective as they were, the administrators could not convince the public to accept the exoffender into the community. Yet, ironically, while women's roles in the community were severely restricted, society did continue to accept the exoffenders as servants working for upright Christian families.[21]

## THE SITUATION TODAY

These historic factors continue to affect female offenders. First, the treatment of incarcerated women today still reflects the sex role stereotyping. Second, although women have played a major role in improving conditions in institutions for female offenders, they have perpetuated those role stereotypes. And third, sex role stereotypes continue to affect the exoffenders' opportunity to succeed in the community. This is a conclusion based largely upon the writer's firsthand experience as the project director of a rehabilitation program in the New York City Correctional Institution for Women.

In 1929, the New York City Department of Correction attempted to explain the increase in the number of imprisoned women by stating:

> It is possible, of course, that the comparative emancipation of woman, her greater participation in commercial and political affairs and the tendency towards greater sexual freedom may be playing their part in bringing about this situation.[22]

Recent statements concerning the reported rise in the crime rate among women continue in the same vein. In 1975, Rita J. Simon wrote:

> As women's opportunities to commit crimes increase, so will their deviant behavior, and the types of crimes they commit will much more closely resemble those committed by men.[23]

Simon's thesis is supported by Freda Adler who contends that, as cultural restraints disappear because of the women's rights movement, women will enter the criminal arena on an equal footing with men.[24] According to the New York City Department of Correction, Simon and Adler, the emancipation of women leads to increased criminality and incarceration. Thus, the myth that the emancipation of women from the traditional roles of wife and mother will lead to increased criminality finds continued support. Wife and mother remain the socially acceptable roles. The perpetuation of the myth has contributed to society's fears and misunderstanding by equating equal rights and opportunity for women with delinquent behavior. (As in the first peak period of the "cult of true womanhood," the statements by the New York Department of Correction, Simon, and Adler have been made during a time of unusual domestic insecurity characterized by major political, economic, and social changes as well as an organized movement fighting to increase the rights of women. The second peak period of the American obsession with women's role in society—the resurgence of the "cult of true womanhood"—occurred in the 1920s after women won the right to vote. We are presently in a third peak period.)

Yet the myth denies some basic historical facts. Poor women have always been overrepresented in penal institutions. From 1932, when the first jail for women opened in New York City, to the present, the jail population has been predominantly poor, uneducated, and unskilled. When employed, these women have worked in factories or as domestics or waitresses.[25] Incarcerated women in New York City are neither emancipated nor are they participants in the women's movement; rather, these women are victims of denied economic opportunities. In 1976, the superintendent of the New York Correctional Institution for Women, Essie O. Murph, called them "the bottom of the barrel."[26]

The role of middle- and upper-class women in determining treatment also remains relatively unchanged since the nineteenth century. Because of their own backgrounds, they continue to perpetuate the concept that the woman's proper role is wife and mother. Staff in the New York City Correctional Institution for Women attempt to establish a homelike environment in the jail with flowers, pictures, and draperies; and inmates are taught domestic skills. Treatment is oriented toward exposing the female offender to an "acceptable" lifestyle and to values deemed desirable. Rehabilitation means instilling in offenders "certain standards of sexual morality and sobriety and preparing them for their duties as mothers and homemakers."[27]

Like her predecessors, the present superintendent perpetuates the stereotypical sex role by referring to the institution as a home and insisting that each inmate act and dress as befits a "lady." In 1970, superintendent Murph said, "We're a lot like a family here. . . . This is a home for most of them."[28] Until recently, detained women were not permitted to wear slacks, and Murph strongly disapproves of slacks worn by civilian female personnel.[29] She does not consider such apparel "ladylike."[30]

Other women's organizations seeking to bring about improvement for the female offender also maintain traditional expectations. Since 1955, the Women's Prison Association, the Friendly Visitors, and the New York City Junior League have offered the incarcerated women in New York City the choice of training programs, but all are premised on the traditional societal attitudes and cultural role expectations for women.[31] In the nineteenth century it was servant-housekeeper; in the twentieth century, waitress-typist. Members of those organizations may have supported the women's movement, but few if any ever brought the ideas into the jails.

Any attempts to establish training programs in jail which could prepare the women for skilled, well-paying jobs have met with failure. Companies such as New York Telephone and IBM explained that it was not economical to bring in machines and an instructor for the few eligible women; apparently, these companies did not consider the possibility of permitting the women to continue the program of study after their release from jail.[32] Government policy makers have been unwilling to allocate money for training programs for women on the premise that women do not support themselves or their families. But in 1970, approximately 70 percent of the inmates were single workers with full responsibility for support of their families.[33]

While female superintendents are still allowed a greater range of experimentation than is permitted in male facilities, neither the administrators nor the volunteers employed in special programs have managed to overcome social hostility toward the offenders. Inmates leaving penal institutions today still face a hostile society in which jobs, housing, and training programs are either nonexistent or of poor quality.

To be fair, the fault is not entirely with prison administrators. In some cases, female offenders have refused training in nontraditional fields even though wages would be high.[34] Many of these women leave jail only to go back on the welfare rolls and back to their old way of life.

## A WARNING

There are inherent dangers in the myth that the emancipation of women leads to criminal behavior. First, it misdirects and confuses investigation into the causes of female crime. Second, it denies the reality that many wives and mothers—as well as single women—have worked outside the home. Finally, and most important, it denies the fact that our jails and prisons are populated largely by poor women. In so doing, it obviates the need to seek the real reasons for this situation.

# NOTES

1. David W. Lewis, *From Newgate to Dannemora: The Rise of the Penitentiary in New York, 1796-1848* (Ithaca, N.Y.: Cornell University Press, 1965) pp. 73-75, 162-63.

2. Barbara Welter, "The Cult of True Womanhood: 1820-1860," in *Our American Sisters: Women in American Life and Thought,* Jean E. Friedman and William G. Shade, eds. (Boston: Allyn and Bacon, 1973), pp. 96-123; and Andrew Sinclair, "Ladies, Not Women," in *The Woman Question in American History,* Barbara Welter, ed. (Hinsdale, Ill.: Dryden Press, 1973), pp. 66-67.

3. Welter, "The Cult of True Womanhood," pp. 96-123; and David B. Davis, *Homicide in American Fiction, 1789-1860: A Study in Social Values* (Ithaca, N.Y.: Cornell University Press, 1957), pp. xiii, 148.

4. Robert E. Reigel, *American Women* (Rutherford, N.J.: Farleigh Dickinson University Press, 1970), p. 58, and Davis, *Homicide in American Fiction,* pp. 154-55.

5. Estelle B. Freedman, "Their Sisters' Keepers: An Historical Perspective on Female Correctional Institutions in the United States: 1870-1900," *Feminist Studies,* vol. 2, no. 1 (1974), pp. 78-79.

6. Caesar Lombroso and William Ferrero, *The Female Offender* (New York Philosophical Library, 1958), p. 152.

7. Davis, *Homicide in American Fiction,* p. 177.

8. Lewis, *From Newgate to Dannemora,* pp. 94-95, 162.

9. Ibid., p. 163.

10. Ibid., p. 164.

11. Ibid., pp. 164-65.

12. Ibid., p. 143.

13. John F. Richmond, *New York and Its Institutions, 1609-1872* (New York: E. B. Treat, 1972), p. 319.

14. Ibid, pp. 317-19.

15. Ibid., pp. 457-58; and Freedman, "Their Sisters' Keepers," pp. 79-80.

16. Allen F. Davis, *Spearheads for Reform: The Social Settlements and the Progressive movement 1890-1914* (New York: Oxford University Press, 1967); and Page Smith, *Daughters of the Promised Land* (Boston: Little, Brown, 1970), pp. 255-58.

17. Freedman, "Their Sisters' Keepers," pp. 77-78; and Robert W. Smuts, *Women and Work in America* (New York: Schocken Books, 1971), pp. 112-113, 119.

18. Philip Klein, *Prison Methods in New York State* (New York: Columbia University Press, 1920), pp. 105–06; and Ibid., p. 88.

19. Lewis, *From Newgate to Dannemora,* pp. 238–41.

20. Blake McKelvey, *American Prisons: A Study in American Social History Prior to 1915* (Chicago: University of Chicago Press, 1936), p. 214.

21. Richmond, *New York and Its Institutions,* pp. 319, 457–58; Freedman, "Their Sisters' Keepers," pp. 79–80; and Klein, *Prison Methods in New York State,* p. 324.

22. The city of New York, Department of Correction, *Annual Report,* 1929, pp. 13–14.

23. Rita J. Simon, *The Contemporary Woman and Crime,* Crime and Delinquency Issues (Rockville, Md.: National Institute of Mental Health, Center for Studies of Crime and Delinquency, 1975), p. 48.

24. Freda Adler, The Rise of the Female Crook," *Psychology Today,* November 1975, pp. 42, 46–47, 112–114.

25. The City of New York, Department of Correction, *Annual Report, 1931,* pp. 103, 114, 117, 121, 129, 132–133; *Annual Report, 1955,* p. xxvii; and New York City Correctional Institution for Women, "Inmate Demographic Profile, March 1975 – December 1975," in Women's Development Unit Project, *Annual Report, January 1, 1975–April 9, 1976,* p. 18, Appendix H.

26. Interview with Essie O. Murph, Superintendent, New York City Correctional Institution for Women, Jan. 16, 1976.

27. Rose Giallombardo, *Society of Women: A Study of Women's Prisons* (New York: John Wiley, 1966), p. 7.

28. Kathryn W. Burkhart, *Women in Prison* (Garden City, N.Y.: Doubleday, 1973), p. 137.

29. One of the major reasons for Superintendent Murph's prohibition of slacks was her contention that these would be used as a form of role identification for potential homosexual liaisons among female inmates. In March 1977, the Legal Aid Society of New York won its dress-code case brought on behalf of detained prisoners against Superintendent Murph. Thereafter, detained women were permitted to wear slacks. To prevent jealousy or conflict between detained and sentenced women, Superintendent Murph had uniform slacks supplied to the sentenced women.

30. Murph interview.

31. Women's Prison Association, "Profile, Open Door Project," 1974; and City of New York, Department of Correction, *Annual Report, 1960,* p. 49.

32. Murph interview.;

33. Ibid.; and New York City Correctional Institution for Women, p. 18.

34. Ibid.

TWENTY-TWO

# Imprisoned Women and Their Children*

### BRENDA G. McGOWAN AND KAREN L. BLUMENTHAL

Before making any specific recommendations for change, it is important to specify the rights and responsibilities of each of the major parties that must be considered as changes are implemented. These are summarized in Table 1.

When the rights and responsibilities of inmate mothers and their children are outlined in this way, it becomes clear that there is no single answer to the problems of children of women offenders. To develop coherent policies and programs for this population, we must clearly articulate and balance the rights of the individual versus those of society, the rights of children versus those of parents. Clashes and compromises are inevitable, but there are many areas in which needed changes may be identified.

## VIEWS OF SURVEY RESPONDENTS

As the people most intimately involved with this social problem, and as people likely to have given considerable thought to potential solutions, inmate mothers and correctional administrators who participated in our mail survey were asked for their recommendations for change. The mothers' responses for needed changes in the correctional system tended to cluster in three categories: family-oriented programs and services, increased opportunities for contact with children, and supportive services which should be available to all incarcerated women.

Family-Oriented Programs and Services

The greatest number of suggestions made concerned desired services for incarcerated mothers and their children. Table 2 presents the recommendations for creating and improving family-oriented services.

---

*Reprinted by permission of the publisher, from *The Female Offender*, edited by Laura Crites (Lexington Mass.: Lexington Books, D. C. Heath and Company, Copyright 1976, D. C. Heath and Company).

**Table 1.** *Rights and Responsibilities of Inmate Mothers, Their Children, and the State*

| RIGHTS | RESPONSIBILITIES |
|---|---|
| **Child** | |
| Care and protection by natural parents. | To obey the laws of the state. |
| Adequate and continuous substitute care if natural parents are unable to provide care. | To accept resonable decisions of parents or substitute caretakers. |
| Care or placement in least detrimental alternative. | |
| To express personal preference regarding custody and residence. | |
| Full communication and association with family members. | |
| Adequate health care, education, and social services. | |
| **Mother** | |
| Privacy and freedom from unnecessary state intervention. | To provide adequate care and protection for children to best of ability. |
| Care and custody of children. | To seek adequate care for children when unable to provide such care herself. |
| Due process in proceedings affecting children. | To fulfill parental obligations in accord with state statutes; to ensure that children attend school and receive adequate medical care. |
| **State** | |
| To intervene in parent-child relationship when best interest of child demands it. | To protect welfare of all children; to ensure healthy development of children deprived of care by their own parents. |
| To protect the public interest by appropriate means of law enforcement. | To ensure civil rights (privacy, freedom of association, due process, equal treatment) of all citizens. |
| To impose appropriate penalties or restrictions for those convicted of criminal offenses. | To ensure due process to all those subject to state intervention. |
| | To provide adequate substitute care and placement in least detrimental alternative for children who cannot remain in their own homes. |

**Table 2.** *Family-Oriented Program and Service Suggestions Made by Incarcerated Mothers*

1. Parent education.
    Child psychology, family planning, and family living classes.
    Small groups to discuss questions such as how to explain incarceration to children of various ages, or how to maintain an effective parent role with children who are being cared for by other people.
    Opportunities to work in day care centers to gain experience with children.

2. Counseling-therapy.
    Mothers' discussion groups.
    Family counseling.
    Parents Without Partners chapter.

3. Provisions of information to mothers on matters related to the conditions of their children.
    Liaison worker to check regularly on childrens' care and to inform the mother about the children's conditions.
    Full-time representative of the public child welfare agency at the correctional facility.
    Better communication between the public department of social services and the prison.
    Liaison worker to help mothers locate their children.

4. Programming for children's visits.
    More planned activities for mothers and children during visits.
    Children's day.
    Picnics and other family get-togethers.
    Group overnight outings for mothers and children.
    Holiday dinners at prison for families.
    Opportunity to take pictures of children when they visit.
    Indoor playrooms and outdoor playgrounds for children during visits.

5. Housing for children.
    Nurseries on prison grounds for infants up to one years of age.
    Separate apartments or a separate cottage on prison grounds for mothers and their children.
    Cottages or apartments located near, but not on prison grounds for pre-parole or work-release women and their children.

6. Substitute caretakers.
    Information concerning availability of foster homes.
    Foster homes and group homes for children located close to prison.
    Foster homes for sibling groups.
    Increase number of foster homes (so children need not be institutionalized).
    Improved relationships between foster parents and inmate mothers accomplished by arranging for them to meet prior to the child's placement, encouraging regular visiting, and organizing ongoing discussion groups.
    Visits to mother by child's caseworker.
    Concrete help to regain custody of child and re-establish the home.

**Table 2.** *Family-Oriented Program and Service Suggestions Made by Incarcerated Mothers (continued)*

7. Services for children in the community.
   Special educational programs.
   Day care services.
   Pre-school program.
   Liaison between school personnel and women prisoners.
   Provision for gifts to children on birthdays and holidays.

8. Miscellaneous.
   Maternity leave.
   Permission for prisoners to receive pictures of their children in the mail.
   Information for inmate mothers about effects of incarceration on mothers and children.

**Table 3.** *Recommendations Made by Inmate Mothers Concerning Contacts with Their Children*

1. Number of contacts.
   More visits, telephone calls, and furloughs than currently allowed.
   Unlimited visits.

2. Length of contact.
   Longer visiting hours, telephone calls, and furloughs.
   Visits—overnight to one week.

3. Quality of contact.
   "Contact" visits (physical contact between mother and child).
   More appropriate settings for visits on prison grounds.
   Occasional visits with children off prison grounds (e.g., parks).
   Fewer correctional staff present during visits.
   More private telephone calls.

4. Facilitating visits.
   Visiting days and times varied (e.g., more weekdays, after school hours) so that it is easier for caretakers to bring children.
   Escort for unaccompanied children.
   Transportation directly supplied or caretakers reimbursed for the costs of transportation.
   System established whereby caretakers pool transportation for visits by children.
   Mandatory visiting policy so that visitation rights may not be legally denied or denied by agency or person(s) with custody of the children.
   Caretakers (husbands, foster parents particularly) urged to bring children to visit.

### Contact with Children

Many of the mothers' suggestions related to their desire for increased contact with their children. (See Table 3.) Although visiting seemed to be the primary concern, many recommendations were also offered concerning phone calls, furloughs and leaves.

### Supportive Services for Inmates

Most of the service recommendations made by the mothers related directly to their children, but many women indicated that their competency as parents could not be separated from their physical, emotional, and economic concerns. (See Table 4).

We certainly endorse many of these inmate mothers' recommendations. We also support the suggestions made to us by correctional officials who were anxious to promote the concept of community responsibility for the correctional system. They suggested, for example:

- Hiring ex-offenders who have found legitimate means of solving their problems as staff in correctional facilties.
- Recruiting minority group staff for facilities in which a large portion of the inmates are members of minority groups.
- Initiating programs for staff in correctional facilities to sensitize them to the family concerns of inmates.
- Involving community residents in planning and policy development and securing provisions for inmates in correctional facilities.

## INNOVATIVE PROGRAMS

Fortunately, some communities have already introduced programs aimed at enhancing the familial ties of women offenders. Ranging from parent education to community release, these programs vary in the extent to which they strengthen family bonds, but each effort suggests alternative ways of responding to the needs of women offenders and their children. The Purdy Treatment Center for Women in Washington was described in chapter 1. Other examples include:

### Oregon Women's Correctional Center

This state correctional facility has developed an "integrated services project" staffed by a social worker and a vocational rehabilitation counselor

**Table 4.** *Supportive Service Recommendations Made by Inmate Mothers*

1. Therapy/counseling.
   More psychiatric and social work staff, easier access, fewer delays once treatment is requested.

2. Legal services.
   Information regarding parental rights.
   Legal representation in custody and divorce cases.

3. Medical services.
   More physicians and nursing staff.
   Inspection of sanitary conditions.
   Contraceptive counseling.

4. Financial aid.
   Information regarding public assistance.
   Increased allowances.
   Direct financial assistance immediately after release from prison.

5. Drug treatment programs.
   Group sessions with ex-addicts.
   Lowered age for methadone use.

6. Recreational programs.
   Crafts, sports, religious programs.

7. Vocational and educational opportunities.
   Better educational programs.
   Specialized training programs in nursing, homemaking, secretarial work, child care, cosmetology, and technical trades.
   Expanded work-release programs.
   Increased prison wages.

8. Post-release services.
   Social services.
   Counseling (to ease readjustment of parent and child).
   Housing.
   Mediation with former employers.
   Work opportunities.
   Financial support.
   Babysitters.

9. Other.
   Opportunities to speak to outside groups.
   Better shopping facilities in the canteen.
   Better library.
   More outside speakers.
   Personal grooming courses.

from the State Department of Human Resources, and a corrections counselor from the prison. This team is responsible for maximizing resources currently available in the facility and community, developing new resources, providing more effective patterns of service, and coordinating and facilitating the services and programs of other state agencies. A key member of this team is the social work representative from the Children's Service Division, who tries to convey to each resident at the *beginning* of her stay that he views her as a person with familial roles and responsibilities, that he is available to render help on any family problems, and that he would welcome seeing her regularly or whenever she has a specific problem. The services most often provided by this worker are counseling with individuals and family groups and liaison-advocacy activities with relatives and representatives of various community agencies. For example, he encourages visits to the mother by caseworkers, children, and foster parents; serves as the mother's liaison with members of the mother's family, the courts, schools, and other community agencies; and attempts to ensure that the dependent children of residents get the financial aid to which they are entitled. In all of the facility's programs, heavy emphasis is placed on the utilization of community-based educational and training programs.

## Minnesota Correctional Institution for Women

A weekly mother's discussion group is conducted at this facility by two family life educators from the Minneapolis Family and Children's Services. The family life educators who lead the groups serve as facilitators of the group process, information givers and teachers, and liaisons and advocates between the inmates and the community. Group discussions cover the following topics: how to explain incarceration to children, problems of separation, child development concepts, family reunification, family origin and its effects, rights of mothers in prison, and reentry into the community.

## The South Forty Corporation

This is a private, nonprofit organization whose purpose is to rehabilitate prisoners and to facilitate their successful return to society. The organization runs several special programs for residents in New York prisons, two of which have special revelance for children of women prisoners. The first, the South Forty Hills Project at Bedford Hills Correctional

Facility for women, is a "motivational-vocational" program which prepares a group of twenty women for study release, work release, or parole release. One of the key components of the program is the community resource session, in which guest lecturers share their knowledge of training programs, community projects, educational opportunities, and human services. The second program is the Family Service Project. A family service counselor functions as counselor, liaison, and advocate. An important part of her job is helping to maintain the parent-child relationship in every possible way by helping children visit their parents and opening channels of communication.

## Mabon Odyssey House

This is a therapeutic community in New York City which houses drug addicted mothers and their children. The program is designed to develop self-awareness, a positive self-image, and the capacity to take responsibility for one's own actions. It relies heavily on group encounter sessions as a therapeutic modality, but also employs individual therapy, vocational counseling, and activities therapy. The women are expected to spend a certain portion of each day with their children, but the children are cared for in group quarters and certain residents have assigned duties in the nurseries. Many women enter the Mabon program because, unlike other therapeutic communities for addicts. they are permitted to care for their children. The program is designed to help women develop positive relationships with their children, learn basic mothering skills, and make realistic plans for themselves and their children after release.

## New Jersey Division of Youth and Family Services

This state child welfare agency has developed a liaison program with the New Jersey Correctional Institution for Women in which a social worker is assigned to the prison to help pregnant inmates make plans for their expected children and to meet regularly with mothers of children in foster care. In conjunction with this program, the agency developed a special foster home located near the prison for three to five infants who are born while their mothers are incarcerated. Any mother who is within a year of parole and not "on discipline" can request to have her child placed in the home; after placement the mother is encouraged to spend one day a week in the foster home developing a relationship with her child and learning to provide adequate care.

Iowa Community-Based Corrections Program

This program, which was designated as an exemplary project by the
National Institute of Law Enforcement and Criminal Justice, offers several alternatives to commitment to a correctional facility. The four
major components of the program are pre-trial release screening, pre-
trial community supervision, the county-administered probation unit,
and the community-centered correction facilities. The ultimate goals of
this program, and of the many similar programs developed in other
communities, are to protect the community from additional crime and
to help the defendant become more integrated into the community by
utilizing community resources. A higher percentage of women than men
receive services in the community during the pre-trial period because
women present less risk to the community and are much less likely to
leave the community or to fail to appear for trial since they often have
strong family ties. Promotion of family life is not a major objective, even
though there is a clear recognition of the value and importance of familial ties throughout the program. Although the benefits for children of
women offenders served by this program appear to occur more by accident than by design, the program could be used to enhance family life if
it were designed to provide services such as family counseling and parent
education.

    We conducted no formal evaluation of any of these programs. The
program administrators are quick to point out their many problems and
limitations. However, efforts such as these are important because they
represent an attempt to deal with the familial needs and responsibilities
of women offenders, and suggest some of the types of programs which
might be introduced in other communities.


## RECOMMENDATIONS FOR CHANGE

Programmatic changes such as those recommended by inmate mothers
and prison administrators and those attempted in the agencies described
above are essential. But the development of small, isolated programs for
women offenders and their children—no matter how innovative and
effective—is not enough. To meet fully the needs of this population, it is
necessary to modify some of the basic policies of the criminal justice
system and to make changes at each significant point in this system.

    The primary recommendation we must make is that, *insofar as pos-
sible, women should be diverted from the criminal justice system.* As
discussed earlier, the mounting criticism of the criminal justice system

has created widespread support for depopulation of prisons and the development of community alternatives to incarceration.[1] Only a small proportion of the women in prison have been convicted of crimes of violence. Certainly, those women who pose a danger to the community must be incarcerated, but alternative forms of punishment such as fines and community-service work assignments, restitution and intensive probation supervision are feasible for most of the female inmate population. The potential benefits to these mothers and their children are obvious.

Unfortunately, despite increasing support for diversion programs and strong evidence suggesting that incarceration is an ineffective rehabilitative tool, there is no evidence that promises a sharp reduction in inmate population in the immediate future. What can be done now to ensure the welfare of the children of women who do enter the criminal justice system and are incarcerated? We believe the following principles are basic to any attempts to answer that question:

1. The child's welfare should be considered at each point in the criminal justice system.
2. Although the correctional system may not have the capacity to improve poor mother-child relationships, it has a responsibility to protect existing family ties and to engage in efforts to minimize any potential damage to the child resulting from the mother's incarceration.
3. If the state deprives the child of parental care by incarcerating the mother, it has a responsibility to insure the welfare of the child during the mother's imprisonment.
4. Inmate mothers should be treated not simply as individuals in need of training and rehabilitation but also as members of family units with specific parental rights and responsibilities.
5. The criminal justice and social welfare systems must develop closer policy coordination and service integration to meet the needs of inmate mothers and their children.

In accordance with these principles, the state should assume responsibility for initiating the following series of policy and programmatic changes at each point in the criminal justice system.

## At the Time of Arrest

*The police department* should develop guidelines regarding the responsibilities of an officer making an arrest of a parent with dependent children. These guidelines should require that all adults be asked if there are any children for whom they have sole responsibility, and if so, that these parents be given an opportunity to explain the situation to their children and to make appropriate arrangements for their care. If the parent(s) are not able to make private arrangements, the arresting officer should be required to make a referral to the responsible child welfare agency.

*Child welfare departments* should develop guidelines to aid police and court officials in situations where children should be referred for care and describe procedures to be followed in such cases. The child welfare department should maintain readily accessible emergency foster homes or group homes for children requiring temporary care when their mothers are detained. To expedite planning for children at the time of arrest and arraignment, consideration should be given to the feasibility of assigning child welfare liaison workers to police departments and criminal courts. In addition, training programs should be offered to personnel in the criminal justice system regarding the developmental needs of children and the ways officials could minimize potential harm to children while carrying out their duties.

## During the Pre-Trial Period

*The judiciary* should require pre-trial investigation and probation workers to report fully on the defendant's family responsibilities and to make appropriate referrals for child welfare services when necessary. In addition, the judiciary should assume responsibility for developing guidelines regarding the detention of mothers (or single parents) with dependent children and the custody of their children. Such guidelines should take into account the risk of separation for children.

*Detention facilities* should develop services designed to enhance each mother's capacity to fulfill her parental responsibilities and to minimize the effects of separation on her children. These services should include the provision of adequate information regarding placement alternatives, open-visiting policies for children and caretakers, and easy access to telephones and mail so that open communication can be maintained.

## After Conviction

*The judiciary* should develop guidelines for the sentencing of women or single parents with dependent children. Such guidelines should prohibit the use of out-of-state, indeterminate, or lengthy sentences which are likely to have an adverse effect on the parent-child relationship, except when the protection of the community requires such a sentence.

The judiciary should also develop clear guidelines regarding grounds for termination of parental rights for children of offenders. Such guidelines should place primary emphasis on the current and future needs of the child; the parent's status as a convicted felon or prisoner should not be the determining factor in a decision to terminate parental rights.

*The child welfare department* should provide all incarcerated parents with full information about placement alternatives for their children. If a mother chooses to place her child informally with a relative or friend, the child welfare department should assess the adequacy of the child's living situation, ensure that the child's caretaker has proper legal authority to care for the child, and provide all the financial benefits (AFDC or foster care payments) and services guaranteed by law.

If the mother chooses to place her child in foster care voluntarily, or if, after appropriate hearings, the decision is made by the state to place the child in a more appropriate home pending the mother's release from prison, the child welfare department should encourage the mother's participation in the placement process, provide her with full continuing information about the child's progress in care, and make provisions for regular contact between mother, child, and foster parent.

If parental rights are terminated by judicial action or voluntary surrender by the parent(s), the child welfare department should act as expeditiously as possible to secure and authorize a suitable permanent home for this child.

## During Incarceration

*State correctional agencies* should assume responsibility for developing smaller, community-based facilities so that women can maintain family and community ties during their incarceration.

*Correctional facilities* should review current visiting policies and make necessary revisions to encourage children of all ages to visit frequently at convenient times in pleasant surroundings; for example, abolish restrictions on length and frequency of visits, provide transportation to the facility, create special visiting areas, and develop facilities for extended and overnight visits. Correctional facilities should also move immediately to grant free and reasonable telephone and mail privileges to inmates to encourage frequent communication between parents and children.

Correctional facilities should develop guidelines for granting emergency furloughs to mothers when problems arise regarding their children's care or adjustment.

Correctional facilities should establish programs designed to enhance inmates' capacities to fulfill their parental obligations, such as parent education programs and liaison programs between the prison and schools, hospitals, and other community agencies.

Correctional facilities should be required to establish a range of high quality educational and vocational training programs that would prepare women to obtain decent employment after their release. They could be trained, for example, as computer programmers, bookkeepers, home health aides, beauticians, chefs, or secretaries.

Correctional facilities should examine the feasibility of establishing halfway houses providing housing and supportive services for mothers and children and "mother release" programs similar to existing work-release programs.

*Community social welfare agencies* should study the feasibility of establishing family support services for inmates, such as child development classes, mothers' discussion groups, parent-child counseling, family legal services, and liaison programs between mothers, children, caretakers, and community agencies.


After Release

*Parole boards* should develop guidelines for reviewing cases of inmates eligible for release which consider the family responsibilities of potential parolees.

*Parole officers* should be required to inquire about parolees' children and to help mothers secure services and resources necessary to help them provide adequate care.

*The child welfare department* should provide the necessary services and financial benefits to mother so that they can resume custody of their children as quickly as possible whenever they show serious intent to re-establish a home for their children. In addition, the child welfare department should provide intensive after-care services to mothers and children to strengthen the family unit during the difficult readjustment period.

## RESPONSIBILITY FOR CHANGE

The changes proposed are directed toward enhancing societal responsibility for meeting the needs of this neglected population through public agencies and officials. However, there is much that women's groups, prisoners' rights organizations, child advocates, and other concerned citizens can do to raise concern for the needs of inmate mothers and their children and press for public action to meet such needs.

The question of who should take responsibility for which programs must be decided in relation to existing needs and resources in the local community. One means of drawing attention to the problems of inmate mothers and their children is through mass media; another is for interested groups to ask official agencies what they are doing to address the needs of this population.

For example, at the federal level, the Bureau of the Census should be asked to collect data on the children of inmates when making the census of Persons in Institutions: How many children do inmates have? How old are they? Where are they living? Similarly, the Department of Justice should be asked to collect more adequate annual and single-day census data on women arrested, detained, and incarcerated in federal, state, and local prisons and jails. At the state level, questions should be addressed in criminal justice agencies regarding the number of children affected by the arrest, detention, and/or incarceration of their mothers during a year, and administrators of local correctional facilities should be asked for data about the children of their inmates.

Officials in local criminal justice and social welfare agencies should be queried on a variety of issues. For example, police departments should be asked about their procedures for processing a female arrest. Do they inquire whether the woman has dependent children and, if so, who is available to care for them? Is she given time to talk with her children and make arrangements for their care? When a responsible relative cannot provide care, are the children referred to the public child welfare agency? Similarly, probation officers, public defenders, and judges should be asked how they handle women who have dependent children. Do they know where to refer the children? Do they always ask women about their children? Correctional officials should also be questioned about relevant policies and procedures. For example, how many of the inmates have children? How often are children permitted to visit and where? Can inmates make telephone calls to their children's caretakers? Can emergency care be arranged if the children are experiencing problems?

It is equally important for child welfare officials to be reminded of their responsibilities to these children. Are child welfare workers available in the courts and correctional facilities to help the mother plan for her children? Do they have foster homes accessible to the prison? Are informal caretakers provided the same supports and services as foster parents? What are their policies regarding discharge of children following their mother's release from prison?

Posing questions such as these to responsible public officials is an essential first step in the advocacy process. Monitoring alone seldom produces change, but it can create the necessary pressure for change by focusing public attention on specific failings and inadequacies of official agencies. Moreover, questions of this type should provide advocacy groups with the data they need to evaluate how such children are treated in their community and to select possible targets for change.

In addition to monitoring, there are other important actions which advocacy groups can take. For example, at the legislative level, there should be strong lobbying for bills aimed at:

- Decriminalizing prostitution and other victimless crimes.
- Providing a wider range of sentencing options such as fines and community work assignments.
- Increasing funding for community-based correctional programs.
- Strengthening preventive services and after-care programs for children in their own homes.
- Widening eligibility for foster care payments to include all relatives caring for dependent children.

Litigation might also be an effective means of expanding the rights of inmate mothers and their children. For example, legal rights organizations might attempt to bring suits aimed at establishing the child's right to maintain a relationship with his mother or to be freed for adoption. This could involve challenges to restrictive visiting, telephone and mail policies, out-of-state incarcerations, inadequate provisions for transportation, and denials of furlough. Other court challenges might be directed toward establishing the child's right to financial support and adequate care and supervision during the time the mother is incarcerated. In states in which there are work-release programs, it might be possible to file an equal protection suit on behalf of women whose primary work is child care in order to justify establishment of "mother-release" programs.[2] And termination of parental rights solely on the grounds of incarceration or criminal conviction might be challenged on the grounds of cruel and unusual punishment.

There are, of course, many other approaches advocacy groups could take. There are also a number of critical direct services which could be provided by interested community groups:

- A parent's rights handbook should be prepared and distributed to all defendants with dependent children describing their rights and responsibilities in regard to their children and the community service options available to them and their families.
- Discussion groups, child development and homemaking classes, family counseling, and family law classes should be offered to mothers in correctional settings.
- Individual and group counseling should be offered to children of offenders to help them deal with the many problems they may experience as a result of their parents' imprisonment.
- Specialized foster homes and group residences should be developed for children of offenders in order to increase the range of child-care options available to inmate mothers.
- Volunteer transportation services should be developed for families of offenders.
- Family liaison programs should be established in which volunteers would act as mediators and advocates for inmate mothers in the outside community.
- Work opportunities, housing resources, and social support networks should be developed for families attempting to reunite after the mother's release from prison.

In the past, community groups have shown little interest in these children. There are several explanations for this. First, this is a relatively small population for whom there are no simple solutions and for whom there is no obvious base of community support. And, as a group, inmate mothers are often difficult to work with. They have frequently been disappointed by other volunteer groups and tend to be suspicious and guarded with outsiders. Prison officials may also create barriers for the advocate by their insistence on complicated security measures, limited visiting hours, and restrictive telephone privileges, which make it difficult for outsiders to communicate with inmates. Confidentiality may be used as an excuse for not providing necessary information. Finally, both the inmates and their keepers—for different reasons—are likely to convey the impression that it is a hopeless situation and nothing can be done to help.

Yet we believe there is some basis for optimism at the present time. Emerging prisoners' rights, women's rights, and children's rights groups all provide natural constituencies for children of women offenders. Much could be accomplished if these groups were to focus some of their attention on the needs of this population. Further, we were astounded by the amount of interest and the unanimity of responses we received in our survey of correctional administrators and inmate mothers. These groups should certainly be receptive to any advocacy efforts, and they have pointed out clear directions for change.

In conclusion, we would like to stress that the importance of attending to the needs of inmate mothers and their children should not be minimized. The Committee for the Study of Incarceration, an interdisciplinary group composed of several of the leading national authorities in the criminal justice field, recently published a report of a four-year investigation in which they noted:

> Law, in a good society at least, must preserve not only the society but its ideals and values as well. And, in so doing, it must balance its desire for stability and order against other values. Security, safety, survival may be fundamental—but there are limits. A good society must examine the methods of its survival to make sure that that which survives is still worthy. For that reason, one of the truest indices of the quality of life in a state is the way it responds to those who defy its laws.[3]

Our intent in this report has not been to romanticize the plight of inmate mothers or to suggest that convicted criminals should not be held responsible for their actions. But the familial responsibilities of women offenders and the welfare of their children should be considered at each point in the criminal justice process. The state must constantly seek to balance its obligation to protect the general welfare with its responsibility to protect the rights of individual children. Certainly, no humane society, either through ignorance or neglect, should tolerate the punishment of children for the offenses of their parents.

## NOTES

1. See Michael S. Serrill, "Critics of Corrections Speak Out," *Corrections,* March 1976, pp. 3–8, 21–29, for further discussion of this point.

2. See Richard Palmer, "The Prisoner Mother and Her Child," *Capital University Law Review,* vol. 1 (1972), pp. 127–144, for further discussion of the "mother release" concept.

3. Willard Gaylin and David J. Rothman, "Introduction," in Andrew Von Hirsch, *Doing Justice: The Choice of Punishments* (New York: Hill and Wang, 1976), p. xxxviii.

TWENTY-THREE

# Gender Differences in Prisoner Subcultures*

LEE H. BOWKER

In this article, we discuss differences between male and female subcultures in American correctional institutions. There has been a considerable outpouring of literature on both male and female prisons in the past decade (Bowker, 1977)—so much so that Rasche (1974) refers to the most recent era of studies on female criminality as the prison studies era. This article compares prisoner subcultures rather than prisons as institutions. To draw attention to certain key differences between male and female subcultures, the material has been organized around nine specific points of comparison. These are the severity of criminality of the inmates, the importation versus the deprivation theories of the origin of prison subcultures, similarity of prisoner roles to street roles, prisoner opposition to staff members, homosexual love, pseudofamilies, sub rosa economic structures, sexual victimization, and other forms of victimization.

## THE CRIMINAL SEVERITY OF PRISONERS

There are two opposing ideas about the relative criminality of male and female inmates. The first is that because women are generally less criminal than men on the streets, they are also less criminal than men in prison. In contrast, the second idea is that the criminal justice system constitutes a series of filtering processes through which criminals must go before reaching the final depository of a correctional institution—filtering processes that are more extensive for women than for men, so that proportionately fewer women finally reach a correctional institution. Having been filtered more extensively, these women are more severely criminal. That is to say, the less severely criminal felons are

---

*Revision of a paper delivered at the annual meeting of the American Psychiatric Association, 1979.

more likely to be diverted away from serving time in prison if they are female than if they are male.

There is not a great deal of evidence on this question, and what there is is inconsistent. Cochrane (1971) found that female prisoners in a Michigan sample differed more from a control group of females than male prisoners did from their analogous control group. In Louisiana, Sutker and Moan (1973) found that females were more likely to be incarcerated for homicide, forgery and checks, and drug offenses than males. This particular pattern of offenses suggests a lower degree of criminality than the males, who committed more crimes having a closer association with patterned violence over an extended period of time. Finally, Panton (1974) compared matched groups of male and female corrections admissions in North Carolina on their Minnesota Multi-phasic Inventory (MMPI) profiles, finding that male prisoners were more pessimistic, irritable, emotionally immature, and complaining, while female prisoners were more withdrawn, less confident about their ability to cope in the market place, and generally deviant. Males were characterized by a problem with authority, while females seemed to feel isolated and insufficiently gratified in their social relationships.

If we measure the criminality of inmates in terms of the number of arrests or the number of previous sentences served in prison, then male prisoners will usually be found to be more severely criminal than female prisoners. It is likely that the same result would be found if we were to look at types of offenses rather than length of criminal record. In prisons, the least criminal inmates are commonly known as "square Johns"—people still committed to the norms and values of law-abiding society. "Square Johns" tend to be made up of passion murderers (who, being lifers, make up a larger proportion of prisoner populations than one would think from the murder rate) and property offenders who committed crimes not involving any violence. These latter offenses include the white-collar crimes of forgery and fraud as well as many more direct forms of theft. In most correctional systems, a higher por-portion of women than men are incarcerated for such crimes. On this basis, it appears that the less severely criminal women are not necessarily filtered out to a greater extent by the criminal justice system than the less severely criminal men. Filters may be operating but on dimensions other than severity of criminality, such as the degree of conformity to traditional sex-role stereotypes. In any case, there is some evidence that if one controls for the number of previous offenses, females do not get better treatment by the courts than males. Taking all of this evidence into account, it appears fair to say that inmates in male prisons are, in general, more severely criminal than inmates in female prisons.

## IMPORTATION VERSUS DEPRIVATION THEORIES OF PRISONER SUBCULTURES

Sykes (1956) and Clemmer (1940) were among the first to hold that prisoner subcultures developed because of the severity of deprivations in correctional institutions. The only theory that has emerged to challenge this deprivation theory was put forth by Irwin and Cressey (1962). They believed that prisoner subcultures were essentially imported from the larger society and were merely a concentration of lower-class and criminal norms, values, and beliefs. Researchers on male prisoner subcultures have long since agreed that the only intelligent position is that both theories explain part of the origin and maintenance of prisoner subcultures, while neither is fully adequate if taken by itself. Bowker (1977) suggests that the relative value of the two theories in explaining prisoner subcultures in a given institution depends largely on the severity of deprivations in that institution. The more severe the deprivations, the greater the adequacy of the deprivation theory in explaining the prisoner subculture and the weaker the contribution made by the importation theory.

The fieldwork done by Giallombardo (1966) at the Federal Reformatory for Women, Alderson, West Virginia, focused on the extent to which the responses made by women in the prison social structure were a reflection of cultural expectations for the female sex role outside of the prison. She found that the women had lower cohesion and loyalty than men seemed to have in correctional institutions. Giallombardo argues that women bring norms, values, and beliefs into the prison with them that are consistent with sex role stereotypes, and that imported norms, values, and beliefs dominate the nature of prisoner subcultures in female institutions. Propper's (1976) study of homosexuality in female institutions supports Giallombardo's position. She found that the differences between seven youth institutions accounted for only 4 percent of the variance in the young women's homosexual behavior, while their degree of preprison homosexuality explained 29 percent of the variance. Only 12 percent of the young women who had never engaged in homosexual behavior before entering an institution admitted doing so while incarcerated, as compared with 71 percent of the young women who had been introduced to homosexuality before the current institutionalization.

There is no study that claims that the deprivation theory of prisoner subcultures is the best explanation for the origin of prisoner subcultures in female institutions. The evidence seems to indicate that the deprivation theory applies more fully to male institutions than to female institutions, while the reverse is true of the importation theory. Actually, this is what one would expect considering that conditions and services in male institutions tend to be physically more depriving than those in female institutions. However, we must keep in mind that the crucial deprivation variable is not physical deprivation as measured by scientific researchers but rather felt deprivation as experienced and expressed by the inmates. It is possible that although female institutions may be physically less depriving, they may be perceived by their residents as being subjectively more depriving because of gender differences in socialization in the larger society and the unique effects of being separated from the children they have given birth to.

It is reasonable to argue that males are often socialized to depend on themselves (rugged individualism), while females tend to be socialized to concentrate more on interpersonal support systems. Imprisonment combines the deprivation of sustained interpersonal support from family and friends with an environment in which prisoners provide only a minimal level of support for each other in dealing with the problems of convict life. This situation may be more damaging to females than to males. This position has been taken with respect to self-destructive behavior in prisons by Fox (1975). Fox's argument is that the inability to play meaningful socially approved roles is more problematic for incarcerated women than the physical deprivations of imprisonment. In his view, much of the self-destructiveness found in female prisons is due to inadequate interpersonal security and responsiveness in times of personal crisis.

## SIMILARITY TO OUTSIDE ROLES

Except for the small number of co-correctional institutions, male and female prisoners both face the problem of deprivation of extensive relations with the opposite sex. Physical sexual deprivation is probably more easily dealt with by most prisoners than socio-sexual deprivation. If a man is no longer intimately associated with a woman who plays a feminine role, thus highlighting his masculine role, how can he be sure that he is a man? Exactly the same question applies to incarcerated women. Both subcultures have solved this problem by the creation of substitute gender roles within correctional institutions. In male institutions, there are "queens" and "punks." "Queens" are men who have a history of consensual homosexual behavior outside the institution, and who do as much as possible to dress and act like women while within the prison. Since they constitute only a very small proportion of the prisoner population, the prisoner subculture requires additional feminine roles, and this social problem is solved by "turning out punks." These prisoners are generally younger offenders, perhaps with slighter builds and less facial hair, who are forced to play feminine roles by the threat of physical violence. The feminine behavior engaged in by "punks" is not limited to overt sexuality but includes all of the other ways in which "kept women" are "kept" in the larger society.

In women's prisons, it is useful to create complementary masculine roles to facilitate dyadic gender behavior. This is accomplished through the creation of the "butch" role, the incumbents of which cut their hair short and dress and act like men as much as possible. Interestingly enough, the research literature is unanimous in agreeing that women who play masculine roles in prisons have higher status than women who play feminine roles, so the pattern of status differentiation by gender that exists in larger society is fully replicated in female prisoner subcultures just as it is in male prisoner subcultures.

## OPPOSITION TO STAFF MEMBERS

Discounting the rare cases of effective treatment institutions, prisoner subcultures in both men's and women's prisons are characterized by a considerable degree of opposition to staff members. The strength of opposition to the staff seems to be directly related to both the severity of criminality of the inmates and the severity of the physical deprivation that they suffer in the institution. It evolves from this that we should expect there to be a lower degree of opposition to the staff in most women's prisons than in most men's prisons, and an examination of the literature reveals nothing that is inconsistent with this expectation.

The future does seem to hold any alterations in the balance of deprivation between male and female prisons, but it may be that the relative criminality of male and female prisoners will change over time. Hannum et al. (1973) examined changes in the characteristics of prisoners at the Iowa Women's Reformatory between 1960 and 1970, finding that more recent prisoners scored higher on the MMPI depression and schizophrenia scales, but that they had fewer previous incarcerations. Staff members at the Iowa Women's Reformatory felt that the more recent prisoners were more difficult to handle and more emotionally disturbed than the earlier prisoners, but there was little objective evidence to support their opinions. Adler's (1975) thesis of the "new female criminal" suggests the possibility that female prisoners are becoming much more violent and criminal than they were in the past. Morton (1976) takes the contrasting position that there have been few changes in the female prisoner population over the years. She says that most female offenders have not been motivated by the women's liberation movement since they are from the lower class and have had no contact with it. There is no parallel argument about the increasing criminality of prisoners in male correctional institutions, for statistics from almost every state show both a steady increase in the percentage of violent crimes committed by men as a prelude to incarceration and a parallel increase in violent crimes committed by men against fellow prisoners and staff within institutions. Considering all of this evidence, it seems likely that both male and female prisons will experience increasing opposition to staff in the coming years, but that the difference between male and female prisons will stay about the same.

## OVERT HOMOSEXUAL LOVE

With heterosexual love objects kept at a distance, prisoners must decide to what extent they are willing to develop substitute ties to their same-sex companions. The idea of engaging in loving homosexual behavior appears to be much more threatening to male than to female prisoners. As a result, there is comparatively little homosexual love found in prisons for men. Some men do settle down with stable homosexual relationships, but a more common pattern appears to be coerced homosexuality or prostitution in which there is perhaps an economic transaction or violent aggression but a minimum of tender loving care. The situation in women's prisons is very different. The emphasis is more on love than on physical sex. Most homosexual behavior in women's prisons occur in a context of a loving relationship so that it is integrated into a total interpersonal experience. For men, there is little love, and the experience of overt sexuality tends to be segregated from the caring relationships that they may have with their friends. A further difference is that many of the most intense love relationships in women's institutions do not include overt homosexual behavior at all. The idea of two lovers sending notes back and forth to each other without intending to engage in overt sexual behavior is unheard of in most men's prisons. This gender difference is reminiscent of the traditional teenage dating system in which females tend to be more love oriented and males to be more sex oriented.

## PSEUDOFAMILIES

In the late 1920s, Ford observed that inmates in an Ohio institution for women formed pseudofamilies complete with parents, children, grandparents, aunts, and cousins. The familial ties involved some jealousy and passive-aggressive role playing of the sort that we find in traditional male-female role relationships. The pseudofamilies functioned on an emotional rather than a physical level, providing a meaningful social life and interpersonal support for female prisoners. In the 50 years since Ford's article was published, there have been dozens of descriptions of pseudofamilies in institutions for women, and contemporary descriptions of pseudofamilies do not seem to be even slightly different from the first published accounts of these social structures. Furthermore, descriptions of pseudofamilies from different regions of the country and even from abroad are also remarkably similar. The only significant variation is that there are a very few studies of female institutions (see, for example, Ward and Kassebaum, 1965) in which no pseudofamilies are reported.

The similarity in pseudofamily structures across time and regional and national boundaries is brought into bold relief by the contrast with male institutions, in which there are never any pseudofamilies. This gender difference is the strongest piece of evidence in support of Giallombardo's (1966) theory that the behavior of female prisoners is largely determined by sex-role conventions in a larger society, a theory that was given additional support in her later study of three institutions for juvenile delinquents (1974). Having been socialized to concentrate their energies on family relationships, women presumably miss these relationships more than men do and therefore create pseudofamilies to replace the lost familial relationships.

## SUB ROSA ECONOMIC STRUCTURES

Prisoners attempt to mitigate the material deprivation of their situation by engaging in a sub rosa economic system through which stolen, smuggled, and manufactured items are illegally circulated within the prisoner subculture in return for money, script (prison money issued by the administration), or tobacco, which are the three traditional mediums of exchange in prisons. Sub rosa economic structures exist in both male and female institutions but are more fully developed in male institutions. The main reason that they are so extensively elaborated in male institutions is probably that male institutions are much larger than female institutions, and size is a major determinant of the complexity of economic systems. A sound reason is that male prisoners seem to require a greater diversity of sub rosa items and services to support their subcultural activities than do female prisoners. While the illegal drug distribution system seems to be fairly similar in male and female institutions, male institutions are characterized by much more gambling and therefore much more banking (illegal loansharking by prisoners) and also by a heavier use of illegal weapons manufactured within the prisons. As Williams and Fish (1974) point out, the "merchant" role that is institutionalized in male prisoner subcultures has no correlate in female institutions.

It is reasonable to assume that since the development of sub rosa economic systems is a response to economic deprivation during imprisonment, the greater the level of deprivation, the more elaborate the sub rosa economic system. In view of the fact that material deprivations tend to be less severe in female than in male correctional institutions, one would expect that the sub rosa economic systems in female institutions would be less fully developed. This point, combined with differences of scale and the greater diversity of items and services used in male prisoner subcultures, explains the gender differences in prisoner sub rosa economic systems that have been observed by researchers.

## SEXUAL VICTIMIZATION

Women are more likely to experience rape than men on the street, but it is men who are more likely to be raped while incarcerated. Scacco (1975) and Bowker (1980) have provided extensive summaries of the evidence on the prevalence and severity of homosexual rape in male correctional institutions. While some institutions are relatively free of this affliction, there are many other institutions in which large numbers of inmates constantly live in fear of sexual assault. There are relatively few women's prisons where this is true. Some women may be psychologically pressured by others into an overt sexual relationship, but there is rarely any physical coercion. The increase in reports of female sexual assaults in recent years suggests that this situation may be gradually changing. The excess of male over female homosexual rape is not merely a reflection of socialized differences between an orientation toward overt sex and an orientation towards love. Davis (1968) and others present convincing arguments and data in support of the image of prison rape as an aggressive activity aimed at interpersonal dominance rather than sexual gratification. It is interesting that a number of scholars and members of the women's liberation movement have recently made a similar analysis of heterosexual rape on the streets.

## OTHER VICTIMIZATION EXPERIENCES

As Sykes (1956) pointed out, one of the deprivations of imprisonment is the deprivation of adequate personal security. Once in prison, neither men nor women can be sure of the safety of their possessions or their bodies. There is considerable evidence that victimization rates are much higher in prison than in the larger society (Bowker, 1979). This is probably true in both male and female institutions, although the amount of evidence about victimization in female institutions is much smaller and less detailed than the evidence about victimization in male institutions. The Law Enforcement Assistance Administration has funded a national prisoner victimization study, and we should shortly have detailed rates and incident descriptions of victimization in both male and female correctional institutions available to us. At the moment, one can only estimate gender differences in prisoner victimization indirectly through a careful survey of literature. Using this technique, Bowker (1979) found that victimization rates of all types (physical, psychological, economic, and social) seemed to be higher in male than in female correctional institutions.

## CONCLUSION

In this article, we have looked at nine important differences between subcultures in male and female correctional institutions. We have seen that on eight of the nine dimensions examined, gender differences are a matter of degree rather than inherent in the fundamental nature of the prisoner subculture. The exception to this is the existence of pseudo-families, which are found only in female institutions.

We have not attempted to survey the entire literature on female prisons, and as a result have not discussed a number of outstanding studies, both published (such as Hefferman, 1972) and unpublished (such as Simmons, 1975). For a summary of these studies, see the chapter on female prisoners in *Prisoner Subcultures* (Bowker, 1977). It is apparent that the differences between male and female correctional institutions are a product of the interaction between institutional characteristics, including the deprivations of imprisonment, and characteristics that are imported into the prisoner environment from the streets as the prisoners are admitted. The generalization that female prisons are becoming more like male prisons all the time is not entirely accurate. Instead, it would be better to say that male and female prisoner subcultures are continuing to follow different lines of development. Thus, the degree of gender differentiation in prisoner subcultures has not necessarily narrowed over time. It may even have slightly increased during the past decade.

## REFERENCES

Adler, F. *Sisters in crime.* New York: McGraw-Hill Book Company, 1975.

Bowker, L. *Prisoner subcultures.* Lexington, MA: D. C. Heath, 1977.

———. *Victimization in prisons.* New York: Elsevier, 1980.

Clemmer, D. *The prison community.* New York: Holt, Rinehart & Winston, 1940.

Cochrane, R. The structure of value systems in male and female prisoners. *British Journal of Criminology,* 1971, *11,* 73–79.

Davis, A. Sexual assaults in the Philadelphia prison system and sheriff's vans. *Transaction,* December 1968, *6,* 9–16.

Ford, C. Homosexual practices of institutionalized females. *Journal of Abnormal and Social Psychology,* January-March 1929, *23,* 442–448.

Fox, J. Women in crisis. In H. Toch. (ed.), *Men in crisis.* Chicago: Aldine, 1975, 193–203.

Giallombardo, R. *Society of women: A study of a women's prison.* New York: John Wiley, 1966.

———. *The social world of imprisoned girls.* New York: John Wiley, 1974.

Hannum, T., Manne, J., Betz, E., and Rans, L. Differences in female prisoner characteristics—1960–1970. *Corrective and Social Psychiatry and Journal of Applied Behavior Therapy,* 1973, *19,* 39–41.

Hefferman, Esther. *Making it in prison, the square, the cool, and the life.* New York: John Wiley, 1972.

Irwin, J., and Cressey, D. Thieves, convicts and the inmate culture. *Social Problems,* Fall 1962, *10,* 142–155.

Morton, J. Women offenders: Fiction and fact. *American Journal of Corrections,* July-August and November-December 1976, *38,* 36–37 in 38(4) and 32–34 in 38(6).

Panton, J. Personality differences between male and female prison inmates measured by the MMPI. *Criminal Justice and Behavior,* December 1974, *1,* 332–339.

Propper, A. *Importation and deprivation perspectives on homosexuality in correctional institutions: An empirical test of their relative efficacy.* Unpublished doctoral dissertation, University of Michigan, 1976.

Rasche, C. The female offender as an object of criminological research. *Criminal Justice and Behavior,* December 1974, *1,* 301-320.

Scacco, A. *Rape in prison.* Springfield: Charles C. Thomas, 1975.

Simmons, I. *Interaction and leadership among female prisoners.* Unpublished doctoral dissertation, University of Missouri-Columbia, 1975.

Sutker, P., and Moan, C. A psychosocial description of penitentiary inmates. *Archives of General Psychiatry,* November 1973, *29,* 663-667.

Sykes, G. *Society of captives.* Princeton: Princeton University Press, 1956.

Ward, D.A., and Kassebaum, G. *Women's prison: Sex and social structure.* Chicago: Aldine, 1965.

Williams, V., and Fish, M. *Convicts, codes and contraband: The prison life of men and women.* Cambridge, MA: Ballinger, 1974.

TWENTY-FOUR

# Reform School Families[*]

BARBARA CARTER

Inmate culture in a girls' reform school is best understood as a complex of meanings through which the girls maintain continuity between their lives inside and outside of the institution; and as social forms established to mitigate and manage the pains of confinement and problems of intimate group living. The informal world of reform school girls is one of make-believe families, homosexual courting relations and adolescent peer group culture. It is the world of the adolescent girl on the outside, imported into the institution and appropriately modified to fit the formally structured world of the institution.

## LOVE AND ROMANCE: GOING WITH GIRLS

Adolescent concern with boy-girl love relationships is no less intense for girls in the institution than it is for adolescents in the world outside of

---

*Published by permission of Transaction, Inc., from *Society,* Vol. 11, No. 1. Copyright © 1973 by Transaction, Inc.

the institution. But for these girls, many of whom have gotten into trouble because of their association with boys, there are no boys around with whom to explore courtship, romance and love. To fill the painful void created by the total absence of boys, the girls turn inward to each other and create their own world of love relationships.

"Going with girls" is a relationship which attempts to capture the characteristics and qualities of the traditional adolescent boy-girl relationship. Girls in the institution go with girls for much the same socio-emotional reasons that boys and girls in the society at large go with each other: they seek recognition, companionship and emotional involvement.

Courtship in the reform school allows a girl to acknowledge a romantic and symbolically heterosexual attachment to another girl. While in part a state of mind and a world of fantasy, this acknowledgement is objectively concretized, like its outside counterpart, by pleas for and declarations of love, flirting and jealousy; by the exchange of letters and verbal messages; and generally, by seeking out a present or prospective courting partner in a variety of informal settings. These courting relationships, like boy-girl relationships in the external world, provide the substance for everyday social conversations.

Smiles, stares, glances, pushes, pats and name-calling take on important and exaggerated meaning for the conversational and romance lives of the training school girls. Physical contact per se is a relatively minor component of the courting relationships and is most often manifested in hand-holding, touching and, to a lesser extent, by kissing. For most girls more extensive physical contact appears to be both undesirable and/or unattainable. The vast majority of the courting relationships are emotional and symbolically sexual rather than physical.

Generally, informal group pressure encourages but does not demand that one go with girls. The decision to do so is entirely voluntary. The threat of force, or its actual use, is neither a socially accepted nor practiced way of inducing girls to participate in the courtship system.

Despite the absence of overt coercion and in the presence of formal restrictions against it, somewhere around 70 percent of the girls participate in the courtship system. This estimate is based on my own counting and familiarity with the declarations and activities of the girls. Girls participating in courting activities estimate that close to 90 percent of all girls go with girls. The specific estimates of the noncourting girls cluster around 50 percent. The few staff estimates elicited tended to be considerably lower and most often characterized as "not many." It is clear that estimates about the extent of participation in the courting system are influenced by one's relationship to that system.

## COURTSHIP RULES

"Butch" and "femme" are the two pivotal roles in the courtship system. Auxiliary roles are the "stone butch," the "half-ass butch," the "jive butch" and the "stone femme."

The butch is that position in the courtship system assigned to the girl who assumes the masculine role in the courting relationship. An important part of being a "good butch" is learning to look the part. In a setting where real sex differences are nonexistent, nuances of dress, hair style, carriage and posture take on great social significance.

In summary, then, to be a butch simply means to "act the part of a boy." However, a butch may still show interest in some traditionally feminine activities like knitting, crocheting and sewing. Also she may, like the other girls, decorate her room with dolls, stuffed animals and bric-a-brac. The butch is permitted to play a role without assuming an identity which implies a "real" or permanent commitment. She is permitted to maintain an image of herself as female. It is this permissiveness which gives rise to the distinction between the butch and the stone butch. The butch plays a role while the stone butch purports to have accepted an identity.

A girl may be a butch for the duration of her stay in the institution, or she may be a butch one day and a femme the next—a butch in one relationship and a femme in a concurrent relationship. Most of the terms used by girls in describing roles in the courtship system are terms taken from black culture. That this is so reflects the dominance of the soul orientation in reform school life. For example, the label "half-ass butch" is applied to the girl who calls herself a butch but generally fails to play the part. The black societal counterpart is "half-ass nigger."

The term "jive butch" is most frequently used to describe the butch who courts many girls at once without being "serious" about any. Its equivalent on the outside is the playboy. To call a butch jive is at once to offer a complement and a criticism; to be jive means that one is popular; but to openly exploit that popularity is bad. The black societal counterpart is "jive nigger."

The female counterpart of the butch is the femme. Within the reform school culture the femme affects in an exaggerated fashion behavioral patterns culturally associated with femininity. Most girls perceive this as just acting "natural." A femme is expected to take pride in her personal appearance and to wear jewelry, make-up and lipstick to make her attractive to butches. The femme is expected to be submissive or, as the girls say, "to do what the butch tell her." She is expected to "obey" her butch.

At any given moment in the courting system femmes probably out-number butches by at least two to one. This uneven distribution, of course, contributes to the internal dynamics of "going with girls" by further allowing butches—as scarce commodities—to assume a role of dominance by defining the terms of the courting relationship. The *single* most important factor determining this distribution is race. Within the context of the institution, race becomes a highly visible constant for imagined sex differentiation. Blacks, grossly disproportionate to their numbers in the institution, become butches, and whites, equally dispro-portionately, become femmes. The most common and desirable arrange-ment is a relationship consisting of a black butch and a white femme.

Whether black girls become butches because they have been social-ized to be more aggressive than white girls, or are more aggressive because they have become butches, is unclear. I am inclined to believe that the two are mutually reinforcing: the black girls are in fact "tougher" than the white girls but their toughness is made acceptable and manageable to white girls by having the blacks become the symbolic masculine figures in a social context which is microcosmic of a society that assigns toughness and power to males and not females.

A second argument is that the purpose of creating symbolic males in an all-female population is to permit the vast majority of girls to con-tinue to maintain their pre-institution identities as "feminine people." One might then argue that due to past and present position in society, black girls are more willing to temporarily give up their female roles for certain high-status rewards.

## THE DYNAMICS OF COURTSHIP

Courting relationships in the reform school, like teenage courtships on the outside, are highly charged emotionally and often short-lived. Girls frequently estimate that during the course of nine to 12 months in the institution, the typical girl may go with anywhere from five to ten girls, with five or six girls being the most common estimate given.

Despite, and maybe because of the relatively short duration of most courtships, going with girls is one of the most alive, emotionally intense and conversationally consuming experiences of the girls. These relation-ships are the source of considerable anxiety for many girls. Girls talk about, dress for, "show-off" for and look forward to seeing each other, even momentarily and at a distance. Girls are excited and joyous when things go well and sometimes angry or sad when things go badly.

Daily courtship relations revolve around the exchange of written and verbal messages; the sharing of "goodies" and the exchange of small gifts; the arranging and engaging in momentary and ·public rendezvous; hand-holding, smiles, glances, kisses, petty jealousies and continually recapturing these moments in conversations with friends.

The single most prominent feature of going with girls is the regular exchange of "pen notes." These illegal written communications are saved, hidden and treasured by the girls who receive them. The themes of loneliness, frustration and a need for love are common to most of the letters.

A code for various phrases is used. Presented below are some of the most common phrases.

| | | |
|---|---|---|
| 1 4 3 | I love you |
| 2 1 6 | As a sister |
| 2 2 6 | As my mother |
| 2 2 3 | As my man |
| 2 4 3 | Go fuck off |
| 2 2 4 | Go to hell |
| 2 2 5 | As my woman *or* It is quits |
| 2 1 8 | As a daughter |
| 1 3 3 | I dig you |
| 3 2 4 | Pen me back *or* Pay me back |
| 6 3 7 | Always and forever |
| 2 6 8 | We belong together |
| 2 1 7 | As a brother |
| 4 4 6 | True love always |
| 4 2 3 | Kiss my ass |
| 4 2 4 | Take me back |

The codes reflect the sense of a need for secrecy, but also seem to create some emotional distance. For example, in face-to-face encounters girls are far more likely to say, "1 4 3" than "I love you."

---

Love Is Here and Now You're Gone, I'm
Your Puppet, Hello Stranger, Respect, Ain't
No Mountain High Enough, Reach Out

Time — To pen you
Place — My lonely room
Thought — Of you

Reason — I love you
Desire — To be with you
Hope — We meet on the outs
Wish — You were here now!
Want — You and your loving
Need — You and your loving
Care — For you
Hurt — By love
Love — You
Hate — I hate —— (I hope she drops dead)
Happy — Not now
Sad — Yes
Mood — Confused
Songs — I Do Love You, Stand by Me, Since I Lost My Baby

Say Love,

Time plus pleasure permits me to write you these few sweet lines. Hon I hope I did not upset you but I just had to tell you. And if I did not tell you when I did decide to tell you which I probably would you would have either been angry or hurt because I didn't tell you before. Paula I do love you and I mean it but hon I don't know how to prove it to you but believe me I'll do anything to prove it to you. Hon, I want you to go to board and go home why should you suffer because of me oh sure you'll say you're not suffering but I'll know and deep down you will too. And if you go home and behave I'll probably be able to see you in June or even on my Xmas weekend and remember one thing even if we don't meet on the outs or for that matter ever see each other again remember there will always be someone else that you will love and be happier with than me.

You may not think that now but when you do meet that someone you'll look back and say Pony really knew what she was talking about and then after a while you'll forget me and then it will be hard for you to think that we were more than friends but I hope that doesn't happen to us but if it does, well that's life and boy life sure is hard. Isn't It?

Well I got to go see you tomorrow sometime I hope

1 4 3
6 3 7

Little Miss Supreme

P.S. But promise me never again as long as you live to touch that
Dope! and I mean it hear?
Well good night and       1  4  3
                          6  3  7

---

This love note is typical of those which the girls regularly write to each other. 1 4 3 means
"I love you" and 6 3 7 means "always and forever."

A common pattern observable at recreational activities is the informal sorting of femmes and butches into separate groupings. These
groupings are often seen as some combination of the sorting of symbolic
males and females to discuss their respective partners and activities and
as an informal grouping of blacks (butches) and whites (femmes). In first
discussing this phenomenon with the observer, one femme vividly
recalled how she had been told to leave an informal grouping of butches,
some of whom were her close friends, because the conversation was to
be about things which she, as a femme, should not hear. With respect to
the second basis for groupings (race), the observer notes that a considerable portion of conversation content for butches centers around the
recounting of preinstitution experiences, events and places known to the
blacks coming from common urban area ghettos.

The dynamics of the courtship system can be elaborated further by
describing the everyday language of courtship. Girls talk about "digging" girls, and this is their way of saying that one girl is attracted to
another and would like to enter into or continue a courting relationship.
Talk about who is "digging" whom is very common. A girl may communicate this particular attraction for another girl by penning a note or
more informally by a variety of nonverbal gestures such as stares, smiles,
winks, pushing or hitting. Presented below is one girl's description of
how the observer could identify when one girl is "digging" another. "If
that name keeps popping up. They keep bringing it up and you get
suspicious. That's what Lee did with Helen. We were talking about cars
and she said, 'Don't Helen look cute today.'" To accuse a partner of
"digging" another girl is to charge her with unfaithfulness. Such accusations of jealousy are common and lively features of the courtship drama.
These accusations, often true, lead to many break-ups. While butches
and femmes probably make an equal number of accusations, butches are
more likely to take the initiative in ending relationships. This is so
because femmes are more numerous than butches and consequently, it is
easier for butches to find new partners than for femmes to do so. Then
too, femmes are less likely to end relationships when partners are suspected of being unfaithful because there is a general consensus that

butches, like males, are to some extent "jive." That is, butches, like men, are expected to be playboys.

Girls also talk about "rapping." Girls "rap" to each other, but especially butches to femmes. Rapping is variously described as, "You make a girl think you like her," "You talk bull," or "Play up to her." "Rapping" is the act of artistically persuading one to believe the impossible or improbable. Historically, it is similar to the art of making the master believe that he is loved by his slave.

"Slobbing" is the local and graphic vernacular for "French" kissing. Though frequently described as a "natural" feature of courting relationships, this activity seems to occur as frequently, if not more so, between noncourting partners as it does between courting partners. "Slobbing" is perceived as one of the "big" things that girls can engage in. It certainly carries a greater penalty from the school's administration than writing pen notes. Physical contact for most courting partners seldom goes beyond "slobbing." Most girls say that this limitation is imposed by the girls themselves, but a small number do see it as an expedient reflecting the absence of opportunities for more extensive contacts. The actual amount of "slobbing" occurring in the institution is open to debate. Some girls estimate that it is a frequent activity and say that about three-quarters of courting partners slob each other; others place the figure higher and some estimate that it is an activity in which as few as one-third of the courting girls are engaged.

While the dominant relationship in the romance complex is the courting relationship, marriage relationships are also acknowledged. Except for the name, and a ceremony which accompanies it, it is usually impossible to distinguish between courting and marriage. Girls, however, say that marriage relationships, like those relationships in the external world, imply a degree of permanence, stability, faithfulness and commitment not necessarily implied by a courting relationship.

Most courting girls do not get "married." "Marriage" relationships last no longer than the more common courting relationships, and girls may get married one day and divorced several days later. Many girls involved in courting simply refuse to get married on the ground that it, unlike courting, is "too unrealistic."

One girl summed up the meaning of marriage by saying, "It means that they like each other a whole lot more than kids just going together. They have to stay together or get a divorce. The girl takes the last name of the butch."

Marriages, like most other activities, take place during recreational periods in the presence of other girls. Like marriages on the outside, they are performed by preachers. Any butch may become a preacher simply by performing a marriage. (There are few female preachers in the outside world and none in the institution.) The marriage ceremony varies both with the style of the preacher, the setting, the risk of discovery, and the amount of time available for performing the ceremony. It may be as simple or as embellished as the preacher desires, but always consists of the lines "Do you *(pen name)* take *(pen name)* to be your lawfully wedded butch/femme." Each marriage must be witnessed by at least two people, but more are usually present, often standing as camouflage or lookouts.

Divorces most often seem to occur because partners lose interest in each other, though it is reported that some girls simply get divorced before they leave the institution, maybe to denote a real end to a symbolic existence. Below is a brief description of how one girl described her divorce and the circumstances surrounding it.

> She quit me for no reason at all. I wasn't going with anybody. At first I thought she was jealous or something, but she wasn't. She just said that she wanted to go with Thelma. [Have you had other breakups like this?] No we haven't. We quit each other before but usually we were back together in five minutes. . . . Yet we got a divorce. A preacher divorced us. [Did you have to stand together?] No. It was a one-way divorce. I didn't want to get it. She told me that she wanted a divorce and I said no. I thought she would just forget all about it but she didn't. Then the girl who divorced us told me that we were divorced. [What did you do when told about the divorce?] I turned in her dirtiest pen note. She lost her weekend and everything. But I don't care. I'm glad. She hurt me.

New girls learn the langugage and etiquette of courting by talking with, listening to and observing their peers as they act out the daily courtship drama. These girls learn that it is a voluntary activity which "gives you something to do" and which "helps to pass the time." But, too, they learn of the verbal ambivalence of even those girls who participate in the system: that going with girls is "fun" and "exciting" but also "wrong," "crazy," "sick" and "stupid"—and that one can get in trouble for it. They learn that the staff officially and usually informally disapproves of it and that one can really get in trouble for a "dirty pen note" if it is discovered. They learn that some matrons who are otherwise accepting get really upset when they hear girls talking about going with girls and that a few staff members also see it as a "game" and will laugh or smile when they overhear girls talking about it. Mostly they learn that it's best to try to keep going with girls a secret.

Most girls stop going with girls when they leave the institution, for they know that "it's only something you do up here," and "once you leave you forget all about this place." After all, almost everybody prefers life on the outside to life inside, and boys to girls.

## HAVING A FAMILY

In recreating life on the outside, the girls do not stop at boy-girl relations. Just as they miss having boy friends, they long for their mothers, fathers, sisters and brothers. The following is a typical letter written by one of the girls to her family at home.

Dear Ma and Dad

I hope this letter finds you in the best of health.

Ma and Dad I lonely and blue and I need you very much, more than I did before, because I know How much you & the kids mean to me now. I never knew how much yous mean tell now. So I am asking for yours and Dad forgives. Please! take me back I need you and I need your love.

I know you say she only fooling around so she can come home, but am not I mean every word I am saying to you. Ma please take me in your arms and love me like you do the other kids. Please! Rock me and hold me in your arms Ma. Someone said to you (You can have alot of fathers but you can only have one mother. Cause she the one who brought you in this world. I believe that if only you would let me love you and you love me. Ma please understand what I am trying to say, Well thats all for now. Please forgive me.

I already forgave you and ready to try again.

Love & Kisses & Hugs

Dena

Dena writes from the heart and paints a plea for love, acceptance and affection. Her letter, unfortunately, is typical of many I read during my fieldwork at the Girls' Reform School.

Dena, like many girls at the school, is estranged from her family and feels an intense loneliness for them. Families, both loved and hated, are everyday topics of conversation for the girls, their visits anticipated and letters anxiously awaited.

Girls in the institution talk about and long for their families. Yet there is little that one can do about families on the outside except write to them, wait for their visits, hope for an infrequent weekend, send apologies, and ask for forgiveness and acceptance. Perhaps this is the reason that girls create their own make-believe familial relationships within the institution.

Girls use kin terminology to describe a variety of close relationships between them and other girls in the institution and speak of having "sisters," "brothers," "mothers," "fathers" and "daughters." Kin relationships generally lack the tone of emotional excitement so characteristic of the courting relationships, and the vast majority of girls acknowledge not just one but several make-believe relatives on the grounds. This commonly ranges from a low of two or three relatives to a high of 14 or 15. Girls most typically have about four to seven family relations. Having family relations distinguishes courting from non-courting friends and thus reduces feelings of jealousy, suspicion and distrust among courting partners involved in multiple relationships.

I have found it convenient to divide kin relationships into two broad categories: macro- and microfamily groupings. Girls speak of the macrogroupings as "grounds families," meaning that these families are institution-wide. The most popular groupings at the time of my research were the Robinsons and the LaMonts. Girls simply identified themselves as belonging to one of the "grounds families" and often took the family name as their pen note surnames. Belonging to a large family grouping seemed to convey some positive status on girls. The major function of these groupings presently seems to be to provide a sense of social rather than emotional integration.

When asked about the history of the two dominant macrofamilies the responses ranged from "don't know" to constructions of a recent past. Many times I was told that the Robinson family, the larger of the two families, was started up in the fall of 1966 by two girls who were "married" to each other. Others reported that the Robinson and LaMont surnames have been used by the girls for many years. Thus the girls have attempted to create a past and legitimate the families and interrelationships.

One becomes a member of a family grouping simply by being asked or so identified by someone who is already a member. Getting out of a family is as simple as getting into it. A girl simply declares that she no longer wants to be in that family.

From the perspective of the girls the large grounds family groupings are seemingly less important on the level of day-to-day interaction than are the smaller, comparatively more closely knit nuclear and sibling groups into which the girls also organize themselves.

A sizeable number of girls are mothers or daughters, and an even larger number of girls acknowledge sister or brother relationships. (Interestingly, there are no "sons." A girl assuming a butch role in a courting relationship will usually become a brother to another girl or even a daughter. In most cases it seems that a girl identifying herself as a butch will not have a parent unless she has alternated between the roles of butch and femme.) It is not uncommon that a girl will be a mother or father in one relationship, a sister or brother in another, and a daughter in still another.

In general, girls who acknowledge kin relations regularly write pen notes to each other, send verbal messages, share with each other and exchange small gifts. These girls seek out each other and talk together at recreational activities, hold hands, exchange affectionate hugs and kisses, and often move in the same circle of friends. In terms of observable content, these relationships are practically indistinguishable from courting relationships. Importantly, however, these relationships lack the talked-about glamour and excitement of the courting relations. Of course in the outside world adolescent girls take families for granted and talk, instead, about boyfriends.

A sister or brother, most commonly a sister, is frequently the first kin relation to be acknowledged by a girl on the grounds and this tie is frequently established within a week or two of a girl's arrival at the institution. Some girls establish these ties within a few days after their arrival but others do not choose or are not chosen until much later. One girl, for example, reported that she was at the institution for five months before she acknowledged a kin relation. At the time of our conversation she acknowledged five sisters, several brothers, an aunt and uncle (both unusual since the term "aunt" is usually reserved for matrons) and a host of "good friends" described as "not worthy" of being called sisters and brothers. Another girl, however, reported that on her first day at the institution she received six pen notes with several of them containing requests for a sister relationship. At present this girl is in the Robinson ground family and acknowledges a mother, two daughters, four sisters and two brothers.

Mother-daughter relations are less common than sibling associations, and the girls seemed at a loss to describe the parent-child relationship. In explaining why she had chosen a particular girl as her daughter, one girl said it was, "because I like her. She's little. I don't know, I like little people. If they're smaller than me they can be my daughter." Mothers are nearly always older than their daughters. Girls typically describe those who become mothers as "more mature girls."

Mothers give advice, provide a sense of security and help meet material needs. Parents assume some responsibility for socializing their children into the informal culture of the institution. When asked to describe the relationships which commonly exist between parent and child on the grounds, the girls almost always say that the parent tells the child what to do, how to behave and how to avoid trouble. One in fact frequently hears parents, as well as girlfriends and relatives, telling the girls to "be good" or "You'd better make A-Party" (for girls who have adhered to all school rules for the week) or to obey the matrons.

Family members on the grounds, like the idealized concept of families on the outside, "like" and "care" for each other. The girls themselves see the parental role as being one which provides the child with a sense of emotional security, social direction and physical protection. The parent fulfills the desire to nurture; the child has her need to be nurtured fulfilled. These are intensely personal needs which cannot be fulfilled by the formal structure of an institution.

The child-parent relationships are effective channels for socializing recruits into life on the grounds: it is an informal but powerful channel of social control. The girls want to protect their social system and to maintain a comfortable social order where staff discipline is minimal. To the extent that parents (and other kin and friend relations) express concern about the behavior of their children by telling them to "be good" or "make A-Party" and children obey these commands, the child-parent unit becomes an important informal source of support for the formal structure's emphasis on discipline and order. To the extent that the entire enterprise is successful, parents become informal social control agents of the formal institutional structure.

Families—parents, daughters, sisters and brothers—are important to adolescents both inside and outside the institution. For these adolescent girls on the inside, plagued by real family conflicts and often social and emotional estrangement and certainly physical separation, make-believe families function to fill a void not otherwise filled by the institution. There is some interaction between girls and matrons characteristic of child-parent interaction, and though girls may develop special attachments for certain matrons, these attachments clearly do not erase the need for make-believe families. In the final analysis, say the girls, even most of the "nice" matrons are people who just *work* at the institution. Furthermore, not even the matrons themselves feel equipped to provide the 25 girls in their cottages with the "love and affection" they are perceived as needing.

These reform school girls have attempted, consciously and subconsciously, to affect their restricted environment, finding ways to compensate not only for their incarceration but also for deprivation in their lives outside of the institution. Make-believe boyfriends, girlfriends and families provide, at least temporarily, the romantic, sibling and parental relationships that these girls crave.

# CONTRIBUTORS

Emily Stier Adler, Department of Sociology and Social Welfare, Rhode Island College

Alan Block, Department of Criminal Justice, University of Delaware

Karen L. Blumenthal, Consultant, Special Services for Children, New York City

Lee H. Bowker, Department of Criminal Justice, University of Wisconsin, Milwaukee

Ann Burgess, School of Nursing, Boston College

Barbara Carter, Department of Sociology, Federal City College, Washington, D.C.

Meda Chesney-Lind, Department of Sociology, Honolulu Community College

Sandra Dudley, Department of Sociology, Bowling Green State University

Clarice Feinman, Department of Criminal Justice, Trenton State College

William Feyerherm, Department of Criminal Justice, University of Wisconsin, Milwaukee

Peggy C. Giordano, Department of Sociology, Bowling Green State University

A. Nicholas Groth, Director, Forensic Mental Health Department, Harrington Mental Health Clinic, Southbridge, Massachusetts

Lynda Holmstrom, Department of Sociology, Purdue University

Eugene J. Kanin, Department of Sociology, Purdue University

Sandra Kerbel, Department of Sociology, Bowling Green State University

Brenda G. McGowan, School of Social Work, Columbia University

E. Eugene Miller, Administrator, Women's Detention Center, Washington, D.C.

Imogene L. Moyer, Department of Sociology and Criminal Justice, Old Dominion University

Mildred Pagelow, Department of Sociology, University of California, Riverside

Stanley R. Parcell, Department of Sociology, Purdue University

Susan C. Randall, Department of Sociology, Southern Methodist University

Vicki M. Rose, Department of Sociology, Southern Methodist University

Rita J. Simon, Department of Sociology, Law, and Communications Research, University of Illinois

Carol Smart, Department of Sociology, Trent Polytechnic, Nottingham, England

Darrell J. Steffensmeier, Department of Sociology, Pennsylvania State University

Richard Symanski, Department of Geography, University of Texas, Austin

Garland F. White, Department of Sociology and Criminal Justice, Old Dominion University

Pamela Wood, Attorney